WESTERN WOMEN AND
IMPERIALISM

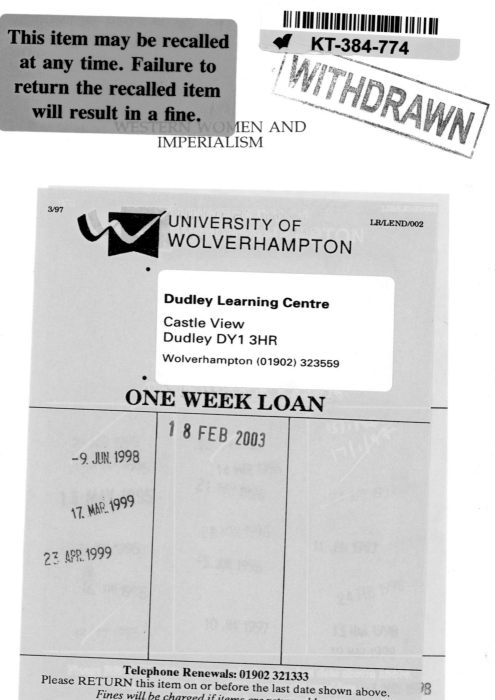

WESTERN WOMEN AND IMPERIALISM

Complicity and Resistance

EDITED BY

NUPUR CHAUDHURI

AND

MARGARET STROBEL

INDIANA UNIVERSITY PRESS

Bloomington and Indianapolis

The paper used in this publication meets the minimum requirements of American National Standard for Information Sciences—Permanence of Paper for Printed Library Materials, ANSI Z39.48-1984.

Manufactured in the United States of America

Library of Congress Cataloging-in-Publication Data

Western women and imperialism : Complicity and resistance / Nupur Chaudhuri and Margaret Strobel, editors.
     p.   cm.
   Includes index.
   ISBN 0-253-31341-4 (alk. paper). — ISBN 0-253-20705-3 (pbk. alk. paper)
     1. Women—Europe—Colonies—History—19th century.   2. Women—Europe—Colonies—History—20th century.   3. Women—Great Britain—Colonies—History—19th century.   4. Women—Great Britain—Colonies—History—20th century.   5. Imperialism—History—19th century.   6. Imperialism—History—20th century.   I. Chaudhuri, Nupur.   II. Strobel, Margaret, date.
HQ1587.C66   1992   91-809
305.42'094—dc20

1 2 3 4 5   96 95 94 93 92

CONTENTS

ACKNOWLEDGMENTS

We wish to thank the many people who assisted the birthing of this volume. Cynthia Enloe encouraged our co-editing the special issue of *Women's Studies International Forum* from which several essays were reprinted. Her moral and concrete support was critical. Various anonymous reviewers gave helpful comments on individual articles and on the entire volume as a whole. Indiana University Press staff was a pleasure to work with and paid careful attention to the details that threatened to overwhelm the project and us. Finally, we thank technology: without long-distance phones, international electronic mail, and faxes, the volume would have taken even longer to produce, thereby straining our authors' patience past its limits.

Nupur Chaudhuri
Margaret Strobel

WESTERN WOMEN AND IMPERIALISM

INTRODUCTION

Since the 1970s, a marked resurgence of interest in colonial matters has occurred, at times verging on colonial nostalgia.[1] Banana Republic, an insulting term used to describe Central American nations whose oligarchies were supported by United States fruit companies and United States foreign policy, is unabashedly used as a trade name for a line of safari clothes. In the 1980s, as viewers, we have been treated to feature films and television series on Africa.[2] Popular British media have also released a number of feature films, television programs, and documentaries on India under the British rule, a flowering that Salman Rushdie has named the "raj revival."[3] To complement the heightened interest in colonial matters, biographies, autobiographies, and novels have been published and reissued. White women feature prominently in these feature films, television series, and writings.

Along with popular attention, scholarly interest in white colonial women has grown as well. The articles collected here represent a portion of research, published and in progress. The popular and scholarly attention being paid to this subject at this time raises important issues of historical interpretation and present concerns.

In Britain, awareness of a colonial past has never died. The term "raj revival" refers to a sentiment that, despite mistakes, the British performed a valuable service in ruling India because of the backwardness of its people. The politics involved do not relate solely to the past; they involve justification for a late twentieth-century conservative ideology of white racial superiority as well.[4] Defense of the empire certainly became more acceptable during Margaret Thatcher's Conservative administration of the 1980s. This explosion of romantic images of Western women in the empire is reminiscent of how juvenile literature of late nineteenth- and early twentieth-century Britain emphasized the theme of empire to inculcate ideas of imperialism and nationalism among a large and impressionable youthful audience.[5] However, in this case the audience is large, impressionable, and adult. In the United States, alongside a rejection of an interpretation of the country's past as imperialist by many mainstream intellectuals as well as the general public, there is a keen voyeuristic interest in the British empire.

Reading about or watching film images of Europeans in colonial settings is one way for white people in both the United States and Britain to expand

their horizons beyond the narrow borders of their own societies. Unfortunately, colonial nostalgia about Africa, India, or the Middle East typically
lacks a historical and specific understanding of the colonial context, central
to which was the exploitation of indigenous peoples: the racism of imperialism. "Seeing the world" (and "the Other") through colonial nostalgia in
no way challenges white European and North American viewers' and readers' hegemonic position in today's world.

Moreover, recent colonial nostalgia is notable in its efforts to coopt feminist consciousness and activism. In an increasingly conservative political
climate, it is hardly surprising to find feminism manifested as an interest in
famous, "heroic," white women in colonial settings. Such representations
contain and diffuse the revolutionary potential of feminism to attack ineq-
uities of gender, race, and class. This the popular media has done in its
representations of Isak Dinesen and Beryl Markham, for example, against
the backdrop of an inadequately contextualized history of colonialism.[6]

Although popular interest in colonial history is relatively new, scholarly
interest in imperialism dates to the beginning of the century. Imperialism is
a concept that signifies any relationship of dominance and subordination
between nations, including the modern form of economic control. Colonialism is the specific historical form of imperialism that involves direct military, economic, and political control.[7] The first attempt at serious analysis
was made by J. A. Hobson in 1902, with *Imperialism: A Study*. Since the
publication of V. I. Lenin's *Imperialism, the Highest Stage of Capitalism* in
1916, Marxists have recognized imperialism's place in the evolution of
modern capitalism. To Marxists, colonialism expresses the changing character of the hegemony exercised by the capitalist West over the rest of the
world.[8] However, Patrick Brantlinger, the author of *Rule of Darkness: British
Literature and Imperialism, 1830–1914,* has pointed out that Marxist analyses
of ideology have not always paid adequate attention to racism, even while
they have much to say about imperialism as the last stage of capitalism and
as a form of false consciousness.[9] Writing in the 1950s and 1960s, Frantz
Fanon, Albert Memmi, and O. Mannoni contributed a profound sense of
the psychological dynamics of racism under colonialism.[10]

Their analyses have been further augmented by Edward Said's analysis
of the cultural and intellectual processes that inhere in imperialism. In his
Orientalism, Said described Orientalism "as a kind of Western projection on
to and will to govern over the Orient." Said maintained that

> during the nineteenth and twentieth centuries the Orientalists became a
> more serious quantity, because by then the reaches of imaginative and ac-
> tual geography had shrunk, because the Oriental-European relationship
> was determined by an unstoppable European expansion in search of mar-
> kets, resources, and colonies, and finally, because Orientalism had accom-
> plished its self-metamorphosis from a scholarly discourse to an imperial
> institution.[11]

In the last decade, some scholars have also started to explore how the West in the colonial period defined indigenous culture and space. Research of scholars with non-Western roots has started to provide new dimensions to colonialist discourse. For example, many historians of India transferred their attention from studies of the nationalism of the middle class to analyses of peasant movements or subaltern movements and revolts.[12] Western scholars have also broadened their scope of investigation. In studying colonialism as a historical phenomenon, some have explored the impact of colonial encounters on Western historical experiences; a few have examined how imperialism expressed Victorian values; several have probed into traditions by which colonizers legitimized relations of authority; and others have discussed how late nineteenth- and early twentieth-century literature embodied an ideological justification of empire.[13]

In general, theories about colonialism have stressed its "masculine" nature, highlighting the essential components of domination, control, and structures of unequal power. The colonial experience itself, expressed in terms of political and economic power and dominance, has been a major focus of historical study. For the most part, scholarship has reinforced the common belief among imperialists that colonies were "no place for a white woman."[14] Consciously or unconsciously accepting the "masculine" attributes of colonialism, most scholars have simply excluded or marginalized Western women from the focus of their studies. Those few who have commented on the role of Western women in the colonies have emphasized the racist attitudes of white women and their luxurious lifestyle compared to their sisters at home.[15] They have not analyzed the complexity of the roles played by Western women in colonial history.

Scholars of women's history trained in the history of Third World areas have been particularly inspired to write the histories of indigenous women, rather than of white people. Scholars trained only in United States and European women's history, until recently, saw the empire as being of marginal significance to their explanatory framework. The result has been the neglect of the role of Western women in the colonies.

Recent political developments, however, have propelled the study of Western women and imperialism to the center of scholarly enterprise. As feminist theory, women's history, and women's studies have matured, accompanying the growth of feminism as a powerful social movement, the numerically dominant white practitioners of these scholarly fields have been forced to examine and evaluate white women's part in imperialism as well as in other forms of class and cultural exploitation. The critical understanding of subjectivity that has evolved from this scholarship has made each of us, whether white and European/North American or representatives of the formerly colonized and culturally dominated, approach the study of Western women and imperialism as part of a process of studying not only others, but also ourselves. This process continually poses issues of contemporary values in the examination of past value systems, compli-

cated by our desire to find resistance when, often, we actually face complicity.

Until recently, the historians of empire and scholars who worked in
women's history functioned in intellectual isolation. By the late 1970s, students of colonial history had found traditional imperial history disintegrat-
ing in the face of postcolonial political sensibilities.[16] The study of Western
women in colonial settings is but the most recent reconstruction of now
fast-changing imperial history, one that rejects the notion of empire solely
as male space (ideology to the contrary), or even of imperial history as
solely constituted by what the policy makers in London or in other Western
capitals attempted to achieve. Furthermore, scholars of colonial history
have begun to discover that, over time, the imperial agenda shaped gender
ideology and practice for both colonizers and colonized. New insights
about colonialism have opened up unexplored historiographical vistas, and
women's history and imperial history have found that they share common
territory.[17]

Since the late 1970s, a number of works have been published that have
attempted to refute the stereotypically negative image of Western women
as participants in empire. Many of these works are more descriptive than
analytical and tend to oversimplify.[18] By the mid-1980s, scholars of women's studies and imperial history started to delve into the complexities of
Western women's lives in the colonies.[19] By challenging established opinion, these scholars created a new paradigm and charged a new way of
studying Western women's experiences in the colonies. This work, focusing on gender, opened the way to the new analyses that increasingly demanded an understanding of the interactions of gender, race, and class
that have now become the new focus of women's history and women's
studies.[20]

What, then, will be the focus of women's history and women's studies in
the 1990s? In her article, "Feminism and History," Judith M. Bennett, a historian who writes about medieval women, calls upon historians not to create a fixed division between women as victims and woman as agents who
have created their own spaces, cultures, and lives. She maintains that

> to emphasize either one without the other, creates an unbalanced history.
> Women have not been merely passive victims of patriarchy; they have also
> colluded in, undermined, and survived patriarchy. But neither have women
> been free agents; they have always faced ideological, institutional, and prac-
> tical barriers to equitable association with men (and indeed, with other
> women). . . . Women have a large part to play in this historical study of pa-
> triarchy, not merely as victims, but also as agents. Women's support has al-
> ways been crucial to the endurance of patriarchy; hence we must examine
> and understand the motivations of women who have colluded in their own
> oppression.[21]

This collection of essays on Western women's experiences in the colonies follows Bennett in exploring both their complicity with colonialism and their resistance to it. The essays focus on interactions between gender, race, and class. The authors in *Western Women and Imperialism: Complicity and Resistance* offer analyses of both complicity and resistance by Western women to the cultural values dominant during an imperialist era. They juxtapose feminists and social reformers of varying stripes and pro-imperialist women of different levels of consciousness and thereby offer the reader many important insights into the workings of race and class ideologies within imperialism.

Since Great Britain controlled the largest Western colonial empire for over seventy-five years and contained the greatest diversity of imperialist practice, this collection on Western women's experiences emphasizes the British colonies.[22] In India, both direct and indirect imperial systems were practiced simultaneously. Direct rule meant that imperial interests were promoted and protected by abolishing indigenous administrative institutions and social practices in favor of new ruling institutions and bureaucracies that maintained a small number of Western salaried agents at the higher levels and used selected indigenous men at the lower echelons. By contrast, in colonies administered by indirect rule traditional political institutions and social practices were maintained, subject to treaties or agreements with the traditional rulers and administered by resident agents whose aim was to accomplish colonial objectives through the facade of indigenous leadership.

Although a bureaucratic structure with a small number of paid European officials formed the core of the Indian Civil Service governing much of India, the indigenous rulers of Indian princely states were given the permission to maintain their separate existence in terms of governance and social practices so long as they received a resident agent and maintained allegiance to the colonial power. Fieldhouse has aptly described the dualism of the Indian colonial system: it set itself to preserve even while it innovated.[23] The British government gradually adopted direct rule over an ever larger part of India in the nineteenth century as it proved impracticable to work first through traditional Indian agents and institutions and then increasingly through their chartered company agents.

Thus the colonial framework in India offers an illustration of a wide spectrum of governance possible under the empire. The complexities of women's roles in a colonial atmosphere need to be approached across the many forms of colonial systems that existed. Both the length of its history and its prominence as a colonial establishment within the largest colonial empire in the modern world, as well as the range of imperialist policies practiced, have made India an attractive area of research. This, in turn, has prompted a seeming disproportion of articles on India in this collection.

Africa represented the second major arena of European colonialism in the nineteenth and twentieth centuries. Trading relations preceded formal colonial rule, which was established in sub-Saharan Africa in the last quarter of the nineteenth century. The European empires in Africa practiced both direct and indirect rule. More significant in terms of actual impact on indigenous populations were decisions to encourage white settlement in some areas under British control, notably South Africa, Kenya, and Northern and Southern Rhodesia.

It is necessary to take up the issue of how to proceed when opening a new field of scholarship such as "gender and imperialism." First efforts cannot always provide a neat structure for beginning to think about the issues involved. The essays that follow have the virtue of showing some of the prominent areas that will reward future exploration. They raise questions about Western women's complicity and resistance to dominant cultural values during an imperialist era. The essays encourage the reader to consider the multiplicity of voices, variety of assumptions, and different understandings of empire represented by activist women who used the implied—and sometimes explicit—power of race and class to negotiate their own agenda within the colonial scene.

In this collection, both Susan L. Blake and Mervat Hatem have analyzed writings of late nineteenth-century and early twentieth-century Western and indigenous writers to show the kind of images these writers presented to their audiences. Ewart S. Grogan's *From the Cape to Cairo* (1900), Mary Hall's *A Woman's Trek from the Cape to Cairo* (1907), and Frank Melland and Edward Cholmeley's *Through the Heart of Africa* (1912) are a part of a Cape-to-Cairo subgenre of African travel literature. In "A Woman's Trek: What Difference Does Gender Make?" Susan L. Blake analyzes these narratives contrasting the one female author with the three male authors. Hall's argument—that ordinary travelers, especially women, can travel in Africa—clearly "refutes the imperial wisdom that 'Africa is no place for white women.'" Hall, like Mary Kingsley and other Victorian and early twentieth-century narrators, mixes endorsement of empire with accounts of personal experience that undercut imperial notions of superiority. For example, Blake examines Hall's ability to grant reciprocity and subjectivity to an African chief, in contrast to the male writers' domination or objectification of such chiefs. In relating to the African chief as an equal, Hall rejects racial superiority as a source of power and replaces it with a sense of shared class superiority.

In "Through Each Other's Eyes: The Impact on the Colonial Encounter of the Images of Egyptian, Levantine-Egyptian, and European Women, 1860–1920" Mervat Hatem analyzes the writings of one English, one French, one Hungarian, three Levantine-Egyptian, and three Egyptian female authors. The Western women's expressed superiority toward the Egyptian women is quite similar to that of Western feminists and missionary women toward Indian women. Hatem finds that Levantine women, as immigrants in Egypt and often Christians, were able to view Eastern and Western women less stereotypically and forge a critique of the cultural nationalisms and gender oppression of both Egyptian and European women.[24] She concludes that "by thinking of themselves as all powerful and free *vis-à-vis* Egyptian women, Western women could avoid confronting their own powerlessness and gender oppression at home." And the images that all these women created help us understand the sources and causes of tension among them then that continue, in modified forms, to the present.

The complex dynamic of complicity and resistance in Western women is examined by Julia Clancy-Smith in "The 'Passionate Nomad' Reconsidered: A European Woman in *L'Algérie Française* (Isabelle Eberhardt, 1877–1904)." A Russian emigré to French North Africa, Eberhardt holds a contradictory reputation as both "an enemy of France" and being "profoundly Algerianized." In actuality, argues Clancy-Smith, her story reveals that "a European woman labeled by officials as disorderly, undesirable, and marginal was . . . central to—even emblematic of—the colonial encounter." Eberhardt transgressed European norms of gender and civilization by embracing Islam (taking as her spiritual mentor a female sufi saint), dressing as an elite Arab man, and claiming male prerogative. Yet her self-exploration was made possible by French colonial power, and, in the end, she became a player in French imperial politics.

Other European women were equally complex, if not as flamboyant. Helen Callaway, Dorothy O. Helly, and Mrinalini Sinha examine the roles of such women as Flora Shaw, Annette Akroyd Beveridge, and others in actively maintaining and strengthening colonialism in Africa and India.

Flora Shaw, as the colonial editor of *The Times* of London during the 1890s, and later, as wife of Lord Lugard (the architect of the British policy of indirect rule in Africa), played a leading role in legitimizing the conquest and domination of other lands in the name of civilization and development. Until the present, Shaw has been ignored by both historians and women's studies scholars, perhaps because imperial historians have preferred male actors, while feminist women's studies scholars have chosen to resurrect more "politically correct" women with whom they feel greater affinity. Helen Callaway and Dorothy O. Helly's "Crusader for Empire: Flora Shaw/Lady Lugard" analyzes Flora Shaw's life and writings within the world she experienced to add a more textured understanding of gender, ideology, and imperialism. Callaway and Helly question whether Shaw contrasts with or shares the views of other women of her generation, prominent or not. They compare her with Olive Schreiner (1855–1921), Beatrice Webb (1858–1943), and Mary Kingsley (1862–1900) to place Flora Shaw, arch imperialist, within a spectrum of attitudes held by other contemporary women who are viewed today more sympathetically than is Shaw.

In describing the people and customs of Antarctic France (now Brazil), Michel de Montaigne (1533–92) wrote: "Each man calls barbarism whatever is not his own practice; for indeed it seems we have no other test of truth and reason than the example and pattern of the opinions and the customs we live in. There [in one's own country] is always the perfect religion, the perfect government, the perfect and accomplished manners in all things."[25] This sixteenth-century attitude of Europeans toward non-Europeans was equally true in the nineteenth and twentieth centuries, and it was manifested in various ways through the activities of British women in India and Africa.

In the early 1880s the British community in India became embroiled in a controversy that linked gender and racial/national issues. The Ilbert Bill would have allowed Indian judges to try cases involving Europeans. Opposing this bill, memsahibs held public meetings and drew up petitions. In her article " 'Chathams, Pitts, and Gladstones in Petticoats': The Politics of Gender and Race in the Ilbert Bill Controversy, 1883–1884," Mrinalini Sinha examines the reasons for white women's objections to the Ilbert Bill. Western women opposed being tried by "native" judges because they feared loss of prestige and dignity from judges who, in their view, held "barbaric" views about the female sex; they also believed that isolated white women would become victims of "native" lust. Memsahibs' agitation may have had an impact; the version finally passed by the colonial government was so vitiated as to prompt few objections from them.[26] By analyzing memsahibs' political mobilization against the Ilbert Bill, Sinha explicates how gender ideology and racial ideology were both implicated in the colonial pattern of domination.

Among British women who went to India were a small number whom indigenous reformers invited or who took it upon themselves to reform existing indigenous cultural and social systems. While sympathetic to Indians, these reform-minded women generally subscribed to the notion of superiority of their own culture and political systems. Barbara N. Ramusack's "Cultural Missionaries, Maternal Imperialists, Feminist Allies: British Women Activists in India, 1865–1945," focuses on five activists: Mary Carpenter, Annette Akroyd Beveridge, Margaret Noble/Sister Nivedita, Margaret Gillespie Cousins, and Eleanor Rathbone. Annette Akroyd Beveridge generally looked upon Indians as inferior, which explains why she became a pivotal force in opposition to the Ilbert Bill. Among these five women, Margaret Noble had the most contact with the Indian women and men who were not educated elites. Margaret Cousins was the first to cooperate almost exclusively with Indian women in her organizational and political activities on their behalf and to serve as a mentor to younger Indian women. (Cousins's relationship with Kamaladevi Chattopadhyay, a radical social and cultural activist, is quite similar to Le Brun's relationship with Sha'rawi in Egypt, as described by Hatem.) Perhaps Noble's and Cousins's Irish background helped them empathize with colonized Indians. Although Noble, Cousins, and Rathbone were active supporters of Indian nationalists and their demand for self-government, all five women continued to think that the colonial government was a major factor in the improvement of the condition of Indian women. Ramusack terms these five women "maternal imperialists" because "in various ways these British women activists embodied a benevolent maternal imperialism. They were frequently referred to as mothers or saw themselves as mothering India and Indians."

The attitude of other feminists in Britain toward colonized women embodied many aspects of these "maternal imperialists." Moreover, argues Antoinette M. Burton in her essay "The White Woman's Burden: British Feminists and 'The Indian Woman,' 1865–1915," middle-class Victorian feminists viewed Indian women both as passive subjects and as examples against which to gauge their own progress. According to Burton, "although Indian women of the period were active in social reform and feminist causes of their own making, many British feminists insisted on creating them as passive colonial subjects partly in order to imagine and to realize their own feminist objectives within the context of the imperial nation into which they sought admission." The empire, far from being outside women's sphere, was central to it, Burton contends. In insisting upon their right to citizenship, suffragists and suffragettes not only claimed their right to be part of the political nation but also demanded to take their part in the political empire.

Nancy L. Paxton explores Burton's and Ramusack's subjects further in "Complicity and Resistance in the Writings of Flora Annie Steel and Annie Besant," drawing primarily upon two women's autobiographical writings. Paxton suggests how their experiences of living in India under the British raj shaped their analyses of race, class, and power, and discusses the subsequent impact of this experience on their understanding of feminism. By a detailed comparison of the positions both took on these issues, Paxton illuminates "the largely undocumented role that imperialism played in shaping British feminism in the second half of the nineteenth century." Following Adrienne Rich's formulation of resisting women being "disloyal to civilization," Paxton argues that Steel's feminism was compromised by the power she claimed as a civil servant's wife under the raj; Besant enacted her disloyalty to the British empire through support of Indian nationalism, while sacrificing some of her feminist principles in the process of supporting Theosophy.

Empire provided opportunities to maternal imperialists, feminist allies, and activists to test their independence from the constraints of patriarchal society. The experiences of British nurses in colonial West Africa is another example of how Western women took advantage of opportunities opened by imperialism, while at the same time resisting its restraints. In the late nineteenth century, the consolidation of British rule and the growth of European communities on the west coast of Africa brought an immediate demand for improved medical care. Leading colonial officials' wives established the Colonial Nursing Association in 1896. In "The 'White Woman's Burden' in the 'White Man's Grave': The Introduction of British Nurses in Colonial West Africa," Dea Birkett examines the careers of British nurses who went to West Africa for adventure, authority, and enhanced status.

But instead of emphasizing their nursing skills, Birkett argues, colonial authorities wanted them to complement and bolster male authority in a limited, strictly feminine role, which prompted the nurses to rebel.

Where some sought opportunity for independence and adventure
through nursing, others, British and American women missionaries, went
to the colonies to transplant Western values and culture. The latter part of
the nineteenth century found many female missionaries working in India;
they were committed to substantially changing the social norms that affected Indian women's lives. In "A New Humanity: American Missionaries' Ideals for Women in North India, 1870–1930," Leslie A. Flemming
claims that the commitment of American women missionaries was often
couched in a rhetoric that stressed women's low status in Indian society
and urged conversion to Christianity as a means of raising women's status.
In addition, Flemming argues that missionaries also saw themselves as
agents of change, carrying values culturally superior to those embodied in
the rigid structure of relations between the various Hindu *jatis* (kin-based
subcastes) and between Hindus and members of other religious communities. Focusing on American Presbyterian women missionaries, Flemming
argues that they offered to Indian women a vision of womanhood strongly
oriented toward domestic roles; they did not, despite their self-construction as change-agents, offer Indian women radically new roles. Nevertheless, because of their emphasis on education, physical well-being, and voluntary activities that took women outside their homes, the missionaries
encouraged Indian women to begin breaking down the strong public-
private distinctions that characterized much of North Indian life and to assume roles not previously available to them in Indian culture.

White American and European Protestant church boards began to establish missions in Africa in the nineteenth century as they had in India. These
churches frequently appointed African-American missionaries, whose
work is examined by Sylvia M. Jacobs in "Give a Thought to Africa: Black
Women Missionaries in Southern Africa." Jacobs shows that the relationship of African-American missionaries with Africa and Africans was both
ambivalent and contradictory. They shared prevailing white perceptions of
Africa as a "Dark Continent" that needed civilizing, yet they came to be
seen as promoting unrest among Africans. Examining activities of nine
African-American women missionaries in Southern Africa, Jacobs discusses how imperialism, gender, and race limited their roles as missionaries in Africa. In order to be successful in their missionary works, they had
to be careful not to offend European imperialists. They were viewed by
their mission boards and by their male colleagues as second-class missionaries, and, with the rise of Jim Crow in the United States, Africans and African-Americans were treated with comparable racial prejudice.

Believing in their own racial and cultural superiority, the majority of
Western women and men rejected indigenous institutions and cultures of
the colonies. In "Shawls, Jewelry, Curry, and Rice in Victorian Britain,"

Nupur Chaudhuri indicates that British wives' negative attitudes regarding the use of Indian goods and dishes was almost totally confined to the colonial environment. Examining accounts from women's periodicals, newspaper advertisements, cookbooks, household manuals, and memsahibs' private letters, Chaudhuri argues that memsahibs served as a major channel for Indian artifacts and mediator of Indian tastes to a segment of upper middle-class and middle-class Victorian women in Britain. This material transport fostered a mutually beneficial economic system, outside the mainstream economic structure of the country, for memsahibs and their sisters at home.

We have already mentioned that historians have blamed Western women for creating racial tension by widening the gap between the colonizers and the colonized. In "White Women in a Changing World: Employment, Voluntary Work, and Sex in Post–World War II Northern Rhodesia," Karen Tranberg Hansen challenges this thesis. She has shown that "it was class relations, and in particular the insistence on British class-bound practices, that contributed to growing racial tensions in Northern Rhodesia during the late colonial period." In addition, Hansen questions the usefulness here of the notion of "incorporated wife": white women tested other roles than that of wife in the late colonial period in Northern Rhodesia, a period characterized by greater economic and sexual freedom than before.

These essays touch upon themes that merit considerable further exploration and point to others. Thinking about gender in this context was connected with thinking about race. Wrapped in the language of science, structures and assumptions of both proved difficult to transcend.[27] The West African nurses analyzed by Birkett acted in ways that preserved hierarchies of race and culture while opening to question hierarchies of gender. A similar pattern can be found in Burton's examination of British suffragists and suffragettes. African-American missionaries described by Jacobs challenged hierarchies of race but accepted hierarchies of culture. Those Western women examined by Sinha who opposed the Ilbert Bill saw a particular (Indian) configuration of gender hierarchy as evidence of Indian cultural inferiority. Traveler Mary Hall, Blake's assessment suggests, transcended racial and cultural difference while reaffirming class hierarchy. Those Western women who embraced Indian culture, such as Sister Nivedita or Annie Besant, perhaps rejected in a profound way the scientific thought that undergirded Western notions of evolution, race, culture, and gender. Indeed, the study of individuals, most strikingly in this volume Isabelle Eberhardt, reveals how intertwined and jumbled were concepts of racial, cultural, and gender identity. Moreover, these aspects of identity appear to have been situational as well. The memsahibs that Chaudhuri studies, however much they distanced themselves from Indian culture in India, found it to be a resource (in terms of both economics and identity) once they returned to England.

Some of these essays clearly show that, for many of these Western women, rethinking gender roles in their society proved difficult when dealing with the ideology of imperialist motherhood.[28] Indeed, some of the least overtly imperialist women, as Ramusack illuminates, spoke and acted in a maternal idiom, substituting a hierarchy of age for one of race or gender. Indeed, one of the most powerful gender role messages passed on by Western women, for example, as missionaries, was their vision of motherhood.[29]

This collection of essays emphasizes the complex part played by Western women in both sustaining imperialism and resisting or undermining it. The link between pro-imperial and anti-suffrage politics, embodied in but not limited to Flora Shaw, is striking, even if the converse linkage (anti-imperialist and pro-suffrage politics), as Burton argues, was not inevitable and strong. The images of indigenous women transmitted by feminists, missionaries, memsahibs, and travelers contributed to defining and explicating the empire to people back home.[30]

Several essays introduce an inadequately examined feature of colonial life: sex, sexuality, and sexual control.[31] Paxton argues that a "view of sexuality as a dangerous force" was central to Steel's and Besant's spiritual self-concepts and identity. In a later period in colonial Northern Rhodesia, Hansen finds irregular sex—premarital, extramarital, and interracial—to be unsettling to the keepers of "civilized standards."[32] The sexual double standard granted European men sexual access to indigenous women as concubines and prostitutes. More needs to be discovered in terms of indigenous women's views of and responses to sexuality in the colonial context.[33] Regulation of European and indigenous people's sexuality was one component of colonial rule, whether it was exercised by the provision of regulated prostitution for colonial troops or the manipulation of health policy regarding venereal disease.[34]

These essays demonstrate that Western women influenced the contours of colonial history. Further studies will reveal nuances, for example the different gender ideologies of missionaries from different countries, ethnic groups, and denominations and their implications for indigenous people.[35] Explorations into cultural interchanges in the domestic sphere, enlarging upon Chaudhuri's work and expanding into other areas of childbirth and childrearing, for example, will further flesh out our sense of the gendered social and cultural implications of imperialism.

NOTES

1. The editors thank Dorothy O. Helly and Helen Callaway for their extensive suggestions and comments.

2. *Out of Africa* is a feature film about Isak Dinesen, the Danish writer (Karen

Blixen) who lived in and drew inspiration from colonial Kenya. *Out of Africa* has been followed by a long television special about Beryl Markham, the first person to fly west from London to North America and, incidentally, Blixen's rival for the affections of Kenyan white hunter Denys Finch-Hatton. Both events, naturally, surround the reissuing of their respective biographies, autobiographies, and writings. The uncritical perspective of *Out of Africa* is counterpoised by the film (and book) *White Mischief*, which reveals the seamy underside of the Happy Valley scene on whose margins Blixen lived. In none of these is Africa more than the backdrop. In contrast, the film *A World Apart*, directed by Shawn Slovo, tells from a daughter's viewpoint a fictionalized autobiographical tale of white engagement in Africa, based on the life of Ruth First, a South African opponent of apartheid.

3. Salman Rushdie, "The Raj Revival," *The Observer* (April 1, 1984): 19; also quoted by Joanna Liddle and Rama Joshi, "Gender and Colonialism: Women's Organization Under the Raj," *Women's Studies International Forum* 8 (1985): 521.

Since the nineteenth century, India has provided European authors background as an exotic world of color, romance, and adventure. Following that tradition, Ruth Prawar Jhabvala wrote the Booker Prize–winning novel *Heat and Dust* (New York: Harper and Row, 1975), which was released as a film in 1983. M. M. Kaye's adventure and romance *The Far Pavilion* (New York: St. Martin's, 1978) has been dramatized for television. Paul Scott's *Jewel in the Crown* (New York: William Morrow, 1966, 1968, 1978), a reissued quartet of novels about the last days of the raj, also appeared as a BBC television series. In response to the public's interest in colonial settings, the film version of E. M. Forster's *A Passage to India* (New York: Harcourt Brace Jovanovich, 1924) was released in 1985. *Clive of India* and *War on the Springing Tiger* were two documentaries that dealt with the Indian subcontinent.

4. Rushdie, p. 19; Liddle and Joshi, p. 528.

5. Louis James, "Tom Brown's Imperialist Sons," *Victorian Studies* 18 (1973): 89–99; Patrick H. Dunae, "Boys' Literature and the Idea of Empire, 1870–1914," *Victorian Studies* 24 (1980): 105–21; J. S. Bratton, "Of England, Home, and Duty: The Image of England in Victorian and Edwardian Juvenile Fiction," in *Imperialism and Popular Culture*, ed. John M. Mackenzie (Manchester: Manchester University Press, 1986), pp. 73–93.

6. Cf. Cynthia Enloe, *Bananas, Beaches and Bases: Making Feminist Sense of International Politics* (1989; Berkeley and Los Angeles: University of California Press, 1990), pp. 51–52. See footnote 2.

7. Harry Magdoff, *Imperialism* (New York: Monthly Review Press, 1978), pp. 117, 139.

8. D. K. Fieldhouse, *Colonialism, 1870–1945* (London: Weidenfield and Nicholson, 1981), pp. 2–5.

9. Patrick Brantlinger, *Rule of Darkness: British Literature and Imperialism, 1830–1914* (Ithaca: Cornell University Press, 1988), p. 10.

10. Frantz Fanon, *Black Skin, White Masks: The Experiences of a Black Man in a White World*, trans. Charles Lam Markmann (1952; New York: Grove Press, 1967); Albert Memmi, *The Colonizer and the Colonized*, trans. Howard Greenfield (Boston: Beacon Press, 1967); O. Mannoni, *Prospero and Caliban: The Psychology of Colonization* (New York: Praeger, 1964).

11. Edward W. Said, *Orientalism* (New York: Vintage Books, 1979), p. 95.

12. Here we are using the word "subalterns" as defined by Ranjit in his "On Some Aspects of the Historiography of Colonial India," in *Subaltern Studies* 1 (1982). Malek Alloula, *The Colonial Harem* (Minneapolis: University of Minnesota Press, 1986); Rana Kabani, *Europe's Myths of Orient* (Bloomington: Indiana University Press, 1986); Kumkum Sangari and Sudesh Vaid, eds., *Recasting Women: Essays in Colonial History* (New Delhi: Kali for Women Press, 1989); Liddle and Joshi, pp.

521–29; Mrinalini Sinha, "Manliness: A Victorian Ideal and Colonial Policy in late Nineteenth-Century Bengal," Ph.D. diss., SUNY at Stony Brook, 1988); Chandra Mohanty, "Under Western Eyes: Feminist Scholarship and Colonial Discourse," *Feminist Review* 39 (1988): 61–88; Gauri Viswanathan, *Masks of Conquest: Literary Study and British Rule in India* (New York: Columbia University Press, 1989) are some important works done by scholars who have non-Western roots.

13. Dorothy O. Helly, *Livingstone's Legacy: Horace Waller and Victorian Mythmaking* (Athens: Ohio University Press, 1987); Fieldhouse; V. G. Kiernan, *The Lords of Human Kind: European Attitudes towards the Outside World in the Imperial Age* (London: Weidenfield and Nicolson, 1976); C. C. Eldridge, *Victorian Imperialism* (London: Hodder & Stoughton, 1978); Ronald Hyam, *Britain's Imperial Century, 1815–1914: A Study of Empire and Expansion* (London: Batsford, 1976); John Saville, "Imperialism and the Victorians," in *In Search of Victorian Values: Aspects of Nineteenth-Century Thought and Society*, ed. Eric M. Sigsworth (Manchester: Manchester University Press, 1988); J. M. Mackenzie, *Propaganda and Empire: The Manipulation of British Public Opinion, 1880–1960* (Manchester: Manchester University Press, 1984); W. Baumgart, *The Idea and Reality of British and French Colonial Expansion 1880–1914* (Oxford: Oxford University Press, 1982); Bernard S. Cohn, "Representing Authority in Victorian India," and Terence Ranger, "The Invention of Tradition in Colonial Africa," in *The Invention of Tradition*, ed. Eric Hobsbawm and Terence Ranger (Cambridge: Cambridge University Press, 1983); Bob Dixon, *Catching Them Young: Political Ideas in Children's Fiction*, vol. 2 (London: Pluto Press, 1977); and Brantlinger.

14. Helen Callaway, *Gender, Culture, and Empire: European Women in Colonial Nigeria* (Urbana: University of Illinois Press, 1987), p. 5.

15. For example, Percival Spear, *The Nabob* (London: Oxford University Press, 1967); Mark Nadis, "Evolution of the Sahibs," *The Historian* 19 (1975): 425–35; J. K. Stanford, *Ladies in the Sun: The Memsahibs in India, 1790–1860* (London: The Galley Press, 1962); and to a lesser extent, Kenneth Ballhatchet, *Race and Sex and Class under the Raj* (London: Weidenfield & Nicolson, 1980).

16. Richard Voeltz, "Still out in the Midday Sun? Women, Popular History, and the Relevance of the Study of Imperial History," (Paper presented at the American Historical Association conference, Cincinnati, 1988).

17. See Anand Yang's review essay in *Women's Studies International Forum* 13 (1990): 407–8; Ann L. Stoler, "Making Empire Respectable: The Politics of Race and Sexual Morality in Twentieth-Century Colonial Cultures," *American Ethnologist* 16 (1989): 634–60.

18. V. Bamfield, *On the Strength: The Story of the British Army Wife* (London: Charles Knight, 1974); Pat Barr, *The Memsahibs: The Women of Victorian India* (London: Secker and Warburg, 1976); Margaret MacMillan, *Women of the Raj* (London: Thames and Hudson, 1988) are examples of popular history.

19. Callaway; Claudia Knapman, *White Women in Fiji, 1835–1930: The Ruin of Empire?* (Sydney: Allen and Unwin, 1986); Mary Ann Lind, *The Compassionate Memsahibs: Welfare Activities of British Women in India, 1900–1947* (New York: Greenwood Press, 1988) are some examples of these scholarly writings. See Susan Bailey, *Women and the British Empire: An Annotated Guide to Sources* (New York: Garland Publishing Company, 1987).

20. Jane Haggis, "Gendering Colonialism or Colonising Gender? Recent Women's Studies Approaches to White Women and the History of British Colonialism," *Women's Studies International Forum* 13 (1990): 105–15.

21. Judith M. Bennett, "Feminism and History," *Gender and History* 1 (1989): 262–63.

22. Fieldhouse, p. 29.

23. Fieldhouse, pp. 32–33.

24. For a discussion of these issues in the Indian context, see Partha Chatterjee, "Colonialism, Nationalism, and Colonialized Women: The Contest in India," *American Ethnologist* 16 (1989): 622–33.

25. *Oeuvres complètes,* ed. Albert Thibaudet and Maurice Rat (Paris: Gallimard, 1962), p. 203. The English translation is from Donald M. Frame, ed. and trans., *The Complete Essays of Montaigne* (Stanford: Stanford University Press, 1965), pp. 152, 200.

26. MacMillan, pp. 222–23.

27. Joyce Avrech Berkman discusses these ideas in situating her subject in *The Healing Imagination of Olive Schreiner: Beyond South African Colonialism* (Amherst: University of Massachusetts Press, 1989).

28. Anna Davin, "Imperialism and Motherhood," *History Workshop Journal* 5 (1978): 9–65.

29. Nancy Hunt discusses how missionary societies found single women problematic in " 'Single Ladies on the Congo': Protestant Missionary Tensions and Voices," *Women's Studies International Forum* 13 (1990): 395–403.

30. Janaki Nair analyzes several major themes in this discourse in "Uncovering the Zenana: Visions of Indian Womanhood in Englishwomen's Writings, 1813–1940," *Journal of Women's History* 2 (1990): 8–34.

31. Ann Stoler's work examines sexuality and sexual control as one aspect of colonial culture; see her article cited above and Stoler and Frederick Cooper, "Introduction: Tensions of Empire: Colonial Control and Visions of Rule," part of a special issue of *American Ethnologist* 16, no. 4 (1989). Ronald Hyam's *Empire and Sexuality* (Manchester: Manchester University Press, 1990) is the most recent, if controversial, effort. A criticism of his articles on this subject is found in Mark T. Berger, "Imperialism and Sexual Exploitation: A Response to Ronald Hyam's 'Empire and Sexual Opportunity,' " *The Journal of Imperial and Commonwealth History* 17 (1988): 83–89. Ballhatchet's was an early and useful analysis.

32. Hansen explores European notions of Northern Rhodesian African women's sexuality in "Body Politics: Sexuality, Gender, and Domestic Service in Zambia," *Journal of Women's History* 2 (1990): 120–42.

33. See Margaret Strobel, *European Women and the Second British Empire* (Bloomington: Indiana University Press, 1991), chapter 1. For prostitution, see Luise White's *The Comforts of Home: Prostitution in Colonial Nairobi* (Chicago: University of Chicago Press, 1990), and for Indian courtesans, see Veena Talwar Oldenberg's "Lifestyle as Resistance: The Case of the Courtesans of Lucknow, India," *Feminist Studies* 16 (1990): 259–87.

34. See Carol Summers, "Intimate Colonialism: The Imperial Production of Reproduction in Uganda, 1907–1925," *Signs* 16, no. 4 (1991): 787–807.

35. An early and valuable exploration of this theme is Marcia Wright's *German Missions in Tanganyika, 1891–1914: Lutherans and Moravians in the Southern Highlands* (London: Oxford University Press, 1971).

Images of One Another

A WOMAN'S TREK

WHAT DIFFERENCE DOES GENDER MAKE?

Susan L. Blake

In the preface to her 1907 narrative *A Woman's Trek from the Cape to Cairo,*
Mary Hall claims that a woman's point of view will make her book different
from the usual account of African travel:

> As I am the first woman of any nationality to have accomplished the entire
> journey from the Cape to Cairo, I think perhaps a simple account of how I
> managed to do it quite alone may be of some interest to many who, for var-
> ious reasons, real or imaginary, are unable to go so far afield. I hope that a
> book, written from a woman's point of view, minus big game romances,
> and the usual exaggerations incidental to all things African, may be accept-
> able. (P. v)

Hall here addresses the question in the foreground or background of the
several recent studies of Victorian women travelers in Africa: In the relation
of European travelers to empire, what difference does gender make?[1]

Implicit in this question is the hope that women, colonized themselves
by gender, might recognize and oppose colonization based on race. As
Catherine Barnes Stevenson observes,

> the attitudes of women travellers toward imperialism and toward Africans
> are not easily categorized. In general, . . . most Victorian women travellers
> accept the notion of British superiority and sanction the presence of Britain
> in Africa. However, within this general framework of acceptance, they fre-
> quently voice strong criticism of their country's treatment of specific situa-
> tions or particular African tribes.[2]

At one extreme, the activist journalist Florence Douglas Dixie, who devoted her South African sojourn and narrative to the restoration of the
Zulu king deposed by the British in 1879 and later championed the causes
of the Irish, animals, and women, made in the course of her career, if not

explicitly in a single text, the feminist connection between restrictions on women's rights in Britain and British imperialism abroad.[3] At the other extreme, Daisy Chown, the timid author of a 1927 narrative tellingly subtitled *A Woman's **Wanderings** from the Cape to Cairo* (emphasis added), repeats unquestioningly both imperial attitudes toward Africans and popular stereotypes of independent women. Most Victorian and early twentieth-century women narrators, however, including Mary Hall and her better-known role model Mary Kingsley, mix endorsements of empire and accounts of personal experience that undercut it. In the endorsements of empire, they follow, though often less emphatically, the conventions of men's narratives. It is in the narration of incident—the fiction of the traveler-protagonist encountering Africa—that the differences between male and female travel narrators' relations to empire emerge.

We can see the differences in men's and women's representation of the relationship between traveler and Africa by comparing the narration of incident in *A Woman's Trek* with that in two nearly contemporaneous Cape-to-Cairo narratives by men: *From the Cape to Cairo: The First Traverse of Africa from South to North* by Ewart S. Grogan (with one chapter by Arthur H. Sharp), 1900, and *Through the Heart of Africa* by Frank H. Melland and Edward H. Cholmeley, 1912. Despite the Cape-to-Cairo claims of their titles, neither Grogan nor Hall started a continuous trek in Cape Town; both started in Portuguese East Africa, justifying their titles by previous travel in South Africa. Thus their itineraries are comparable to that of Melland and Cholmeley, who trekked to Cairo from Northern Rhodesia. But both the Cape-to-Cairo claim—inspired by Cecil Rhodes's dream of laying a transcontinental rail and telegraph line to secure the "backbone" of Africa for Britain—and the anatomical metaphor of Melland and Cholmeley's title reveal the implicit imperialism of all travel by Europeans in the empire. The similarity of the routes all of these writers followed and the contemporaneity of their narratives help to isolate the differences in their relations to empire attributable to gender.

Among any three individuals, of course, gender is not the only difference. Grogan, Melland (the actual writer of *Through the Heart of Africa*), and Hall also differ in age, class, marital status, profession, temperament, and how much we know about their circumstances and motivations. But these differences are related to gender. Grogan, the fourteenth of twenty-one children of a rich estate agent, became one of the most outspoken, outrageous, and long-lived members of Kenya settler society and the subject of an admiring biography. At the time of his trek he was in his early twenties, had been "sent down" from Cambridge for playing pranks, had spent a couple of years fighting the Ndebele in South Africa, and was looking for a way to impress his prospective father-in-law.[4] He represented himself, however, as a person of public significance, the surveyor and legitimator of Rhodes's Cape-to-Cairo connection. Melland, listed in *Who Was Who among English and European Authors 1931–1949*, seems to have followed a typical

career path for a servant of empire: graduate of Shrewsbury and
colonial official in Northern Rhodesia, representative of Northern I
in London, husband, father, editor, and journalist on African to
trek was sponsored, in effect, by the civil service, for it was his means of
travel home on leave, at the age of thirty-one after nine years in Africa, and
he was allowed time after his return to write it up. Different as they were,
Melland the civil servant and Grogan the free-lance adventurer both had
upper middle-class backgrounds, public school and university opportunities, and a sense of role, whether official or self-claimed, in the work of empire. In these respects, they were both typical of male travelers in the age of
empire, most of whom had some function in colonial institutions, which
were themselves part of the sequence of all-male, middle- and upper-class
institutions—from public school to London club—of British public life.[5]

Mary Hall, by contrast, has no public identity except as the author of *A
Woman's Trek* and a later narrative of a trip around the world. According to
public records, she was born in 1857, the daughter of a master gasfitter in
the lower-class London district of Southwark, and died in 1919 in a modest
row house she did not own in genteel Hampstead. She was admitted to
membership in the Royal Geographical Society in 1913 and left an estate of
over seven thousand pounds at a time when most estates were under one
thousand. Her rise in class appears to have been assisted by her brother, a
surveyor and land agent who lived in a Hampstead mansion and left an
estate of 180,000 pounds when he died in 1908. She never married, was in
her late forties when she traveled in Africa, and, according to her obituary,
started traveling for that most common of reasons attributed to women,
her health.[6] She is as typical of Victorian women travelers as Grogan and
Melland are of men. As the title of Dea Birkett's composite biography of
Victorian women travelers, *Spinsters Abroad,* emphasizes, women who had
the freedom to travel were almost all single; they often had to wait for this
freedom until the death of parents or husbands left them with money and
without responsibilities; and, unless they were missionaries, they traveled
for travel's own sake because, except for the church, the institutions of empire excluded women. In a segregated society, few distinctions between individuals on opposite sides of the divide are unrelated to the basis of segregation.

As both travelers and narrators, individual Europeans stand somewhere
between Africa and empire. In relation to Africa they are like imperial powers. They undertake to conquer, grasp, or assimilate challenging lands and
alien peoples. They exercise the power they have (wealth, stamina, inge-
nuity, flexibility) to gain more power (knowledge of land, people, flora,
fauna; knowledge of self; sense of achievement). They requisition food,
shelter, carriers, and guides and return cash, medical attention, and
glimpses and tokens of European culture. Like the empire, they both assert
authority over and depend upon the people they encounter. The narrative
representations of their relationships with Africa and Africans constitute

models for the national relationship between Self and Other that is empire. "How I managed to do it" conveys "how it can, and should, be done." At the same time, the individual's experience with Africa is mediated by the empire, "how it is presently being done." Thus the representation of the relationship between Self and Other in travel narratives offers both an ideal conception of empire and a critique of the conception in practice.

The single situation that brings into sharpest focus the relationship between Self and Other in these travel narratives is also their common denominator, the daily negotiation for hospitality. Mary Louise Pratt, writing about eighteenth- and early nineteenth-century narratives, calls the meeting between the traveler at the head of a caravan and the chief at the head of a village a "courtly encounter."[7] In the imperial period, however, the encounter is not necessarily courtly. It holds the potential for domination as well as dialogue, and its representation dramatizes the narrator's understanding of authority, dependency, and reciprocity.

Ewart S. Grogan, who claims that the twin purposes of his journey were to survey the Cape-to-Cairo transportation route and to shoot big game, is undoubtedly one of the writers from whom Mary Hall distinguishes herself. In the tradition of explorer-heroes, the protagonist of *From the Cape to Cairo* lives in constant combat with Africa. He stalks and drops dangerous animals, cuts through a thousand miles of papyrus swamp, overcomes hostile Dinkas, purges the country of cannibals, whips his servants into honesty, and tortures his porters into alacrity. He has consistent difficulty obtaining provisions. After a string of what he considers inhospitable receptions, Grogan reports:

> At Gombi, things reached a climax, the chief telling me that he wanted no white men in his country, that the Portuguese forced them to work for nothing, and demanded a 5 r. hut tax, that my men would obtain no food, etc. etc., *ad nauseam*. In thirty seconds he was prone, and taking a severe dose of hippo-whip before his astonished band of elders; he rose refreshed and brought me flour and fowls, guides to show me game, and a guide to Chiperoni for the morrow. (P. 50)

The relationship between Self and Other here is clearly that of subject to object. As Grogan the protagonist fells the chief without a word, Grogan the narrator raises only to dismiss the chief's claims to subjectivity: his sovereignty over his country, his position among the elders, his reason, his language. In a potential dialogue, Grogan speaks with his weapon; since he can overcome the chief with his hippo-whip, he need not answer his argument. The source of his authority is his power.

As he makes explicit in countless assertions and innuendoes, Grogan's relationship with the chief at Gombi is his model of empire. His task as a surveyor is to overcome the physical obstacles of the land for a rail route that is itself a means to conquer the land for trade, settlement, and political

Illustration by A. D. McCormick after a sketch by Ewart S. Grogan, *From the Cape to Cairo: The First Traverse of Africa from South to North*, 1900.

control. He recommends forced labor for Africans, admires German colonial methods because they allow force, extends the application of Lord Salisbury's equation of "civilization" and "subjugation" from land to people (pp. 318–19). His model of empire also puts him in conflict with the Colonial Office, which, with "sickly, unreasoning philanthropy" (p. 358), imagines Africans have rights (that is, subjectivity) and fails to exercise British power. Grogan embeds this conflict in his statement of the purpose of the narrative:

> to convince my readers that the trans-continental communication by electricity and steam, so far from being the wild dream, treated with such shameless cruelty by those whose range of vision is limited to the end of their nose, is now, thanks to the land-accumulating, wind-raising, and administrative ability of Mr. Rhodes, and provided that the scheme can be kept free from the blighting touch of British Red Tape, a looming reality of the near future temporarily dependent on Throgmorton Street. (P. xv)

He identifies with Rhodes, the individual visionary (from whom he solicited an introduction to the book), against timid and sluggish social organization. Grogan's power does not come from the empire; rather, such power as the empire is willing to exercise comes from individuals like himself and Rhodes.

Grogan's concept of power is not only personal but sexual. Early explorers commonly represented the African land as female and its exploration as sexual conquest. In this account, Grogan represents his meeting with the chief at Gombi as rape. He applies the phallic whip to the "prone" chief as though in accordance with locker-room advice on how to handle a woman. And the result—"he rose refreshed and brought me flour and fowls"—confirms the wisdom of that advice: the chief really liked it, and it restored him to his (servile) nature. For Grogan, the source of authority is power, the source of power, manhood.

Although the announced purpose of *From the Cape to Cairo* is to prove the practicability of the Cape-to-Cairo connection, the motive throughout is to prove Grogan's manhood. This is why, in the concluding chapters of advice to the Colonial Office, "The Pursuit of Big Game" takes its place between "The Swamps of the Upper Nile, and Their Effect on the Water-Supply of Egypt" and "Native Questions." Like the archetypal quest hero, Grogan the protagonist tests himself against treacherous terrain, wild animals, and unworthy men and proves himself the true heir of his father, Rhodes. The story that Grogan conceived his trek in the midst of an unfavorable interview with his prospective father-in-law suggests that Grogan the traveler even undertook these tests to win the hand of the princess.[8] The humiliation of the chief of Gombi is only a particularly explicit incident in a narrative of racial conquest rooted in gender.

Frank Melland and Edward Cholmeley in *Through the Heart of Africa* present a sharp contrast to Grogan. They are using the better part of their home leave to trek across Africa because they are "interested . . . in the African native and the possibilities and development of his country" (p. 2). Where Grogan bags big-game trophies, they collect ethnographic information. Where Grogan has to bully local chiefs into supplying provisions, they find ready hospitality.

One gracious reception is provided by Muchereka, a female sultan in German East Africa:

> [H]er reception of us was an amusing mixture of dignity, familiarity, and respect. She got in a handshake, when we were off our guard, provided us with stools until our chairs arrived, invited us to pitch our tents close to her own compound, . . . and gave us the use of a comfortable and well-built *nsaka*, or half-open shelter, just outside it.
>
> We tried the experiment of inviting her to have a cup of tea with us when she came round to pay a call in the afternoon. She accepted with alacrity; and, sitting on her chair, which she had brought with her, her husband and court squatting on the ground at her side, showed by her enjoyment of two cups sweetened with plenty of sugar, that it was not an unfamiliar beverage. . . . She had already presented us with a pot of beer, of which we found quantities in process of brewing on our arrival, and later twice repeated the gift, invariably tasting it herself before it was handed to us. It was a little thin at first, but evidently grew mellow within the next few

From Frank H. Melland and Edward H. Cholmeley,
Through the Heart of Africa, 1912.

hours, and the penetrating harangue to which she treated her husband
shortly after the middle of the following night testified to its potency when
taken in sufficiently generous doses. (Pp. 46–47)

In this smoothly recounted meeting between travelers and Africans, conflict is not only absent, but unthinkable. Its place is taken by detailed description, which serves both the narrators' acknowledged purpose, to communicate as much information as possible about the land, peoples, and
colonial administration in the countries they traverse, and their implicit
purpose, to demonstrate the ease with which, thanks to their experience in

the Colonial Service and the natural manners of English gentlemen, they travel unbeaten tracks.

There is a conflict in the narrative, however, between the apparently objective description and the evaluative framework. On the one hand, the relationship between description and evaluation reinforces the narrators' self-representation as gentlemen; only the assumption of Muchereka's inferiority makes their attention to the details of her hospitality—the stools, the "well-built *nsaka*"—seem objective, that is, open-minded, rather than simply observant. On the other hand, in the characterization of Muchereka, description escapes the bounds of evaluation and calls attention to their narrative manipulation. The narrators attempt to take control of the relationship between themselves and Muchereka by referring to the tea party, potentially the interaction between two subjects, as an "experiment," in which a subject acts upon an object. But the description of Muchereka, sitting on her chair, surrounded by her court, enjoying her tea, even getting in a handshake, reveals her acting like a subject. When the narrators speak of her "mixture of dignity, familiarity, and respect" as "amusing," they are objectifying her very subjectivity.

Muchereka is "amusing" because she is out of her place in two respects: as an African assuming social equality with Europeans and as a woman dominating her husband and other men. In the last sentence, the narrators manage, by the dexterous use of elevated diction and subordinate clauses, to characterize Muchereka as a drunken shrew while simultaneously representing themselves as gentlemanly scientists too well bred to notice a lady's departure from universally accepted standards of decorum, though too thorough to overlook ethnographically interesting evidence of the potency of the local beer.

Unlike Grogan, Melland and Cholmeley do not claim personal credit for their success with Africans. They do not differentiate themselves from each other or from the office and class they represent. Not until "one of us (Cholmeley)" gets sick does Melland get trapped into using, briefly, the pronoun "I" (p. 122). "Of ourselves," they say in the first paragraph, where other narrators mention childhood ambition or influence,

> we need merely say that, after years of residence in the Northern and least known province of Rhodesia, with a thorough acquaintance with the ordinary ways of reaching and leaving the continent, inspired by a craving to know something more of what lay beyond us, we decided to travel home by the countries to the North of us, instead of by the more beaten tracks. The probability that our acquaintance with a similar country would enable us the better to observe and more justly appreciate what we saw than the traveller or sportsman paying perhaps his only visit to the continent, helped to encourage us in the hope that a journey that was bound to occupy at least the greater part of our vacation leave would not be without result as a useful and educative experience. (Pp. 1–2)

Their easy relations with Africans throughout their trip both confirm the prediction that their "acquaintance with a similar country" will facilitate their travel and validate that "acquaintance," which is the training and perspective of the British Colonial Service. Their comment on the hospitality of the villages in German East Africa is telling: "Though one might expect it from one's own natives, it was a pleasant surprise to find it extended to total strangers in a foreign territory" (p. 13). If the British colonial way of relating to Africans elicits such friendliness even in a territory where, as they will emphasize, colonial methods are quite different, it is evidently appreciated by the Africans and based on a true understanding of their character.

Melland and Cholmeley derive their identity and authority from the role of colonial officer, which is based on the role of gentleman, which is grounded in the code of chivalry, "a model of altruistic relations between the powerful and the weak, the rulers and the ruled, the autonomous actor and his dependents, and what was considered to be the strong male and the physically fragile female."[9] Chivalric altruism depends—as Melland and Cholmeley's account of the tea party with Muchereka shows—on the weakness, dependency, and fragility of all categories of people other than upper-class English men. Grogan acts out the chivalric myth as a knight errant, cleansing the land of monsters and villains. Melland and Cholmeley take the role of benevolent *seigneur*, beloved of his dependents. Their conception of the ideal relation between Self and Other is gentler than Grogan's but just as objectifying and just as specifically male.

As a woman, Mary Hall had no access to her male contemporaries' reasons for African travel. In the opening pages of her narrative, she presents herself as the generic traveler: "I have always been interested in seeing fresh countries and peoples, and have ever considered travelling the most delightful method of studying geography. . . . In 1904, when South Africa was still uppermost in all minds, I decided to turn my steps in that direction" (p. 2). She is interested, but unengaged, in her country's fortunes abroad (*"when* South Africa," not *because*), motivated instead by a personal appetite for new experience.

The argument of her narrative is that ordinary travelers, particularly women, can travel in Africa. It is supported by references to comfortable hotels and convenient trains in colonial southern Africa and Egypt and by accounts of amicable relations with porters and villages in the less known and therefore more interesting territory between. Hence, instead of concluding, as Grogan and Melland and Cholmeley do, with a chapter about the implications of her experiences for the colonial administration, she ends her "simple account" in Khartoum, over a thousand miles before the end of her trip, because, thanks to a connection by riverboat and "very luxurious train," the Cairo-to-Khartoum segment is now "within the reach of the ordinary tourist" (p. 418).

From Mary Hall, *A Woman's Trek from the Cape to Cairo*, 1907.

Hall is aware that as a woman she also lacks the typical male traveler's advantages in dealing with Africans—firearms and the acquaintance with some African languages provided by experience in the colonial service or the military. In the one conventionally hair-raising episode in *A Woman's Trek*, she deals with the issue of a woman's vulnerability. In German East Africa, she travels with an escort of two *askari*, or "native soldiers," provided by a colonial officer anxious about the safety of a white woman traveling alone. Soon after one of these *askari* rejoins the party with a guide obtained from a village, Hall notices that they are being pursued by "hordes of natives . . . racing helter-skelter down the hill . . . brandishing their spears above their heads" (p. 206). She dismounts from her hammock and waits—for two anxious pages, picturing herself as St. Sebastian stuck with spears—to talk to the chief.

I, a solitary white woman faced the dusky chief, and the parley began. . . .

His anger was at white heat, but outwardly he was very calm and dignified, and stated his case concisely.

"Your soldiers," he said, "have been to the village in my absence, and
seized one of my men, besides carrying off spears which were dropped by
others in their flight."

I expressed my regret, and told him that it was not with my sanction that
this had been done. . . . I said that I should be very glad if he would allow
some one to come with me as far as the next river, and he answered to the
effect that nothing would give him greater pleasure . . . but he could not
spare the one we had taken as he was a herdsman and was needed to milk
the cows.

I felt that I had taken a new lease of life when we came to this amicable
understanding. There was a visible stir among the men in the background,
who began to feel that "the white Queen" and their own Sultan were evidently coming to terms, and that bloodshed would be unnecessary. I think
my own porters had remained so calm because they never doubted the om-
nipotence of the white skin to overcome every difficulty.

The Sultan posed for his portrait, which I greatly prize as a memento of
one of the most thrilling incidents of my life. He then presented me with a
brass wire bracelet from his arm, and I returned the compliment with much
salt, after which we parted the best of friends.

Had the chief and his followers been more hasty, or less willing for an
explanation, the consequences might easily have proved fatal to me, but as
it turned out, the incident was a striking example of what can be effected by
a little courtesy even among so-called savages. . . .

We continued on our way for about 8 miles, and camped on an eminence
in a dry atmosphere. I had not been there long when word was brought to
me that the Sultan had sent me a fine goat as a present, so I felt I must have
impressed him as favourably as he had impressed me. (Pp. 209–10)

Like Grogan's and Melland and Cholmeley's this is a story of a successful
encounter between traveler and Africans. But Hall's success is quite different from that of either Grogan or Melland and Cholmeley. Grogan's success is to overpower the chief of Gombi physically on the trail. Melland and
Cholmeley's is to overpower Muchereka narratively, in the text. Hall's is to
achieve reciprocity, both on the trail and in the text.

Where both Grogan and Melland and Cholmeley relate to African chiefs
as subject to object, Hall relates to the Sultan as subject to subject. She acknowledges his potential power over her; presents him as three-dimen-
sional, with inward anger as well as outward dignity; lets him speak for
himself in direct quotation; and admires his self-presentation, his concise
style. The structure of her account—the dialogue, the parallelism of " 'the
white Queen' " and "their own Sultan," the exchange of compliments and
gifts—emphasizes parity and reciprocity. In fact, to call herself "the white
Queen," in imitation of the American May French Sheldon, an imperious
anomaly among women travelers, who in a similar situation reached for
her gun, is out of character and serves no purpose except rhetorical bal-

ance.[10] The conclusion—"I felt I must have impressed him as favourably as he had me"—balances Hall's right to evaluate the Other with his right to evaluate her. The courtesy to which she attributes the success of this encounter is the recognition that the Other has a point of view and the right to express it. She attributes courtesy as much to the chief "willing for an explanation" as to herself, and she inscribes it in the structure of the account.

How can Mary Hall construct a reciprocal relationship between herself and an African chief when Ewart Grogan, Frank Melland, and Edward Cholmeley cannot? Like her male contemporaries, Hall participates in the chivalric structure of social relations, but her position in it is split—superior in race, inferior in gender. Her reciprocal relationship with the Sultan reflects, on the one hand, the Victorian lady's subordinate gender position. She is accustomed to feeling vulnerable, to deferring to men. The Sultan as she represents him relates to her like a composite of the European men she meets, some of whom attempt to discourage her from pursuing her "ambitious project" (p. 50), others of whom do everything they can to assist her. The language she attributes to the Sultan in paraphrase, "nothing would give him greater pleasure," characterizes him as the courtly gentleman with whom she is familiar. Her ability to consider *his* impression of *her* reflects the fact that the Victorian lady, herself Other in a male-dominated society, is trained to see herself from a gentleman's point of view.

On the other hand, Hall's reciprocal relationship with the Sultan represents her effort to affirm herself as a woman, an autonomous Self and traveler, against the position of lady, dependent Other, offered by the chivalric myth. In the typical exploration narrative, the antagonist is Africa itself. In this episode, however, the antagonist is not the African, for all his spear-brandishing army, but the double-pointed imperial myth of female fragility and African savagery that provokes the African's anger. Hall invokes this myth with the opening image of the "solitary white woman" awaiting attack by "hordes of natives," then inverts it: the "savage" is a gentleman; the "protection" provided by the colonial officer is nearly fatal; the vulnerable woman's power, courtesy, is more effective than the imperial power represented by firearms; and any reader who has taken the bait of the opening image to anticipate the worse-than-death implicit in the myth has been caught. *A Woman's Trek* refutes the imperial wisdom that "Africa is no place for a white woman." The encounter with the Sultan shows that the myths of race and gender underlying this injunction are interdependent. If Africans are savages, unarmed women must be vulnerable. Conversely, if woman's power, courtesy, is to work, Africans must respond to it; they must be courteous themselves. The validation of a woman's strength requires African subjectivity.

Hall thus rejects racial superiority as a source of power because it is inseparable from gender superiority. She must, however, assure herself and her readers that she controls her caravan. This she does by replacing the authority of race with that of class. Her relations with the chief and other African royalty are reciprocal; with her servants and porters, maternal. Hall's assessment of her situation when the *askari* leave her party illustrates her class-differentiated application of courtesy, as it reinforces the superiority of courtesy to force and the corrective power of experience over myth:

> The whole caravan was now without a firearm of any description, and still eight or nine days must elapse before I could expect to be under the protection of Europeans once more. . . . nevertheless I had a feeling that we should now get along better with the people *en route*, which proved to be the case. The porters by this time were really no trouble; like children they were quick to see that I meant what I said, and I was very careful never to give an order unless I intended it should be obeyed, so that I had them quite under control. (P. 238)

Courtesy, as its association with chivalry reminds us, is not egalitarianism. Applied to the porters, it means consistency of authority. But the substitution of a sense of class superiority for racial superiority undermines the premises of empire. It transforms the cliché that Africans are childlike from a justification of imperialism to an attitude toward servants. It allows Hall, unlike either Grogan, to whom Africans' claims to leadership in their own societies are irrelevant, or Melland and Cholmeley, to whom they are amusing, to acknowledge the social distinctions Africans themselves make and to regard African society as parallel to English. It is her own divided and self-contradictory position as a woman in English society that leads Hall to this implicitly anti-imperial relationship to Africa.

Hall directs attention to this divided position in a comic account of her arrival in the colonial town of Blantyre after her first stretch of overland travel. As the encounter with the Sultan dramatizes Hall's relationship with Africa, the entry into Blantyre dramatizes her relationship with Europe in Africa.

> The porters, tired as I knew they must have been, put on a spurt, assumed the same hilarity they had displayed at the start, and we approached the hotel in great form. The few people who live there were just returning from a walk (it was Sunday) and, much to my dismay, we arrived simultaneously at the door, so that I had to dismount more or less in public. As I have remarked, there is a knack in getting into a machila: there is also one in getting out, which I unfortunately had not then acquired, so all I could do was to roll out, in a most undignified manner, a disorganised mass at the onlookers' feet. People sometimes attach a good deal of importance to first impressions: I can only hope that the few who witnessed my *debut* at Blantyre have long ere this forgotten theirs of me! (P. 47)

As there is a knack to getting into and out of a machila, there is also a knack to setting out on the trail and returning to town, to relating to Africa and to Europe, slipping between the roles of Self and Other, traveler and lady. Hall introduces herself in this passage as a traveler, then endeavors to convert the image of traveler to that of lady. The opposition between traveler and lady contains that between Africa and Europe. The traveler identifies with the Africans—"we approached the hotel in great form"; the lady with the Europeans' view of such hilarity. Hall's entry into Blantyre parallels her encounter with the Sultan. In both episodes, an unknown outsider bears down on a scene of social stability, but this time, the outsider is the lady traveler. As the fearsome chief turns into a gentleman, the disruptive traveler turns into a lady. As Hall revises her first impression of the Sultan, she hopes the people of Blantyre (and her readers) will forget their first impression of her. If she wants us to forget the image of her rolling out of the hammock, however, she describes it unforgettably. And her ladylike apology for unladylike behavior parodies itself as well as the standards of ladyhood.

Hall's irony fingers and keeps open the split between traveler and lady. This split pervades women's travel narratives. It appears in the paired questions Hall and others ask: Will I manage? How will I look? It appears in Mary Gaunt's alternating anxiety and triumph; in Stella Court Treatt's divided self-image, frivolous in pretty frocks, serious in boy's shorts; in Mary Kingsley's "baffling polyphony of narrative voices."[11] As her photograph of the Sultan is a memento of Hall's relationship to Africa, her portrait of herself rolling out of the hammock is a memento of a woman traveler's problematic relationship to Victorian society. Grogan and Melland and Cholmeley leave no ironic self-portraits. They no more wonder how they look to colonials in Africa or their fiancées, mothers, and readers back home than they wonder how they look to Muchereka and the chief of Gombi. For the roles of African traveler and Victorian gentleman coincide. The relationships of both men and women travel narrators to Africa are functions of their gendered relationships to their own society. Grogan and Melland and Cholmeley represent their relations with Africans in ways that fulfill different aspects of the Victorian concept of manhood. Hall represents her relation with the Sultan in a way that both fulfills and resists Victorian expectations of a lady. "A woman's point of view" does not guarantee a reciprocal relationship with an Other, but it opens a crack in the concept of Self through which to examine the concept of Other.

NOTES

1. I am grateful to the National Endowment for the Humanities, Lafayette College, and the University of Iowa's University House for support in the development of this essay. A version of this article appeared in *Women's Studies International Forum* 13, no. 4 (1990): 347–55; reprinted with the permission of Pergamon Press.

2. Catherine Barnes Stevenson, *Victorian Women Travel Writers in Africa* (Boston: Twayne, 1982), p. 11.

3. Ibid., pp. 41–86.

4. Leda Farrant, *The Legendary Grogan: The Only Man to Trek from the Cape to Cairo: Kenya's Controversial Pioneer* (London: Hamish Hamilton, 1981), pp. 7, 19–20.

5. Helen Callaway, *Gender, Culture, and Empire: European Women in Colonial Nigeria* (London: Macmillan, 1987), p. 14.

6. *The Times,* London (5 Dec. 1919): 11b.

7. "Scratches on the Face of the Country; or, What Mr. Barrow Saw in the Land of the Bushmen," in *"Race," Writing, and Difference,* ed. Henry Louis Gates, Jr. (Chicago: University of Chicago Press, 1986), p. 150.

8. Farrant, pp. 19–20.

9. Callaway, p. 40.

10. May French Sheldon, *Sultan to Sultan: Adventures among the Masai and Other Tribes of East Africa* (Boston: Arena, 1892), pp. 330–31.

11. Stevenson, p. 147.

REFERENCES

Birkett, Dea. *Spinsters Abroad: Victorian Lady Explorers.* Oxford: Basil Blackwell, 1989.

Callaway, Helen. *Gender, Culture, and Empire: European Women in Colonial Nigeria.* London: Macmillan, 1987.

Chown, Daisy. *Wayfaring in Africa: A Woman's Wanderings from the Cape to Cairo.* London: Heath Cranton, 1927.

Court Treatt, Stella. *Cape to Cairo: The Record of a Historic Motor Journey.* Boston: Little, Brown, 1927.

Dixie, Florence Douglas. *In the Land of Misfortune.* London: Richard Bentley and Son, 1882.

Farrant, Leda. *The Legendary Grogan: The Only Man to Trek from the Cape to Cairo: Kenya's Controversial Pioneer.* London: Hamish Hamilton, 1981.

Frank, Katherine. *A Voyager Out: The Life of Mary Kingsley.* Boston: Houghton Mifflin, 1986.

_____ . "Voyages Out: Nineteenth-Century Women Travelers in Africa." In *Gender, Ideology and Action: Historical Perspectives on Women's Public Lives,* edited by Janet Sharistanian, 67–93. Westport, Conn.: Greenwood, 1986.

Gaunt, Mary. *Alone in West Africa.* New York: Charles Scribner's Sons; London: T. Werner Laurie, n.d. [1912].

Grogan, Ewart S., and Arthur H. Sharp. *From the Cape to Cairo: The First Traverse of Africa from South to North.* London: Hurst and Blackett, 1900.

Hall, Mary. *A Woman in the Antipodes and in the Far East.* London: Methuen, 1914.

_____ . *A Woman's Trek from the Cape to Cairo.* London: Methuen, 1907.

Kingsley, Mary H. *Travels in West Africa.* London: Macmillan, 1887; London: Virago, 1982.

Melland, Frank H., and Edward H. Cholmeley. *Through the Heart of Africa.* Boston and New York: Houghton Mifflin, 1912.

Oliver, Caroline. *Western Women in Colonial Africa.* Westport, Conn.: Greenwood, 1982.

Pratt, Mary Louise. "Scratches on the Face of the Country; or, What Mr. Barrow Saw in the Land of the Bushmen." In *"Race," Writing, and Difference,* edited by Henry Louis Gates, Jr., 138–62. Chicago: University of Chicago Press, 1986.

Russell, Mary. *The Blessings of a Good Thick Skirt: Women Travellers and Their World.*
    London: Collins, 1986.
Sheldon, May French. *Sultan to Sultan: Adventures among the Masai and Other Tribes of
    East Africa.* Boston: Arena, 1892.
Stevenson, Catherine Barnes. *Victorian Women Travel Writers in Africa.* Boston:
    Twayne, 1982.

THROUGH EACH OTHER'S EYES

THE IMPACT ON THE COLONIAL ENCOUNTER OF THE IMAGES OF EGYPTIAN, LEVANTINE-EGYPTIAN, AND EUROPEAN WOMEN, 1862–1920

Mervat Hatem

The importance of cultural nationalism in understanding the history of the relations between Middle Eastern and European women, their problems, and the related images they have of themselves and of each other has yet to be recognized and explored. The present study will attempt to show how the writings of European Orientalist and Egyptian nationalist women, during the period from 1862 to 1920, presented idealized and partial images of one another. Because they viewed each other as alien, they were not able to relate to each other's experiences, learn from them, or to integrate them into an understanding of the dilemmas that were also their own.[1]

The period under discussion combined a semi-colonial phase (1862–82) with a very harsh colonial phase (1882–1920). During the first phase, Egyptian resistance to the informal but substantial European colonial influence spreading in the economic, social, and political arenas became more focused and organized as part of the 'Arabi revolution (1881–82). The revolution, headed by Ahmed 'Arabi, a high-ranking Egyptian officer in the army, was initially supported by the Egyptian landowning class, which along with the army pushed for the establishment of new parliamentary institutions. These changes would have curtailed the autocratic power of the Khedieve (the title of the Egyptian ruler then) and diminished the increased intervention by the European (largely British and French) advisor in the affairs of the heavily indebted Egyptian government. Eventually an alliance between the Khedieve and the Europeans, along with an anxious Egyptian landowning class, succeeded in undermining the revolutionary forces and paved the way to the British occupation of Egypt in 1882.

The colonial phase (1882–1920) witnessed the development of a heavy-handed imperial system that was intensely felt by all classes. During that period, the different British high commissioners and their civil servants emerged as the effective administrators of the country.[2] Resentment by some public figures of the Egyptian landowning class regarding their exclusion from the affairs of government, coupled with the rise of nationalist intelligentsia (of which Malak Hifni Nasif and Nabawiya Musa, the two pioneering women discussed in this chapter, were members), contributed to the widespread support of the Egyptian delegation (the Wafd) that met with the British commissioner in 1919 to ask for Egyptian independence. The exile of members of the Wafd led to the outbreak of a mass rebellion against the British and the granting of formal independence to Egypt in 1923.

The discussion of the images produced by Egyptian, Levantine-Egyptian, and European women, who are the focus of this study, reflects the changing relationship between European and both groups of Egyptian women under the conditions of semi-colonial and colonial control discussed above. The three Europeans analyzed here lived in Egypt at different historical points in the period between 1862 and 1914. It was their voices that produced and shaped the images of Egyptian women presented to the national and the European publics. Starting with 1892, however, the indigenous voices of Levantine-Egyptian and Egyptian women begin to influence the national discussion of women's position in society through their own magazines, their articles in mainstream journals, and their own books.[3] They also began to establish direct contacts with the European and national public opinions during the first decades of the twentieth century.

The emergence of Levantine-Egyptian and Egyptian women's autonomous voices had more of a dramatic impact on Egyptian public opinion than they did on the European ones. The old European images of Middle Eastern woman proved to be resistant to change. Similarly, Egyptian romantic and competitive images of European women remained unchanged. Despite the asymmetry of power between European and Egyptian women under conditions of colonial rule, it is useful to examine the similar uses each group made of their images of one another to push for some changes and to avoid some others.

European women writers saw Egyptian women as largely circumscribed by seclusion through the harem institution. In contrast, Egyptian women envied European women's unrestricted freedom. The relationship between these images and the reality experienced by the two groups of women was far from simple or direct. As far back as the 1860s, Egyptian and Levantine women had increased their access to private education and to missionary schools.[4] During the 'Arabi revolution, Egyptian women, of all classes, played an important role in supporting the revolution.[5] The significance of these changes was not reflected in the images produced by the European women writers. Similarly, the writings of Egyptian and Levantine women did not appreciate how the European women who settled in Egypt and those who married Egyptian men were privately and publicly restricted by European as well as Egyptian patriarchal rules.

The images of the "secluded" and "unfree" Egyptian woman as well as those of the "free" and "publicly visible" European woman are curiously related. They focus the discussion on external appearances and not their meaning and/or their underlying reality. They also project onto the other what is feared the most in oneself. By thinking of themselves as all powerful and free *vis-à-vis* Egyptian women, Western women could avoid confronting their own powerlessness and gender oppression at home. For Egyptian women, the defense of Islam and some of its restrictive institutions allowed them not to own their power to transform society. They were critical of the liberty of Western women that was not put to the explicit service of the family and society. Similarly, Western women avoided the discussion of how their own patriarchal system penalized them for exercising a certain degree of liberty in their personal lives by taking Egyptian husbands and mates. By making public equality the measure of their freedom, they avoided the discussion of the weight of the patriarchal rules governing their personal lives.

In this paper, I want to argue in favor of a double critique of European Orientalist and Egyptian nationalist writings which contributes to a "decentered" discourse in which numerous relationships among multiple subjects are explored. I will analyze how some Egyptian, some Levantine-Egyptian, and some European women were influenced by and, in turn, participated in the cultural production of gender and national ideologies during the period 1861–1920. Since a particular ideology interacts with the external and the internal world of its actors, I want to explore how the increasing nationalization of their cultures, women's conflicting needs of symbiosis (solidarity with other women and men) and autonomy (definition of their difference), and the colonial encounter between Egypt and Europe shaped the multiple and recurring images that Egyptian and European women produced of themselves, of each other, and the relationship between both.

The authors I have selected for discussion represent the views of three important groups of women who were part of an intense debate on the roles that women played in Egyptian society and their relationship to the roles that women played in Europe. Huda Sha'rawi (1879–1947), Malak Hifni Nasif (1886–1918), and Nabawiya Musa (1890–1951) were the three pioneering Egyptian women of that period. They published articles, lectured, and organized women contributing to the change of the roles and the images of women. Warda al-Yazji (1838–1925), Zeinab Fawaz (1860–1914), and May Ziadah (1886–1941) represented the views of the Lebanese and the Palestinian women who settled in Egypt and were actively involved in the ongoing debates. Finally, the English Lucie Duff Gordon (1821–69), the Hungarian Marie Torok, and the French Eugenie Le Brun (died 1908) were European women who resided in Egypt and wrote about their experiences and views of Egyptian women to European audiences. In the conclusion, I will discuss the way these images help us understand the contradictory relationships that women have to their patriarchal systems and that they have with women of other cultures as they struggle for liberty and equality.

The Changing Lives of Egyptian Women: Rebels and Pioneers

The personal lives and public roles of Malak Hifni Nasif, Nabawiya Musa, and Huda Sha'rawi reflected the many changes that were taking place in their society. The spread of state education for women and the incorporation of women into the labor force represented a process by which different sections of Egyptian society were nationally integrated. This process offered women many opportunities. It allowed Nasif to become the first woman to obtain a primary school certificate (1900) and also a teacher's diploma.[6] Musa was to become the first woman to get a high school certificate in 1907.[7] Both Nasif and Musa were middle-class women who worked as teachers, with Musa becoming the first Egyptian woman to become school principal and inspector at the Ministry of Education. While Nasif's and Musa's education and work experience reflected their middle-class background, Sha'rawi's lack of formal education was more typical of the aristocracy. She was taught at home and continued to be secluded.

Nasif, Musa, and Sha'rawi contributed to the nationalist and social discussions of the time in different ways. Musa was vocal in her criticism of British educational policies. She ridiculed the anglicization that led to the hiring of British teachers even for the teaching of Arabic grammar.[8] She also expressed her resentment at the harassment of Egyptian teachers by English inspectors.[9] Nasif, who used the pen name of *bahithat al-Badiya* (the bedouin researcher), took up writing on women's issues at *al-Jarida,* a very influential and respected liberal publication, which supported the redefinition of women's roles and the use of those changing roles as a measure of the social development of the society. Nasif's reaction to the widely discussed reforms regarding the education and the unveiling of women, which were suggested by the Egyptian judge Qasim Amin as part of his discussion of the liberation of women, was distinctly nuanced. It reflected a greater understanding of the complex emotional dynamics involved in sexual desegregation. While she supported Qasim Amin's call for the education of women, Nasif opposed his advocacy of the unveiling of women. To unveil, while both men and women defined the relations they had with one another in largely sexual terms, would be socially disastrous. She argued that there should be a period of transition in which both men and women learned to relate to one another in new ways.[10]

Finally, despite a very conservative family environment, Sha'rawi gradually began to participate in the organizing of women's social groups before the 1919 revolution. With the revolution, the scale and the intensity of her organizing and lobbying efforts on behalf of women were increased. While women had previously been active supporters of the 'Arabi revolution in the 1880s, their participation in the 1919 revolution showed higher levels of participation and effectiveness through boycotting the sales of English goods and waging a media campaign in support of the political leadership of the Wafd that led the revolution and eventually emerged as the majority party in the Egyptian political party system.[11] This earned women a legitimate status as citizens who fought side by side with men in the national struggle. Unfortunately, however, the 1923 constitution did not give women the right to vote.

Musa, Nasif, and Sha'rawi's confrontation with gender inequality inspired resistance, not docile acceptance. Musa was envious of her brother, who was a student at the War College. She asked him to teach her how to read and write but continued on her own until she was able to secretly enroll herself at the al-Saniya Girls' School. After she graduated, she was appointed as a teacher. She then discovered that her male colleagues, who studied at the Teachers' College, earned more than she did because the degrees offered by the male schools were considered to be equal to a high school degree, whereas those offered by the girls' schools were not. She asked a reluctant Ministry of Education for permission to sit for the high school examination given by the male schools and passed it in 1907.[12] She remained the only woman to have a high school degree until the Ministry of Education allowed women to enroll in general high schools in the mid-1920s. The first group of Egyptian women graduated from these schools in 1928.

Although Sha'rawi and Nasif submitted to family-arranged marriages and eventually had to contend with polygamous husbands, they campaigned against the marriage of very young women and the institution of polygamy.[13] Sha'rawi chose to live separately from her husband for seven years because he breached the marriage contract by taking a second wife.[14] Those years she devoted to her own intellectual and personal development.

Musa never married, which was very unusual for an Egyptian woman of the time. She thought that the marital relationship was humiliating to women. In her opinion, wives were treated as domestic maids to their husbands.[15] As a result, she chose to devote herself to a very active and committed public career in women's education. As a senior inspector at the Ministry of Education, she even considered the possibility of studying to become a lawyer. The ministry's refusal of her request to sit for the bar examination led her to criticize its high-ranking officials, which resulted in her dismissal. She sued the ministry, proceeded to argue her case in court, and won.[16] It was then that she raised money and opened her own private school in Alexandria that catered to the needs of the girls of the middle classes.

What the above shows is that these Egyptian women were not particularly docile or restricted to life in the harem. Because both Orientalist (like

\nd Egyptian writers (like Qasim Amin, Abdallah al-Nadim,
{ 'Abdo) had harshly criticized the secluded and uneduca-
..t woman as ignorant, superstitious, and largely unproduc-
these pioneering women were very much interested in distinguishing themselves from the previous generation of women. They tested and
proved themselves in many new areas. While they distanced themselves
from the old definitions of womanhood, they wanted other women to
change and be like them through the exercise of these new roles. Here, the
need to be different and the need to ally oneself with other women clashed
and represented a dilemma for the pioneering women of that generation.
Distance produced by class and education subverted efforts to ally themselves with older women of their own families and class as well as women
of other classes in a larger movement. The colonial encounter with Europe
confronted the Egyptian women with additional dilemmas. They submitted to the national pressure to defend Islam against the European Orientalist writings. The nineteenth- and twentieth-century debates on women's
roles in society, which were started by Egyptian men and then joined by
female writers, sought to contest the claims made by the colonial administrators and the Orientalist scholars about the incapacity of Islam and Muslim society to deal with the issue of gender inequality and new roles for
women. By showing how Islam gave women important rights and how it
was capable of changing its definitions of those roles, nationalists were
challenging the legitimacy of the Western claims used to mobilize European public opinion in support of colonialism and colonial rule. It also
served as an effective means of organizing national opposition at home
against the colonial threat and the new definitions of Islam.

The result was that some Egyptian women, like Sha'rawi, argued that
Islam did not contributed to the subordination of women. In a speech she
gave at the international women's conference held in Rome (March 1923),
Sha'rawi presented the following arguments, which Egyptian male and female writers still reiterate today about the relationship between Islam and
women's rights.

> Egyptian women had equal rights to men until Egypt fell to foreign rule.
> Then Egyptian women became like other Arab women, without laws that
> protected them from male despotism. . . .
> Islam gave women rights they did not have before and which Western
> women are fighting for today. . . . While women's rights are accepted by
> religious law, ignorance prevented them from making use of them. . . .
> As for polygamy, which has been criticized bitterly in the West, the
> Qur'an did not inspire this custom, which existed before Islam. While the
> Qur'an specifies that having four wives is allowed, there are also other
> verses that state that "if you fear that you cannot do them [the different
> wives] justice, then you should have only one."[18]

The nationalist discourse presented above defined foreign rule as the enemy of Egyptian women. There is a vague reference to male despotism, but no discussion of the role that Islam and patriarchs/patriarchy played in the subordination of women.

The participation of women of different classes in the 1919 national revolution against the British legitimized their increased activism for women's rights.[19] What interested the European media, and to a lesser extent the Egyptian public, was the participation of the aristocratic harem women including Huda Sha'rawi (who was the president of the Wafd's Central Committee for Women) in the public demonstrations which challenged the European and the national images of harem women. This international and national attention given to the role played by the aristocratic harem women in the 1919 revolution influenced the development of Egyptian feminism in the 1920s. It alerted the ambitious Huda Sha'rawi, who had up until then only participated in modest social activities, to the possibility of using her new nationalist credentials and wealth, especially after her resignation from the increasingly populist Wafd, to become Egypt's leading feminist leader. From then onward, a nationalist bourgeois feminism emerged as the key approach used to push for women's rights.

The emergence of male advocates of women's rights beginning with Rifa'ah al-Tahtawi's *al-Murshid al-Amin litathqif al-Banat wa al-Banin* (The faithful guide for the education of girls and boys) published in 1872 and Qasim Amin's *Tahrir al-Mar'at* (The liberation of women) published in 1899 complicated the debate on patriarchal domination. Because men were faithful allies during the early phases of the struggle for women's rights, paternalistic strategies for change acquired a certain degree of legitimacy. For example, while Musa criticized men's unwillingness to recognize women's contribution to society and history,[20] she relied on the support of Sa'd Zaghlul, the minister of education at the time, in her numerous confrontations with English inspectors and principals.[21] Ahmed Lutfi al-Seyyid, the editor of *al-Jarida,* the liberal newspaper of the Umma party, encouraged Nasif to publish articles that criticized the male harassment of veiled and unveiled women in the streets and polygamy. Similarly, Huda Sha'rawi continued throughout her long organizing career to expect the various prime ministers to support the efforts of women activists,[22] even though they were clearly ardent protectors of male privilege. The overall result was an ambivalent feminist attack on male privilege, which was seen simultaneously as a cause of the problem and as an important resource for reform. The need for autonomy and the desire for symbiosis with men clashed, affecting the history of the Egyptian feminist struggle for change.

This particular view of men as valuable allies for change explains the somewhat vicious attack by Egyptian women on marriage between Egyptian men and European women. The increased confidence Egyptian women had in their own capacity to be modern made them more competitive with those whom they referred to as "foreign women."

One of Nasif's articles discusses the changing values and attitudes of the

Egyptian middle class and its women.[23] By 1910, marrying a Circassian concubine or a European woman was no longer socially acceptable. Nasif uses the nationalist pride in being Egyptian to persuade middle- and upper-class men to marry educated Egyptian women. In attempting to discourage men from those marriages, she presents the decision to marry a Turco-Circassian or a European as a national danger that produces children with divided cultural loyalties.

Musa discusses the consequences of intercultural marriages in equally strong terms:

> Men are wrong to marry foreign women. They claim that they can influence those women more than they can influence them. The reality disputes those claims. . . . Only ignorant or obstinate men cannot see that women influence their families. . . . A man who marries a Westerner becomes with his children Westerners. As for an Egyptian women, who marries a foreigner (e.g., a Muslim from Persia), she is capable of giving Egypt new Egyptians. This is a fact . . . some men deny for obvious motives. May God help them avoid the wrong path.[24]

As the above makes clear, European women emerged as an "other" in national/cultural and class terms. They were unworthy opponents because they came from the working class. They were also very threatening since they robbed Egyptian women of bright men and eventually produced disloyal young Egyptians. Nationalism defined in sexual and cultural terms was used here by Egyptian women to manipulate men and dissuade them from marrying foreign women.

In addition to the envy and the competition that existed between Egyptian and European women over Egyptian men, Musa, Nasif, and Sha'rawi's writings reveal another source of tension: the goal of catching up with European women. In "Lectures on Women at the Egyptian University," Musa compares the two: "At present, the women of Europe crowd the streets alongside men. They have gone to extremes to uphold their rights and have even asked for the right to vote. In comparison to them, we are still slaves. Men have asked us to wake up, but they have only encountered our laziness and inaction."[25] Musa used the past achievements of Egyptian women and the present success of European women to incite Egyptian women to change. The challenge presented by European women became internalized in most discussions of Egyptian women of the period.

Huda Sha'rawi's relationships with European women were more complicated. She felt comfortable with her European subordinates, that is, her governesses and teachers. She was uncomfortable, however, with those she describes as "snobbish intellectuals."[26] For instance, Sha'rawi was approached by Mademoiselle Marguerite Clement, who wanted to give a lecture to Egyptian aristocratic women. Sha'rawi suggested the topic of the attitudes of Western and Eastern women toward the veil. Mlle. Clement agreed but suggested that Sha'rawi find someone older and more important to sponsor the lecture.[27] Princess 'Ayn al-Hayat Ahmed was persuaded to sponsor the lecture, but she arrived late that evening, interrupting the lecture. This disruption caused the Western women who were attending the lecture to criticize Sha'rawi and the Egyptian women as lacking knowledge of proper etiquette. In response, Sha'rawi defensively argued that this was the first public lecture of its kind and that Egyptian women might not have known about the rules European women claimed were broken.[28] The condescending cultural attitude of European women toward Sha'rawi, as a young Egyptian woman, and toward other women of her class was thus another source of tension.

To summarize, Egyptian women were becoming increasingly self-confident about their accomplishments. Their powerful critique of mixed marriages between Egyptian men and European women was an expression of that self-confidence. Because men were seen as supporters and allies in the struggle for change, Egyptian women criticized their decision to marry European, especially working-class, women. They doubted the claims that men could transform their European wives and children into loyal Egyptians, emphasizing the power women had in the private world of the family. Both Egyptian and European women were assumed to exert significant influence over men and children.

In this process of defining the relationship they had with European women, Egyptian women produced split images of them. The idealized European woman was "free" after having fought for her rights. She was also hard working. Although these ideal traits were admired, Egyptian women developed hostile attitudes to certain groups. They presented working-class European women as "manipulative" for having cleverly attracted and married Egyptian middle-class men. Sensitive to the loss of the original greatness that Egyptian women claimed historically, they also resented the patronizing attitudes of European middle-class women.

Levantine-Egyptian Women: Immigrants and Citizens

The Levantine-Egyptian women in our study were educated middle-class women. Warda al-Yazji, the daughter of a well-known literary writer, worked as a teacher when she was young. She started writing poetry and migrated from Lebanon to Egypt with her children in middle age. In Egypt, she continued to write until she died in 1925. In contrast, Zeinab Fawaz came from a poor, working-class family, but she learned to read and write as a companion of the daughters of a rich family in southern Lebanon.[29] She then migrated to Egypt in the 1880s where she started a career in newspaper writing. She also produced many literary works and became a well-known figure in her own right. Finally, May Ziadah left Palestine for Cairo with her parents at the age of twenty-two. There she worked as a tutor for the daughters of an aristocratic family that owned the journal, *al-Mahrousa*, where her father worked as editor and where she published her early French poems.[30] Eventually, she learned to write in Arabic and had her own literary salon, which was frequented by both male and female literary figures of the time.[31]

The Lebanese, Palestinian, and Syrian immigrants who settled in Egypt in the second half of the nineteenth century were categorized by the Egyptians as Levantine, that is, as coming from different parts of Greater Syria or the Levant, as it was known in earlier times. They spoke Arabic and were very much a part of the culture of Egypt. Egyptians did not consider them to be outsiders like the Europeans, whom they categorized as "foreigners." They did, however, recognize their difference and hence referred to them as Levantine.

While the Egyptians distinguished members of this group by their place of national origin, the British colonial administrators and Western writers set them apart from the rest of the population by dealing with them as members of a new Christian minority in Egypt. This latter characterization was very Orientalist. It used Christianity as a basis for defining cultural difference and disregarded the many other elements that determined cultural identity. It also assumed that Lebanese and Palestinian immigrants were all Christian, which was inaccurate. Zeinab Fawaz, the working-class writer, for example, was a veiled Muslim women. But both elements of their identify, the fact that they were born and/or brought up in different parts of Syria and, for many, their adherence to the Christian faith, held significance for their views on European and Egyptian women and themselves.

Because an active state with an adequate infrastructure did not exist in Syria during the nineteenth century, there was greater reliance in the Levant on missionary schools. The schools' mission status accounts, in part, for the different levels of education among Christian and Muslim girls, since many Muslim families were uncomfortable with sending their children to these schools. Levantine women who attended these schools internalized many Western influences and values. Their sympathetic discussion of European women reflected many of those influences and set them apart from other Egyptian women.

Levantine-Egyptian nationalism was less anti-Western than was Egyptian nationalism, because Lebanon and Palestine remained free of Western colonial rule until 1920. Levantine women like al-Yazji, Fawaz, and Ziadah were less apologetic about advocating the synthesis of what they called their Eastern (a precursor of what later on became known as an Arab) identity with that of the West. In Egypt, where the British had become de facto rulers in 1882, this same goal was somewhat discredited. From then on, the Westerners became colonizers whose formal and informal domination was important to resist if one was to become independent.

Moreover, the British gave the new Levantine immigrants many privileges because they imagined them to be potential allies who could be mobilized for the goal of making Egypt a multiethnic society. The new immigrants supported rather than resisted the British ideology of modernism because it offered the potential of an effective synthesis of the Western and Eastern cultures. As Ziadah argued,

> If we do not keep up with the changing rhythm of life, we condemn ourselves to idiocy despite our intelligence. . . . If as inhabitants of these countries, we do not become strong by learning modern ways and keeping up with the pace of the world, we will be conquered and enslaved.[32]

While there were Egyptian male advocates of modernism, like Tahtawi, Amin, and al-Seyyid, they were never representatives of the mainstream. For Egyptian middle- and upper-class women, modernism was a tricky ideal that associated change with the potential betrayal of one's own culture. Levantine-Egyptians were not less nationalistic than other Egyptians. Ziadah was concerned with protecting Arab culture from conquest and keeping its people free. In other parts of the same article, she underlines the fact that Western civilization borrowed extensively from the Arabs and suggests that Arabs can, in turn, "use the West as a source of inspiration for new/modern forms and techniques without losing our personality."[33]

Zaynab Fawaz's book *al-Dur al-Manthur fi Tabaqat Rabat al-khudur* (The dispersed pearls among the different classes of goddesses of the household) (1894), defines the relationship between East and West as part of a discussion of the relationship between Egyptian and European women in an equally interesting way. "History," she writes, "which is the best of all sciences, is largely dominated by men. Not a single one of those male historians had dedicated a single chapter in which to discuss women who represent half of humankind."[34]

Fawaz felt equally jealous for the neglect of Eastern and Western women's history. She offers biographies of important Eastern and Western women, which helps one trace their histories and accomplishments. The biographies do not emphasize the differences between the two groups of women, but rather the similarities of their virtues and contributions to society. Included in this long list of biographies are philanthropic women, the mothers of great kings, heroic and literary figures, and women active in social associations and public professions. The images of Eastern and Western women that emerge out of this voluminous work emphasize the common and changing roles that women have played historically as mothers and philanthropic figures as well as their increased present participation in the public world. Even in the discussion of those new roles, Fawaz does not see major differences between Eastern and Western women. She cites many in both groups as taking on those new roles.

Warda al-Yazji participates in this discussion of the relationship between Eastern and Western women by offering a more complex view that underlines the bonds of solidarity as well as points of tension. She argues that by challenging many of the assumptions made about women and their role in society, European women have contributed to the cause of women elsewhere and especially in the Middle East. Here, the existence of a common cause and the generalized rewards of the struggle are made clear. The progressive message of European women as they struggle for more equal rights contrasts with the chauvinistic cultural nationalism of European women working as teachers in the Middle East. While al-Yazji accepts the former enthusiastically, she rejects the latter unequivocally.[35]

Ziadah's writings addressed other concerns in this complex discussion of the relations between East and West. She shared some of Malak Hifni Nasif's nationalist fears about the disintegration of the East as a result of the influx of Western cultural influences,[36] but she thought that Japan offered an example of how such an interaction does not necessarily have to end with subordination.[37] Ziadah was also skeptical of how much progress Western women achieved in their own societies. She saw women in general as making slow progress. This continued emphasis on the similarities between Eastern and Western women distinguished the views of the Levantine-Egyptian women from other Egyptian women.

The differences that existed between the views of the Levantine-Egyptian and other Egyptian women were not strong enough to isolate them from one another. Many of Ziadah's books were devoted to the study of the lives of key Egyptian women in this period. She wrote biographies of Aicha Timur (whose poems, published in the 1870s, established her as a pioneering literary figure), Malak Hifni Nasif, and Warda al-Yazji. Timur gave al-Yazji a copy of her book of poems and they corresponded.[38] She also wrote a poem praising Fawaz's above-mentioned book.[39] Ziadah participated in the lecture series organized by Egyptian women and attended by European women at the Egyptian University. It was through this series that she became acquainted with Sha'rawi, Nasif, and Musa.[40]

Since Ziadah wrote biographies of Timur and Nasif, it might be useful to examine the images that she offered, as a Levantine-Egyptian woman, of her Egyptian counterparts. Ziadah wrote a very sensitive study of Timur's life. She admired Timur's accomplishments given her seclusion, her early marriage, and the lack of family support for her artistic talents. She also showed a sensitive appreciation of the constraints Timur faced as well as her resourcefulness.[41]

Although Timur was not Ziadah's contemporary, Nasif was her friend. In her biography of Nasif, Ziadah expressed her fondness for Nasif's femininity and sense of humor. She also admired her intelligence. As a result, Nasif emerges as a well-rounded person, despite the fact that Ziadah disagreed with her on a number of different issues. Ziadah defends the missionary schools that Nasif criticized for neglecting to teach their students Arabic and Islamic history. Ziadah, who attended one of those schools, commends them for teaching their students European languages and argues that Arabic and Islamic history should be taught by the family.[42] Like Nasif, Ziadah did not support marriages between Egyptian men and European women, because they hurt both Egyptian women and the homeland. She thought, however, that love was possible between partners of different nationalities.[43] In the age of nationalism, Levantine-Egyptian women might have felt the dilemma of being simultaneous Egyptian and Levantine, that is, non-Egyptian. For those who considered the Levantine-Egyptians to be of a different nationality and hence unacceptable marriage mates, Ziadah argued that love could bridge the differences.

In conclusion, the key Levantine-Egyptian women discussed in this section were as confident as their Egyptian counterparts about their changing roles as women. Their images of other women, whether they were Egyptian or European, were nuanced. They appreciated the cultural traditions and dilemmas they had in common with Egyptian women, but they did not share their view of European women as an enemy. Although they did not romanticize the progress made by Western women, they had great admiration for them as positive role models. More importantly, they were critical of European cultural chauvinism, advocating instead the importance of synthesizing modernism and Middle Eastern cultures. Ziadah used the modern concept of love to avoid being marginalized by Egyptian cultural nationalism, which might have treated Egyptian-Levantine women as less attractive marriage mates.

European Women: The Orientalist as Insider

The European women who are the focus of this section came from upper- and middle-class backgrounds. Lucie Austin was brought up by parents who were members of the English intellectual and literary circles. She married Sir Alexander Duff Gordon. When she contracted tuberculosis, she traveled to Egypt in 1862 in search of a drier climate and remained there until she died in 1869. Lady Gordon, who lived primarily in Upper Egypt, was part of an increasing European presence (in the form of tourists and/or settlers) throughout the land, even in this remote region, often considered to be the Egyptian hinterland. During her seven years in Egypt, she wrote letters that described her experiences and that were eventually published in 1865, attracting considerable attention. In contrast, the French Eugenie Le Brun and the Hungarian Mary Torok were brought up in middle-class families, which gave them adequate education but not financial security. This partially explains their decisions to marry economically secure foreigners. Both converted to Islam upon marriage. The mixed marriages of Le Brun and Torok were part of a very large wave of intercultural marriages, which followed the British occupation along with a new Egyptian belief in the superiority of everything European, including the attractiveness of European women as marital partners for middle- and upper-class men.

Torok married Khedieve Abbas II, who ruled Egypt from 1892 to 1914, when he was expelled by the British. Le Brun married Husayn Rushdy, who eventually became prime minister (1914–17). Both women wrote books about their experiences in Egypt. Le Brun wrote *Harems et Musulmanes d'Egypte* under the pseudonym Niya Salima ("good intentions") in 1900 in Paris. Torok, who took the name Djavidan Hanum after her marriage, published a book after her divorce entitled *Harem Life*, which deals with her life in the royal harem in Egypt and in Turkey.

These three European women, who settled in Egypt between 1862–1920, were influenced by the production of popular images about "the Orient" in their original societies. These images were derived largely from European travelers' accounts and the various translations of the *Arabian Nights.* The Muslims, with their exacting rituals (especially the fasting of Ramadan, which fascinated the authors), their veiled, beautiful, and erotic women and despotic cultures and political systems, served to define the boundaries between East and West in the women's writings.

Although they were critical of Western understanding of particular aspects of Egyptian culture, they made use of their association with the West to maintain a powerful position in Egypt. Privileges granted to their states (whether financial, political, or social) were extended to them as individual citizens. Gordon took her grievances to the English consul in Egypt who attended to them. When Western privileges and protection were withdrawn from Djavidan Hanum and Le Brun because they married Egyptian men, they felt vulnerable and helpless in an alien land and culture.[44]

Gordon's "radical liberalism," which led her to argue that Christianity and Islam were two equally great religions, a radical position in discussions of the Orient at the time, did not lead her to repudiate the key Orientalist assumption about the essential differences between the Orient and the West. In her writings, the two cultures remained separate. Similarly, their "naturalized status" (i.e., conversion to Islam, marriage to Egyptian men, and long residence in Egypt) did not lead Djavidan Hanum and Le Brun to repudiate all of their Western assumptions about Eastern inferiority. This was difficult for a number of reasons. In the semi-colonial Egyptian society and later on in a colonized Egypt, both rulers and ruled (the latter somewhat uneasily) accepted the power and the superiority of everything Western. This constrained and influenced the interactions between European and Egyptian women as well as the European women's relations with Egyptian men. Even though the European women under discussion considered themselves to be naturalized Egyptians, their past views and identification with the West determined their writing concerns: for example, they addressed Western audiences whose flawed understandings of Egypt and the Egyptians they wanted to correct, but did not particularly challenge assumptions about the superiority of the West and the inferiority of the East.

The writings of Gordon, Djavidan Hanum, and Le Brun are different from other Orientalist writings in that they attempt to present Islam and the Egyptians in a somewhat favorable light. Duff Gordon described Egyptian tolerance of religious and cultural differences (whether of Muslims or Copts) in Upper Egypt and contrasted it with European intolerance of those same differences.[45] As new converts to Islam, Djavidan Hanum and Le Brun made the conventional Muslim distinction between Islam as a religion and the distortions that the corrupt religious establishments and men had introduced into it.[46] They also argued, like other Muslims of their class, that Islam gave women important rights.[47] Their defense of Islam, while new and different from the usual Orientalist presentations, must have appeared self-serving to Europeans, however, since both converted to Islam. The presentation of Islam as a humane religion made their conversions more acceptable.

The social and political convictions of the women discussed, as well as the periods within which they were writing, explain their varying attitudes as insiders/outsiders to Egypt. Gordon's liberalism stimulated her to view Islam as a religious equal. The following statement summarized those views:

> I am very puzzled to discover the slightest difference between Christian and Muslim morality or belief—if you exclude certain dogmas—and in fact, very little is felt here. No one attempts to apply different standards of morals or of piety to a Muslim or a Copt. East and West is the difference not Muslim and Christian.[48]

Gordon was writing in the 1860s, a period when an informal European presence, coupled with a relatively active Egyptian state, permitted the interesting religious dialogue she and her Egyptian male friends entered into. They all became convinced of the "real unity of faith," whether Christian or Muslim.[49] Her Egyptian male and female friends also expressed their admiration for European science and rules of government.[50] Following the British occupation of Egypt in 1882, this kind of discourse by Egyptians came to an end because it could be used to support the continued colonialization of Egypt. In fact, the British colonial administration had this in mind when it made Lady Gordon's *Letters from Egypt* required reading in all Egyptian public schools during the colonial period.[51] The *Letters'* simultaneous portrayal of Egyptian rulers as corrupt and the Europeans as benevolent must have been very useful in combating the rise of nationalist sentiments among the students and legitimizing continued British control of Egypt.

The French Le Brun, writing in the late 1890s, was affected both by French support for the emerging Egyptian nationalism and the liberal ideology of an emerging bourgeoisie to which her husband belonged. Her interaction with the many distinguished liberal friends of her husband like

Shaykh Mahammed 'Abdou, Qasim Amin, and Sa'd Zaghlul allowed her to develop some appreciation for the changes taking place. It also biased her views of what these changes meant to women.

She described, for instance, the uproar that Qasim Amin's *Tahrir al-Mar'at* (The liberation of women) had caused in upper- and middle-class households and harems. The harem, which she had described as largely concerned with gossip about marriage, birth, death, and fashions, had become preoccupied with Qasin Amin's offensive criticism of the women of the harem.[52]

Le Brun's description of how Egyptian women were now involved in the public debate of Amin's book reflected the changing concerns and interest of the harem women. The passage also showed the condescending attitudes that Le Brun had toward both average Muslim women and women of the harem. She thought that the average woman deserved Amin's contempt because she was not literate. Le Brun presented the harem women as having misunderstood what Amin said. Le Brun prided herself, however, as having understood what he intended. Because she did not take the objections of Egyptian women seriously, she could not be critical of some of Amin's misogynist views of them. Amin's advocacy of reforms aside, he accused Egyptian women, in general, of being ignorant and lifeless beings who did not use any of their mental or physical capabilities. In his opinion, these ignorant Egyptian wives had no way of appreciating the moral and social accomplishments of men and could not, therefore, be capable of loving their husbands.[53] Even though Le Brun's marriage to Rushdy made her part of the harem, she clearly dissociated herself from these women by seconding the criticism voiced by Amin.

Djavidan Hanum was the most politically and socially conservative of the three European women under discussion. The survival of the old-style imperial system in Hungary and her acceptance of its arbitrary character in Egypt explained the ease with which she accepted royal privilege and her defense of her husband's character flaws, including his meanness to her. She also shared her husband's condescending Turkish attitude to Egypt and Egyptians.

When Torok converted to Islam, she first took the Arabic name Zubaida, then changed it to the titled Turkish name Djavidan Hanum. (*Hanum* was the Turkish equivalent of "her royal highness.") She was particularly enamored of the luxury of the royal harem; it compensated for the isolation that harem life imposed on her and that she chose by having only European friends. She may have known Le Brun, but Le Brun's identification with European liberalism and Egyptian nationalists might explain why they were not or could not be friends.

Djavidan Hanum's limited understanding of the political events of this turbulent period, combined with an uncritical acceptance of Abbas II's personal weaknesses (his greed, his miserly spending habits, his infidelities, and his pettiness) made her account of her experiences in Egypt a very good example of the alienated and alienating experiences some European women had in Egypt. This she accepted in the name of a very masochistic type of heterosexual love.

The writings by the European women under discussion on Egypt and Egyptians were Orientalist in a number of ways. They shared the view that European settlers could be interpreters of this alien culture to the West. Moreover, the images of Egyptian men and women that appeared in the writings of Gordon, Djavidan Hanum, and Le Brun would have been very objectionable to an Egyptian audience. The three authors were less interested in what Egyptians thought of themselves and more concerned to present a European perspective on Egypt to a European audience who shared many of their values and assumptions. European interest in the women of the harem explains why two of the titles in their three books made some reference to it. It is not clear whether the authors were writing for a male or a female audience. Le Brun begins by leading a female friend to the door of the harem and Djavidan Hanum explains to a more impersonal reader that the word "harem" implies to be forbidden, not permitted, or illegal, but at the same time to be holy, protected, and inviolate.[54] In both cases, the style used is tantalizing and designed to excite interest mixed with fear.

Despite Gordon's emphasis on the noble character of the Egyptians, her descriptions of the women were one-dimensional. They were largely physical. The women were all pretty, with good features, an upright posture, and a strong build.[55] Djavidan Hanum singled out the erotic skills of slave women in the royal harem[56] as the key to understanding that institution and its women. Although she argued that the harem in Egypt was more frugal and practical, something she seemed to regret, she was not interested in exploring those pragmatic aspects of the institution in great detail. She claimed to have pity for the lives of these sexual slaves, but she was also envious of them. Her husband's first wife, Iqbal Hanum, was a slave woman who bore him six children, while Djavidan Hanum had none.[57]

The other traits that Gordon, Le Brun, and Djavidan Hanum dwelled upon in their discussion of Egyptian women were also very stereotypical. Despite the uproar that she notes Amin's book caused within the harem, Le Brun characterized these women as having largely domestic concerns and very little interest in politics, literature, and the arts.[58] Gordon made constant references to how Egyptian men were henpecked by their wives,[59] an observation that Edward Lane and Richard Burton had made in their own writings. Djavidan Hanum focused her attention on a variant of that trait, that is, the shrewdness and cunning of harem women.[60] One gets the impression that Le Brun, Gordon, and Djavidan Hanum would have preferred Egyptian women to be uninformed, meek, and not at all clever. This is ironic since these European women prided themselves on being well informed, clever, and resourceful. Common traits between European and Middle Eastern women were ignored. The mere possibility of the existence of common survival skills, which women everywhere learn, seems to have been too disturbing for European women to acknowledge. It might have led them to speculate about the specific form of their gender oppression. They avoided asking themselves why they felt powerful in the Orient and less so in their own societies. Here, the need for symbiosis (identification with the power of their culture) contributed to an exaggerated emphasis on the differences between the Orient and the West.

In trying to push this distinction between Western and Egyptian women further, Gordon and Djavidan Hanum described their relationships with Egyptian men as based on something supposedly lacking in relationships between Egyptian men and women, that is, love, not erotic pleasure. Their assumption was, of course, that the relationships of Abbas II and Shaykh Yussef (with whom Gordon was probably involved) with their Egyptian wives were largely physical and that only with European women did these men feel love. This particular split between love and erotic pleasure was largely European in conception and superfluous to Egyptians. It served to transform European sexual inhibitions, which was a disadvantage in the competition with Egyptian women, into an advantage.

Insofar as the images offered of Egyptian women failed to point out the changes that were clearly taking place, the authors exhibited another important Orientalist assumption about the permanence of these women's social position. Even though Le Brun was part of many efforts to organize new social and public activities among Egyptian women,[61] she clung to the domestic characterization of harem women. Similarly, Gordon mentioned the freedom of the Bedawi young woman (Shaykh Yussef teaching his daughter how to read and write and Mustafa Agha teaching his daughter English)[62] but she still argued that the Egyptian women she saw were not any different from those discussed in the Scriptures and the Arabian Nights.[63] In a parallel vein, Djavidan Hanum chose to emphasize the continuity of the old notions about the harem into the present. There was no mention in her discussion of the educated or the socially active princesses of the royal family in Egypt like Nazli Fadel, who had her own literary salon, princess 'Ayn al-Hayat Ahmed, who sponsored the lecture series on women that Sha'rawi organized, or princess Fatma Ismail, who funded the building of the Egyptian University.[64] Le Brun, Gordon, and Djavidan Hanum's decision to emphasize the old images, despite the changes taking place around them, testifies to the power of Orientalist assumptions over those who write about the Middle East. Furthermore, change was deemphasized because it would also have robbed European women of their position of superiority and privilege. Once again the need to assert one's difference was satisfied at the expense of observing and analyzing the implications of existing similarities.

What about the European images of Levantine-Egyptian women? The following anecdote from Gordon offers a useful insight into the complex relationship that existed between these two groups.

Mme. Mounier described Rachel's stay with them for three months at Luxor, in my house, where they lived. She hated it so, that on embarking to leave she turned back and spat on the ground and cursed the place inhabited by savages where she had been *ennuyée à mort*. Mme. Mounier fully sympathized with her and thought no *femme aimable* could live with Arabs, who are not at all *gallants*. She is Levantine and I believe half Arab herself, but hated here and hates the Muslims. As I write this I laugh to think *galanterie* and Arab in one sentence.[65]

The above passage describes the cultural dynamics that governed the relations between the Levantine-Egyptians and Europeans. The Europeans considered themselves and other Christians to be more civilized than the Arabs who were Muslim. This was the reason why Rachel set apart Mme. Mounier, who was a Levantine Christian, from the Arabs/Muslims. Because they shared Christianity as a common bond, Rachel proceeded to share with Mme. Mounier her racist feelings toward the Arabs and their way of life. Because to be associated with the Muslims was tantamount to being uncivilized, Mme. Mournier wanted to dissociate herself from the place where she lived as well as that part of her identity that was Arab. Unfortunately for Mme. Mounier, Gordon laughed at her affected Westernized critique of the Arabs for their lack of gallantry. In an equally racist remark about Mme. Mounier and Arabs in general, Gordon chuckled at the inclusion of gallantry and Arabs in the same sentence. The implication here was that such a linkage was not only laughable but nonsensical.

I have argued, so far, that the European authors under discussion shared many of the old images and assumptions of other writers. One image that appeared more prominently in the writings of European women under discussion was that of the Egyptian man. Lucy Duff Gordon dealt with and referred to them constantly as children.[66] Djavidan Hanum picked the childish nickname *mon poupon* for her husband.[67] She often disguised herself as his bodyguard to escape the restrictions of the harem and seemed to believe she was quite capable of protecting him if there was any need to. Somehow by assuming that Egyptian men were children, they were effectively neutered and ceased to be threatening. The alleged tameness of Egyptian men was expressed by Le Brun in a different way. She told Huda Sha'rawi that she married Husayn Rushdy because, unlike European men, Muslim men were safe. They were prohibited by their religion from drinking and gambling. After watching her sister suffer from the abuse of an alcoholic husband who gambled, she vowed to select someone who was different.[68] Even though Shaykh Yussef, with whom Gordon fell in love (and most probably had an extended relationship), was the only Egyptian to whom she referred as manly and more of an equal, when she first met him she was forty-four and he was thirty. The age difference made theirs another "safe" relationship.

One can only speculate about why European women needed to make

Middle Eastern men both childish and tame. They might have felt more secure and/or powerful in these relationships. Unfortunately, most discovered that it was a false sense of security. Husayn Rushdy did drink. Le Brun felt very insecure about this and about being lumped with her other working-class nationals, who were less educated and refined and consequently despised by the Egyptian bourgeois class, especially its women.[69]

For Djavidan Hanum, having a husband who was childish in his ways did not protect her from eventual divorce. Since she never had any children, she suffered the fate that the Egyptian patriarchal system devised for childless women. Being European and/or having a childish husband did not provide her with the security she needed.

Finally, Gordon lived with the considerable anxiety and fear of being discovered in an illicit affair by both European and Egyptian patriarchies.[70] The fact that Shaykh Yussef was younger, belonged to another class, nationality, faith, and was himself married served to throw people off for a while. Eventually, however, many acquaintances knew of or at least suspected the liaison.[71] In the end her deadly illness (tuberculosis), coupled with the fact that this affair broke many taboos, led everybody to pretend that it did not happen.

While many of the European women discussed were capable individuals, their status in Egyptian and European societies continued to be determined by their relations to men. In Egypt, Gordon's social standing was enhanced by the access she had to male circles as a desexualized elderly English woman. Djavidan Hanum's and Le Brun's status were determined by their marriage to distinguished Egyptian men. All used their experiences in Egypt with those men to secure their fortunes as writers on the Orient in Europe. Gordon, Le Brun, and Djavidan Hanum found ready and interested audiences in Europe, which they were eager to address.

These were not necessarily audiences that were sympathetic to women. Gordon was afraid that the publication of her letters would give away her affair and bring condemnation. Le Brun and Djavidan Hanum were condemned in European circles for having married Egyptian men. At the end of her book, Djavidan Hanum mentioned that she was excluded from her fatherland and could not go home.[72] Le Brun wrote under the pseudonym of Niya Salima (good intentions) to avoid harsh judgments by both French and Egyptian readers. Since the book was published in France in French, it probably was not widely read in Egypt. Huda Sha'rawi, who was told by Le Brun about the book, read it and recommended it to May Ziadah, who mentioned having used it in the research she did on the nineteenth-century harem and its effect on the life of Aicha Timur.

There were many tensions and fears that kept European and Egyptian women apart. To begin with, European women's access to Egyptian men created considerable friction between them and Egyptian women. European women used their access to men to overcome their subordinate position as women in Egyptian society. This type of empowerment had its limits in the sexually segregated system under discussion. The alternative mode of empowerment, which was not explored extensively, would have utilized the female dominated world. The special friendships that Huda Sha'rawi and Eugenie Le Brun, May Ziadah, and Malak Hifni Nasif had with one another were exceptional. It is interesting to note that while the relationship between Ziadah and Nasif seemed to be between equals who could disagree with one another and still be friends, that which existed between Sha'rawi and Le Brun resembled the more traditional relationship between mentor and protegé. While the former allowed the two to grow and feel free together, the latter was based on the inequality between them—in age, experience, and culture. Le Brun took it upon herself to educate Sha'rawi by introducing her to Western culture and suggesting to her the evils of the veil and seclusion.[73] This type of a one-sided cultural exchange represented a condescending European approach and attitude toward women of other cultures. Its hierarchical character was compounded by the age difference between the two. It was an obstacle to an open-ended dialogue about their experiences as women living under different patriarchal systems of control.

Conclusion

Cultural nationalism in its Orientalist or anti-colonialist discourses gave women the very traditional role of the protectors and conveyors of cultural definitions of gender. The images European and Egyptian women produced of themselves and of each other were not different from those produced by their dominant cultures. It was Levantine-Egyptian women, with their simultaneous links to the two cultures, who tried to use the traditional roles of women as producers and preservers of cultural definitions to criticize the new and old definitions of women's roles in the East and West.

The other serious danger that cultural nationalism posed for the women under discussion is that it prevented them from developing an appreciation for the varied mechanisms of control developed by different patriarchal systems. By emphasizing public equality, Gordon, Le Brun, and Djavidan Hanum paid less attention to the patriarchal mechanisms of control that still dominated their private lives. While these women criticized the seclusion and the privatization of Egyptian women, they did not challenge their own relative loss of freedom within the marriage institution and their subordinate role in heterosexual relations.

While Nasif, Sha'rawi, and Musa were consistently critical of the private mechanisms of patriarchal control as they manifested themselves in early marriages and polygyny, the nationalist emphasis on modernization (defined as women's access to education, work, and public discussion) eventually made them adopt, like European women, public participation as the only measure of liberty. For the two groups of women, the new gendered roles only served to hide the more archaic hierarchical relations that continued in the family and that also spilled into the public arena, accounting for the restricted forms of access to the existing professions and equally restrictive definitions of women's contributions to society. Similarly, Levantine-Egyptian women's enthusiastic embrace of modernism made them focus less attention on the personal as a key arena.

The modern ideology of cultural nationalism further distorted the progress of women in different societies by introducing misleading cultural comparisons that made "other foreign" women, not men, the relevant frame of reference for the discussion of equal rights. By accepting the contention that they were superior to women from other cultures, European women's attention was diverted from the fact that they continued to be subordinate to European and other men with whom they came into contact. Similarly, Egyptian and Levantine-Egyptian women were encouraged to base their superiority vis-à-vis European women on combining education and public activity with their culturally defined roles as wives and mothers. Their acceptance of what was, and continues to be, described as "the best of the two worlds" is an obstacle to the thorough critique of the new and old patriarchal rules that oppress them.

NOTES

1. An earlier version of this chapter appeared in *Women's Studies International Forum* 12, no. 2 (1989); reprinted by the permission of Pergamon Press. To save space, many of the citations and quotes have been shortened or omitted. All of the quotes from Arabic sources in this chapter are my translations.

2. Abdel ʿAzim Ramadan, ed., *Mudhkarat Saʿd Zaghlul* (Cairo: al-Hayʾat el-Misriyat al-ʿAma lil Kitab, 1988), pp. 639–48; Naguib Mahfuz, *Hayat Tabib* (Cairo: Dar al-Maʾarif, 1963), pp. 62–64.

3. Ijlal Khalifa, *al-Harakat al-Nisaʾiyat al-Haditha* (Cairo: al-Matbaʿt al-ʿArabiya al-Haditha, 1973), pp. 22–26.

4. Muhammed Kamal Yahya, *al-Juzur al-Tarikhiya li Tahrir al-Marʾat al-Misriyat* (Cairo: Al-Hayʾat al-Misriyat al-ʿAma lil kitab), chapter 4.

5. A. M. Broadly, *How We Defended ʿArabi and His Friends* (Cairo: Research and Publishing Arab Center, 1980), chapter 28.

6. Latifa Salem, *al-Marʾat al-Misriyat wa al-Taghiur al-Ijtimaʾi* (Cairo: al-Hayʾat al-Misriyat al-ʿAma lil kitab, 1984), p. 18.

7. Salah ʿIssa, *Hawamish al-Maqrizi* (Cairo: Dar al-Qahira lil Nashr wa al-Tawziʿa, 1983), p. 195.

8. Emile Fahmy Shenouda, *Saʿd Zaghlul: Nazir al-Maʿrif* (Cairo: Dar al-Fikr al-ʿArabi, 1977), p. 60.

9. Ibid.

10. Malak Hifni Nasif, *Al-Nisaʾiyat* (Cairo: al-Jarida, 1910), pp. 10–11.

11. Amal al-Sobki, *Al-Harakat al-Nisaʾiyat fi Misr bayn al-Thawratayn 1919 and 1952* (Cairo: al-Hayʾat al-Misriyat al-ʿAma lil kitab, 1986), pp. 13–17.

12. ʿIssa, pp. 195–96.

13. Thomas Philipp, "Feminism and National Politics in Egypt," in Lois Beck and Nekki Keddie, eds., *Women in the Muslim World* (Cambridge: Harvard University Press, 1978), p. 283; Huda Sha'rawi, *Mudhakarat Rai'dat al-Mar'at al-'Arabiya al-Haditha* (Cairo: Dar al-Hilal, 1981), pp. 249–55.

14. Sha'rawi, pp. 81–83.

15. Nabawiya Musa, "Zakrayati," *al-Fatat*, no. 48 (September 28, 1938) , pp. 19–20.

16. Salem, pp. 109–10.

17. Yahya, pp. 69–75.

18. Sha'rawi, pp. 253–55.

19. Mervat Hatem, "Egyptian Upper and Middle Class Women's Early Nationalist Discourses on National Liberation and Peace in Palestine (1922–44)," *Women and Politics* 9, no. 3 (1989), pp. 49–70.

20. Nabawiya Musa, "al-Muhadarat al-Nisa'ya fi al-Jami'at al-Misriyat," in al-Ahram, ed., *Shuhud al-'Asr* (Cairo: Al-Ahram, 1986), pp. 40–41.

21. Shenouda, pp. 68, 136.

22. Sha'rawi, pp. 261, 323.

23. Nasif, p. 14.

24. Musa, "al-Muhadarat," p. 38.

25. Ibid., p. 34.

26. Sha'rawi, p. 94.

27. Ibid., p. 115.

28. Ibid., p. 119.

29. Fawzia Fawaz, *Husn al-'Awaqib* (Beirut: al-Majlis al-Thaqafi li Lubnan al-Janubi, 1984), p. 13.

30. Rose Ghurayyib, *May Ziadah: al Tawahuj wa al-'Aful* (Beirut: Mu'assasat Nufal, 1978), pp. 31–32.

31. Amy Khayr, in Hasayn 'Omar Hamadah, ed., *Ahadith 'An May Ziadah* (Damascus: Dar Qutayba lil Nashr, 1983), pp. 115–16.

32. Ghurayyib, p. 121.

33. Ibid., pp. 120, 122.

34. Zaynab Fawaz, *al-Dur al-Manthur fi Tabaqat Rabat al-Khudur* (Cairo: al-Matb'at al-Amiriyat, 1894), p. 5.

35. Warda al-Yazji, *Hadiqat al-Ward* (Beirut: Dar Maron 'Abboud, 1984), pp. 95, 97.

36. Ghurayyib, p. 134.

37. Ibid.

38. Al-Yazji, pp. 54–55.

39. Fawaz, *al-Dur*, p. 3.

40. Sha'rawi, pp. 86–87.

41. Ghurayyib, pp. 145–54.

42. Ibid., p. 133.

43. Ibid., p. 135.

44. Djavidan Hanum, *Harem Life* (London: Noel Douglas, 1931), p. 299; Sha'rawi, p. 81.

45. Lucie Duff Gordon, *Letters From Egypt* (London: Virago Press, 1983), p. 31.

46. Djavidan Hanum, pp. 12–17; Sha'rawi, pp. 97–98.

47. Djavidan Hanum, pp. 12–27; Sha'rawi, pp. 98–99.

48. Gordon, p. 177.

49. Gordon, pp. 165, 190, 198–201, 227, 291.

50. Ibid., pp. 107, 164, 235–36.

51. Muhammed 'Auda, "1882: 'Am Ahdath Misr al-Kubra," *Rose al-Yusef* (February 11, 1982), p. 6.

52. Niya Salima, *Harems et Muselmanes d'Egypte* (Paris: Felix Juven, 1900), p. 46.

53. Qasim Amin, *Tahrir al-Mar'at* (Cairo: Dar al-Ma'rif, 1970), pp. 43, 58.

54. Djavidan Hanum, p. 11.
55. Gordon, pp. 20, 21, 96–97, 147, 238.
56. Djavidan Hanum, pp. 96–101, 147.
57. 'Issa, p. 93.
58. Niya Salima, p. 44.
59. Gordon, pp. 43, 79.
60. Djavidan Hanum, pp. 144–45.
61. Sha'rawi, pp. 99–100.
62. Gordon, pp. 96–97, 104, 125.
63. Ibid., pp. 21, 53–54.
64. Sha'rawi, pp. 117–23.
65. Gordon, p. 171.
66. Ibid., pp. 117, 140.
67. Djavidan Hanum, p. 196.
68. Sha'rawi, p. 98.
69. Ibid.
70. Gordon, p. 213.
71. Ibid., pp. 182, 183, 266.
72. Djavidan Hanum, p. 299.
73. Sha'rawi, pp. 96–100.

Imperial Politics

THE "PASSIONATE NOMAD" RECONSIDERED

A EUROPEAN WOMAN IN *L'ALGÉRIE FRANÇAISE* (ISABELLE EBERHARDT, 1877–1904)

Julia Clancy-Smith

> As a nomad who has no country beside Islam
> and neither family nor close friends, I shall
> wend my way through life until it is time for
> that everlasting sleep inside the grave.[1]

In the spring of 1897 a young Russian woman and her mother arrived for the first time in Bone (Annaba), a thoroughly Europeanized port on the Mediterranean coast of Algeria, which by then had been uneasily under French rule for nearly seventy years. The two women had gone to North Africa seeking refuge from personal tragedy and domestic unhappiness. There they offended the smug sensibilities of Bone's European residents by spurning the city's modern French neighborhoods for a modest house in the older Arab quarter. Before the year was out, Isabelle Eberhardt (1877–1904) buried her mother, Madame de Moerder, in the Muslim cemetery located outside Bone's northeast gates since both women claimed to have converted to Islam.[2] For the next seven years, Eberhardt regarded North Africa, particularly Algeria, as her true homeland, much to the dismay of the civilian settlers. Forced on several occasions back into "exile" in Europe by hostile colonial authorities and poverty, Eberhardt's sensational death during a desert flash flood in 1904 finally allowed her to remain permanently in her country of adoption.

Algerian historiography of the past 132 years appears as the "imperial man's world" par excellence.[3] The history of *L'Algérie française* even today is peopled almost exclusively by men, whether French military "heroes" like General Bugeaud, celebrated in colonial hagiography, or Muslim resistance figures such as Amir Abd al-Qadir, venerated as an early nationalist leader by the Algerians. One of the few exceptions in the fin-de-siècle period is the enigmatic Isabelle Eberhardt; no other individual from Algeria's hybrid European society has been the object of so much passionate attention. Immediately after her death, a number of works devoted to Eberhardt were published along with some of her own writings; soon thereafter, the author of *The Oblivion Seekers* fell into literary and historical oblivion.[4] The past decades have witnessed a revival of interest in the "passionate nomad," who has become somewhat of a cult figure. The growing body of literature on Isabelle Eberhardt demands critical analysis, as does the life of this flamboyant woman.[5]

Many of the recent works fall into three different, although related, categories: the history-cum-nostalgia for the colonial past in which biographies of heroic white women constitute a subgenre; second, studies that portray Eberhardt as a protonationalist and even as a protofeminist; and last, works written by the formerly colonized, particularly Algerians attracted by Eberhardt's sympathy for Islam and Arab North African civilization.[6] Few, if any, recent studies examine her squarely within the proper historical perspectives—European Orientalism of the late nineteenth century, on the one hand, and the peculiar colonialism of Algerian *pied-noir* society which, as Eberhardt arrived on the shores of Africa, was just reaching maturity, on the other.[7] By placing this woman within these two mutually reinforcing systems of domination, she becomes less of an anomaly or a social aberration. If she became a cause célèbre in French Algeria it was not—as both her detractors and admirers claim—because she truly was "an enemy of France," nor was she, as others have asserted, "profoundly Algerianized."[8] I will argue instead that Eberhardt was a collaborator in the construction of French Algeria. Moreover, her ambiguous niche in the imperial social order reveals in unambiguous ways how gender, class, and race fused to produce the half-breed of colonization. Thus, a European woman labeled by officials as disorderly, undesirable, and marginal was in fact central to—even emblematic of—the colonial encounter.

A Life of Her Own: Geneva, 1877–1897

Most biographers divide Eberhardt's life into two neat segments, which wrongly suggests that there was little political connection—beyond youthful, romantic yearnings for the exotic—between the young woman of stifling Geneva and the Isabelle Eberhardt of the Sahara.[9] Nevertheless, she (and many like her, both male and female) was a cultural exile long before leaving the European continent. More importantly, Eberhardt was a participant of sorts in imperial ventures before setting foot in North Africa at the close of the century. Conversion to Islam, membership in an Algerian *sufi* (mystical) order, and marriage to an Arab Muslim only heightened her personal involvement in the French colonial enterprise.

By the early nineteenth century, Paris and other European cities were already deeply influenced by Orientalism, defined by Edward Said as a field of study, a mode of thought and discourse, and as a "Western style for dominating, restructuring, and having authority over the Orient."[10] As Eberhardt was growing to troubled adolescence in the 1880s, many peoples of Asia and Africa were either already under various forms of colonial control or soon to be; most of northern Africa bordering the Mediterranean represented an imperial backyard for France and Great Britain.[11] Travelers and officials who had spent time in the "Orient," returned from Egypt, Tunisia, or Algeria laden with Eastern curios and cultural artifacts. These added panache to world's fairs held in London and Paris and furnished European drawing rooms—paradoxically the matrix of the cult of bourgeois domesticity—with the bric-a-brac of subjugated non-Western societies.[12] Colonial exhibitions and drawing room exoticism both advertised Western global hegemony and provided a powerful stimulus for many bored Europeans to travel to the East.

The illegitimate offspring of an Armenian Orthodox ex-pope turned anarchist, Alexandre Trophimovsky, and an aristocratic German woman, Isabelle Eberhardt was raised in a wildly eccentric household located in one of Geneva's sedate suburbs. Tutored at home by the nihilist Trophimovsky, who within the family was as much an autocrat as the Russian tsars he conspired against, Eberhardt and her hapless siblings were raised to despise middle-class and Christian morals. She received an extensive education at the hands of her oppressive father—classical and European languages as well as Arabic, history, geography, philosophy, etc.—which provided the only relief in childhood from the morbid atmosphere of the family compound. From an early age, she wore only male clothes and was taught to ride a horse as vigorously as any man, two formative influences that served her well later in North Africa but also may have contributed to the "fluidity" of her own gender identification.[13]

As a girl she dressed up in the romanticized costume of a *spahi* or a bedouin, read Pierre Loti's *Aziyade* (published in 1879), as well as colonial novelists, and later, while still in Switzerland, corresponded regularly with a French lieutenant stationed at an Arab Bureau in the Algerian Sahara.[14] She also took as one of her many lovers a youthful diplomat assigned to the Turkish consulate in Geneva. A dark, Levantine Armenian converted to Islam, Rehid Bey fed her fantasies, sexual and otherwise, about the "mysterious Orient."[15] At the age of eighteen, two years before her initial trip to Africa in 1897, she donned the Arab garb of a "dashing desert cavalier" for a photograph in one of Geneva's studios where Europeans could indulge in the fiction of an Eastern voyage without leaving home.[16] The next year she fashioned a "Muslim" identity for herself by employing the pseudonym "Mahmoud Saadi" in her letters written in Arabic to an Egyptian litterateur living in political disgrace in Paris. Isabelle Eberhardt was an Orientalist writer, actress, and playwright in-the-making. The costumes and part of the script had been constructed in Europe; what was lacking was an adequate mise-en-scène.

Her first journey to Algeria in 1897 at the age of twenty was motivated by emotional distress as well as ambition. Unlike many other European women of her class and generation, she was never involved in any social campaigns or political causes in the Continent before setting out for the colonies.[17] However, one (and perhaps two) of her unstable brothers dabbled briefly in the subversive politics—and drug dealings—of the expatriate Russian anarchist community in Geneva; already in her teens she may have acquired a fondness for opiates from her brother, Augustin.[18] She always claimed to eschew politics, although this was more out of political naiveté than an ideologically motivated rejection.

While she was beginning to publish articles, using male and female noms de plume, in avant-garde Parisian literary magazines, she felt the urge to travel—at last—to the long dreamed of Dar al-Islam.[19] There she would establish her credentials as a writer and secure some measure of financial security. At the same time, she and her mother could flee the enervating melancholia of their home in Geneva, dominated by the abusive Trophimovsky, and hopefully build a new life in colonial Algeria. In one sense, Eberhardt's motives for going to North Africa did not differ from those of other European immigrants, particularly from the poorer, overpopulated southern Mediterranean countries. However, unlike the lower-class Maltese and Corsicans, who outnumbered the French in Algeria by the turn of the century, she also embarked on a voyage of self-discovery as much as self-promotion.[20] And her journey can be seen as a contrived pilgrimage to achieve the sort of liminal states conferred by cultural dépaysement, normally only the privilege of the privileged. (And Eberhardt was, in many respects, very much the aristocrat, despite her vagabond ways.)

Thus, as was true for a whole host of disaffected, peripatetic Europeans, the invented "East" represented an antidote to mental anguish, social malaise, or personal angst, a haven whose facade of social liberation was underwritten by colonial subjugation. Eberhardt's trips to Algeria were preceded by nearly half a century of French military "pacification" in North Africa, which had rendered travel to and within the region a relatively safe matter.[21] Paradoxically her self-discovery through travel to foreign places would only be partially, if ever, realized. She landed in the bigoted, self-righteous community of Bone whose inhabitants suffered from acute "status anxiety," as did most other members of colonial society.[22]

L'Algérie française : "Ici, c'est la France"

By the end of the century, Algeria had become as vital to France's imperial self-confidence as India was to Great Britain's sense of global superiority; still the country presented a myriad of unresolved contradictions. As David

Prochaska nicely put it: "Algeria was a French colony—the colonizers maintained hegemony over the colonized, and at the same time Algeria was not a French colony—it was an integral part of France. In short, Algeria had been incorporated but not integrated into France in 1870, ingested but not digested."[23] And the obstacles to full digestion were not only the Muslim Algerians but also the large numbers of non-French Europeans living there, people such as Isabelle Eberhardt and her mother. In effect, a "secondary colonization" existed in which the French-born lorded it over the southern Mediterranean groups (or the *petits blancs* as they were disparagingly called); all Europeans, no matter what origins, despised the Algerian Muslims. Like other colonial societies, class, race, and ethnicity together formed the infrastructure of social stratification. Nevertheless, "the Algerian melting pot did not dissolve individual European ethnic differences, but instead created a heady new Mediterranean stew—what later came to be known as the pied-noir community."[24] Thus, Algeria was very much an "imagined community" whose heterogeneous, and potentially antagonistic, components were kept in unsteady equilibrium by the creation of the Algerian Muslim Other. In the eyes of the *colons*, Isabelle Eberhardt compromised that equilibrium by fraternizing, both culturally and sexually, with those relegated to the "other side of the tracks," and in so doing, she threatened to expose the phantasms of the invented community.[25]

Soon after her arrival in Bone, the young Russian woman provided idle tongues with ample ammunition for malicious gossip. Dressed in Arab male garb—fez, turbans, etc.—Mahmoud Saadi, as she called herself, wandered through the streets and markets at all hours of the night, at times unaccompanied, at others, with Algerian male companions.[26] Already quite conversant in classical Arabic, she perfected her spoken Arabic by hanging out in the quintessential space for Mediterranean men, irrespective of religion or culture—the popular café; there she may also have indulged in what was later to become an addiction—her passion for hashish. Avoiding the company of the European settlers, whom she found insufferable, Eberhardt prayed at the city's mosques—dressed as a man—and sought to deepen her knowledge of Islam by studying with local Muslim scholars. In cultivating friendships within Bone's Muslim community, she not only ignored gender boundaries but class divisions as well, frequenting all manner of people, the great and the humble. And on the few occasions when she dressed as an Algerian woman, several young Arab men sought her hand in marriage.[27]

All of this naturally shocked and horrified the European community, which was as conservative in defining gender roles as traditional Muslim society was.[28] Civilian *pied-noir* opprobrium, however, was replaced by growing official consternation over Eberhardt's public and private behavior. She may have participated—inadvertently—in a popular Muslim riot against the abuses of the colonial regime in the months following her mother's death. Fearing reprisals and fleeing her creditors, she took off to the Sahara where she fell in love with "that mysterious void known as the great Sahara," the nomadic way of life, and perhaps with a few of the desert's male denizens.[29] A noble at heart and in matters of finance (she borrowed money shamelessly, mainly from her Muslim friends), Eberhardt retreated back to Geneva in 1898 when her funds gave out and news of Trophimovsky's deteriorating health reached her.[30] Her father's death and the prospect of married life with an Oriental in a non-Oriental setting—Rehid Bey, by then posted to Holland, had proposed to her—impelled her back to North Africa in the summer of 1899. In Tunis, she further scandalized both the Europeans and the Tunisians, who had been placed under a French protectorate in 1881.[31]

Fin-de-siècle Decadence and Colonial Control

Drugs, alcohol, sexual digressions, and other kinds of amusement were cultivated as an art form in fin-de-siècle Paris and other European capitals, at least among certain classes. And transvestism, whether employed to circumvent social strictures upon ordinary females or indulged in as a tantalizing pastime by urban demimondaines, was not frowned upon in some social milieux.[32] Wearing disguises—often costumes appropriated from other cultures—was a passion; Pierre Loti, whom Eberhardt admired fiercely, frequently donned Turkish or Berber clothing to escape from himself and make his mark on Parisian society.[33] Isabelle Eberhardt, who visited Paris on several occasions in 1900, would not have been terribly out of place in the metropole's sophisticated capital. Yet, in French Algeria, prim and parochial, such comportment could not be condoned, at least not in public and thus within view of the Muslims whose domination was justified by the principle of innate European moral and cultural superiority.[34]

Moreover, the premise of Western superiority undergirded another operative myth in the period—that of "assimilation." Manipulated by colonial administrators to sooth liberal consciences in the metropole and to dampen political activism by the few Muslim *evolués* (evolved), assimilation held that some Algerians would someday enjoy the same privileged civil status already conferred upon the *colons*.[35] But first they had to become culturally like Frenchmen. Isabelle Eberhardt's extravagant attempts to "go native" threw assimilationist theory into disarray by suggesting that indigenous culture had its own intrinsic merits. The fact that Eberhardt, who at least by birth came from the upper ranks of European society, had crossed class and racial lines to mix freely with those at the very bottom of the colonial hierarchy could not be tolerated.

Most writers opine that Algerian Muslim society was more tolerant of Eberhardt because she had ostensibly embraced Islam, joined a sufi order, and dressed like an upper-class Arab man, which gave her access to male public and, particularly, religious spaces.[36] Nevertheless, it must be emphasized that Eberhardt had the weight of the French imperial system behind her—however reluctantly—when she entered sacred spaces normally off limits to Europeans of whatever gender and to Algerian Muslim women. While she did establish true friendships with the colonized, the Arab Muslims were relatively powerless and had no choice but to tolerate whatever she chose to do. Moreover, her claims to being a fervent Muslim—while buttressed by Eberhardt's apparently scrupulous observance of the daily prayers and ritual fasting—were compromised by her growing penchant for alcohol, drugs, and illicit sexual unions, all absolutely forbidden by Islamic law. Thus, she flouted the norms of both societies; more serious still to the colonizers, she mocked the European myth of moral ascendancy over the Muslims.

During her first journey to the Sahara in 1899, Eberhardt had discovered the desolate beauty of the oasis of El Oued, the "town with a thousand white domes." Perhaps the Sahara would prove less socially confining than the settler towns of the north. El Oued was part of the Algerian desert that was then under military administration; the coastal regions had passed under civilian rule after 1870. The officers responsible for the region's security were suspicious of this European woman dressed in Arab garb. Some suspected her of involvement with Methodist missionary efforts, others of being an English spy. While she cast herself in the role of a nomad, riding wildly over the dunes with bedouins, Foreign Legion types, and the riff-raff of caravans, and reveling in her apparent total freedom, the military bureaucracy was tracking her movements. She had to obtain a permit from the Arab Bureau to travel into the deep south—there were administrative limits to exoticism as lived.[37] If their European counterparts in Algerian cities were beset by status anxiety, military officials were obsessed by fears of insurrection; this led them to assign more political importance to this disorderly Western woman (or man?) than she deserved. While Eberhardt professed to dislike the French military—for nonpolitical reasons—she was quite comfortable in the company of officers, and later agreed to aid them in the takeover of southeastern Morocco.

Chased for a second time from North Africa by poverty and ill health at the end of 1899, Eberhardt returned the next summer intent upon settling permanently in El Oued, although she was still a Russian citizen. In the oasis she first encountered the man who eventually became her husband. Slimene Ehnni was a junior officer in the *spahis*, a Muslim and, significantly, a French citizen, one of a handful of Algerians to enjoy this status. Eberhardt followed him from posting to posting with his military contingent until her official expulsion from the country in 1901 as an "undesirable." It was also at this time that she began keeping a journal of her wanderings and musings. In her diary, she often excised the European presence in its cultural and, above all, political manifestations, just as the colonial literary and pseudoscientific production on Algeria's history banished the Algerian and the Islamic from its pages.[38] Yet what Eberhardt re-inserted in her works as genuinely North African, Arab, and Muslim was only partially true, if that. As stated above, she arrived in the country already imbued with the Orientalist fable as told in Europe. What she saw and how she perceived it had already been filtered—indeed, veiled—by earlier Orientalist writers, like Loti, whom Eberhardt may consciously or unconsciously have emulated.[39]

The Diary: Writing as Expatriation

As exposed in the diary, Eberhardt's views of Africa, the North Africans, and Islam are generally—though not always—informed by the same kinds of sentimental stereotypes and racist caricatures employed by other less unconventional writers of the period.[40] Rather than a subversive text—that is, one which offered a counter-reading of indigenous society and culture—her writings may have confirmed the worst European biases regarding the Muslims' innate inferiority and thus their unworthiness for political equality. "The beloved fateful land of Barbary"—Mediterranean Africa—was, for Eberhardt, intoxicating, heady, pungent; her descriptions of Algeria's coast are reminiscent of the *pied-noir* maxim that "L'Algérie monte à la tête" (Algeria goes to your head).[41] In contrast, the Sahara is "mysterious" and a "bewitching and magnificent expanse" where indigenous life is "slow and dreamy." The desert's inhabitants are described—using staged, photo-graphic-like clichés—as "primitive men," "biblical," and belonging to "primitive humanity." As for Islam, the religion is "mysterious and dream-like," brings "ecstasy," and, of course, demands fatalism and total resig-nation before God, the latter representing the single most pervasive (and inane) stereotype of Islam among Westerners then, as even today.[42]

Algerian men fare scarcely better in the diary. They "all resemble one an-other" physically, their collective Arab persona is one of "harshness and violence," attributes which did not discourage Eberhardt from initiating countless sexual liaisons with indigenous men. Even the beloved Slimene, whom she married in a civil ceremony in Marseille in October of 1901, is described as childlike and in need of tutoring to instruct him in "all the things he does not know [i.e., Western civilization], which is a tall or-der."[43] Thus, the paternalism of the colonial order was recreated in Eber-hardt's sexual relationships. Ironically, marriage with Slimene conferred French nationality upon her and the right to return to Algeria later that year, despite the expulsion decree and official opposition. This was the ul-timate challenge to the colonial order of things. Isabelle Eberhardt, a Rus-sian and thus a part of the "foreign peril," became a citizen of France by virtue of marriage to an Arab Muslim. (Marriages between Muslims and Europeans were exceedingly rare in this period.)[44] Cultural expatriation had its rewards.

But what of her views of women, both European and colonized? Eberhardt's diary says little about females, for whom she betrayed scant empathy or even interest. In general, the female character provides a negative foil to the male personality: "invincible will and integrity [are] two traits that are so hard to find in women." Aside from her own mother, for whom she displayed sincere affection, Eberhardt judged harshly the few European women that she wrote about: "a horrible revolting creature" was how she described one unfortunate French lady.[45] These sentiments are probably representative of her attitudes toward Western women as a social category. While Eberhardt's own gender conflict (and the snubs she encountered from straitlaced European women) may have fueled her distrust of and distaste for females, there was another dimension to this.

In a settler colonial society, such as Algeria, where racism was rooted in the notion of cultural superiority, European women were the vanguard of the *mission civilisatrice*, the divinely ordained civilizing mission of France. "White" women defined social distance from, and political control over, the Muslims; Islam was intrinsically inferior to Western civilization precisely because of female status in the Other's holy law and culture. Thus, women were the measure of all things, particularly in the last decade of the century when a new sociocultural synthesis had finally emerged, that of the *pied-noir* community. Moreover, the civilizing mission had as one of its goals the de-Orientalization of the Oriental, who was to be assimilated culturally to the West, forcibly or otherwise, at least in theory. By "making Algeria French," the colonial agenda, in Eberhardt's mind, threatened to remove the exotic backdrop so necessary for her own cherished expatriation.[46]

While Arab women are dealt with a bit more sympathetically in the diary, they are usually portrayed as passive and resigned, more like strange, decorative objects, exiles in their own land.[47] The one exception is an Algerian female saint and mystic, Lalla Zaynab (1850–1904), who befriended Eberhardt in 1902. Due to her piety, advanced Islamic learning, and ability to work miracles, Lalla Zaynab was immensely powerful within her own Arabo-Berber society; she was also an ascetic and had taken a vow of celibacy. Overlooking the European woman's dissolute ways, Zaynab welcomed Eberhardt to the family sufi *zawiya* (lodge or monastery) in the Sahara, consenting to be her spiritual mentor and confidant. This relationship between a colonized woman, whose life was wholly devoted to self-abnegation, and a Western women, whose manic personality impelled her to sensual excess, is remarkable in the annals of North African history.[48] Eberhardt's profession of Islam and her membership in a sufi order probably gave her an entrée into Zaynab's circle as did the Arab custom of hospitality and courtesy toward guests.[49] Yet as important was the fact that their friendship developed in the Sahara—away from the centers of European implantation with their increasingly rigid lines of social demarcation. In the desert, which was overwhelmingly inhabited by indigenous Algerians, there was no need to maintain the fiction of assimilation.

Despite the innocuous nature of the friendship, the colonial police closely surveyed Eberhardt's visits to Zaynab, seeking to discover the subject of their conversations.[50] In part, this was related to concerns about assuring the Sahara's political calm on the eve of a planned military sweep into neighboring Morocco. In addition, army officials held the mistaken belief that the European woman exerted influence over the North Africans because of her command of Arabic, conversion to Islam, and her involvement with a sufi brotherhood. This might be turned to France's advantage.

A Colonial Accomplice in Spite of Herself?

By 1902 colonial authorities regarded Eberhardt as more than a debauched eccentric; a bitter debate over her conduct was waged in the colonial press. When she and her Arab husband, Slimene, settled in Tenès, an ultraconservative and politically divided *pied-noir* town, a press campaign was launched against the couple, with Eberhardt as the principal target of vituperation. Observing her preference for the company of the Muslims or—worse still—for a few resident French "Arabophiles," the town's administrators accused her of spreading hostile propaganda among the Algerians; others charged that she was setting herself up "as some kind of prophetess."[51] By then she enjoyed the support of a small cohort of liberal French journalists, among them the well-known writer, Victor Barrucand. Barrucand defended her in the newspapers and offered her the position of special correspondent with the newly created daily, *El Akhbar*, in 1903. Mounting hostility toward Eberhardt among settlers in northern Algeria probably convinced Barrucand to send her to the desert that year to cover General Lyautey's "absorption" of southeastern Morocco.

By 1903 the only obstacle to a vast French empire stretching from southern Tunisia to West Africa was Morocco. A proponent of yet another colonial myth, that of *pénétration pacifique*, Lyautey's aim was to weaken the Moroccan Sultan's authority over the truculent tribes of the ill-defined border regions between the two countries. This policy of "colonialism on the cheap" sought to avoid costly, protracted warfare in gaining new territories; it also demanded winning local indigenous allies who would not resist the French army's "gentle pushes" onto Moroccan soil. From the oasis of Ain Sefra, Eberhardt, dressed in male garb and using her assumed name of Mahmoud Saadi, sent back accounts of French military activities to Barrucand in Algiers—in addition to spending much time with Foreign Legion soldiers in cafés. Eventually introduced to the commanding general, she agreed to perform some reconnaissance missions to advance Lyautey's "peaceful penetration." In effect, she became a paid, although unofficial, agent of the "Deuxième Bureau" which conferred upon her a horse, complete liberty of movement, and enough money to subsist on. This was the lifestyle she had long craved but which had been denied her by the European settlers in northern Algeria out of fear of her cross-cultural fraternizing and cross-gender behavior. Ironically, Eberhardt may also have struck the bargain with Lyautey to redeem her tarnished reputation as anti-French.[52]

In General Lyautey she found a kindred spirit. The general genuinely admired her precisely because she was a "réfractaire" (rebel) and scorned the hypocrisy of *pied-noir* bourgeois society. And being a career officer, Lyautey shared the military's latent hostility to the civilian colonial administration.[53] Moreover, Lyautey, like Eberhardt, desired that the "Orient" remain Orientalized and not be "degraded" by debasing mixtures of European modernity. By 1904 Eberhardt's dispatches to *El Akhbar* began to betray the general's influence, particularly her op-ed pieces on proper tactics for winning new lands and peoples for France. "It would not be impossible for us to gain some profit from our conquest and to organize it without disturbing Morocco's illusion that it possessed these regions."[54]

Eberhardt's affiliation with the Qadiriyya sufi order convinced the general that she alone could perform a delicate diplomatic mission in 1904.[55] Seeking to neutralize potential political opposition in the contested Algerian-Moroccan areas, Lyautey commissioned her to visit the sufi shaykhs of the regionally powerful Qnadsa (or Kenadsa) brotherhood and prepare the way for the French advance. Posing as a young Muslim male scholar in search of mystical learning at the Qnadsa zawiya, Eberhardt was warmly received by the head shaykh, Sidi Brahim, who was aware of her identity and intentions. Given an austere cell in which to live, pray, and meditate, she soon grew weary of her guise as an aspiring mystic since she was deprived of alcohol, drugs, and sex and kept more or less in isolation. Some sources credit her with a pivotal role in convincing Sidi Brahim to accept France's "protection" and thereby renounce allegiance to the Moroccan sultan.[56] It seems more likely that Eberhardt, less and less enthused by the rigors of true monastic life, was able—at best—to furnish information on the Qnadsa to the French command back in Ain Sefra. In effect, Sidi Brahim had out-manipulated her and indirectly Lyautey, by forcing the European woman to play fully, for the first time, the role in which she had long cast herself: an expatriate seeker of mystical truth.

Suffering from bouts of malaria and probably syphilis in its advanced stages, Eberhardt refused Sidi Brahim's offer of escorts so that she could push further west into Moroccan territory. Instead she returned in October of 1904 to Ain Sefra, where an autumn flash flood engulfed the hut she was residing in; her body was discovered in the attire of an Arab cavalryman surrounded by the muddied pages of her writings. She had drowned in the desert.[57]

Grief-stricken, Lyautey arranged a Muslim burial for Eberhardt in the cemetery at Ain Sefra. Yet the general refused the deceased one final honor. Her tombstone was not inscribed with the preferred masculine name of Mahmoud Saadi; rather, the feminine "Lalla Mahmoud" was employed.[58] Lyautey had the scattered remnants of Eberhardt's manuscript sent to Victor Barrucand, who already possessed some of her earlier, un-published works. In 1905, Barrucand published selections from her writ-ings (to which he added his own sensational prose) under the melodra-matic title of *Dans l'ombre chaude de l'Islam*. The book was a bestseller for the period, going into three editions and selling thirteen thousand copies. In addition to listing himself as co-author (and cashing in on the royalties), Barrucand exoticized Eberhardt's life even further, inserting suggestive material that bordered on the pornographic.[59]

Nevertheless, if Eberhardt had become a sort of colonial apologist in her press articles—once again due to her political immaturity—a profound transformation can be detected in the many stories and literary sketches she wrote in the period just before her death. No longer the dreamy, cliché-ridden Orientalist prose, her fiction presents painfully realistic, almost ethnographic, accounts of indigenous life in its confrontation with a con-quering, alien civilization.[60] Paradoxically, by shedding one set of assumptions—that of Orientalism—about the Arab-Islamic world, she was seduced by another—Lyautey's heterodox notions of pacification through peaceful cooptation underscored by the threat of superior military might.

Eberhardt had desperately sought not only to adopt another culture, but also to construct another gender identity through writing and living as a passionate nomad. Yet her story was appropriated—and exploited—by one of her dearest male associates, Barrucand. Likewise, her other close male companion, Lyautey, imposed a female (and false) identity upon Eberhardt in the grave. She was, thus, confined to a European literary harem in co-lonial North Africa, a victim of her own thirst for exoticism which, like Orientalism and imperialism, was a male-dominated endeavor.

From Europe to Africa and Back Again

Part of Europe's flotsam and jetsam thrown up on the French-ruled shores of Africa, Isabelle Eberhardt resembled T. E. Lawrence in her frantic, re-lentless search for the glamor of strangeness. Algeria was her private the-ater; French colonialism provided the staging, the North Africans offered backdrop color. Eberhardt not only dabbled in that archetypal colonial genre—the European travel account—but also embodied the genre itself; she was the most outré expression of travel as expatriation. In a diary entry of 1901 she stated:

> there are women who will do anything for beautiful clothes, while there are others who grow old and grey poring over books to earn degrees and status. As for myself, all I want is a good horse as a mute and loyal companion, a handful of servants hardly more complex than my mount, and a life as far away as possible from the hustle and bustle I happen to find so sterile in the civilized world where I feel so deeply out of place.[61]

But political expatriation is very often an act of cultural appropriation. Like Loti, André Gide, and many others, Isabelle Eberhardt attempted to appropriate another culture and its ways; her principal tactic was that of gender manipulation, which was partially the product of her own deeply felt gender conflict. Gender transvestism permitted her to engage in cultural transvestism, which ultimately rendered her marginal to both cultures—the hybrid European community of French Algeria and Muslim North African society. Isabelle Eberhardt was an extreme example of cultural hyphenation. Yet it can be argued that she was representative—indeed totemic—of the entire colonial enterprise in *L'Algérie française*, which today lives on in the collective memories of *pied-noir* communities, forcibly repatriated after 1962 on the northern shores of the Mediterranean.[62]

NOTES

1. Isabelle Eberhardt, *The Passionate Nomad: The Diary of Isabelle Eberhardt*, trans. Nina de Voogd, intro. and notes by Rana Kabbani (Boston: Beacon Press, 1987), 2; hereafter cited as *Diary*.

2. David Prochaska's *Making Algeria French: Colonialism in Bone, 1870–1920* (Cambridge: Cambridge University Press, 1990) is a first-rate study of French colonialism. Prochaska contrasts British India, where the attraction of the summer hill stations was precisely the absence of large numbers of Indians, to French Algeria: "(W)ere not the European settlers, the *pieds-noirs*, so firmly ensconced in Bone that there was little need to get away—at least from the Algerians?" (p. 208). Whether North African or Indian, the carefully nurtured myth of Western superiority dictated that Europeans observe special behavioral norms in front of the natives.

3. Women, whether European or indigenous, are notably absent in the two standard historical studies of Algeria, Charles-André Julien, *Histoire de l'Algérie contemporaine (1827–1871)*, vol. 1 (Paris: Presses Universitaires de France, 1964) and Charles-Robert Ageron, *Histoire de l'Algérie contemporaine (1871–1954)*, vol. 2 (Paris: Presses Universitaires de France, 1979). The Algerian war of national liberation, 1954–62, produced a number of heroines, such as Jamila Boupasha, whose story is told by Simone de Beauvoir and Gisèle Halimi, *Djamila Boupacha: The Story of the Torture of a Young Algerian Girl Which Shocked Liberal French Opinion* (New York: Macmillan, 1962).

4. Isabelle Eberhardt, *The Oblivion Seekers and Other Writings*, trans. Paul Bowles (San Francisco: City Lights, 1975). The title for this collection of stories and sketches was inspired by one of Eberhardt's pieces written in 1904 immediately before her death. Paul Bowles, himself a cultural exile living in Morocco for decades, might be considered as a sort of latter-day American version of Eberhardt in his capacity as a writer and professional expatriate.

For a critical analysis of the work on Eberhardt from 1904 until 1982, see Simone Rezzoug, "Etat présent des travaux sur Isabelle Eberhardt," *Annuaire de l'Afrique du Nord* 21 (1982): 841–47; Rezzoug rightly characterizes these works as "numerous but of poor quality," 841. In addition, Eberhardt's biography inspired at least two plays: *L'Esclave errante* (*The Wandering Slave*), which opened at the Théatre de Paris in 1924; and *Isabelle d'Afrique* (1939). In 1987 a surrealistic film was made on her life with the unfortunate title of "There Was an Unseen Cloud Moving."

5. In his *Femmes d'Algérie: Légendes, traditions, histoire, littérature* (Paris: La Boite à Documents, 1987), Jean Déjeux devotes a chapter to Isabelle Eberhardt, the only entire chapter on a European woman in Algeria, 207–56. His bibliography, 337–41, lists at least sixty works on her.

6. The question of why Eberhardt's story, once forgotton, is now remembered needs to be raised. In addition to recent biographies, Eberhardt's own writings, including her diaries, are being republished both in French and in English translation. As Margaret Strobel and Nupur Chaudhuri point out in the introduction to the present work, the answer lies in the nature of late twentieth-century sensibilities. Nevertheless, the current rage for colonial backdrops in literature and cinema—romantic cross-cultural escapism—has an invidious side. In this global village we call our own, the colonial moment conjures up false images of a past stability and order when Africans and Asians "knew their place" and had not yet emerged as both a challenge and threat to the West. The re-publication of the writings of female travelers, for example the travel account of Edith Durham (1863–1944), first published in 1909 and republished as *High Albania*, intro. John Hodgson (Boston: Beacon Press, 1985), is evidence of this nostalgia. An analysis of present-day interest in Eberhardt among Algerians is found in Déjeux, *Femmes*, 239–56.

7. The origins of the term *pied-noir* are still disputed in the literature on French Algeria. Here the term is employed to designate the European settlers—at first mainly French in nationality but later from all over southern Europe—who arrived in Algeria as colonists soon after the initial French invasion of 1830. Originally intended to settle land expropriated from the indigenous Muslim Algerians, the *colons* eventually clustered in cities and towns. By the end of the nineteenth century, the *pied-noir* community had evolved into a culturally hybrid society that was, in many respects, distinct from France and from the French of the metropole.

8. The colonial newspaper, *Petite Gironde,* described her as an "enemy of France" and Eberhardt, significantly, felt compelled to refute this accusation in her letter of April 27, 1903, cited in Déjeux, *Femmes*, 253. Paul Catrice in his "Femmes écrivains d'Afrique du nord et du proche orient," *L'Afrique et l'Asie* 59, no. 3 (Paris, 1962): 23–44, published the year of Algerian independence, characterized Eberhardt as being of "Russian origins but profoundly algerianized," 24.

9. Edmonde Charles-Roux in his *Un Désir d'Orient: Jeunesse d'Isabelle Eberhardt, 1877–1899* (Paris: Bernard Grasset, 1988), entitles chapter 5, which deals with Isabelle's departure for North Africa, "Ruptures."

10. Edward E. Said, *Orientalism* (New York: Pantheon Books, 1978), 3.

11. For the intellectual antecedents of nineteenth-century Orientalism and imperialism, see Ann Thomson's *Barbary and Enlightenment: European Attitudes towards the Maghreb in the Eighteenth Century* (Leiden: E. J. Brill, 1987).

12. There were a number of "Expositions Universelles" held in Paris during the nineteenth century, for example in 1867 and in 1889; on the World Exhibition as part of the colonial encounter, see Timothy Mitchell, "The World as Exhibition," *Comparative Studies in Society and History* 31, no. 2 (1989): 217–36.

13. The toll that Trophimovsky's nihilist philosophy exacted from the five children in his care was high (only Isabelle was certainly his own child; Augustin's paternity remains doubtful; the rest were from Madame de Moerder's marriage to a Russian officer in the tsar's army). Two of Eberhardt's brothers and a niece committed suicide; several fled the family when the opportunity for freedom arose. On Isabelle Eberhardt's early life, see Cecily Mackworth, *The Destiny of Isabelle Eberhardt* (London: Quartet Books, 1977); and Annette Kobak, *Isabelle: The Life of Isabelle Eberhardt* (New York: Knopf, 1989). Her sexual identity is a complex affair; she may have

been in love with her brother, Augustin, for awhile, according to Kobak, *Isabelle,* 31–37.

14. Mackworth, *The Destiny,* 20–25. The *spahis* were Algerian Muslim troops in the service of the French colonial army.

15. Ibid., 24–25.

16. Kobak, *Isabelle,* 33. Popular Orientalism reached its height in the late nineteenth century as seen in the European fad for "chinoisérie" and Ottoman furnishings and dress. World's fairs and colonial exhibitions not only displayed expropriated Oriental cultural artifacts but also the colonized peoples themselves to gawking European audiences; this represented cultural imperialism-cum-voyeurism at its worst. The photographer's appropriation of other cultures and civilizations was not limited to European studios. For a fine discussion of the colonial postcard and colonized women, see Malek Alloula's *The Colonial Harem,* trans. Myrna Godzich and Wlad Godzich (Manchester: Manchester University Press, 1987); the title of the French edition, *Le Harem colonial: Images d'un sous-érotisme* (Geneva-Paris: Editions Slatkine, 1986), is more accurate.

17. Eberhardt's attraction to French Algeria contrasts sharply with the pull-push factors that brought British women to India; see Antoinette M. Burton's "The White Woman's Burden: British Feminists and 'The Indian Woman,' 1865–1915," in the present volume.

18. Mackworth, *The Destiny,* 26–36.

19. Kobak, *Isabelle,* 38–47. A tendency toward necromania is already manifest in her early writings; this later developed into a fascination with graveyards and obsession with death as seen in her diaries.

20. In some respects, Eberhardt resembled other women travelers of the period who sought social mobility, self-assertion, and liberation through treks in foreign yet conquered lands. Like Mary Kingsley, she was clearly a "tortured soul"; see Helen Callaway's review of Katherine Frank's *A Voyager Out: The Life of Mary Kingsley* and of Dea Birkett's *Spinsters Abroad: Victorian Lady Explorers* in *Women's Studies International Forum* 13, no. 4 (1990): 405. In large measure, the relative ease of travel was due to refinements in the "tools of empire" — tremendous changes in communications technology made it feasible to reach Asia or Africa rapidly. Eberhardt noted in her journal (*Diary,* 17–18) that the sea crossing from Marseilles to Algiers in 1900 took roughly twenty-four hours, which is still true today. Thus the social phenomenon of women travelers at the turn of the century was the product of three interrelated forces: transformations in European female status that made it acceptable for women, even unaccompanied by men, to journey alone; the "New Imperialism," which made northern Africa into Europe's southern frontier; and significant advances in travel technology.

21. The progressive "pacification" of places like Algeria is reflected in the changing titles of European travel literature during the course of the nineteenth century. From the "expeditions" of the early conquest period (1830–c. 1850) to later travel accounts entitled significantly, "scenes from the sunny south," the forced domestication/appropriation of the Algerians' culture and land is clear.

22. Prochaska, *Making Algeria,* 204.

23. Ibid., 137.

24. Ibid., 155.

25. The notion of imagined communities is taken from Benedict Anderson's provocative work, *Imagined Communities: Reflections on the Origin and Spread of Nationalism* (London: Verso, 1983). While Anderson's main focus is the "invention" of the nation-state and nationalism, one could argue that this invention went hand-in-hand with imperialism/colonialism. Of course, all communities, whether national or not, are imagined and invented to a certain degree.

In French Algeria, the *pied-noir* community, despite—or perhaps because of—its diverse ethnic/linguistic components, came close to embodying an invented or imagined subnational political and ideological entity. By the turn of the twentieth century, this entity had its own peculiar spoken patois or dialect, a distinct political culture and literature, and thus a collective awareness of its own subjective existence. (On the emergence of pied-noir culture, see Prochaska, *Making Algeria French*, 206–29.) Nevertheless, it was a highly volatile community since class lines did not always, in reality, match racial-ethnic divisions between white Europeans and Muslim Algerians. Moreover, the Europeans were highly stratified socially, and deeply-rooted antagonisms existed between the metropole and the settlers. Therefore, these potentially disruptive social (and political) faultlines among the Europeans were kept in a steady state by *colon* fears or phantasms of indigenous insurrection, violence, and sexuality.

26. As Mackworth, *The Destiny*, 39, correctly points out, cross-gender dressing (i.e., women clothed as men) was acceptable for some strata of Algerian Muslim society in certain situations, although it was certainly not the norm. Eberhardt's preference for male disguises undoubtedly scandalized the Europeans of Bone more than its indigenous inhabitants. As a recent biographer of Gertrude Bell (another well-known female traveler in the Middle East during exactly the same period) observed, the wearing of trousers by European women was "an almost unheard of sartorial departure for a woman." H. V. F. Winstone, *Gertrude Bell* (New York: Quartet Books, 1978), 58.

Eberhardt's ability to pose as a man was aided by her physical appearance; a French woman who had known her in Tunis described Eberhardt in the following way: "She lived like a man—or a boy, because she was far more like one, physically. She had a hermaphrodite quality—she was passionate, sensual, but not in a woman's way. And she was completely flat chested . . . her beautiful hands were tinted with henna, her burnous was always immaculate." Lesley Blanch, *The Wilder Shores of Love* (New York: Schuster, 1954), 293.

27. Mackworth, *The Destiny*, 37–45; Kobak, *Isabelle*, 50–57; and Charles-Roux, *Un Désir*, 329–42.

28. In "Rethinking Colonial Categories: European Communities and the Boundaries of Rule," *Comparative Studies in Society and History* 31, no. 1 (1989): 134–61, Laura Ann Stoler observes that European women were the "custodians of morality," and that colonial (white) prestige and female honor were closely linked.

29. Despite the mass of publications devoted to her, the chronology of Eberhardt's life in North Africa is far from certain. Some works claim that she returned at the end of 1897—after her mother's death—to Geneva, for example, Marie-Odile Delacour and Jean-René Huleau in the annotated edition of Isabelle Eberhardt, *Oeuvres complètes: Ecrits sur le sable*, vol. 1 (Paris: Bernard Grasset, 1988), 23; another work states that she took off briefly for the Sahara (L. Blanch, *The Wilder Shores*, 295); still another that she took part in the revolt of March 1899 in Bone (Kobak, *Isabelle*, 62–65). The quote is from the *Diary*, 10–11.

30. Eberhardt's indolent lifestyle was often financed by the Algerians whom she importuned to lend her money; *Diary*, 24, 25, 45.

31. Kobak, *Isabelle*, 81–86; and Mackworth, *The Destiny*, 46–49.

32. Eugen Weber, *France, Fin de Siècle* (Cambridge, Mass.: The Belknap Press of Harvard University Press, 1986), 27–50.

33. Lesley Blanch, *Pierre Loti: Portrait of an Escapist* (London: Collins, 1983), 146.

34. The view that most Europeans held of the indigenous Algerians was expressed by Hubertine Auclert in *Les Femmes arabes en Algérie* (Paris: Editions Littéraires, 1900), 3: "In Algeria, there is only a very small elite minority of Frenchmen who would place the Arab race in the category of humanity."

35. On the myth of assimilation, see Martin D. Lewis, "One Hundred Million Frenchmen: The 'Assimilation' Theory in French Colonial Policy," *Comparative Studies in Society and History* 4, no. 2 (1962): 129–53.

36. For example, Mackworth, *Destiny*, 39.

37. Ibid., 56–63; and *Diary*, 56–58.

38. Eberhardt often sublimated the worst abuses of the colonial regime in its treatment of the indigenous population. When she does describe the workings of European imperialism, it is usually to lament the fact that modernity was eroding the aesthetic appeal of the picturesque, quaint, and "traditional" in North African life. For example, in the *Diary*, 32, she states that: "Arab society as one finds it in the big cities, unhinged and vitiated as it is by its contact with a foreign world, does not exist down here [in the Sahara]."

39. For example, in the *Diary*, 31, she quotes a passage from Loti's *Aziyade* in which he depicts a moonlit graveyard in Istanbul; she then compares Loti's fantastic landscape to her own landscape artfully composed of a cemetery in the Sahara under moonlight.

40. Alain Calmes, *Le Roman colonial en Algérie avant 1914* (Paris: Harmattan, 1984); and Albert Memmi, ed., *Anthologie des écrivains français du Maghreb* (Paris: Présence Africaine, 1969). For critical assessments of French colonial perceptions of the colonized Other, see the collected works contained in *Le Maghreb dans l'imaginaire français: la colonie, le désert, l'éxil* (Aix-en-Provence: Edisud, 1985), and Julia Clancy-Smith, "In the Eye of the Beholder: Sufi and Saint in North Africa and the Colonial Production of Knowledge, 1830–1900," *Africana Journal* 15 (1990): 220–57.

41. Eberhardt's descriptive writings bear an uncanny resemblance to those of Albert Camus: there is, however, another more important parallelism in their works. While she often makes only oblique references to the political underpinnings of the colonial system of domination, Camus in his two most celebrated novels, *L'Etranger* (1942) and *La Peste* (1957), deliberately omits, for the most part, the Algerian Muslims who by then outnumbered the Europeans by at least eight to one.

42. *Diary*, 7, 10, 41, 23, 28, 79, 20, 68.

43. Ibid., 20, 79, 88.

44. Prochaska, *Making Algeria French*, 207.

45. *Diary*, 4, 21.

46. In the *Diary*, 91, she states that: "Despite the riff-raff French civilisation has brought over her, whore and whoremaster that it [France] is, Algiers is still a place full of grace and charm."

47. Ibid., 4, 25, 35.

48. I have deliberately employed the term "manic" in a clinical sense to imply that Eberhardt may have suffered from acute manic depression. Some writers, notably Rana Kabbani in her introduction to *The Passionate Nomad*, v, suggest that she was afflicted by anorexia nervosa. I would argue instead that her somatic or physical conditions (amenorrhea, lack of breasts, lanugo, etc.) were a function of drug and alcohol addiction, which were in turn manifestations of manic-depressive psychosis; cf. Rudolph M. Bell, *Holy Anorexia* (Chicago: University of Chicago Press, 1985).

49. Eberhardt's first visit to Zaynab in 1902 is described in Eglal Errera, ed., *Sept années dans la vie d'une femme: Isabelle Eberhardt, lettres et journaliers* (Arles: Actes Sud, 1987), 188–90; on Lalla Zaynab and the sufi *zawiya* of al-Hamil, see Julia Clancy-Smith, "The Shaykh and His Daughter: Coping in Colonial Algeria, 1830–1904" in Edmund Burke III, ed., *Struggle and Survival in the Modern Middle East, 1850–1950* (London: I. B. Tauris, and Berkeley: University of California Press, 1992); and on the friendship between Lalla Zaynab and Isabelle Eberhardt, see Julia Clancy-Smith, "The House of Zaynab: Female Authority and Saintly Succession in Colonial

Algeria, 1850–1904," in Nikki Keddie and Beth Baron, eds., *Shifting Boundaries: Women and Gender in Middle Eastern History* (New Haven: Yale University Press, 1992), 254–73.

50. Kobak, *Isabelle*, 191.

51. Ibid., 204. Opposition to Eberhardt may have taken more violent forms than mere character assassinations in the colonial press. In 1901, she was attacked by a knife-wielding Algerian male in the Sahara, and narrowly escaped death. The authorities "solved" the affair by attributing it to Muslim hostility toward Christians. However, some journalists at the time suspected that the colonial regime had paid her assailant to do away with a disorderly and embarrassing foreign woman; see Robert Randau, *Isabelle Eberhardt: Notes et souvenirs* (Paris: La Boite à Documents, 1989).

52. Kobak, *Isabelle*, 207–19; and Ursala K. Hart, *Two Ladies of Colonial Algeria: The Lives and Times of Aurélie Picard and Isabelle Eberhardt* (Athens, Ohio: Ohio University Center for International Studies, 1987), 98–100; the Deuxième Bureau was a French intelligence service that normally relied upon indigenous (paid) informers; see also Mackworth, *The Destiny*, 192.

53. General Catroux, *Lyautey, le Marocain* (Paris: Hachette, 1952), 86–88.

54. A quote from one of Eberhardt's reports cited by Kobak, *Isabelle*, 215.

55. Eberhardt had joined the Qadiriyya sufi order sometime in 1901 disguised as an Arab male (although Algerian females were also members of the order), and befriended the brotherhood's local elites in the Algerian Sahara. There are suggestions, however, that the sufi notables admitted her into their inner circle for political reasons—they believed she was secretly allied with French authorities, and thus sought to make use of the European woman; see Kabbani's notes to the *Diary*, 111, notes 25 and 27.

56. Hart, *Two Ladies*, 100–101, states that "Sidi Brahim had become a major lever in French penetration and there seems little doubt that Isabelle had had a hand in making it so." However, once again, this attributes to Eberhardt more political clout than she really had.

57. Accounts of her death are found in: Kobak, *Isabelle*, 231–38; and Mackworth, *The Destiny*, 219–23; Blanch in *The Wilder Shores*, 285, appears to have been the first to point out the irony of her drowning in the desert.

58. Hart, *Two Ladies*, 109.

59. Isabelle Eberhardt, *Dans l'ombre chaude de l'Islam*, edited by Victor Barrucand with a biographical essay on her life (Paris: Librarie Charpentier et Fasquelle, 1906); Kobak, *Isabelle*, 241, offers a fine analysis of why the book was so appealing to European audiences.

60. Kobak, *Isabelle*, 217. An example of the transformation in her writing is seen in the short story entitled "Outside" published in *The Oblivion Seekers*, 19–22.

61. *Diary*, 59.

62. Nostalgia for the colonial past has recently produced a number of sentimentalized works devoted to the *pied-noir* community in Algeria, for example, Marie Cardinal's *Les Pieds-Noirs* (Tours: Belfond, 1988).

CRUSADER FOR EMPIRE
FLORA SHAW/LADY LUGARD

Helen Callaway and Dorothy O. Helly

> Well, [Flora Shaw] . . . is a fine handsome
> woman and very clever and possessed of a
> power of which I am not. She has got
> imperialism in place of ordinary human
> feelings *or* religion *or* sympathy *or* chivalry.
> She represents the official view perfectly.[1]

Mary Kingsley 1899

Dame of the British Empire

Studies of Western women who took part in the British colonial enterprises show them as both resistant to and complicitous with men's policies and activities. Women's stands on issues of gender, "race,"[2] and class are shown to have been immensely varied and many-stranded, located in complex historical situations. Comparatively little work has been done on women who actively promoted imperialism with its ideology of the innate superiority of the "English gentleman" and the privileged position of the English race entitling it to rule over other peoples. The case of Flora Shaw (1852–1929) reveals a woman of incisive intellect who, as colonial writer for *The Times* of London from 1890 to 1900, used her strong powers of communication in the politics of imperialism.

Shaw toured the frontiers of the British Empire to gain firsthand knowledge for her reports. During this critical decade when European nations intensified their competition for overseas possessions, particularly in Africa, she wrote over five hundred articles on economic and political issues in the colonies, vigorously supporting British expansion, by military force if necessary. Her views—well-researched and cogently expressed—reached leading policy-makers at least once a week to inform and influence their decisions. In close touch with many leading statesmen of the day, she played an active political role, not merely reporting events, but helping to shape the jingoistic discourse of a new and more aggressive imperialism rising in the 1890s. She herself became deeply involved in political controversy.

After her retirement from *The Times* on grounds of ill health, she married Sir Frederick (later Lord) Lugard, then High Commissioner of Northern Nigeria. As a "Governor's Lady," she continued her dedicated support for imperial interests through her writings, her work for various philanthropic causes, and the strong promotion of her husband's career. Her refugee work during the First World War earned Lady Lugard public recognition in her own right as Dame of the British Empire, a title eminently befitting her career as a whole.

How does the study of an individual woman imperialist extend our understanding of the interweaving of gender, class, and race in the British imperialist enterprise? Shaw was at once a product of her class and an agent in shaping its imperial ambitions. Her ideas derived from her upper middle-class position with its base in the military and political establishment of the day. In terms of gender, her life reveals a strong determination for self-creation: at each stage, she assessed her situation to find new opportunities. During the Victorian era, when most upper middle-class women lived dependent lives at the margins of public affairs, Shaw guarded her autonomy and acted on the larger stage of political events according to her own vision.[3] Yet she did not support any movement to change the accepted gender roles of her time; indeed, she was anti-suffrage. By examining her relations with three male empire-builders—Cecil Rhodes, Sir George Goldie, and Lord Lugard—we discover her strong identification with the imperial ideology of masculinity and male "heroes of empire." In her direct political maneuvers, she acted through men; in her writings, she used the screen of anonymity conventional for *The Times* of that period. She had to negotiate the tension between her professional work, viewed as masculine, and her womanhood, as did other outstanding contemporary women engaged in the politics of imperialism—such as Beatrice Webb, Mary Kingsley, and Olive Schreiner, with whom we make comparisons. An analysis of Flora Shaw's life within its historical frame reveals new perspectives on the ambiguities and complexities of Western women's involvement in imperialism.

Journalism as Active Politics

Shaw's gender strategies show a double consciousness. While following the code of feminine decorum in her social life, she deliberately undertook professional work considered unsuitable for a woman. She studied political economy, developed sharp analytical skills, and through political journalism moved into male public space. Margery Perham assessed the effects of gender in Shaw's work: "She always wore black and she never played the woman as a short cut to her professional objectives. Even so, her beauty . . . seemed to add a glow even to her purely intellectual activities. Public men, however cautious, found it surprisingly easy to give away official information to such an interviewer."[4] Flora Shaw manipulated to her advantage the contradiction between her image as an attractive, dignified upper middle-class woman and her professional role as a keenly intelligent political writer. As a woman, she understood that her journalism provided the means she otherwise did not have for influencing public affairs.

In an intimate letter to her husband during their early years of marriage, she reflected upon her work of the previous decade. She summed up her sense of purpose: "I never thought of my work exactly as journalism, but rather as active politics without the fame."[5] She had no interest in fame, she claimed, using conventional gender discourse: "I daresay that is only the bent of a woman's mind. We are brought up that way—rather to shun than to court public notice." Among her journalistic achievements, she listed:

> To have helped to rouse the British public to a sense of Imperial responsibility and an ideal of Imperial greatness, to have had a good share in saving Australia from bankruptcy, to have prevented the Dutch from taking South Africa, to have kept the French within bounds in West Africa, to have directed a flow of capital and immigration to Canada, to have got the Pacific cable joining Canada and Australia made, are all matters that I am proud and glad to have had my part in.

Her assessment of her work, "in the company of lions," as she put it, exhibits the gratification of power exercised, the claim to a substantial role in making history, and a consciousness of herself as a woman. Fame aside, she clearly discerned the dimensions of political power that she had commanded through her journalism. The authors of *The Story of The Times* devote an entire chapter to her, concluding: "Flora Shaw was certainly more than a reporter and commentator; in matters affecting the Empire she was a crusader."[6]

Shaping Her Career

Some understanding of Flora Shaw's imperial commitments can be gained by reviewing her social background.[7] She was born in 1852, her mother from a prominent family in Mauritius related to the French aristocracy and her father the second son in a family of the Anglo-Irish gentry. He was then a captain, who later rose through the ranks at the Royal Military Arsenal at Woolwich to retire as major-general. Her paternal grandfather was Sir Frederick Shaw, an Anglo-Irish politician of some renown who, like his father before him, had served in parliament and (at the death of his older brother) succeeded to the baronetcy. During Flora's childhood, the Shaws spent long summers at the family estate in Kimmage, outside Dublin.

Shaw learned the lessons of gender at an early age. Her mother, a chronic invalid, bore fourteen children and died in her early forties. An elder daughter, Flora took charge of teaching the younger children when she herself was only thirteen. After a season as a debutante, when she refused marriage, she nursed her mother in her final illness and managed the large household on a straitened budget. With the remarriage of her father, she left home at age twenty to earn her living in the respectable position open to young women of her class, as a housekeeper-governess, in her case with family friends.

Although Flora had no formal schooling, she became fluent in French during visits to her mother's relatives in France and she undertook extensive reading encouraged by eminent mentors. When John Ruskin came to Woolwich in 1869 to lecture, he adopted the seventeen-year-old Flora as a protégée on the same pattern as other bright young women he had fostered. He introduced her to the elderly Carlyle, whose strong views on patriotism, masculinity, and imperial power had recently come to the fore during the campaign supporting Governor Eyre of Jamaica in the controversy over his brutal suppression of a black Jamaican uprising.[8] Ruskin's enthusiasm for imperial expansion apparently inspired Cecil Rhodes among other future empire-builders. In his inaugural address in 1870 as Slade Professor of Art at Oxford, Ruskin heralded England's duty:

> To found colonies as fast and as far as she is able, formed of her most energetic and worthiest men; seizing every piece of fruitful waste ground she can set her foot on, and there teaching these her colonists that their chief virtue is to be fidelity to their country, and that their first aim is to be to advance the power of England by land and sea.[9]

At Ruskin's suggestion, Flora Shaw wrote a children's novel, *Castle Blair*, published in 1877 and reprinted in numerous editions. This story takes place on an Anglo-Irish estate where the spirited young hero aids a plot to free the Irish tenants from the hated English agent. By the conclusion of the story, the lad regrets his mistaken ideas and looks forward to his future role as benevolent landlord. In Shaw's novel, the considerable sympathy the children of the gentry show for the wretched conditions of the tenants serves in the end only to reinforce the paternalist values of the Victorian social hierarchy and the political status quo.

With this success, Shaw was asked to write for *Aunt Judy's Magazine*, a popular children's magazine, which published her next two novels in serial form. She wrote two further books for young people. While Shaw portrayed realistic settings, she drew most of the characters as simplistic embodiments of good or evil and constructed plots with fast-moving action full of coincidences and inconsistency. She did not, like Olive Schreiner in her first novel, *The Story of an African Farm* (1883), probe her own experiences for new meanings and directions.

Certain recurring themes give insights into Shaw's deeper values. In these stories it is the boys who are rebel leaders, to be saved from their excesses by virtuous young women. This pattern of gender behavior follows ideas of chivalry revived during this period in the elite public schools and in numerous writings, including Ruskin's popular lectures published as *Sesame and Lilies* (1865). Again, the theme of gentlemanly honor pervades these books, carrying with it the wider meaning of a hierarchical social order based on inheritance, the ruling class exercising its prerogatives of power and wealth while using the rhetoric of paternalistic responsibilities. Her children's books were thoroughly of their period in supporting class stratification and gender subordination.

While becoming financially self-sufficient through her children's stories, Shaw explored the world of charity work in the slums of London's dock area. In the East End, like other young women of her class, she discovered the "social evils" of her day—overcrowded housing, sweated labor, incest, and prostitution involving girls under sixteen. She wrote in her diary:

> It is not possible to look round in this part of London without a numbing sensation of despair. . . . The beauty of many of the children, the brightness of the young people, only seems in one mood to make it worse. . . . they are to be drawn into the whirlpool of sin, they are to become inhuman and degraded, and the laws which make this so are too strong for us. Private charity, while I admire it, seems to me utterly insufficient. It is like bailing out the sea with a tea-cup, or trying to sweep up the sands of the shore. . . . the head tells me all the time that this kind of work is a satisfaction of the heart, but no real remedy.[10]

This experience did not impel her to become an investigator of economic conditions intent on political reform, as it did Beatrice Webb, who also confronted these conditions in the East End in the 1880s but turned to Fabian socialism. Instead, Shaw believed England's poverty could be solved by colonization of distant lands.[11] She envisioned that her role in promoting such a policy could be to write, not children's fiction, but serious journalism.

In 1883 Shaw rented a room in a cottage in Abinger, in the Surrey woods, later to become her permanent home. Here she developed a close friendship with a neighbor, George Meredith, who fostered her aspirations to become a journalist. He introduced her to his friends in the literary and political world, including the editor of the *Pall Mall Gazette*, W. T. Stead, an imperialist who strongly believed in the power of the press to direct public policy. Stead promised to consider publishing any letters she sent from Gibraltar and Morocco, where she was to spend the winter of 1886–87 accompanying family friends. She was alert to imperial issues. Discovering the political prisoner, Zebehr Pasha, exiled from Egypt by the British government of occupation, she recorded his life story. With its publication, Zebehr gained his release and for the first time Shaw experienced the impact of her journalism as active politics.[12]

Accompanying family friends to Egypt in the winter of 1888–89 enabled Shaw to become the accredited correspondent for two newspapers, the *Pall Mall Gazette* and the *Manchester Guardian*. She confidently arranged interviews with Sir Evelyn Baring (later Lord Cromer), in charge of the British occupation, and, under the patronage of Zebehr Pasha, gained entry to Muslim harem life in Cairo. Her reports showed her incisive understanding of political and financial matters and her distaste for the narrowly circumscribed lives of upper-class Egyptian women. Returning to England, Shaw wrote articles almost daily for these newspapers. Recognition as a highly competent political journalist came in the fall of 1889, when Flora Shaw took on a special assignment to represent the *Manchester Guardian* at a major European conference in Brussels to set out an international code for dealing with the slave trade in Africa.

Colonial Editor of *The Times*

C. F. Moberly Bell, whom Shaw had met in Egypt, became Assistant Manager of *The Times* early in 1890. He discussed the future development of the newspaper with her; both were enthusiastic to have much greater coverage of the empire. In response to a specimen column she wrote at his invitation, he told her, "If you were a man you would be Colonial Editor of *The Times* to-morrow."[13] But a slower approach was required to override the prejudices of the Editor and the Proprietor. Hard work, a sharp sense of news analysis, and the self-confidence of her class eventually gained her a place on *The Times* as its first Colonial Editor.

Success came from the arresting quality of her reporting during her travels on assignment for the newspaper. In 1892 she sailed to South Africa, where she investigated the diamond mines at Kimberley and gold mines at Johannesburg, and then went on to Pretoria to interview President Kruger—sending back her reports in the form of "Letters." Her vivid descriptions of life and work in South Africa presented readers in London with an overwhelming sense of firsthand knowledge about conditions of mining, prospects for agriculture, and problems of labor, white and black. She reiterated the theme that South Africa was "nothing less than a continent in the making": "Everything that is written of the material resources of this astonishing country must read like exaggeration, and yet exaggeration is hardly possible. The fertility of the soil is no less amazing than the mineral wealth." She argued that Dutch land interests could be reconciled with English commercial enterprise: "What English supremacy demands . . . is railway development, customs union, . . . [and] above all, an increased white population. . . . the steam-engine has become a more effective instrument of empire than the cannon."[14]

From London, Moberly Bell wrote her, "I think I can honestly say that nothing of the sort published in the paper since March 1890 (when I arrived) has created such comment . . . never have I so often heard the term 'Remarkable' applied so generally and by so many different sorts of people as to your letters."[15] Her achievement brought authorization to sail on to Australia, New Zealand, and across the Pacific to Canada. She made her way visiting farms and factories and talking to politicians, managers, and laborers. After more than a year abroad, she returned to London to wide acclaim for her articles and an appointment to the permanent staff of *The Times*. As its Colonial Editor she earned the substantial annual salary of £800, higher than other women journalists of her day.[16] *The Times*, more than any other newspaper, both reflected and shaped the opinions of the educated classes who ruled the nation. Writing fortnightly columns and numerous articles on colonial affairs, Shaw brought the empire to the breakfast table of those actively engaged in politics.

Shaw traveled for the newspaper later in the decade as well. Learning of gold discoveries in the Klondike, she spent five months in 1898 traveling in the wilds of the Canadian far north—the gold fields of the Yukon, Labrador, and the trading stations of the Hudson Bay Company. Attacking the official corruption she discovered in the administration of the Yukon district, her *Times* "Letter from the Klondike"—picked up by the Canadian press—placed her again in the middle of political controversy. Several times she made plans to travel more extensively in Africa, but none of them came to fruition. In 1895, she proposed crossing the continent from west to east, entering at the Niger River, crossing Lake Chad, and coming out through the Mahdist-controlled Sudan. She planned to travel with an interpreter through the Niger region, but otherwise alone. This bold idea was turned down by the Manager. Again in 1899, Shaw urged him to allow her to take a trip through Africa from Cairo to the Cape. She worded her request with a dash of humor: "I really have a practical gift for travelling without hurting myself. The reason is chiefly that I am able to make myself thoroughly comfortable everywhere. When I slept soundly on shingle in the Klondike, the men told me that I ought to try sand, which, they say, is the hardest thing there is. Obviously the desert is required to complete my experience."[17]

Cecil Rhodes and the Jameson Inquiry

The Victorian age has been called one of hero-worship, and high in popularity were the explorers, soldiers, and administrators of empire. From a military family herself, Flora Shaw identified with aspirations of the great empire-builders of her day. As a woman, she could not become such a hero, but she achieved the limits of the possible—as a fearless global traveler and a journalist who could sway public opinion and influence the reputation of empire-builders.[18]

Shaw developed a great and lasting admiration for Cecil Rhodes

(1853–1902). They kept in touch on his visits to England and on her tour of South Africa; he found the Colonial Editor of *The Times* a useful ally. In a letter to Lugard, one of those repelled by Rhodes's unscrupulous methods, Shaw defended him and, by implication, her own imperial vision: "I cannot help thinking, that if you were brought into personal touch with Mr. Rhodes and could realise, as I do, the absolutely unsordid and unselfish nature of the devotion which he gives to the imperial cause, you would acknowledge the ennobling influence of a great conception, and much of your prejudice would disappear."[19]

In the early summer of 1897, the extent of Shaw's involvement in imperial politics became dramatically exposed to public view when she was called before a Select Committee of the House of Commons at two separate sessions—on May 25 and July 2. This parliamentary inquiry sought to place responsibility for the military incursion into the Transvaal at the end of 1895 led by Dr. Leander Starr Jameson, close colleague of Rhodes and administrator of Rhodesia for the British South African Company. Jameson's position was that he was aiding European "Uitlanders" (non-Afrikaners) who were rebelling against Kruger's government for curbing their "political liberties," their right to vote. Rhodes, with his gold mining interests in the Transvaal, had been secretly supplying them with arms to ensure the victory that would bring the Boer republic once more within the British Empire.

When incriminating telegrams between Shaw and Rhodes were discovered, she was suspected of being a link in a collusion between him and the Colonial Secretary, Joseph Chamberlain. The evidence strongly suggests, and many contemporaries were convinced, that she was deeply involved in the events leading up to the raid. From the diary of anti-imperialist Wilfred Blunt comes the comment made to him by a member of Parliament that Flora Shaw was "really the prime mover in the whole thing . . . [the one] who takes the lead in all their private meetings, a very clever middle-aged woman."[20]

Mary Kingsley, a few years later, described her as being "as clever as they make them, capable of any immense amount of work, as hard as nails and talking like a *Times* leader all the time. She refers to the *Times* as 'we' and does not speak of herself as a separate personality and leads you to think the *Times* is not a separate personality either."[21] Because of Shaw's identification in the public mind with the newspaper, her loyalty to Rhodes and Chamberlain, and her own dubious actions, her appearance before the Select Committee became a supreme test of her ability to avoid damaging revelations.

She had to negotiate gender through a minefield of politics. On the eve of her first interrogation, the Editor, G. E. Buckle, warned her "against proffering too much unsolicited information, and making speeches to the Committee," clearly implying that as a woman she was not to be trusted in such a public arena.[22] Shaw did lecture the Committee, but only to compliment them that they, unlike the general public, would be able to understand that the telegrams referred to the "Jameson Plan" for a miners' uprising against President Kruger, and not the "Jameson Raid." Put on the spot about whether she had cabled Chamberlain's views to Rhodes, she replied that she had made educated guesses about the Colonial Office position from her general knowledge of the political situation.

Shaw evaded key questions and acquitted herself with great intellectual agility, refusing to implicate either *The Times* or the Colonial Secretary in the planning of the insurrection. In the draft report of the Committee, her sharpest interrogator, Liberal member of Parliament Henry Labouchere, commented wryly: "The recollection of the lady was somewhat defective."[23] Five years later he recounted: "A more difficult lady to induce to say what she did not want to it would be difficult to find. Her manner was most charming. When asked a question, she went off at a tangent, and made a clever speech on things in general. . . . And so well did she do it, that had I persisted in an attempt to get the answer I should have been regarded as a ruffian lost to all sense of courtesy towards a lady anxious to tell me everything. . . . I got nothing out of her that she wished to conceal, but I conceived an unbounded admiration of her charm and her cleverness."[24]

On this episode, Margery Perham concluded, "It would certainly seem that under the spell of Cecil Rhodes she had improperly mixed up her professional and her private action. But those who would judge, as Goldie seems to have done, that here for once she was betrayed by her sex, should remember how many men were swept into allegiance by the force of Rhodes's personality."[25]

Sir George Goldie and Nigeria

With Sir George Goldie (1846–1925), the professional and personal sides of Shaw's life meshed in a different way. She met him first in 1891, when she was in her late thirties and coming into her own as a formidable political journalist. During the following years, she became an intimate friend and reported on Goldie's achievements as creator of the Royal Niger Company. Although the evidence is sparse, Shaw apparently fell in love with this charismatic figure.

Goldie had grown up in a large country mansion on the Isle of Man. Trained as a soldier, he used his inheritance to escape a conventional life. He lived for three years with an Egyptian mistress in the Sudan and later eloped with his family governess, Mathilda Elliot. Goldie sustained close bonds with his wife, but according to his biographer, he was "not a faithful husband." After visiting West Africa in 1877, Goldie saw the possibility of amalgamating the trading firms competing with each other on the Niger River. His efforts enabled Great Britain, at the Berlin conference of 1884–85, to claim a predominant position over the region of the Niger basin.

The name "Nigeria" was coined by Flora Shaw in an article in *The Times* on January 8, 1897, to designate the territories under the jurisdiction of the Royal Niger Company headed by Goldie.[26] A few months later, his successful military campaigns at Bida and Ilorin secured British authority in these troubled areas. Shaw's articles placed Sir George Goldie within the discourse of heroic imperialism. In her editorial on March 4, she effused, "It is difficult to speak too highly of the brilliancy of this achievement." And in her column on March 30, she called on imperial precedents: "The Battle of Bida takes, in Nigerian history, the place held by the Battle of Plassey in the history of India." She also wrote two long and highly laudatory articles on the Royal Niger Company appearing on April 17 and 19. In the view of Goldie's biographer, "This was crude propaganda."[27]

In Shaw's defense, it might be noted that hers was by no means the only glowing praise for Goldie. Mary Kingsley wrote in her *West African Studies* that his company showed "how great England can be when she is incarnate in a great man, for the Royal Niger Company is so far Sir George Taubman Goldie."[28] Goldie himself wryly acknowledged: "What with the *Saturday* comparing me to Clive and the *Daily News* to Cortes, I fear I shall cease to be the retiring man you have hitherto known, and shall become a notoriety-hunter."[29] In this year of Queen Victoria's Diamond Jubilee, the rhetoric of imperialism had reached its most overblown style.

Flora Shaw's affections were caught up in her admiration for this "hero of empire." Apparently, she believed that if Goldie were free, he would marry her. When his wife died unexpectedly in 1898, she must have waited for a proposal that never came. Just what happened remains unknown. An estrangement occurred that affected Shaw so deeply she became ill for many months. She resigned from *The Times* in 1900 and before long accepted a proposal from another empire-builder.

Marriage to Sir Frederick Lugard

Not long after Flora Shaw met Goldie, she also made the acquaintance of Captain Frederick Lugard (1858–1945). The son of a missionary mother and clergyman father, Lugard became an officer in the Indian army. He sought escape from a devastating love affair by going to Africa and soon found an imperial cause. Praised by Joseph Chamberlain in Parliament for his services in East Africa, he wrote an acclaimed two-volume account of his work, *The Rise of Our East African Empire*. Shaw met him, in fact, when he made an ill-advised visit to *The Times* to see its prospective reviewer and was surprised to find a woman. Chiding him for not observing the proper conventions, she nevertheless reviewed his work favorably, calling it "the most important contribution that has yet been made to the history of East Africa."[30] Over the following years, *The Times* continued to support Lugard's positions and projects in Africa. When Shaw's relationship with Goldie foundered, her friendship with Lugard deepened.

As High Commissioner of Northern Nigeria and recently knighted, Sir Frederick returned on home leave in 1901 and proposed marriage. After some hesitation, she agreed, stating her feelings clearly: "You once said you would win my *love*. I, too, hope to win yours. . . . We cannot force it. Let us not try on either side: but let us be content to marry as friends." She added a few days later: "We shall both of us wish to work on. The greater part of our energy must always be given to the public thing."[31] She was now in her late forties, he six years younger, both fully committed to serving an ideal of empire—in her words, "this conception of an Empire which is to secure the ruling of the world by its finest race."[32]

Their quiet wedding, without guests, took place the following year in Madeira. Lugard had only a few weeks' leave and they were soon on the steamship to Nigeria. Flora Lugard's letters to her niece give vivid, rather romantic descriptions of the journey, showing her anticipation of this new phase of her life. Reaching Zungeru, Lugard's new capital in Northern Nigeria, she proudly announced to Moberly Bell: "Empire-making goes on here on a scale to suit you."[33] Her longest letter, nearly the length of a government dispatch, she wrote to Joseph Chamberlain, as a friend from her years in journalism, but also as the Colonial Secretary to whom she could advance her husband's cause. Warmly inviting him to make a visit to this part of his imperial estate, she set out the details of the "almost incredible" progress achieved by Lugard in such a short time in Northern Nigeria, emphasizing the lack of manpower and resources, and the doctor's concerns at the strain of overwork on his health.

Against her hopes, Flora Lugard did not flourish in the humid, malarial climate. She described the adverse effects of the climate on Europeans: "a distinct lowering of vital force showing itself in loss of energy, irritability of nerves, depression of spirits, premature ageing etc."[34] She felt the isolation of Zungeru, a tiny cantonment of a half dozen mud bungalows for as many British officers, who were not allowed to bring their wives. Cut off from her previous colleagues and the London political scene in which she had played such a vital part, she had little to do each day except read and write letters. Unlike Sylvia Leith-Ross, who arrived there a few years later and was so captivated by Fulani women that she learned their language, Flora Lugard felt only the absence of European civilization.[35]

As High Commissioner, Lugard spent almost all his waking hours at work, seven days a week; he had monosyllabic moods and hated being interrupted.[36] His new wife saw him only at meals. Under medical orders not to go out in the sun, she admitted in a letter to Moberly Bell that she now spent the greater part of her time "in solitary confinement."[37] She confessed deeper anxieties about her relations with Lugard in a letter to her niece: "We have probably to get over a little difficult time first until we have learned how to manage our lives."[38] Lady Lugard's health worsened and, after little more than four months, the doctor ordered that she be sent home. The disappointed "Governor's Lady" would now have to continue her wifely role in England, rather than by her husband's side. Writing and speaking in the metropolitan center would once again be her way of empire-building.

The Making of an Imperial Statesman

Despite this inauspicious beginning to their marriage, Lady Lugard spent the remaining twenty-five years of her life helping to advance Lugard's career to his eventual recognition as the foremost British colonial administrator in Africa and the reward of a peerage. With mutual admiration and a united purpose, they transformed the friendship on which they had based their partnership into a deep and sustained love, evident from the affectionate intimacy of their letters. Marriage did not erase her sense of individual identity; her support for Lugard's work became the way for her to continue her self-designated role as a crusader for empire.

Lugard welcomed the strong backing for his career she provided by means of her articles and lectures, her easy entry to the Colonial Office, and her active social life in London's influential political circles. According to his brother, however, Lugard privately commented about her lecture at the Royal Society of Arts on Nigeria, "She might have left me my part of Africa."[39] Taking on ambitious research, in a burst of energy she turned out a five-hundred-page book, *A Tropical Dependency*, published in 1905.[40] Nearly two-thirds of the book covers what she called "an outline of the ancient history of the Western Soudan," a mixture of myth and history ranging from the Phoenicians to the Fulani, told with sweeping panache, citing only a few references and without a bibliography. Central to this book is an implied scale for measuring racial superiority and inferiority, based mainly on color. In Nigeria, she accorded superior qualities to the northern Muslims, with the thesis that they had driven inferior black races toward the sea. Her frontispiece map showed a series of mythical inhabitants along the coast—Lam-lam, Rem-rem, Dem-dem, Gnem-Gnem—representing a "cannibal belt."

The main political message came across clearly in her introduction: the recently acquired non-white areas of the empire required special attention to be given to questions of "tropical administration." She argued: "The administration of this quarter of the Empire cannot be conducted on the principle of self-government as that phrase is understood by white men. It must be more or less in the nature of an autocracy which leaves with the rulers full responsibility for the prosperity of the ruled."[41] In the final section, confessing her possible bias, she gave a detailed account of the steps taken by Lugard as High Commissioner, first to "pacify" large areas of the country, bringing slave-raiding to an end, and then to introduce his administrative framework with the principles of "indirect rule." She presented a specially bound copy to King Edward VII and copies to the Prime Minister, Colonial Secretary, and other leading politicians. With this book, and his own published report on Nigeria of 1904, the name of Lugard became synonymous with new and vigorous colonial administration in tropical Africa.

Unable to negotiate special terms of service that would have given him alternately six months in Nigeria and six months in the Colonial Office setting up a new "tropical" administration, Lugard resigned in 1906. The following year he was appointed Governor of Hong Kong, where ceremonial duties made the presence of Lady Lugard important. In her notes for Lugard's biography, Perham commented, "It seems that a good woman was wanted in H. Kong and the appt. was as much of *her* as of him."[42] From 1907 to 1912, despite serious illness, Flora Lugard made extensive journeys to Japan and China and helped gain the support necessary for establishing the University of Hong Kong.

Lugard's next posting returned him to Nigeria with the mandate to amalgamate the Northern and Southern Protectorates. Meanwhile, Lady Lugard used her influence to uphold the empire in the divisive politics of Irish Home Rule by supporting the Ulster camp. With the onset of the First World War and the invasion of Belgium, almost overnight she shifted plans for housing women and children in the event of an Ulster uprising to providing hostels for Belgian refugees. For this work, in 1916, she was made Dame of the British Empire.

In her biography of Lord Lugard, Margery Perham gives Lady Lugard fulsome praise for her strong support of his career as a leading colonial administrator. Later critics of Lugard argue that her writings, lectures, and lobbying of politicians constituted a campaign not only to advance her husband's reputation—at the expense of his predecessor, Sir George Goldie—but to promote a particular version of imperialism that was autocratic and conservative.[43] Lady Lugard belonged wholly to the age of empire. She translated her fervently held belief in its greatness first into her career of journalism as active politics and then into her marriage partnership for advancing her husband's, and her own, political power to attain their united goals.

Gender, Ideology, and Imperialism

"Imperialism" as a word first entered the vocabulary of politics in Britain in the 1870s, to become by 1900 the term "used to denote the most powerful movement in the current politics of the western world."[44] As Colonial Editor of *The Times* during the 1890s, Flora Shaw played a leading role in creating and disseminating this discourse, which legitimated the conquest and domination of other lands in the name of civilization and development. The ideology of imperialism cannot be separated from gender asymmetry and class hierarchy: ideas of dominance moved in concentric circles from male authority in the domestic scene, to upper-class privilege in governing the national arena, to the rightness of English rule over other people around the globe. This ideology grew in intensity during the last decade of the nineteenth century to pervade the consciousness of the nation. *The Times,* as the leading newspaper, and its Colonial Editor helped to generate and spread this dynamic discourse.

As a powerful crusader for empire, Flora Shaw might be considered a woman unique in her time, a limiting case. Her position may explain her "double invisibility": neglected both by historians who see the record in terms of male actors and by feminists who, understandably, prefer to resurrect women with whom we feel greater affinity. Yet the question must be confronted: as a woman imperialist, does she stand in contrast to other women of her generation or were her basic attitudes more or less shared by other prominent women and by many others not in the political limelight?

Feminists of the period protested gender inequality in some of its manifestations, yet many endorsed ideas of empire as paternal responsibility. Women on the political left, Beatrice Webb a leading figure, sought government action to redress poverty and alleviate class deprivation, while supporting the broad outlines of imperialism. Only a few contemporary women associated imperial domination abroad with gender and class inequalities at home.[45]

The similarities and differences in Flora Shaw's ideas show up in comparisons with other outstanding women of her time—Olive Schreiner (1855–1921), Beatrice Webb (1858–1943), and Mary Kingsley (1862–1900)—the subjects of recent biographies with revealing feminist insights.[46] Both Shaw and Webb were self-consciously upper middle-class; Shaw throughout her life promoted the interests of her class, while Webb deliberately fostered Fabian socialism. Kingsley felt insecurity in her mixed class background, her father from a prominent literary family, her mother a servant; in imperial politics, she sided with the traders against upper-class establishment interests. Coming from South Africa, with an English mother and a German missionary father, Schreiner became "a literary success, a political disturbance, a friend of the troublemaking intellectuals of her time"; her writings, passionately expressed and inconsistent with one another, cut across the dominant ideas of the day.[47]

While growing up, all these women became aware of the inequalities of gender in their families. None had formal schooling and all were burdened with household duties and caring for invalid parents or young children. Highly motivated for self-education, they placed themselves under male mentors, whose professional status validated their protégées' intellectual endeavors. As women with active careers in the public eye, all challenged Victorian ideology concerning womanhood, while conforming to feminine conventions of dress and behavior. Shaw and Webb both married late but claimed to regret their childlessness. Kingsley publicly repudiated being labelled a "new woman" and wanted to marry, but she remained single throughout her brief life. Schreiner yearned to go beyond gender restrictions to personhood and empowerment, yet she extolled the ideal of motherhood. Marrying late, she deeply mourned her inability to become a mother after the death of an infant daughter and numerous miscarriages.

Although all were aware of how gender stereotypes imposed constraints on women's lives, only Schreiner publicly analyzed the structure of gender subordination and called for women's full emancipation. She was honored as the most distinguished member of the suffrage movement in South Africa, but resigned from the Women's Enfranchisement League when its definition of the voting qualification was changed to exclude black women.[48] Webb signed a petition against suffrage for women in 1889, and though she later recanted, she concentrated her efforts on publicizing the cause of Fabian socialism.[49] Of the four, Mary Kingsley took the strongest stand *against* feminism, even speaking against votes for women to suffragists at the Fawcett Society.[50] In her early womanhood, Shaw apparently discussed women's rights with George Meredith; later with her husband and imperial-minded friends, she joined the anti-suffrage movement. Her friend Mrs. Ethel Moberly Bell claimed in a letter to Lord Cromer: "*The Times* has done more for the anti-suffrage cause than any other paper."[51]

The relation of imperialism to anti-suffrage for women becomes clear in the literature of the *Anti-Suffrage Review*. An editorial setting out the complementarity of the sexes as an argument against women's suffrage called for "saving women from the immeasurable injury of having their sex brought into the conflict of political life, [and] . . . saving the Empire from a most hazardous experiment (which, whatever its other result might be, would undoubtedly cause a weakness at the heart)."[52] Allowing women to vote for Parliament challenged imperial constructions of gender.

Although not crusaders for empire like Shaw, these other women took it for granted that the British Empire represented—at least in theory—the highest form of civilization and potential justice. They differed radically, however, on their vision of the best relationship between Britain and its overseas territories. Webb believed it was necessary for the British Empire to triumph over the Afrikaners in 1899. Kingsley fought against direct Colonial Office rule in West Africa because she favored placing the region under the governance of British traders. Schreiner denounced the capitalist profiteering of Rhodes's chartered company in Rhodesia and its callousness to Africans, yet she upheld the Afrikaner republics' demand for autonomy without condemning their demand for unlimited, obedient, cheap African labor.[53]

In terms of race, all were more or less caught within the social Darwinist, evolutionary thinking of their day and did not question the superiority of white civilization. Schreiner protested both the Boer sexual exploitation of

African women and the brutal treatment of Africans by British capitalism, and she denounced the failure of government policy in South Africa to consider African welfare. Yet her writings also demonstrate her conviction that the English, Boer, Bantu, Hottentots, and Bushmen constituted a hierarchical scale of "civilization" and that "racial purity" must be preserved.[54] Kingsley, knowledgeable in the scientific anthropology of the day, similarly accepted the "inferiority" of Africans, but she claimed for them the right to "advance along their own lines" in terms of their own institutions and social structures. She was the only one of these women who came into close touch with Africans in any sustained way, inviting educated Africans to her home in London and, in Africa, living in huts in their villages, attempting to understand their lives within their cultural settings. Shaw, in contrast, viewed Africans only at a physical and psychological distance, as servants and workers. For her, Africans were important as laborers to serve European economic needs; propagating the contemporary view that the "negro races" were inferior to the "civilized" Europeans, she believed that exposure to "civilization" could only bring them benefits.

Rhodes represented a critical touchstone of difference among Shaw, Kingsley, and Schreiner. Shaw never lost faith in the imperialist goals that this empire-builder envisioned for southern Africa, while Kingsley felt something close to contempt for Rhodes and his followers.[55] Schreiner was for some time as keen an admirer of Rhodes as Shaw, considering him "a genius and one of the most remarkable men of the century."[56] But she also saw "the worms of falsehood and corruption creeping" upon him and considered his policy toward Africans a deliberate "sop to the Boers."[57] Condemning him for the Jameson Raid, she still expressed personal sympathy for him when he lost his political position at the Cape. His policies in Rhodesia then led her to condemn him and his chartered company publicly in her novel *Trooper Peter Halket of Mashonaland* for brutally massacring the African people, taking their land, and seizing the women.[58]

What can we conclude from such comparisons? They enable us to place Flora Shaw, arch imperialist, within a spectrum of attitudes held by other contemporary women who are viewed today more sympathetically. Such comparisons alert us to the need for a more nuanced reading of women's lives within the dominant discourses of their time and to search, critically, for the context and intent of their writings and actions. To dismiss Shaw or any of these women as racists and participants in contemporary imperialism without understanding their personal experiences and springs of motivation, their complexities and ambiguities, leaves us with labels, not history. Exploring Flora Shaw's life and writings within the world she experienced allows a more textured understanding of gender, ideology, and imperialism.

NOTES

1. The authors wish to thank the relatives of Flora Shaw/Lady Lugard—Mrs. Louise Grant, Lt. Col. Peter Guyon and his wife Rosemary, Wing-Cmdr. Dennis Ryan, and Mrs. Shelagh Meade—for relating their memories of her. We also thank for helpful comments on a first draft of this essay Susan Hallgarth, Darline Gay Levy, Barbara Sicherman, Laura Strumingher, and our editors Nupur Chaudhuri and Margaret Strobel. For aid in finding sources, we are grateful to archivists Melanie Aspey (*The Times* Archives, London) and Alan S. Bell (Rhodes House Library, Oxford), and to Joseph Baylen, Mary Bull, Judith Godfrey, Fred N. Hunter, A.H.M. Kirk-Greene, and Patricia Pugh. This research was supported (in part) by two grants from The City University of New York PSC-CUNY Research Award Program, made to Dorothy O. Helly.

The epigraph is taken from Mary Kingsley in a letter to Macmillan, her publisher, Feb. 19, 1899, Macmillan Papers, British Library. We are indebted to Dea Birkett for this quote.

2. We are using the term "race" throughout as a social construct, not a biological one.

3. Shaw's direct participation on the national stage contrasted with the political roles more commonly played by women in that era, those of political hostess and local government activist. See Pat Jalland, *Women, Marriage and Politics 1860–1914* (Oxford: Clarendon Press, 1986), esp. Part Three, and Patricia Hollis, *Ladies Elect: Women in English Local Government 1865–1914* (Oxford: Clarendon Press, 1987).

4. Margery Perham, *Lugard: The Years of Authority* (London: Collins, 1960), p. 59 (hereafter, Perham II).

5. November 13, 1904, Perham Papers 309/1, f. 25, Rhodes House, Oxford.

6. Oliver Woods and James Bishop, *The Story of* The Times *Bicentenary Edition 1785–1985* (London: Michael Joseph, 1983), chap. 12, p. 182.

7. Enid Moberly Bell, *Flora Shaw (Lady Lugard DBE)* (London: Constable, 1947). Our research suggests this source is not always accurate.

8. Catherine Hall, "The Economy of Intellectual Prestige: Thomas Carlyle, John Stuart Mill, and the Case of Governor Eyre," *Cultural Critique* 12 (1989): 167–96.

9. John Ruskin, *Lectures on Art* (Oxford: Clarendon Press, 1870).

10. Bell, pp. 36–37.

11. On the pervasive rhetoric of colonialism in women's settlement work in the 1880s, see Martha Vicinus, *Independent Women: Work and Community for Single Women, 1850–1920* (London: Virago Press, 1985), pp. 219–20.

12. Perham II, p. 57.

13. Bell, p. 92.

14. *Letters from South Africa* (London and New York: Macmillan, 1893), pp. 39–40, 36, 58–59.

15. August 12, 1892, *The Times* Archives, London.

16. Moberly Bell Letter Books MB 8/84, *The Times* Archives; David Rubinstein, *Before the Suffragettes: Women's Emancipation in the 1890s* (Brighton, Eng.: Harvester Press, 1986) pp. 85, 93 n.79.

17. Bell, p. 225.

18. See Dea Birkett, *Spinsters Abroad: Victorian Lady Explorers* (Oxford: Basil Blackwell, 1989).

19. Bell, p. 173.

20. Wilfred Scawen Blunt, *My Diaries: Being a Personal Narrative of Events 1888–1914* (London: Martin Secker, 1932), p. 226. See also: Bell, pp. 181–95; Elizabeth Longford, *Jameson's Raid: The Prelude to the Boer War* (London: Weidenfeld and Nicolson, new ed., 1982), pp. 250–60; and Robert I. Rotberg, with Miles Shore,

The Founder: Cecil Rhodes and the Pursuit of Power (New York and Oxford: Oxford University Press, 1988), pp. 548–50.

21. February 20, 1899, John Holt Papers, Rhodes House, Oxford.

22. Bell, p. 188.

23. Parliamentary Papers, *Second Report from the Select Committee on British South Africa*, House of Commons, 311 (1897), liii, p. 46.

24. Perham II, pp. 73–74.

25. Perham II, pp. 61–62.

26. *The Times*, January 8, 1897, p. 6. See Perham II, p. 11.

27. John E. Flint, *Sir George Goldie and the Making of Nigeria* (London: Oxford University Press, 1960), p. 258. On his faithfulness as a husband, see Flint, p. 6.

28. Margery Perham, *Lugard: The Years of Adventure* (London: Collins, 1956), p. 648 (hereafter, Perham I).

29. Stephen Gwynn, "An Historical Introduction" to Dorothy Wellesley, *Sir George Goldie: Founder of Nigeria* (London: Macmillan, 1934), p. 68.

30. Perham I, p. 443.

31. Perham II, p. 68.

32. Perham II, p. 81.

33. Perham II, p. 81.

34. Perham II, p. 83.

35. Sylvia Leith-Ross, *Stepping-Stones: Memoirs of Colonial Nigeria, 1907–1960* (London and Boston: Peter Owen, 1983).

36. Perham Papers 302/8, f. 6.

37. Perham II, p. 79.

38. Perham II, p. 79.

39. Perham Papers 302/8, f. 16b.

40. Flora L. Shaw (Lady Lugard), *A Tropical Dependency* (London: James Nisbet, 1905).

41. *A Tropical Dependency*, p. 1.

42. Perham Papers 302/8, f. 15b.

43. I. F. Nicolson, *The Administration of Nigeria 1900–1960* (Oxford: Clarendon Press, 1969); D.J.M. Muffett, *Empire Builder Extraordinary: Sir George Goldie* (Douglas, Isle of Man: Shearwater Press, 1978); and John E. Flint, "Frederick Lugard: The Making of an Autocrat (1858–1945)," in *African Proconsuls: European Governors in Africa*, ed. L. H. Gann and Peter Duignan (New York: The Free Press, 1978), pp. 290–312.

44. Quoted in E. J. Hobsbawm, *The Age of Empire 1875–1914* (London: Weidenfeld and Nicolson, 1987), p. 60.

45. See Susan L. Blake on Lady Florence Douglas Dixie, "A Woman's Trek: What Difference Does Gender Make?" in this volume.

46. Ruth First and Ann Scott, *Olive Schreiner* (New York: Schocken Books, 1980); Joyce Avrech Berkman, *The Healing Imagination of Olive Schreiner* (Amherst: University of Massachusetts, 1988); Deborah Epstein Nord, *The Apprenticeship of Beatrice Webb* (Amherst: University of Massachusetts Press, 1985); and Katherine Frank, *A Voyager Out: The Life of Mary Kingsley* (Boston: Houghton Mifflin, 1986).

47. Elizabeth K. Minnich, "Friendship between Women: The Act of Feminist Biography," *Feminist Studies* 11, no. 2 (1985): 294.

48. First and Scott, p. 262.

49. Nord, pp. 150–52.

50. Frank, p. 281.

51. Brian Harrison, *Separate Spheres: The Opposition to Women's Suffrage in Britain* (New York: Holmes and Meier, 1978), p. 153.

52. *The Anti-Suffrage Review* 26 (January 1911): 2.

53. See especially her long essays, "The Boer," *Fortnightly Review* 59, n.s. (April 1896): 510–40 and "The African Boer," *The Cosmopolitan* 29 (September and October 1900): 451–68; 593–602.

54. See, for example, Olive Schreiner, "Stray Thoughts on South Africa," *Fortnightly Review* 59–60 (1896): 510–40; 1–35; and 225–56. See also Carol Barash, "Introduction," in *An Olive Schreiner Reader: Writings on Women and South Africa,* ed. Carol Barash (London and New York: Pandora, 1987).

55. Frank, p. 263.

56. First and Scott, p. 199. Cf. Richard Rive, ed., *Olive Schreiner Letters,* volume 1, *1871–1899* (Oxford: Oxford University Press, 1988), pp. 175, 189, 208, and 211.

57. Rive, p. 279. See also Rive, pp. 199, 258, and 268, and cf. Rotberg, pp. 402–4.

58. Olive Schreiner, *Trooper Peter Halket of Mashonaland* (London: T. Fisher Unwin, 1897).

"CHATHAMS, PITTS, AND GLADSTONES IN PETTICOATS"

THE POLITICS OF GENDER AND RACE IN THE ILBERT BILL CONTROVERSY, 1883–1884

Mrinalini Sinha

On 9 February 1883, Courtenay Peregrine Ilbert, the law member of the Viceroy's Executive Council in India, introduced a bill to amend the Code of Criminal Procedure in the Indian Penal Code.[1] This measure, popularly known as the Ilbert Bill, was an attempt to remove a racially discriminatory clause, introduced by the Code of Criminal Procedure of 1872, affecting native members of the civil service.[2] Native civil servants, unlike their European colleagues, were denied the right to exercise criminal jurisdiction over European British subjects living outside the chief Presidency towns.[3]

The belated attempt by the government of India to empower native civilians by removing this racial disqualification provoked a "white mutiny," the impact of which was felt most in Bengal. Anglo-Indian officials and non-officials alike offered a concerted opposition to the pro-native bill. The controversy marked a climax in the growing hostility between the Anglo-Indian community on the one hand and, on the other, the politically self-conscious, native middle class, whose chief spokespersons were identified by the Anglo-Indians as "Bengalee baboos."[4]

The heightening of racial tension, especially in Bengal, forced the government of India to reconsider its original proposal. On 25 January 1884, after almost a year of conflict, Act 111 of 1884 was finally passed. However, the spirit of the Ilbert Bill had been compromised. Even though native officials were granted limited criminal jurisdiction over European British subjects living in the districts under their charge, the Anglo-Indians had won a substantial victory: they were assured the right to demand a trial by jury at least half of whose members were European British subjects themselves.

Several scholars of colonial India have examined the political consequences of this controversy and its implications for the future of colonial race relations.[5] They, however, have referred only too briefly to the gender ideology underlying the racial politics of 1883–84. My concern is to highlight the ways in which gender became central to the articulation of this racial conflict, and to examine the ways in which gender ideology and racial ideology were both implicated in the colonial pattern of domination. In this paper, therefore, I will focus on the role of women, particularly white women, both as symbols and as participants in the agitation.

The significance of the Ilbert Bill controversy to white women was recognized by most contemporaries. Many Anglo-Indians interpreted the bill primarily in terms of its implications for white women in India.[6] In fact, the Anglo-Indian opposition received its momentum from capitalizing on the notion that the bill was a blow to the prestige and security of the "pure and defenceless white woman in India." The head of police intelligence in Bengal at the time, Mr. J. Lambert, commented on this strategy. He reported that even though the Anglo-Indian "capitalists" or the business community were behind the agitation, "to make the grievance a general one, they raised the cry of danger to European women and so the agitation spread."[7]

Another equally striking feature of the agitation was the active involvement of white women themselves. The participation of memsahibs in a debate over political policy in India was quite unprecedented. As W. S. Seton-Karr, a former member of the Bengal Civil Service, noted, "One circumstance hitherto unexampled in Indian history . . . is, that Englishwomen have for the first time thought it necessary to descend into the arena of political controversy."[8]

Indeed, the general opinion was that white women were far more vociferous in their opposition to the bill than their male counterparts. The home member of the Viceroy's Executive Council, James Gibbs, observed that the female was "far more unreasonable and active in opposition than the male."[9] Even the viceroy, Lord Ripon, in his communication to Lord Kimberley, the secretary of state in London, wrote that "the ladies are as is often the case hotter than the men."[10] Some native newspapers even went so far as to suggest that the natives had lost the fight over the bill because of the vitriolic campaign of the "white kalis": "white in complexion [but] . . . black at heart."[11] In a parodic but shrewd commentary on the agitation, the *Reis and Reyyet*, a popular native weekly, wrote that the government had given up the bill because white women had refused "to submit to the jurisdiction of the Calibans lusting after the Mirandas of Anglo India."[12]

Although the Ilbert Bill said nothing directly about women, whether white or black, it is scarcely possible to overestimate the importance of gender in the eventual defeat of the bill. There were two major themes in the gender-based arguments against it: first, Anglo-Indians considered native civilians "effeminate" and consequently unfit to try men and women of a more civilized race. One Anglo-Indian woman, explaining her opposition to the bill, wrote: "in Bengal the men are notoriously destitute of manliness, and are most harsh and cowardly in their treatment of the weaker sex."[13] The native males, it was alleged, were unmanly because they held "barbaric" views about the female sex. Moreover, as many Anglo-Indians argued, native men had never had the opportunity of enjoying the company of civilized and sophisticated members of the female sex. It was suggested that since the native civilian's mother was not trained like an "English lady," he was totally unfit for this privilege.[14] As Flora McDonald, a white woman, wrote, "Hindoo women are degraded, they are totally devoid of all delicacy, their ideas and language are course and vulgar, their term of reproach and abuses are gross and disgusting in the extreme. Although they manifest much shyness and outward modesty there is little real virtue of the higher order among them."[15] The wife of another Anglo-Indian official wonders whether the "childish and ignorantly superstitious women by whom the native Magistrate has been, and may be still, surrounded . . . deviate his ideas of our sex."[16]

The opinions of the various officials, which were compiled during the controversy, testified to a very similar evaluation of the potential of the native civilians from Bengal. Mr. J. Munro, the officiating commissioner of the Presidency Division in Bengal, wrote: "The training of natives from their childhood, the enervating influence of the *zenana* on their upbringing, early marriage, a low moral standard resulting from caste distinctions and the influence of centuries of subjugation all tend to hinder the development in Bengalis of those manly and straightforward qualities which under other conditions are found in Englishmen."[17] In the words of R. H. Wilson, the magistrate of Midnapore, "Is it likely that time will ever come when Englishmen in India or elsewhere will acquiesce in a measure subjecting their wives and daughters to the criminal jurisdiction of Judges whose ideas on the subject of women and marriage are not European but Oriental[?]"[18] The state of ignorance among native women, particularly their seclusion in *zenana*s, had become the most convincing proof of the unfitness of native men to try members of a civilized race. These objections against native civilians, it was argued, were especially pertinent when it came to the trial of white women.

The second major theme in the Anglo-Indian argument was the actual physical threat to white women in India if native civilians were allowed jurisdiction over European British subjects. The Anglo-Indians feared that isolated white women would become the victims of unbridled native lust. The suggestion that Bengali magistrates might intentionally misuse their powers over white women was hinted at frequently in Anglo-Indian letters and meetings against the bill. A senior Anglo-Indian officer of the Indian Army wrote,

> Many English officers have English servant girls attached to their families; a native Magistrate, puffed up with importance might set eyes upon one of the girls and make overtures to her. If she refused, as she probably would

do, what would be easier than for this native, acting under the smart of disappointment to bring a case against the girl to be tried in his court? A few
annas would bribe all the native servants of the household and we might
guess the result.[19]

These fears often took on alarming proportions in the minds of white
women who lived in the midst of a large native population. The press
abounded with letters from frightened women in the countryside. The letter of Flora MacDonald, despite the florid prose and sly innuendos, captured the prevailing sentiment eloquently:

> Englishmen try to picture to yourselves a mofussil court, hundreds of miles
> away from Calcutta—in that court a Native Magistrate is presiding with the
> supercilious assurance that a native assumes when he has an Englishman in
> his power. Before that man stands an English girl in all her maidenly dig-
> nity; she has been accused by her ayah for revenge of a loathsome crime, a
> crime that is common among native women; the Court is crowded with na-
> tives of all castes who have flocked to hear an English girl being tried for an
> offence; this motley crowd laugh and jeer; and stare that English girl in the
> face; and spit on the ground to show her the contempt they have for the
> female sex; scores of witnesses are present to give evidence; a native Doctor
> has also been hired for that occasion; witnesses are cross-examined by a na-
> tive pleader; the most irrelevant questions are asked, questions that only a
> native dare to ask. Picture to yourself that girl's agony of shame! By her
> stands her only protector, a widowed mother, who has not the means
> wherewith to secure the protection and counsel of her countrymen. That in-
> nocent girl so kind, so affectionate, so loving, the stay of her widowhood,
> must go from the court with shame, with a blighted name. . . . It cannot be
> that Englishmen renowned for chivalry are willing to subject even the hum-
> blest of their countrywomen to dishonour.[20]

The sexual vulnerability of white women in India struck a responsive
chord in the Anglo-Indian male community. At the infamous Calcutta
Town Hall meeting, Mr. J.H.A. Branson, one of the most notorious speakers of the evening, exploited the "chivalric" sentiment of his countrymen
by urging them to resist any move by the government to place their female
dependents at the mercy of native males. Branson reminded his countrymen that protecting white women was "more than sentiment; it is a sacred
charge of a sacred duty."[21] On his return to England he continued to appeal to the public on behalf of the helpless white women in India. At a
meeting held in London he asked indignantly, "Are you going to support
a Government that thus degrades your race, and thus puts you, what is
more your women, in peril?"[22] His question was answered with a thunder-
ing chorus of "Shame! Shame! We will not."
The London branch of the European and Anglo-Indian Defence Association organized a special protest meeting on 21 August 1883, in the East
End of London at the Lime House Town Hall, to emphasize the threat that

the bill posed to Englishwomen in India. The meeting was widely advertised as one designed to save the defenseless Englishwoman in India. The
card of admission to the reserved seats read "Persecution of English working men and women in India." A placard in front of the hall bore the words
"Appeal to the People of England from Englishwomen in India." A second
placard outside the building stated that the meeting was "in opposition to
Lord Ripon's policy of placing Englishwomen under the criminal jurisdiction of polygamists—Native Magistrates."[23]

In the meantime in Bengal the irresponsible section of the Anglo-Indian
community was making matters worse by giving undue publicity to a few
cases of assaults on white women by native men. One such case, involving
Mrs. James Hume, the wife of the public prosecutor in Calcutta, rapidly
became a cause célèbre within the Anglo-Indian community.[24] Mr. James
Hume, a member of the firm of Sanderson and Upton, had served as the
public prosecutor in a recent case against some Bengali students charged
with rioting outside the Calcutta High Court. These students were protest-
ing the unfair decision by Judge Norris, who had sentenced to prison the
popular nationalist leader from Bengal, Surendranath Banerjea, for contempt of court.[25]

On 11 June 1883, Mrs. Hume was allegedly assaulted by her former em-
ployee, a sweeper called Hurroo Mehter, alias Greedhare Mehter. Mr.
Hume stated that he had found the native on top of his wife on the bath-
room floor. Hume claimed that he had apprehended the native in the act of
assaulting his wife and had given him a sound thrashing. The matter was
then reported to the police and the case was investigated by a magistrate
behind closed doors. The case came up for trial on 30 July 1883 in the court
of Justice O'Kinealy. A Mr. Philips acted as standing counsel prosecuting
the case while the prisoner remained undefended. A mixed jury of Europeans and natives found the prisoner guilty and he was sentenced to eight
years rigorous imprisonment. Yet to the very end the *mehter* refused to ad-
mit his guilt.[26]

There were some glaring inconsistencies in the Humes' story but the case
had to be rushed through the courts and a verdict had to be reached as
soon as possible. The case had received far too much publicity while it was
still *sub judice,* and therefore a quick settlement had become imperative.
The vitriolic Anglo-Indian newspaper in Calcutta, the *Englishman,* made
political capital of this case; it hinted that the "crime was the result of superior instigation" and that student leaders and other middle-class native
politicians were somehow implicated in the assault.[27] The paper, in an attempt to fan the feelings of suspicion and fear in the Anglo-Indian community, urged the formation of a Committee of Safety to protect white women
from the class of natives who "wage[d] war with women."

However, two years later in a private correspondence between a relative
of the Hume family and the then viceroy, Lord Dufferin, a very different
picture of the alleged assault case emerged.[28] Mr. A. O. Hume, who had

been a member of the Indian Civil Service and who on his retirement went on to become one of the founding members of the Indian National Congress, wrote to Dufferin that contrary to the facts made public in 1883, Mrs. Hume and the native sweeper were romantically involved for some six months before the episode. Mr. Hume had caught his wife and the sweeper in a compromising situation and had given them both a sound thrashing. On the advice of his friends, however, the couple agreed to perjure themselves in court and have the *mehter* convicted of attempted rape.

Another case, which received some degree of notoriety in Calcutta, was first reported in the columns of the Allahabad based, semi-official, Anglo-Indian paper, the *Pioneer*.[29] The paper withheld the names of the persons involved in the case, but left enough details to connect it to the family of Judge Norris of the Calcutta High Court. The paper claimed that Norris had received several anonymous threats from the native community after his unpopular decision in the Surendranath Banerjea contempt of court case. One letter allegedly threatened that outrages similar to those committed on the wife of the public prosecutor, Mr. Hume, would be attempted on the females of his household. Following these reports, one night a female guest at the Norris household claimed that a native male had tried to attack her in her bedroom. Before the assailant could be apprehended he had escaped. In the words of one contemporary, "[the case] strongly excite[d] scepticism." A thorough examination by the under deputy commissioner of police, Mr. H. G. Wilkins, revealed that the "failed villainy" was only a delusion in the mind of the young girl. The judge, the examining doctor, and the lady in question later retracted their story and the case was withdrawn.[30]

There were numerous other cases of assaults or attempted assaults on white women reported in the Anglo-Indian press. There was no evidence that these "vile offences" against white women were exceptional to the time or that native politicians were in any way involved in the attacks on white women. Yet the opponents of the Ilbert Bill in India and in England were drawing a connection between it and the attacks on white women in India. The assaults were invariably by natives, usually of the class of *mehters, coolies, khansamahs,* and other menial servants.[31] The Anglo-Indians, however, recognized no difference between these assailants and the class of natives who would benefit from the Ilbert Bill. The *Statesman,* the only Anglo-Indian paper in Calcutta not affected by the general hysteria, observed, "The time is out of joint . . . incidents which, in ordinary times, would have no political significance, are now being seized upon on all hands, and a political significance is attributed to them which, whether it rightly belongs to them or not, has the same effect upon the public mind as if it did."[32]

Senior officials in Bengal did very little to quash the wild and unauthenticated rumors about these assault cases. The lieutenant governor of Bengal, Rivers-Thompson, was a staunch supporter of the Anglo-Indian cause and in his various communications to the viceroy he implied that the assault cases were an indication of things to come if the bill were made into law.[33] The lieutenant governor's chief informant was his subordinate, E. V. Westmacott, the magistrate of Howrah. Westmacott's frame of mind can be gauged from his description of a case involving a native and a white woman that had recently come under his jurisdiction:

> I have also disposed of a case of a dhobie insulting his mistress and challenging her to come out into the road and see what he would do, by giving him six months. His [was] a very heavy punishment for the offence but I think the occurrence of all these cases makes the present an exceptional time and that it is necessary not only to check the growing insolence towards Europeans, but to show that it is not countenanced, as is pretended in some quarters by some officials.[34]

In Britain too the opponents of the bill were drawing a connection between the ability of native civilians to try European British subjects and the assault cases. A retired senior Anglo-Indian official in England, Sir Alexander Arbuthnot, was convinced that there was a political reason behind the cases of assault on white women in India. While heading a deputation to the secretary of state, Arbuthnot used these cases to argue against the extension of criminal jurisdiction to native civilians.[35] The secretary of state rebuked him for implying that there was any connection between these cases and the Ilbert Bill. Later, however, Arbuthnot defended his speech in a letter to the London *Times*. He stated that outrages by natives against white women were rare, and consequently there was no mistaking the significance of at least two such cases in the metropolis at such a time.[36] His letter met with favorable response from a number of quarters in Britain. One writer in the *Times* urged that these outrages were not "pure ruffianism" but were "strongly characteristic of fanatical and race hatred."[37] Lord Lytton, a former viceroy of India, also approved wholeheartedly of Arbuthnot's speech to the secretary of state.[38]

In the British House of Commons some opposition members of Parliament also tried to raise a storm over the Hume assault case. Edward Stanhope, a former Conservative under secretary of state for India, asked the government to respond to the "horrible outrages upon English ladies in Calcutta and Howrah."[39] Stanhope's line of questioning, however, was halted by a counter-question from Mr. O'Donnell, known to be more favorably disposed to native political demands: "Whilst he is on the subject, could not the Honorary Gentleman obtain a statement of annual number of outrages on English women by English men?"

Any "outrage," real or imagined, on a white woman by a native male could move Anglo-Indian males to fits of violence. Throughout the nineteenth century, therefore, white men had jealously guarded white women from native society. As the wife of a senior Anglo-Indian official once wrote: "You must understand that most Europeans of the old school would not allow a lady to accept an Indian gentleman's preferred hospitality. They would not permit her to drive through an Indian town, be a spectator of tent-pegging, or receive an Indian as a visitor, far less dine with him. They would, in short, prefer her to be as wholly absent from every kind of society as are the inmates of zenanas."[40]

Even the hint of any liaison between a white woman and a native man was shocking to the Anglo-Indian community. The Pigot versus Hastie Defamation Case, which came for trial during the Ilbert Bill agitation, highlighted some of the sexual taboos necessary in maintaining the racial division of colonial society. The case involved a white female missionary and was tried in the Calcutta High Court from August to September 1883.[41] Mary Pigot, who ran the Church of Scotland's Orphanage and *Zenana* Mission in Calcutta, had filed a case of defamation against Rev. William Hastie, who was in charge of the General Assembly's institution in Calcutta. Hastie had accused Pigot of, among other things, improper intimacy with a married native Christian, Baboo Kali Charan Bannerjee. Norris, in whose court the case was decided, rushed through the case, arriving at a rather peculiar verdict. He did not agree that there was any ground for the charges made by Hastie, but at the same time he did not entirely vindicate Pigot. Norris found Pigot's relations with Bannerjee not of a "proper character."[42]

The majority opinion in the press, both native and Anglo-Indian, was critical of Norris's decision. The *Englishman*'s defense of Pigot, however, rested on the grounds that no Anglo-Indian lady could *choose* to be familiar with a native male.[43] Commenting on the *Englishman*'s position a native paper wrote: "The *Englishman* refuses to believe that the fair Miranda of the *Tempest*, recently enacted at the High Court, could possibly go wrong with Caliban."[44] The idea of a white woman associating with a native male out of her own choice was scarcely comprehensible to Anglo-Indian society. The case even provoked one district judge in Bengal to write to the *Statesman* pleading for utmost caution in sending white female missionaries to native homes. He urged missionary societies in India to prevent "unmarried ladies to visit alone at houses where they cannot but frequently meet with male members of the Hindoo household in outer apartments."[45] The letter held a special appeal in Bengal where the Anglo-Indian community was already very excited about the cases of assault on white women.

The image of the pure and passionless white woman as the helpless victim of a lascivious native male was a particularly powerful one in colonial society. The sentiment behind this image, and behind much of the Anglo-Indian anxiety over the Ilbert Bill, could be described as "patriarchal racism."[46] This ideology was founded on two complementary aspects: first, the denial of sexual agency to white women and, second, the representation of black men as half animals, with no sexual self-control. In other words, the portrayal of white men as the "natural protectors" of helpless white women legitimated the division of colonial society along racial lines. The Anglo-Indian position against the Ilbert Bill remained true to this spirit. Yet curiously the Anglo-Indian agitation also posed a challenge to one of the foundations of "patriarchal racism." White women, who were at the center of the debate on the Ilbert Bill, decided to join the fray themselves. The mobilization of white women on their own initiative, however, threatened the edifice on which colonial society was built.

White women's contribution to the Ilbert Bill agitation had taken various forms. From February to December 1883 the Anglo-Indian press was flooded with letters of protest from irate white women. Anglo-Indian women were also present in large numbers at the several protest meetings organized by the white community. At the Calcutta Town Hall meeting held on 28 February 1883 white women first made their presence felt. The *Amrita Bazar Patrika*, a leading nationalist newspaper, made special note of the presence of Mrs. J. F. Norris, wife of Judge Norris of the Calcutta High Court, who cheered as speaker after speaker abused the "Bengalee baboos," the chief beneficiaries of the bill.[47]

The women also organized a successful social boycott of supporters of the bill. Henry Beveridge, who was one among a very tiny number of white civil servants in Bengal who supported it, recalled that "English ladies appeared to him often to be drawing their skirts away from him as he passed."[48] From the early months of 1883 there were widespread rumors in Calcutta that the wives and daughters of the nonofficial Anglo-Indian community would boycott all the entertainments of the winter season organized by the government.[49] The winter season in Calcutta was marked by a round of entertainments at the Government House, signaling the return of the viceroy and his entourage from the summer capital in Simla. The women's decision to forego all government sponsored entertainments, therefore, was a major sacrifice. The Government House Levee and Drawing Room, held on 5 December and 7 December respectively, were marred by the boycott. Between ninety and one hundred Anglo-Indian women undertook to formally absent themselves from the Drawing Room.[50] According to a report in the *Pioneer* only 136 "ladies" attended the Drawing Room by Public Entry, of whom nearly 69 were new presentations. There were at least 51 "ladies" who were noted as being "unavoidably absent."[51]

The European and Anglo-Indian Defence Association, which was set up in Calcutta to coordinate the various activities against the bill, recognized the contribution of women to the agitation by electing a few female members.[52] The association also received generous subscriptions from Anglo-Indian women, including one for ten rupees, which had been diverted from *Zenana* work in India.[53] The women also drafted their own separate anti-Ilbert Bill petitions to the viceroy and to the queen.

Not all of these activities of the "ladies," however, was welcomed by their male counterparts. The response to the Anglo-Indian Ladies Committee reflects the uneasiness felt by the Anglo-Indian male community about white women's political activities. The European and Anglo-Indian Defence Association was responsible for "fathering" the separate Ladies Committee against the bill. The Defence Association at its third meeting on 22 March 1883 had announced that a separate "ladies' petition" against the bill should be sent to the queen. Mr. James Furrell, the editor of the *Englishman,* as well as the honorary secretary of the Defence Association, moved a resolution to provide assistance to the "ladies" in drawing up such a petition. The notorious Town Hall speaker, Mr. J.H.A. Branson, seconded the motion; it was passed unanimously and the Defence Association committed itself to provide all necessary assistance to the "ladies" in drafting the petition.[54]

Following the Defence Association meeting, however, nine leading Calcutta memsahibs met independently to discuss the preparation of a Ladies' Petition. This was the beginning of a separate Ladies Committee against the bill. Mrs. Tottenham, the wife of Judge L. R. Tottenham of the Calcutta High Court, was chosen as the honorary secretary of this committee. Mrs. Tottenham was urged to take the initiative in contacting other Anglo-Indian women in the Madras and Bombay Presidencies. It was also decided at this meeting that all the women present would submit for consideration a draft copy of the memorial that would be sent to the queen.[55]

Five days later on 31 March 1883, the women held a second meeting at the house of one of the members. Mrs. Norris, Mrs. Fraser McDonnell, Mrs. J.H.A. Branson, and Miss J. P. Furrell, a relative of the editor of the *Englishman,* were among those present.[56] The list of women involved included the wives of high court judges, Bengal civilians, military men, doctors, barristers, and merchants.[57] At this meeting the various draft memorials submitted by the ladies were read out. It was decided, however, to hold a third meeting to determine the exact form of the memorial to be sent to the queen.

The memorial was finally ready by 18 April 1883. The final draft read that white women in India were apprehensive about the loss of their prestige if the bill were passed and were, therefore, appealing to the queen to intervene and remove the "cruel wound on [their] self-respect." It also pointed to the *"helplessness* [of white women] before an alien tribunal, isolated as [they] should in many cases be from [their] *natural protectors"* (italics mine).[58] Significantly, the final form of the memorial was not the product of the ladies' efforts alone but had been prepared with the help of a Mr. J. G. Apcar, who had been sent by the Defence Association to "assist" the ladies.[59]

When the petition was ready a deputation of the women went to visit Lieutenant Governor Rivers-Thompson to invite his wife to head the list of signatures on the memorial. His official position, however, acted as a restraint and he declined the request on behalf of his wife.[60] The memorial was headed instead with the signature of the intrepid Mrs. Norris. The petition was able to gather a total of 5,758 signatures from Anglo-Indian women all over India.[61]

The Ladies' Petition was an important weapon in the Anglo-Indian arsenal against the bill. Yet the white male attitude toward the women's efforts was at best patronizing. The *Englishman* was amused at the amateur manner in which the women had signed their names on the memorial. All the women had signed their names with their titles, e.g., Mrs. or Miss so-and-so. The paper pointed out the folly: "Mrs. Smith or Miss Smith, as we should have thought every educated person knew is not a signature but a description."[62] The *Civil and Military Gazette*, an Anglo-Indian paper published from Lahore, was also amused at the women's attempt at political activism. One correspondent of the paper wrote, "Who knows or can guess how many mute, inglorious politicians, how many Chathams, Pitts, Beaconsfields, Gladstones in petticoats may have been hidden away, lost to fame and the gratitude of posterity."[63]

If the *Civil and Military Gazette* was patronizing and mildly disapproving of the "ladies' happy occupation to fill monotonous hours," the *Pioneer* voiced its displeasure more directly. It disparaged the "fashionable contagion" that had infected white women in India who met at each other's homes, wrote letters in the press, and had now authored a petition to the queen. The paper believed that women had "somewhat unnecessarily joined the fray." The *Pioneer* was sympathetic to the cause, but it did not think it appropriate that white women should involve themselves in the "masculine" fray. The paper claimed, "there are special reasons in India which emphasize the soundness of the Athenean proverb that she is the best woman who is least observed."[64]

Even a great proponent of the Ladies Committee, the *Englishman*, felt the need to assure its critics that the Ladies Committee was not a permanent committee, but had met only three times with the sole purpose of drafting a petition against the bill.[65] The women too were eager to demonstrate to their white male critics that "no desire for publicity nor any ambition to enter the arena of political strife has prompted this movement."[66]

The Ilbert Bill agitation had brought the activities of Anglo-Indian as well as native women to the center of the political stage. Some native women, especially in Bengal, were drawn into the political arena during the agitation. Sarala Debi, who later became one of the prominent leaders of the anti-British *Swadeshi* agitation in 1905–6, recalled that the female teachers in her Bethune School demonstrated in support of the Ilbert Bill.[67] Kamini Sen, a teacher at the school and the wife of a statutory civilian, was responsible for organizing several pro-bill meetings for the female students of the school. Her students wore badges to show their support for it.[68] The imprisonment of Surendranath Banerjea for contempt of court at the height of the Ilbert Bill controversy further galvanized the Bengali *bhadramahila* to political action. The Bengali Ladies Association convened a meeting with about seventy women in order to express sympathy with Mrs. Banerjea, the imprisoned leader's wife. The *Bengalee* regarded this as a "unique feature," because in the past Bengali women's associations had kept away from politics.[69] In 1883 native women in large numbers came out into the streets in order to publicly demonstrate their support for Banerjea.

Some native political leaders were shrewd enough to recognize the actual and symbolic advantage of native women's participation in national politics. Surendranath Banerjea, at a meeting of the Indian Association, the leading nationalist organization at the time, suggested that henceforth the services of native women should be used "in the political elevation of the country."[70] These leaders hoped that the involvement of native women in national politics would undermine the Anglo-Indian position that natives were unfit for political rights because native women were steeped in ignorance and were rigidly excluded from all public life. Many native politicians, therefore, were quite sanguine about the political participation of native women as long as it furthered the nationalist cause against colonial rule.

It was against this background that a memorial, supposedly written by native women in response to the arrogant petition of the Anglo-Indian "ladies," immediately caught the attention of people in India and in Britain. The memorial first appeared in the columns of the nationalist paper, the *Amrita Bazar Patrika*. The native female memorialists challenged the white women's portrayal of native women and asserted, "We Indian women are not ignorant and enslaved." They admitted that there were, indeed, thousands of ignorant women in India, "as a like number exists in England," but they challenged the generalizations made by Anglo-Indians about the ignorance of the whole native female race. They compared themselves to the white "ladies" who had signed the petition to the queen and declared, "We are not inferior in intelligence or education to the Englishwomen who have come forward to protest the Bill. . . . Some of us have obtained University degrees—among the lady agitators against the Bill there is not a single graduate. Mrs. Tottenham and Mrs. Norris are not B.A.'s, but among us there are B.A.'s who have received first class education at Bethune College."[71] The native signatories were purportedly members of the Bengali *bhadramahila*, belonging to an emerging class of talented and articulate native women.[72] In what appears to be a parody of the Anglo-Indian case against the bill, they urged that "Sir Richard Garth [chief justice of India] and Mr. Croft [director of public instructions in Bengal] may be appointed to bring us and the English ladies who have remonstrated under severe tests, and see if we are not intellectually superior to them. If our superiority is produced the bill should become law at once."

However, on 30 June 1883, little over a month after the first publication of the memorial, the *Bengalee*, edited by Surendranath Banerjea, revealed that the memorial was a hoax which had been perpetrated by the editors of the *Amrita Bazar Patrika*.[73] The latter had come up with the memorial in order to undermine the arguments of the white female memorialists. Even though the memorial was exposed as a fraud it served an important purpose; it had opened up a space for challenging the motives of Anglo-Indians, both male and female, in speaking on behalf of the "native female."

Too many white women had claimed that they had no "unwomanly animosity against [their] fellow subjects the natives" and that they opposed the Ilbert Bill only in the name of the long suffering native woman.[74] Whatever radical edge there may have been in this position was undermined by the political use to which this argument was put. The so-called degraded plight of native women was an excuse that the Anglo-Indians used to justify denying all natives their political rights. There was far too much hypocrisy in the Anglo-Indian propaganda, which depicted selfless "white men [and women] saving brown women from brown men."[75]

The example of the so-called "liberal" white woman, Annette Akroyd Beveridge, was a case in point. Akroyd's support of the opponents of the bill drew a great deal of attention because it gave some respectability to the white woman's position on it.[76] Akroyd, after all, was widely recognized as a "friend of the natives" and was even married to a pro–Ilbert Bill civilian, Henry Beveridge. She had come to India as a Unitarian philanthropist on the invitation of native leaders of the *Brahmo Samaj*, a leading reform society in Bengal.[77] She became involved with native female education at the behest of native reformers. However, her relations with her female pupils or with her native hosts were far from idyllic. She quit her job at the native female school in a cloud of controversy and went on to marry Henry Beveridge.

While her husband was posted in Patna, Akroyd became known for breaking with the norm and hosting "mixed" gatherings of natives and Anglo-Indians at her home.[78] Akroyd's own accounts, however, reveal that she cared very little for the class of educated Bengalis she encountered.[79] Often she found herself on the opposite end of the political spectrum from her husband. For instance, in 1876, when Henry Beveridge supported the native civil service agitation Akroyd was totally unsympathetic to the cause.[80] Once again, on the question of the Ilbert Bill, husband and wife were to take different sides.

Akroyd wrote a strong letter against the bill which was published in the *Englishman* on 6 March 1883. In her letter she asserted that the "ignorant and enslaved" native women bore adequate testimony to the fact that native men were not yet ready to sit on judgment over a more "civilized" race. She condemned the bill in no uncertain terms as a "proposal to subject civilized women to the jurisdiction of men who have done little or nothing to redeem the women of their race, whose social ideas are still on the outer verge of civilization."[81]

Akroyd's husband Henry Beveridge, however, was determined that "Ilbert Bill and Babus shall not divide us."[82] In March 1883 the *Statesman* published a compromise proposal sent by a gentleman signing himself as "H.B."[83] The *Statesman* claimed that the writer was a member of the Bengal

Civil Service.[84] It is possible to speculate that the writer was none other than Henry Beveridge. Beveridge had tried to arrive at some middle ground between the bill's attempt to remove some of the racial disqualifications against natives and the indignation and trepidation that this move had caused among white women in India. He suggested that just as special privileges were accorded upper caste *purdanashin* native women when they had to appear in court, a case could be made for according some special privileges to white women in the courts. White women, he argued, could be excluded from the group of European British subjects who would come under the criminal jurisdiction of native officials. What Akroyd thought of the proposal is not known; but apart from the *Statesman* no other party in Anglo-Indian society was favorably disposed toward this compromise.[85]

In contrast, Mrs. Beveridge's contribution was widely acclaimed in the Anglo-Indian community. The *Englishman* and the *Pioneer* commended her for her role in the agitation.[86] In addition to her letter in the press, she had used her influence in Chapra to get other Anglo-Indian wives to sign a memorial addressed to the viceroy. This memorial, signed by some 732 ladies residing in Bihar, was headed by the signature of Mrs. A. Hudson, the wife of the rabidly anti-Bengali president of the Bihar Indigo Planter's Association. The petition read, "We see that in the social systems of India women are ignorant and enslaved. . . . We see the men of their races insensible to their degradation, if not contented with it. Therefore we assert that men born or bred on such a system are unfitted to become the judges of women of a totally different type of society."[87]

The native community felt that Akroyd's position on the bill had betrayed the hollowness behind her "progressive" posturing. The *Bengalee* expressed skepticism of the intentions of all so-called liberal, white women in India.[88] The *Reis and Reyyet* observed, "these ladies condescendingly invite native gentlemen to their 'at home' parties—but when their sympathy is put to the test, we have the unwanted spectacle of ladies forgetting the tenderness of their sex and taking part in an agitation which it is bad enough that men should take part in."[89]

Mrs. Beveridge, on her return to England in the spring of 1883, was rebuked by some of her own countrywomen for contributing to the racial discord in India. Miss Manning, of the National Indian Association in England, dissociated herself from Akroyd's position.[90] The native papers, the *Bengalee* and the *Hindoo Patriot,* were grateful for the support they received from at least some white women, albeit white women in Britain. The *Hindoo Patriot* published a letter written by a woman of high position in London, assuring her native friends that Akroyd did not speak for all the "progressive" and "independent" women in England.[91] However, there never was any organized support for the bill from white women either in Britain or in India.

The strong-willed Akroyd remained steadfast in her position till the end. In a letter to her husband she claimed to have no regrets whatsoever, for either the content or the tone of her letter to the *Englishman.*

I cannot regret having written the letter to the *Englishman* . . . of a people uncivilized who care about stone idols, enjoy child marriage and seclude their women, and where, at every point the fact of sex is present to the mind. . . . I call it uncivilized in any nation when I see two people together and the notion of their being a man and a woman is the first suggested by their manner, and not the more commonplace one (as in England) of *two people.*[92]

Her defense was that her position on the bill derived not from the "pride of race" but from the "pride of womanhood." This was ironic, considering that Akroyd's statements were derived from the pride of *white* womanhood. She had displayed no desire to understand, far less to accommodate, the position of non-white or native women. Like most of her compatriots in India she remained obsessed by the alleged degradation of native females. Akroyd could not reconcile her position with that of native women, for example those at the Bethune School with whom she probably had had some connections in the past. The native female's own experience of the gender and racial hierarchies of colonial society remained a discordant reality and found no place in Akroyd's woman-centered outrage against the bill. Therefore, Akroyd's claim that she spoke for *all* womanhood could be made only at the cost of silencing the native female's own experience. In the colonial context, any appeal made on behalf of a universal "womanhood" needed to be treated with far more skepticism; invariably such claims served a scarcely disguised racist political agenda.

I have demonstrated, through an analysis of the Ilbert Bill agitation, the ways in which gender and race were implicated in the structure of colonial politics. In the historiography of imperialism the discussion of gender and race has been limited too often to the following question: Were white women or white men more responsible for the racial animosities in the colony?[93] I have shifted the site of the discussion from the above formulation by locating the relations between colonizer and colonized within the larger discourses of gender and of race. I suggest, therefore, that the colonial pattern of domination was determined by the interplay between the discourses of gender and of race. Consequently, in the colonial context, racial ideology was often articulated in gendered terms and gender ideology in racial terms. The Ilbert Bill agitation had made apparent that the Anglo-Indian position, whether it drew blatantly from the "pride of race" or more subtly from the "pride of womanhood," was inextricably tied to colonial power relations.

NOTES

1. A version of this paper was presented at the Eighth Berkshire Conference on the History of Women, Douglass College, 8–10 June 1990. This paper is drawn

from my dissertation, " 'Manliness': A Victorian Ideal and Colonial Policy in Late Nineteenth Century Bengal" (Ph.D diss. S.U.N.Y at Stony Brook, Dec. 1988). In this paper I have used terms, such as "native" and "Anglo-Indian," in their common nineteenth-century sense. The former refers to the indigenous people of India and the latter to the British community in India. Despite protests from the nationalists, the people of India were referred to as "natives" rather than as "Indians"; the latter term was more often reserved for British representatives serving in India.

2. For the background to the Ilbert Bill see Edwin Hirschmann, *"White Mutiny": The Ilbert Bill Crisis in India and the Genesis of the Indian National Congress* (Delhi: Heritage Publishers, 1980), pp. 5–23. For a general discussion of legal inequality in British India on racial grounds, see Nemai Sadhan Bose, *Racism: Struggle for Equality and Indian Nationalism* (Calcutta: Firma KLM Pvt. Ltd., 1981).

3. The legal definition of "European British subjects" as given in Section 4 of the Criminal Procedure Code was vague and arbitrary. It included persons who were neither European nor British and excluded persons who may be in all essential characteristics Englishmen but not of legitimate descent; see *Abstract for the Purpose of Making Laws and Regulations 1883,* vol. 22, p. 13 (henceforth: *Council Proceedings*).

4. The Anglo-Indians used the term "Bengalee baboo" in a loose sense to describe the entire Western-educated native middle class. For much of the nineteenth century, Bengali Hindus had constituted an overwhelming proportion of this class. See Col. Henry Yule and A. C. Burnell, *Hobson-Jobson: A Glossary of Colloquial Anglo Indian Words and Phrases and of Kindred Terms, Etymological, Historical, Geographical and Discursive,* new ed., ed. William Crooke (Delhi: Munshiram Manoharlal, reprint 1968), pp. 44–45.

5. See for instance, Hirshmann, *"White Mutiny"*; S. Gopal, *The Viceroyalty of Lord Ripon 1880–1884* (London: Oxford University Press, 1953); Christine Dobbin, "The Ilbert Bill: A Study of Anglo-Indian Opinion in India, 1883," *Historical Studies Australia and New Zealand* 12, no. 45 (Oct. 1965): 149–66; and S. Ghosh, "The Racial Question and Liberal English Opinion in The Friend of India, from Mutiny to the Ilbert Bill," *Bengal Past and Present* 81, no. 151 (1962): 57–63.

6. In his autobiography, Kipling, who was then a correspondent in India, recalled the bill as a measure designed to place white women under the jurisdiction of native men; see Rudyard Kipling, *Something of Myself: For My Friends Known and Unknown* (New York: Doubleday Doran & Co., 1938) pp. 55–56.

7. Quoted in Hirschmann, *White Mutiny,* p. 105.

8. See W. S. Seton-Karr's speech in *The Ilbert Bill: A Collection of Letters, Speeches, Memorials, Articles, etc., Stating the Objections to the Bill* (London: W. H. Allen & Co., n.d.), p. 113 (henceforth: *Ilbert Bill*).

9. Gibbs to Ripon, *Ripon Papers: India Miscellaneous Public Documents* BP 7/6, Nov. 18, 1883 (henceforth: *IMPD*).

10. Ripon to Kimberley, *IMPD,* BP 7/3, 2 Dec. 1883.

11. *Dacca Prakash,* 24 June 1883, *Report on Native Newspapers of Bengal Presidency* (1883), no. 26, p. 353 (henceforth: *RNBP*).

12. *Reis and Reyyet,* 28 Apr. 1883, p. 196.

13. *Englishman,* 26 Apr. 1883, p. 2.

14. See the parody of the argument in the poem "The Miller and His Men": "and as we don't know his wife or daughter/He can't know us as well as he ough'ter/His principles too are sure to be shady/As his mother's not trained like an English lady," quoted in *Reis and Reyyet,* 7 Apr. 1883, p. 160.

15. *Englishman,* 26 Apr. 1883, p. 2.

16. *Englishman,* 27 Mar. 1883, p. 2.

17. *Legislative Department Papers of Act 1–111 of 1884,* paper no. 55 (henceforth: *Leg. Dept. Papers*).

18. Govt. of Bengal, *Leg. Dept. Papers,* paper no. 55.

19. Quoted in *Reis and Reyyet,* 21 Apr. 1883, p. 182.

20. *Englishman,* 13 Mar. 1883, p. 2.

21. For the text of all the speeches at the Calcutta Town Hall meeting, see *The Friend of India and Statesman,* Supplement, 1 Mar. 1883 (henceforth: *Statesman*).

22. Quoted in *Bengalee,* 17 Nov. 1883, p. 520.

23. Quoted in *Bengalee,* 1 Sept. 1883, p. 409.

24. See Calcutta Town Police Report for 1883, *India Home Department Police Proceedings,* Aug. 1884, B, no. 1.

25. For the background of this case see Hirschmann, "White Mutiny," pp. 181–84.

26. See *Englishman,* 31 July 1883, p. 3 for details of the case.

27. *Englishman,* 26 June 1883, p. 2.

28. Hume to Dufferin, *Dufferin Papers: Correspondence in India,* vol. 78, 4 July 1885 (henceforth: *Dufferin Papers*).

29. Cited in *Bengalee,* 28 July 1883, p. 351.

30. *Bengalee,* 28 July 1883, p. 35; also Hume to Dufferin, *Dufferin Papers,* 4 July 1883.

31. For more information on the assaults on white women during the agitation see Mrinalini Sinha, " 'Manliness,' " chapter 2.

32. *Statesman,* 25 June 1883, p. 2.

33. See, for example, Rivers-Thompson to Ripon, *Ripon Papers: Letters of Rivers-Thompson,* vol. 54, 17 June 1883.

34. Bayley to Ripon enclosing Westmacott to Barnes, 19 June 1883, *Ripon Papers: Letters of Steuart Bayley, 1881–1884,* 26 June 1883.

35. See *Ilbert Bill,* p. 126.

36. *Times,* 27 July 1883, in *Ilbert Bill,* pp. 127–28.

37. *Ilbert Bill,* p. 129.

38. Cited in Sir Alexander Arbuthnot, *Memories of Rugby and India,* ed. Lady Constance Arbuthnot (London: T. Fisher Unwin, 1910), p. 246.

39. *Hansard Parliamentary Debates,* vols. 280 and 282, col. 939–94, cited in Hirschmann, "White Mutiny," p. 189.

40. Lady Wilson (Anne Campbell Macleod), *Letters from India* (London: William Blackwood and Sons, 1911), p. 33. For a general discussion of white women in India see Margaret MacMillan, *Women of the Raj* (New York: Thames and Hudson, 1988).

41. See the discussion of this case in Kenneth Ballhatchet, *Race, Sex and Class under the Raj: Imperial Attitudes, Policies and Their Critics 1793–1905* (New York: St. Martin's Press, 1980), pp. 112–16. For details see the *Pioneer,* 22 Sept. 1883, p. 1. Ballhatchet suggests that Pigot was a Eurasian. However, it appears that Hastie had wrongly described Pigot as an illegitimate Eurasian; she was the daughter of an indigo planter, James, and his wife, Dorothy, see *Englishman,* 7 Sept. 1883, p. 3. Even if Pigot was indeed a Eurasian her case still roused anxieties about the relations of "white women" with native men. In the crisis of 1883 the Eurasian community in Bengal was closely allied to the Anglo-Indian community. The charter of the European and Anglo Indian Defence Association, for instance, included Eurasians, and W. C. Madge, Secretary of the Eurasian Association in Bengal, was prominent in the activities of the Defence Association. Moreover, the Ladies' Petition too had made no distinctions in collecting signatures from white women of pure blood and Eurasian women.

42. For the full text of the judgment see *Statesman,* Supplement, 24 Nov. 1883. The following year an appellate bench overturned Norris's judgment and vindicated Pigot; see *Bengalee,* 19 Apr. 1884, p. 186.

43. See *Englishman,* 27 Sept. 1883, p. 4.

44. *Reis and Reyyet,* 29 Sept. 1883, p. 459.

45. *Statesman,* 3 Oct. 1883, p. 2.

46. The concept of "patriarchal racism" and its implications is from Ania Loomba, *Gender, Race, Renaissance Drama* (Manchester: Manchester University Press, 1989).

47. Quoted from the *Amrita Bazar Patrika* in *Statesman,* 18 May 1883, p. 3.

48. Quoted in Lord William Beveridge, *India Called Them* (London: George Allen and Unwin Ltd., 1947), p. 39.

49. *Pioneer,* 10 Mar. 1883, p. 2.

50. *Bengalee,* 8 Dec. 1885, p. 555.

51. *Pioneer,* 11 Dec. 1883, p. 1.

52. *Englishman,* 12 Sept. 1883, p. 3; 29 Oct. 1883, p. 6.

53. *Englishman,* 23 July 1883, p. 2.

54. *Englishman,* 23 Mar. 1883, p. 2.

55. *Englishman,* 2 Apr. 1883, p. 3.

56. *Englishman,* 7 Apr. 1883, p. 1.

57. *Englishman,* 3 Apr. 1883, p. 2; 7 Apr. 1883, p. 1.

58. *Ilbert Bill,* p. 92.

59. *Statesman,* 16 June 1883, p. 2.

60. Rivers-Thompson to Alfred Lyall, 3 Apr. 1883, cited in Raymond K. Renford, *The Non-Official British in India to 1920* (Delhi: Oxford University Press, 1987), p. 247. See also *India Home Department: Judicial Proceedings,* vol. 2045, June 1883, nos. 146–47.

61. See *Statesman,* 16 June 1883, p. 2.

62. *Englishman,* 25 Apr. 1883, p. 2.

63. *Civil and Military Gazette,* 13 Apr. 1883, p. 3.

64. *Pioneer,* 13 Apr. 1883, p. 2.

65. *Englishman,* 16 Apr. 1883, p. 2.

66. A Letter from a lady on the Committee, *Englishman,* 3 Apr. 1883, p. 2.

67. Sarala Debi, *Jibaner Jharpatra,* cited in Meredith Borthwick, *The Changing Role of Women in Bengal 1849–1905* (Princeton: Princeton University Press, 1984), p. 339.

68. See Usha Chakraborty, *Condition of Bengali Women around the Second Half of the Nineteenth Century* (Calcutta: Burdhan Press, 1963), p. 134.

69. *Bengalee,* 19 May 1883, p. 230; *Statesman,* 14 May 1883, p. 3; *Sanjivani,* 19 May 1883, *RNBP,* no. 22, p. 243. For an account of Bengali women's associations and periodicals in the nineteenth century see Chakraborty, *Bengali Women,* pp. 147–90.

70. Quoted in Borthwick, *Women in Bengal,* p. 339.

71. Quoted in *Civil and Military Gazette,* 7 May 1883, p. 2.

72. The term *bhadramahila* is used by Meredith Borthwick to describe mothers, wives, sisters, and daughters of the many schoolmasters, lawyers, doctors, and government servants who made up the Bengali middle class or *bhadralok;* see Borthwick, *Women in Bengal,* preface, p. xi. Borthwick, who assumes that the memorial was authentic, identifies the signatories as individuals of this class; see pp. 338–39. See also Jana Matson Everett, *Women and Social Change in India* (New Delhi: Heritage Pub., 1979), p. 51.

73. *Bengalee,* 30 June 1883, p. 301.

74. *Englishman,* 3 Apr. 1883, p. 2.

75. This is a paraphrase of Gayatri Chakrovorty Spivak's formulation: White men are saving brown women from brown men, in "Can the Subaltern Speak? Speculations on Widow-Sacrifice," *Wedge* 7/8 (Winter/Spring 1985): 121.

76. See "A Lady's View of Mr. Ilbert's Bill," *Englishman,* 6 Mar. 1883, p. 2.

77. See Borthwick, *Women in Bengal*, p. 91. Also Beveridge, *India*. Annette Akroyd's experiences in India are also discussed in Pat Barr, *The Memsahibs: The Women of Victorian India* (London: Secker and Warburg, 1976).

78. Barr, *Memsahibs*, p. 187.

79. Ibid., p. 167; also Borthwick, *Women in Bengal*, p. 90.

80. Beveridge, *India*, pp. 166–67.

81. *Englishman*, 6 Mar. 1883, p. 2.

82. Quoted in Beveridge, *India*, p. 250.

83. *Statesman*, 27 Mar. 1883, p. 2.

84. *Statesman*, 29 Mar. 1883, p. 2.

85. *Statesman*, 29 Mar. 1883, p. 2; *Englishman*, 28 Mar. 1883, p. 2.

86. *Pioneer*, 10 Apr. 1883, p. 1; *Englishman*, 9 Apr. 1883, p. 2.

87. *Leg. Dept. Papers*, paper no. 28.

88. *Bengalee*, 31 Mar. 1883, p. 152.

89. *Reis and Reyyet*, 17 Mar. 1883, p. 124.

90. Beveridge, *India*, p. 248.

91. See *Hindoo Patriot*, 4 June 1883, p. 266; *Bengalee*, 26 May 1883, p. 241.

92. Letter dated 9 June 1883 quoted in Beveridge, *India*, p. 248.

93. The imperial orthodoxy, which was reiterated in the works of many contemporary historians, blamed the advent of white women in the colonies for the deterioration in race relations. Recently, however, women's historians have tried to right the balance by writing their own glowing accounts of the role of white women in the colonies. For the dangers inherent in such revisionist accounts see an excellent review of some of this literature in Jane Haggis, "Gendering Colonialism or Colonising Gender?: Recent Women's Studies Approaches to White Women and the History of British Colonialism," *Women's Studies International Forum* 13, nos. 1/2 (1990): 105–16.

Allies, Maternal Imperialists, and Activists

CULTURAL MISSIONARIES, MATERNAL IMPERIALISTS, FEMINIST ALLIES

BRITISH WOMEN ACTIVISTS IN INDIA, 1865–1945

Barbara N. Ramusack

The dominant images of British women in India are either memsahibs, the wives of British officials and businessmen, or missionaries, either single women or the wives of male missionaries. They have often been characterized as arrogant exponents of British culture or Christianity as practiced in a Western context and individuals with almost no interest in India, its culture, or its people. More recent scholarship including the essays by Nupur Chaudhuri and Karen Tranberg Hansen in this volume has begun to depict a more sympathetic and complex view of memsahibs both in the Indian and in the African contexts. Although much smaller in number, there were British women outside the formal imperial establishment who came to India because of their declared concern about the condition of Indian women. Five such women whose careers in India parallel the development of British imperial power from firm self-confidence to approaching demise are Mary Carpenter, Annette Akroyd Beveridge, Margaret Noble-Sister Nivedita, Margaret Gillespie Cousins, and Eleanor Rathbone. An examination of their activities provides one avenue of exploring how the categories of race and gender influence efforts to promote social reforms within an imperial relationship. An analysis of the initial attraction of these women to India, their network of contacts within the British imperial establishment and among Indians, and their endeavors on behalf of Indian women forms the basis for an assessment of the shifts in their orientation and activities over the eight decades from 1865 to 1945. The changes delineated reflect much about the British women as individuals, about the evolution of the imperial relationship, and about developments in Indian society, especially in the situation of Indian women.

Larger questions relate to the nature of the boundaries of race and gender within an imperial structure. Interaction across class categories will not be given the same consideration since both the British women and the Indian men and women with whom they interacted were of the middle class in their respective societies, with one notable exception. Thus, is it possible for women from one race or ethnic group to promote effectively reforms or institutions designed to modify or improve the conditions of women of another race or ethnic group in a colonial society that embodies such a pervasive dominant-subordinate power structure? How far can women cooperate or collaborate across racial or ethnic categories? How does the shared category of gender affect the development of movements and institutions designed for the benefit of indigenous women in a colonial setting? Finally, should these British women be labeled cultural missionaries, who preached the gospel of women's uplift based on models evolved in Britain; maternal imperialists, who wanted to socialize immature daughters to their adult rights and responsibilities; or feminist allies, whose effectiveness depended on their own personalities and skills, the institutional and personal alliances they formed, and the state of the women's movement in India when they were active? Perhaps individual women might embody all three roles in varying combinations.

Mary Carpenter

Daughter of a prominent Unitarian minister in Bristol who was the most significant influence on her life, Mary Carpenter (1807–77) was a notable example of the nineteenth-century English spinster who dedicated her life to philanthropy and social reform.[1] She was unusual in that she had received a rigorous, classical education with her brothers so that she might assist in a family-operated school. While teaching, the angular, frail Miss Carpenter had her first contact with India when Raja Rammohun Roy, the founder of the Brahmo Samaj, a rationalist Hindu reform group in Bengal, came to visit her father shortly before his death in 1833.

India was to remain a shadowy concern for three decades while Carpenter pursued a career as a social reformer that focused on the needs of destitute children, who crowded urban streets in industrializing England, and on penal institutions. During the 1860s renewed contacts with Indian male social reformers, most notably a Christmas in 1865 shared with three Hindu students, including Monomohan Ghose, a member of the Brahmo Samaj then in England to compete for the entrance examination of the Indian Civil Service (ICS), revived her interest in India.[2] Krishna Lahiri has also argued that Carpenter was experiencing personal despondency and was looking for new fields of endeavor during these years.[3] The Englishwoman wanted to assist Indian men such as her recent guests who sought to change some social conditions for the women in their own class, but she also implicitly accepted the ethnocentric views of British officials and Christian missionaries that the "degraded" position of Indian women was a major indication that Indian civilization ranked below that of the enlightened British. She joined the movement to "uplift" Indian women.

After her arrival in Bombay in late 1866, Mary Carpenter first considered spending all her time in Bombay Presidency where she was impressed by the commitment to female education. Ultimately she decided to go to Bengal via Madras since she wanted support from the British colonial government, whose capital was Calcutta. Her primary goal was to promote female education, although she also toured penal institutions and became particularly critical of the lack of concern for the rehabilitation of women prisoners.

Throughout her six-month tour, Carpenter displayed ambivalent attitudes toward Indian culture and Indian women. A devout Christian, she was disdainful of what she labeled the superstitious religious practices of Hindus, Muslims, and Parsis. Still she was aware that much opposition to female education among Indians was from fear that it was a preface to conversion, and so she respected Indian concerns and carefully avoided any appearance of proselytization. At the same time she clearly desired to socialize Indian girls into Victorian domesticity. Education was to enable Indian girls to be gracious hostesses presiding over simple, neat homes in which children and husbands would find their moral center.

Carpenter was critical of the elderly male pundits who taught young girls in schools since that practice meant girls would be withdrawn from schools as they approached puberty to avoid contact with the opposite sex. *Zenana* education provided by female missionaries in Indian homes was at best a transitional step since it was "obviously far preferable for young girls to have their minds expanded by seeing something beyond the walls in which they are afterwards to be immured."[4] For Carpenter the key to any expansion of female education was an increase in the supply of female teachers. In her visits to Ahmedabad, Surat, Bombay, Madras, and Calcutta, she met untiringly with Indian male reformers anxious to secure education for their wives and daughters. She lobbied British officials and presented memorials that urged the government of India to give grants to support female normal schools to provide secular female teachers for Indian girls as they already did to train male teachers for boys. Carpenter sought government patronage of this institution for three reasons: first, "as a guarantee to the natives that it is *not* a proselytising institution";[5] second, because the English-women who were needed as principals required the protection of the British government before they exposed themselves "to the difficulties and dangers they would have to encounter in a distant and tropical country"; and third, only the government could ensure the permanency of such an institution.[6]

Her efforts were thwarted by cautious British officials who were more willing to support education that would provide inexpensive male clerks than a more altruistic venture for women who could not be so employed.[7] Carpenter's authoritative personality also offended some white males who might have been allies. In February 1869 Lord Napier, governor of Madras, advised Carpenter that he was "of the opinion that you could do more for the cause of female education by *staying at home and supporting* those who are interested in it."[8] Charles Dall, an American Unitarian missionary in Calcutta, who was upset that Carpenter financially supported some Indian Unitarian establishments but not his, bluntly commented to the American Unitarian Association on 14 December 1869 that "she walks roughshod over everybody and meets her best advisers with rebuke, saying, 'she knows better.' . . . If she could but begin to see how little she knows of India."[9]

On her return to England Mary Carpenter used her celebrity status to awaken public opinion to conditions in India and to English responsibilities to promote social reform in their colony. Besides her memoirs, she published a collection of her speeches in India, spoke before the Social Science Association on both female education and penal reform in India, and had interviews with Queen Victoria, Florence Nightingale, and the secretary of state for India. This propaganda activity became her dominant focus after her effort to assume a direct leadership role in India during three other visits in 1868, 1869, and 1875 failed. In September 1870, in response to a request from Keshub Chandra Sen, the charismatic leader of the Brahmo Samaj, Carpenter founded the National Indian Association to spread knowledge of India in England and understanding of English culture among Indian visitors. The Bengal branch of this association served as a prototype for reform associations among Bengali women.[10]

Annette Akroyd Beveridge

The daughter of a successful business man, public figure, and Unitarian of Stourbridge and his first wife who died in 1849, Annette Akroyd Beveridge (1842–1929) was educated at Bedford College in London during the early 1860s. From ages twenty-two to twenty-seven, her life in Stourbridge was a rather dull routine, as reflected in her diary entries.

> 22 Feb 1865. Bachelors Ball. Very great fun in some things. Not very lively (mentally.) Good Dancing.
> 22 Mar 1865. Read Max Muller & Cicero.
> 16 Jul 1865. To church. Very slow indeed. Won't waste my time again.[11]

The death of her father in 1869 provided the opportunity for new directions. Without any particular career commitment and no financial constraints, Annette Akroyd was ready to follow when Keshub Chandra Sen, the Bengali reformer, proclaimed at the Victoria Discussion Society in London on 1 August 1870:

> I now have the honour to make an urgent yet humble appeal to you Englishwomen—I may say English sisters. I sincerely and earnestly call upon you to do all in your power to effect the elevation of the Hindu women. . . . The best way in which that help can be given is for some of you to embark on the grand and noble enterprise of going over personally to that great country. . . . And what sort of education do we expect and wish from you? An unsectarian, liberal, sound, useful education. (Cheers.) . . . an education calculated to make Indian women good wives, mothers, sisters and daughters.[12]

In many ways Sen's goal of a "useful" education was similar to that of the American missionaries described by Leslie Flemming in her essay in this volume since both wanted women to have greater skills in the domestic sphere and to be helpmates to either Christian or Brahmo Samaj husbands. Here is another example of how Indian men, British officials, and foreign women, whether British or American, would share reform goals for Indian women that did not overtly challenge the patriarchal structure.[13]

When Akroyd arrived in Calcutta in December 1872, she lacked the support of missionary colleagues and introductions to government officials, the latter of which Carpenter enjoyed. She had to confront Indian male attitudes of blank wonder toward her status as an independent woman and then Sen's complex, and to her mind ambivalent, attitudes toward women and female education. Sen had wanted her to teach at his Native Ladies' Normal School, which emphasized the domestic arts, since he argued for gradualism in female emancipation and against Anglicized curriculum and personal habits for Bengali girls. Akroyd aspired to teach a broader curriculum including arithmetic, geography, physical science, reading, writing, and history as well as needlework and household management.[14]

Akroyd did not favor overt Westernization, but she had been offended by the dress of the *bhadramahila* or middle-class, respectable Bengali women, which she considered vulgar at best and immodest at worst. Their heavy jewelry, their transparent muslin saris, and the lack of undergarments, suitable for *purdah,* she found out of place in public spheres into which she tried to draw Indian women.[15] Akroyd did not favor the English gowns proposed by some dress reformers but was particularly concerned to put Bengali women in shoes and stockings. In writing to her sister on the dress of Indian women she reflected on her cultural bias: "I am thrown back on radical questions of modesty and delicacy often, and have to ask myself why are such sights so shocking to me."[16] Her acceptance of Victorian ideals of womanhood influenced not only her concern over the immodest dress of Bengali women but also led her, as it did Mary Carpenter, to want Bengali girls to establish households in which Victorian domesticity would prevail.

Akroyd quickly broke with Sen but continued for awhile to receive support from other liberal members of the Brahmo Samaj and some English officials. In 1873 she opened a boarding school, the Hindu Mahila Bidyalaya, which attracted only five students, so that she could assume overall direction of their lives. Her disheartening struggle to maintain an adequate enrollment, staff, and building demonstrated the accuracy of Mary Carpenter's judgment of the need for government support for female education. Akroyd ended her career as an educational entrepreneur by accepting a proposal of marriage from Henry Beveridge, an independent-minded Indian Civil Service officer who had been a steady subscriber to her school. Her continuing inability to empathize across racial boundaries and to understand the aspirations of Indian women, including those who were educated and socially comparable to herself, led her to take an influential and controversial stance against the Ilbert Bill, which Mrinalini Sinha explores in her essay in this volume. Beveridge then devoted the remainder of her long life to her four children, including Lord William Beveridge, and to learning Persian and Turkish in order to translate the memoirs of Mughal rulers.

Margaret Noble—Sister Nivedita

Conflict within the Brahmo Samaj over the most appropriate curriculum for girls and the proper pace of female emancipation reflected a growing reaction among Hindu social reformers against following Western models. The effort to reconcile Hindu social customs and Western ideals in programs to improve the situation of Indian women emerges in the work of two extraordinary Irish Protestant social and political activists. The first to arrive in India was Margaret Noble (1867–1911), who had taught in various English schools before opening an experimental school for children and adults in Wimbledon. In 1895 she met Swami Vivekananda, a Bengali Hindu reformer who preached a mystical devotion to Siva, the Hindu god who destroys evil, and to Kali, the black goddess who slays demons and reconciles her Bengali devotees to the inevitability of death, and the need to manifest this commitment in social service. Powerfully attracted to Vivekananda's charismatic personality and his appeal to help Indian women, Noble began to study Hindu scriptures, especially the Bhagavad Gita, and the life of the Buddha. After much debate within herself and with Vivekananda, Noble left for India in 1897.[17]

After her arrival in Calcutta, Margaret Noble pursued initiation into the neotraditional, Hindu monastic community founded by Ramakrishna and then led by Vivekananda. She also moved from being a stout defender of the British empire to a sympathetic popularizer of Indian culture and the Indian demand for greater political autonomy.[18] At the time she accepted the social discipline of an orthodox Hindu woman so that she might become a more effective educator of Hindu women.[19] She received the name of Sister Nivedita (she who has been dedicated) and began to observe *ze-nana* restrictions in her Calcutta home, in a lower-class quarter near that of Sarada Devi, the widow of Ramakrishna.[20]

In 1898 on the feast of the goddess Kali, 13 November, Margaret Noble opened her school for Hindu girls. A firm advocate of the kindergarten, her educational goals were only gradually and vaguely defined. At one point she declared that "first and foremost, we must root them in their own past" and then give Indian women the three characteristics of a modern mind, "Scientific standards, geographical conception, historical pre-possessions."[21] Like Akroyd, Noble wanted key elements of a Western education, but unlike her predecessor, she sought a synthesis with Indian culture. Her curriculum usually included both English and Bengali, arithmetic, geography, history, art, sewing, and needlework. Because of her simple life-style and her respect for Hindu customs, Nivedita was able to secure the cooperation of some orthodox Hindu parents of young girls in her neighborhood. When students were irregular in attendance, Nivedita wo

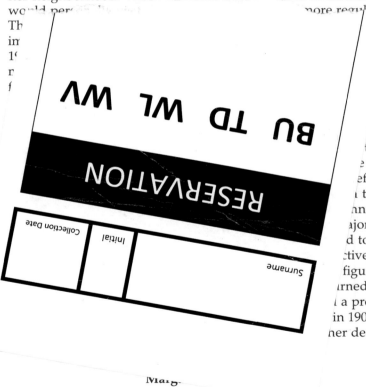

Th
in
1
r
f

y that were
formers. In
ducation for
ial education

es and talents
and, and the
ian women to
to interpret In-
e money for her
ef work during
the more ratio-
na Mission; and
ajor Bengali bota-
d to live indepen-
tive in Indian na-
figure to the more
rned to England to
a pro-Indian infor-
in 1909, she concen-
her death in 1911.

During this same era another red-haired Irish woman, the first one of this quintet who was a self-declared feminist, became interested in India, first through the Bhagavad Gita and then the Theosophical Society headed by

Annie Besant and headquartered in India. Margaret Gillespie (1878–1954) had received a degree from the Royal Irish Academy of Music in Dublin where she met James Cousins, an Irish poet active in the Irish literary revival dominated by W. B. Yeats. They were married in 1903 and Margaret inaugurated their possibly celibate life together by joining her husband in his commitment to vegetarianism at their wedding banquet.[23] During the first decade of her married life she experienced both deepening receptivity to communication with the world of spirits and imprisonment for her work on behalf of the suffragist movement in England.

In 1915 her husband sought and accepted an invitation from Annie Besant to work as a journalist in Madras. The Cousinses soon shifted to teaching at a Theosophical college. After entertaining local Indian women and becoming bored with grading essays from English classes at the college, Margaret formed the Abala Abhivardini Samaj or Weaker Sex Improvement Society in 1916. It provided the model for the Women's Indian Association (WIA) that she and Dorothy Jinarajadasa, another Theosophist, helped to found in 1917 to involve Indian women in public life.

Throughout the remainder of her life in India, Cousins worked in many arenas for feminist causes.[24] In 1917 she formed a deputation of Indian women to petition for the franchise. In 1926 when women first became eligible to run for provincial legislatures, she organized the election campaign for Kamaladevi Chattopadhyay, a former student of hers and a radical social and cultural activist.[25] Later that year she helped to establish the All India Women's Conference (AIWC) that debated the expansion of educational opportunities and the most appropriate curriculum for women. The AIWC soon decided to widen its scope since education was so inextricably related to political and social conditions, and Indian women officers were appreciative of Cousins's role as an intermediary among various Indian regional groups.[26] In 1936 Margaret was elected president of the AIWC, partly to honor her but also because contending factions preferred the neutral figure of a sympathetic Irishwoman.[27] By 1943 Cousins was withdrawing from active participation in Indian political and feminist organizations since, as she wrote, "I longed to be in the struggle against such foreign [British] imbecility; but I had the feeling that direct participation by me was no longer required, or even desired, by the leaders of Indian womanhood who were now coming to the front."[28] Shortly thereafter she suffered a stroke that physically disabled her until her death in 1954.

Eleanor Rathbone

Eleanor Rathbone (1872–1946), probably the most well-known British woman politician who campaigned for social reform measures related to Indian women, was born in London where her father was serving in Parliament as a Liberal member from Liverpool. Educated at Somerville College during the early 1890s, Rathbone remained single and continued her father's social and parliamentary service. Eleanor was committed to the constitutional wing of the suffragist movement, becoming the president of the National Union of Societies for Equal Citizenship in 1919 and being elected to Parliament in 1929. In the public mind she was the principal proponent of family allowances paid directly to mothers. Like Carpenter, Rathbone's Unitarian-Quaker family had also hosted the peripatetic Rammohun Roy, but Eleanor herself did not become involved with Indian women's issues until she was a mature woman of fifty-five.[29]

During her summer holiday in 1927 Rathbone read Katherine Mayo's *Mother India*, a highly popular, polemical work that opened with a graphic critique of the impact of child marriage and other Hindu social customs on the mortality of Indian women. Rathbone's first concern was to determine the accuracy of Mayo's data. She organized a small conference in London to discuss the issues described in *Mother India* and initiated a survey on women in India. Her efforts evoked mixed responses from Indian women and organizations, since Rathbone was trying to study her subject from London without any Indian associates. The AIWC refused to cooperate with Rathbone for several reasons, arguing "that such a Survey cannot adequately and surely be made by women who do not know India by long residence and by sympathetic co-operation in the life of its women."[30] Dhanvanthi Rama Rau, the wife of an Indian official stationed in London, attended the conference at Caxton Hall in October 1929 and heatedly "disputed the right of British women to arrange a conference on Indian social evils in London, where all the speakers were British and many had never even visited India."[31]

In 1929 Eleanor Rathbone was elected to Parliament and launched a double-pronged campaign related to Indian women. First, she lobbied stubbornly to raise the minimum age for Indian women at marriage. This goal meant pressing for more energetic implementation by the colonial government of existing legislation[32] since, as Dagmar Engels has argued, once legislation was passed, British administrators adopted "the Indian [male] definition of a woman's honour and happiness," and did not prosecute offenders since such action would involve entrance into the domestic sphere of the Indian household.[33] Rathbone tried vainly to counter this official reluctance by educating public opinion in both England and India and supporting the passage of more stringent legislation in India. Second, she worked for greater involvement of Indian women in the constitutional governance of India. She sought to have Indian women appointed as delegates to the numerous conferences and commissions that were formulating constitutional reforms for India from 1927 to 1935;[34] she maneuvered for a wider extension of the franchise among Indian women;[35] she sought mechanisms to ensure that Indian women would be members of the reformed central and provincial legislatures. Her only visit to India came in January 1932 when she went to influence testimony being given to the Indian Franchise Committee then collecting evidence.[36] Rathbone faced indifference and some hostility among British officials in London and New Delhi who placed female suffrage and legislative seats in the category of minor minorities (religious communities such as Muslims and Sikhs and caste groups such as the so-called "untouchables" were considered the major minorities) in their correspondence.[37] On the other side, her achievements that were incorporated into the Government of India Act of 1935 seemed insignificant to members of the AIWC, who wanted adult suffrage or nothing. Rajkumari Amrit Kaur, then president of the AIWC, advised Rathbone: "I am sorry I do not *quite* agree with your theory of 'get what you can & make it a basis for getting more.' In a free country like yours—yes—but in a subject country—no—because a start on the wrong basis means disaster ab initio and can never lead to the ultimate true goal."[38]

Patterns of Association

What do these five diverse individuals reveal about the involvement of British women activists in India? Personal characteristics, which several of them shared, were one factor leading them to India and would later influence their effectiveness. Four were single, and none had the social responsibilities linked with biological motherhood when they came to India. All were from families with a deep commitment to forms of Protestant Christianity that these women gradually found did not fulfill their spiritual or emotional needs.[39] This spiritual unease and desire for resolution was also an important factor in the life of Annie Besant, who journeyed from the Anglican Church through socialism to the Theosophical Society and India in her quest for spiritual serenity, as described by Nancy Paxton in her essay in this volume. There was, however, an important difference between Margaret Cousins and Annie Besant in their spiritual submission to Theosophy in that Cousins was an active proponent of birth control in India while Besant came to oppose it and even after she reversed herself never campaigned aggressively for birth control in India.[40]

Most of these women were close to their fathers, whose relatively early deaths allowed the daughters to pursue independent careers. All had more formal education than did most other women of their generation and had assertive personalities. After working in the public sphere in England as educators, social reformers, and suffragists, these women extended their purview to include other women within the British Empire much as Josephine Butler did, as Antoinette Burton has analyzed in her essay in this volume. At a particular point in their lives India offered them an escape from unpleasant personal circumstances or institutional settings that restricted their capacity for social experiments as well as opportunities for professional achievements or spiritual satisfaction.[41] In some ways India served as an environment of alternatives for these women as it did for British men who joined the ICS. Excluded from the ICS, these women went to India as independent activists; they were unlikely memsahibs because of their high level of education and public experience, and unlikely religious missionaries because of their declining enthusiasm for mainstream Christianity.

All of these women viewed their work for Indian women within an imperial political context. All lobbied extensively with British officials, although these men tended to regard the female reformers as busybodies who did not understand the broader political imperatives of maintaining imperial power or local law and order. In order to counter this indifference from British men who did not have reforms for Indian women as a major goal, these women sought to influence British public opinion through their publications, speaking tours, and London-based organizations. As might be expected, Eleanor Rathbone, a member of Parliament, was the most assiduous in cultivating British public and political opinion; but even Noble and Cousins, who saw India as their home, continued to write and lecture in Britain. Although Noble, Cousins, and Rathbone were active supporters of Indian nationalists and their demand for self-government, all five women continued to think of the colonial government as a considerable factor in achieving improvements in the condition of Indian women. By appealing to the imperial power, these women re-enforced its authority in determining the legal context of male-female relationships among Indians. At the same time many Indian political and social leaders were denying the validity of any imperial legislation that affected their personal relationships.[42]

Initially, personal ties based on shared gender were not a key factor in the formulation of programs for the colonized women by these women from the colonizing power. The desire of these British women to help Indian women did not arise from any immediate contact with Indian women. In the nineteenth century, Indian men sought the assistance of British women: Rammohun Roy, Monomohan Ghose, and Keshub Chandra Sen of Mary Carpenter; Keshub Chandra Sen of Annette Akroyd; Swami Vivekananda of Margaret Noble. These men were all from Bengal, where British cultural ideas about ideals of womanhood were first introduced, but also where elite, Western-educated Indian men were led to argue for reform because of concern for the life situations of their wives, daughters, and sisters.[43] In the twentieth century, foreign women stimulated the interest of these British activists: Annie Besant influenced Margaret Cousins and Katherine Mayo influenced Eleanor Rathbone. Finally, only Margaret Noble had more than the most minimal contact with Indian men and women who were not of the educated elite.

Barriers of differing experiences, languages, and cultural attitudes had to be overcome before British women could collaborate effectively with elite Indian women. Carpenter does not give evidence of really knowing Indian women as individuals. Although she refers to Indian men by name in her writing, Carpenter describes Indian women as, for example, the wife of Tagore or Banerjea or a group of underdressed women at a *purdah* party.[44] She had spent much of her life working with dependent children, and she seemed to consider Indian women in the same category. In 1866 Carpenter hosted the first tea party in Calcutta at which both Indian men and women were present. Since she spoke no Bengali, she "explained a portfolio of prints and drawings to a circle of gentlemen, and then requested them to do the same to the ladies."[45] Akroyd learned Bengali but still did not communicate with Indian women on an equal basis nor mention in her writings the personal names of the wives of Keshub Chandra Sen or of her Brahmo supporters. Margaret Noble is a transitional figure. In her religious life Noble had close ties with Sarada Devi and her orthodox companions, and in her educational ventures she was assisted by Indian women, most notably the sister and the wife of J. C. Bose, as well as foreign women, such as the American Christine Greenstidel. Margaret Cousins is the first to cooperate almost exclusively with Indian women in her organizational and political activities on their behalf and to serve as a mentor to younger Indian women such as Kamaladevi Chattopadhyay and Muthulakshmi Reddy, the first woman legislator in India.[46] After her minimal consultation with Indian women in London, Eleanor Rathbone maintained an extensive correspondence with Indian women including some who opposed her views such as Rajkumari Amrit Kaur.[47]

Thus British women activists gradually learned to collaborate with Indian women and work across racial barriers. They became potential allies as they lived for extended periods in India, developed intellectual and personal respect for Indian culture, and were willing to contribute the skills needed at a particular historical moment in reform programs initiated by Indian women. Although Carpenter, Akroyd, and Noble worked mainly in Bengal and Cousins spent most of her Indian career in Madras, the regional setting was less important than the time period in which they were active. When Carpenter and Akroyd were in India, Indian women had begun to form local groups to discuss and promote change in their social conditions, but their meetings were sporadic and conducted in Indian languages in which these two Englishwomen were not comfortable. Margaret Noble knew Bengali, but she remained relatively aloof from the Bengali women's organizations in which women from the Brahmo Samaj were dominant. When Cousins and Rathbone were active in the 1920s and 1930s, elite Indian women activists were using English and so the foreign women had a common means of communication. Cousins was more effective than Rathbone in entering an Indian network since she could utilize the Theosophical lodges in which both European and Indian women had significant leadership roles.

The projects that these British women initiated on behalf of or in cooperation with Indian women reveal how changes in Indian society determined the most effective role for British feminists. None of these women could create the networks necessary to sustain permanent institutions. At first, Carpenter, Akroyd, and Noble sought to establish schools that would produce women who would be suitable wives for Western-educated Indian men or for Indian nationalist leaders. Their schools had very limited enrollments and precarious existences since they lacked the continuity afforded by either governmental grants-in-aid or missionary contributions. They were only stabilized when Indian groups took them over, retaining at most a name and a vague commitment to the ideals of the founder. The spiritual descendant of the efforts of Carpenter and Akroyd was the Banga Mahila Bidyalaya, the first women's liberal arts college in India, founded in June 1876. It soon merged with the Bethune School founded in 1849 to become the Bethune College, which named its main hall after Mary Carpenter. Noble's school, which was heavily dependent on her fundraising tours in the West and donations from Western devotees of Vivekananda, also experienced personnel problems in 1911 when Christine Greenstidel and Sudhira Devi left to join the rival, more Western-oriented Brahmo Samaj School for Girls. Although the written record is silent, it seems that both the American and the Indian woman found it difficult to work with Nivedita, who was increasingly removed from the daily operation of the school but anxious to retain control of its policies. Eventually some of Noble's students opened an institution known as the Sister Nivedita School that was associated with the Ramakrishna Sarada Mission.

Carpenter, Akroyd, and Noble soon realized that education for women was only one aspect of a complex of social factors that needed modification. Thus they all became involved in other Indian organizations: Carpenter in her National Indian Association; Akroyd in the Brahmo Samaj; and Noble in the Ramakrishna Mission and then in nationalist, political groups in Bengal. Carpenter and Akroyd cooperated in these associations with Indian men whose Western education made them more similar in intellectual orientation and organizational style with these British women than were Indian women's groups then emerging. Margaret Noble, living in a slum area of north Calcutta, was the first of these British activists to try to cross class lines as well as to work with orthodox Hindu women, but after the death of Vivekananda she became more involved with Indian male political leaders, such as Aurobindo Ghose, who were committed to Hindu revivalism and political radicalism.

Margaret Cousins was the transitional figure in collaborating with Indian women across racial lines. By the late 1910s she saw the need for regional and national feminist organizations led by Indian women. Her efforts capitalized on the growing organizational sophistication among Indian women who had been working in local groups since the 1860s. The spread of Western education among elite Indian women also meant that they now shared a cultural vocabulary with British women who were sympathetic to Indian culture. Cousins's forty years of residence in India were extraordinary, and her personal sensitivity meant that she was an able ally. Her ability to com-

municate across racial boundaries is reflected in an address of welcome
from members of a small branch of the Women's Indian Association in Tan-
jore, south India:

> Born in Ireland, a land that is suffering untold miseries for some centuries
> past, and a member of the Theosophical Society, you have atonce [sic] a nat-
> ural sympathy for any suffering cause.
>   This sympathy, rare from one of your own colour, except from a Theos-
> ophist, you have shown in abundance by your work for the women of India
> in general and Madras in particular.[48]

Kamaladevi has also reminisced about how Cousins could present plans so
tactfully that the other party accepted them as her own.[49]
  By the 1930s Eleanor Rathbone's well-intentioned, wide-ranging efforts
were both too late and too early. Her campaign for an extension of legal
and political rights demonstrates the increasing difficulty for British
women to work from within Indian organizations as had Noble and Cousins. Indian women now demanded the right to formulate their own objectives and tactics and to disagree with Western feminists over the likely consequences of their strategies. Rathbone's attempt to start an organization
focused on eradicating child marriages was hampered by her London base,
but it was also premature. Single issue organizations were not politically
popular when the dominant emphasis was on a united front to achieve independence. They would become more feasible after independence when
hard decisions had to be made to establish priorities for legislation and the
distribution of scarce resources.

Cultural Missionaries, Maternal Imperialists, or Feminist Allies?

In some ways these women might be viewed as cultural missionaries
preaching a gospel of women's uplift. Like religious missionaries, they
started with the goals of promoting female education, raising the minimum
age of marriage for women, and improving the situation of Hindu widows.
Although they were not overtly working to convert Indian women to
Christianity, Carpenter and Akroyd sought to mold the life-style of Indian
women according to Victorian ideals that reflected Christian influence, as
in their campaign for modest dress. Furthermore, all of these women
thought that Indian women would profit from models, principles, and
techniques derived from European experience. Carpenter had few qualms
about giving advice after a six-month tour of India, deeming her principles
universal in application, although based on decades of work in England.
Akroyd wanted to establish an Indian school based on advanced British
models that were not yet accepted in England itself. Noble sought to apply
the theories of Pestalozzi and Frobel even though she recognized the need

for the integration of Indian myths and art. Cousins used her earlier experiences in the Irish home rule movement and the English suffragist campaign as guides for her activity in India. Rathbone applied the techniques of social science research developed in England that made the subject into an object. In such ways, these women functioned as secular missionaries for Western cultural forms.

Some might label these women cultural imperialists, but perhaps the term "maternal imperialists" is more accurate. In India British political imperialism became paternalistic autocracy. During much of its existence, it was justified as preparation of child-like Indians for self-government, and the ICS officer was described as the *ma-bap,* or mother and father, for the people of his district. In various ways these British women activists embodied a benevolent maternal imperialism. They were frequently referred to as mothers or saw themselves as mothering India and Indians. Carpenter remarked, "In India I am regarded as 'the old Mother,' and I am proud of the title."[50] Sister Nivedita considered herself the daughter of Vivekananda and the mother of her students, but prized the title of Sister most since "We were all 'mother' to them—now, I am 'Sister,' and funny as that sounds, the latter title indicates a more genuine and individual relationship than the former."[51] Margaret Cousins was not referred to as a mother, although Kamaladevi has spoken of her with daughter-like affection. Eleanor Rathbone assumed a "mother knows best" tone when she lectured Indian women on the lessons to be learned from the British suffragist movement.

The use of terms of fictive kinship could have been one way of integrating these women into Indian culture. In India, as elsewhere, mothers can be sources of great affection for their children, and so mother can be a title of honor. Still the mother-daughter relationship involves elements of inequality, and the fact that the mother figures were British and the daughters were Indian heightened the aspects of inequality and suspicions about the motivations of the mothers. The possibility for resentment became acute when Indian women had extensive education and greater political experience. Like maturing daughters or Indian men who organized politically to seek more government positions or greater representation in legislatures, Indian women wanted to be treated as equals. They were increasingly sensitive to unintentional as well as overt gestures expressing inequality or condescension. Thus the women who were most successful in collaborating with Indian women were those like Noble and Cousins who could enter relationships on a basis of equality and respect. Their Irish background and their extended residence in India probably helped them to span the gap between colonizer and colonized as it seemed to influence Annie Besant, who challenged the patriarchal hierarchy of imperialism.

Although this quintet carried political and cultural baggage, they could function as feminist allies when Indian women had particular need of their organizational and communications skills. Therefore, they provide examples of ways in which the boundaries of race, but not class, may be crossed in the imperial context. These activists kept the issue of women's rights and opportunities at the forefront when Indian women had limited access to public arenas or were concentrating on the goal of self-government. They contributed plans and prototypes that Indian men and women could either adopt wholly or partially or discard as they deemed most appropriate. They were articulate and publicized the condition of Indian women through lectures, polemical tracts, newspaper articles, monographs, surveys, and personal memoirs to publics in India and in English-speaking countries. They secured statistical data to buttress pleas for reform; they raised funds for institutions and organizations when Indian women possessed limited control over discretionary funds; they organized deputations and political campaigns with Indian women when Indian men were preoccupied with their own political future. Thus these British women activists provided useful skills at crucial stages of organizational development and were most effective when they worked to achieve the goals set by Indian women.

NOTES

I would like to acknowledge with appreciation fellowships from the American Institute of Indian Studies (1976–77), the Fulbright Faculty Research Abroad Program of the U.S. Department of Education (1981–82), and the Smithsonian Institution (1985), which supported my research in India, and a Summer Fellowship from the National Endowment for the Humanities (1979) for research in England.
A more extended version of this chapter was published in *Women's Studies International Forum* 13, no. 4 (1990): 309–21, reprinted with the permission of Pergamon Press. My analysis for both that version and this one has benefited greatly from the helpful comments of Dagmar Engels, Geraldine Forbes, Allen Greenberger, Mrinalini Sinha, a group of Indian scholars at a Fulbright-sponsored seminar in Calcutta in January 1981, and from a seminar on the Other at the National Humanities Center during 1986–87. Any errors of fact and interpretation are my responsibility.
1. Olive Banks, *The Biographical Dictionary of British Feminists*, vol. 1: *1800–1930* (New York: New York University Press, 1985), 46–48. J. Estlin Carpenter, *The Life and Work of Mary Carpenter* (1879; reprint, Montclair, N.J.: Paterson Smith, 1974); Jo Manton, *Mary Carpenter and the Children of the Streets* (London: Heinemann, 1976).
2. Mary Carpenter, *Six Months in India*, vol. 1 (London: Longmans, Green, 1868), 3–4.
3. Krishna Lahiri, "Mary Carpenter and the Early Crisis in Teacher Training for Women in Calcutta," in *Patterns of Change in Modern Bengal*, ed. Richard L. Park (East Lansing: Asian Studies Center, Michigan State University), 20–22.
4. M. Carpenter, *Six Months in India*, vol. 1, 188.
5. Ibid., 123, emphasis in the original.
6. Ibid., vol. 2, 157.
7. E. C. Bayley, Government of India, to M. Carpenter, 20 July 1867, ibid., 154–55; Lahiri, "Mary Carpenter," 25–29.
8. Bristol Archives, 12693, no. 16, quoted in Manton, *Mary Carpenter*, 209.
9. Charles Dall to American Unitarian Association, 14 Dec. 1869, quoted in

Spencer Lavan, *Unitarians and India: A Study in Encounter and Response* (Boston: Beacon Press, Skinner House Book, 1977), 116.

10. Meredith Borthwick, *The Changing Role of Women in Bengal, 1849–1905* (Princeton: Princeton University Press, 1984), 280.

11. Annette Akroyd Beveridge diary, 22 Feb. 1865, 22 Mar. 1865, 16 July 1865, Beveridge Collections, India Office Library and Records (IOLR), MSS Eur C176/41.

12. William H. Beveridge, *India Called Them* (London: George Allen and Unwin, 1947), 84–85.

13. Dagmar Engels has cogently argued how Indian male reformers and British officials shared ideal gender roles for Indian women that restricted women from having equal rights with Indian men in "The Limits of Gender Ideology: Bengali Women, the Colonial State, and the Private Sphere, 1890–1930," *Women's Studies International Forum* 12, no. 4 (1989): 426–30, 436.

14. Beveridge, *India Called Them*, 89–93; Borthwick, *The Changing Role*, 88–90; David Kopf, *The Brahmo Samaj and the Shaping of the Modern Indian Mind* (Princeton: Princeton University Press, 1979), 34–41.

15. Akroyd Beveridge diary, 26 Dec. 1872, Beveridge Collection, MSS Eur C176/104.

16. Letter to Fanny Mowatt, 20 Mar. 1873, quoted in Borthwick, *The Changing Role*, 252, 243–56.

17. Pravrajika Atmaprana, *Sister Nivedita*, 2nd ed. (Calcutta: Sister Nivedita Girls' School, 1967); Barbara Foxe, *Long Journey Home: A Biography of Margaret Noble (Nivedita)* (London: Rider and Company, 1975).

18. Margaret Noble (Sister Nivedita), *Letters of Sister Nivedita*, vol. 1, ed. Sankari Prasad Basu (Calcutta: Nababharat Publishers, 1982), 11.

19. Margaret Noble (Sister Nivedita), *The Complete Works of Sister Nivedita: Birth Centenary Publication*, vol. 2 (Calcutta: Ramakrishna Sarada Mission, Sister Nivedita Girls' School), 505.

20. Ibid., 293–303.

21. Atmaprana, *Sister Nivedita*, 28–30.

22. Barbara N. Ramusack, "Sister India or Mother India: Margaret Noble and Katherine Mayo as Interpreters of the Gender Roles of Indian Women" (paper presented at Seventh Berkshire Conference on the History of Women, Wellesley College, Wellesley, Mass., 20 June 1987), 4–10.

23. James H. Cousins and Margaret Cousins, *We Two Together* (Madras: Ganesh, 1950), 88–91.

24. Barbara N. Ramusack, "Catalysts or Helpers? British Feminists, Indian Women's Rights, and Indian Independence," in *The Extended Family: Women and Political Participation in India and Pakistan*, ed. Gail Minault (Columbia, Mo.: South Asia Books, 1981), 124–30, 137–43.

25. Kamaladevi Chattopadhyay, *Inner Recesses Outer Space: Memoirs* (New Delhi: Navrang, 1986), 81–82; Kamaladevi Chattopadhyay, interview with author, New Delhi, Mar. 1977.

26. Hilla Rustomji Faridoonji to Kamaladevi Chattopadhyay, 3 Nov. 1927; Sushama Sen to Cousins, 22 Apr. 1928, All India Women's Conference (AIWC) Archives, New Delhi, series 1, file no. 6.

27. Rajkumari Amrit Kaur to Hansa Mehta, 17 Oct. 1936, Hansa Mehta Collection, Nehru Memorial Museum and Library (NMML), New Delhi, no. 5.

28. Cousins and Cousins, *We Two Together*, 740.

29. Banks, *Biographical Dictionary*, 166–69; Mary D. Stocks, *Eleanor Rathbone: A Biography* (London: Victor Gollancz, 1949).

30. Rameshwari Nehru to Rathbone, AIWC Archives, Bombay Report, 1930, p. 32.

31. Dhanvanthi Rama Rau, *An Inheritance: The Memoirs of Dhanvanthi Rama Rau* (New York: Harper and Row, 1977), 170–71; Dhanvanthi Rama Rau, interview with author, Bombay, 16 Mar. 1977.

32. Rathbone to W. Wedgwood Benn, secretary of state for India, 16 May, 1 June, 8 July, 17 July 1930, and Rathbone to Samuel Hoare, secretary of state for India, 30 Nov. 1931, Rathbone Collection, Fawcett Library, London, box 92, folder 2 and B93, F6.

33. Engels, "Limits of Gender Ideology," 428.

34. Letter to *The Times*, 12 Dec. 1927; Rathbone to Wedgwood Benn, 16 Apr. 1931, Rathbone Collection, B92, F2.

35. Rathbone to Sarala Ray, 13 Mar. 1933, Rathbone Collection, B93, F9, no. 2; Rathbone to Lord Lytton, 15 Feb. 1934, Rathbone Collection, B93, F13, no. 26; Rathbone to R. A. Butler, undersecretary of state for India, 15 Feb. 1934, Rathbone Collection, B93, F6.

36. Rathbone, Circular Letters, 1932, Sydney Jones Library, University of Liverpool. I am indebted to Geraldine Forbes for sharing her copies of these letters with me.

37. R. A. Butler to Rathbone, 13 Apr. 1933, Rathbone Collection, B93, F6; Hoare to Lord Willingdon, governor-general of India, 2 Mar. 1934, and Willingdon to Hoare, 3 Apr. 1934, Templewood Papers, IOLR, MSS Eur E240/12 (b).

38. Rajkumari Amrit Kaur to Rathbone, 11 Feb. 1935, Rathbone Collection, B93, F12, I24.

39. J. E. Carpenter, *Mary Carpenter*, 220–21, 294; Cousins and Cousins, *We Two Together*, 87; Foxe, *Long Journey Home*, 15–17.

40. Barbara N. Ramusack, "Embattled Advocates: The Debate over British Control in India, 1920–40," *Journal of Women's History* 1, no. 2 (Fall 1989): 48, 50–51.

41. Borthwick, *The Changing Role*, 58; Cousins and Cousins, *We Two Together*, 240–42; Harriet Warm Schupf, "Single Women and Social Reform in Mid-Nineteenth Century England: The Case of Mary Carpenter," *Victorian Studies* 17, no. 3 (1974): 17.

42. Dagmar Engels, "Age of Consent Act of 1891: Colonial Ideology in Bengal," *South Asia Research* 3 (1983): 107–34; Joanne Liddle and Rama Joshi, *Daughters of Independence: Gender, Caste and Class in India* (London: Zed Books, 1986), 19–38; Mrinalini Sinha, "The Age of Consent Act: The Ideal of Masculinity and Colonial Ideology in Nineteenth-Century Bengal," in *Shaping Bengali Worlds, Public and Private*, ed. Tony K. Stewart (East Lansing: Asian Studies Center, Michigan State University, 1989), 99–111.

43. S. N. Mukherjee, "Raja Rammohun Roy and the Debate on the Status of Women in Bengal," in *Women in India and Nepal*, ed. Michael Allen and S. N. Mukherjee (Canberra: Australian National University, 1982), 163–64.

44. J. E. Carpenter, *Mary Carpenter*, 260–61.

45. M. Carpenter, *Six Months in India*, vol. 1, 183–84.

46. [Muthulakshmi Reddy], *Mrs. Margaret Cousins and Her Work in India*, Compiled by One Who Knows (Madras: Women's Indian Association, 1956), 56–70.

47. Other Indian correspondents included Lakshmi Menon, Rathbone Collection, B93, F14, no. 30 and Rameshwari Nehru, Rathbone Collection, B93, F13, no. 29.

48. Address from WIA, Tirumiyachur, Peralam P. G., 27 Aug. 1921, Reddy Collection, NMML, file no. 2.

49. Chattopadhyay, *Inner Recesses*, 83–84.

50. J. E. Carpenter, *Mary Carpenter*, 310.

51. Noble-Nivedita, *Letters*, vol. 1, 14.

THE WHITE WOMAN'S BURDEN

BRITISH FEMINISTS AND
"THE INDIAN WOMAN," 1865–1915

Antoinette M. Burton

Acknowledging the impact of empire on the British women's movement is one of the most urgent projects of late twentieth-century Western feminism.[1] With few exceptions, historians of the cause have overlooked the historically imperial context of the middle-class British feminist movement, as well as its enduring legacies.[2] And yet the influence of imperial culture[3] on late nineteenth-century feminist ideology should be no more surprising than, for example, the impact of the industrial revolution on women's lives, or that of liberal individualist discourse on the Victorian women's movement.[4] Empire was a fact of life, although the extent to which the average Victorian cared about empire has been a point of controversy recently among historians.[5] Even if imperial consciousness is difficult to measure, few historians today would disagree that a sense of national and racial superiority based on Britain's imperial status was an organizing principle of Victorian culture.

Middle-class Victorian feminists generally shared these assumptions. This chapter emphasizes the imperial context out of which British feminism emerged and examines the imperial assumptions that underlay one British feminist campaign and a variety of British feminist writings during the late Victorian period. Throughout contemporary middle-class feminist discourse "the Indian woman" served as evidence of British feminists' special imperial "burden." Despite both their genuine concern for the condition of Indian women *and* the feminist reform activities of prominent Indian women during this period, many middle-class British feminists viewed the women of the East not as equals but as unfortunates in need of saving by their British feminist "sisters." By imagining the women of India as helpless colonial subjects, British feminists constructed "the Indian woman" as a foil against which to gauge their own progress. Middle-class Victorian feminists not only identified their cause with the British imperial mission, they helped to shape a modern Western feminism which was profoundly influenced by the imperial assumptions of its day.

Liberal bourgeois feminism in Britain contained a number of premises which made it, if not predisposed toward imperialism, then at least compatible with and easily fueled by an imperial ethos. First, both were grounded in the idea of superiority. While Victorian sexual ideology cast woman as the weaker sex, it endowed her at the same time with unquestionable moral superiority, rooted in the ostensibly feminine virtues of nurturing, child-care, and purity. Rather than overturning the Victorian feminine ideal, early feminist theorists used it to justify female involvement in the public sphere by claiming that the exercise of woman's moral attributes was crucial to social improvement. As feminist historians have been arguing for a decade, Victorian feminists exploited assumptions about women's superior moral strength, thereby empowering themselves and other women to take up social service in the name of Victorian womanhood.[6]

Secondly, feminist argument, no less than imperial apologia, was preoccupied with race preservation, racial purity, and racial motherhood.[7] This was in part because it had to be. One of the most damaging attacks made against the case for female emancipation was that it would enervate the race.[8] With women out of the home, the care and feeding of England's children (and by extension the whole Anglo-Saxon race) would be neglected, and the nation would eventually collapse from within. Such diatribes had credibility in late nineteenth-century Britain, when fears of racial deterioration and national decline were considerable.[9] Feminists responded with assurances that not all women would necessarily choose public life and that those who did would not neglect their domestic duties. They argued that women were the "mothers of the race." They inherently possessed equal racial responsibility with men and so deserved equal power in "the councils of the nation."[10]

Anna Davin has conclusively shown how women were induced—by the state, by eugenists, by doctors and reformers—to bear the responsibility for racial strength.[11] But the point must be made that liberal feminists, at any rate, enthusiastically *claimed* racial responsibility as part of their strategy to legitimize themselves as responsible and important imperial citizens—just as they used female moral superiority to justify emancipation. Most feminists believed in the superiority of the Anglo-Saxon race,[12] frequently citing possession of empire as evidence of a superiority that was not just racial but religious and cultural too. The maintenance of racial hegemony was a collective cultural aspiration which feminists tried to use for their own ends—though it could be powerfully turned against them, as the anti-suffragists proved.[13] A strong sense of female superiority combined readily with other assumptions of imperial supremacy to make British feminists conceive of "the Anglo-Saxon woman" as the savior of her race, not to mention as the highest female type.

Lastly, feminism, like imperialism, was structured around the idea of moral responsibility. In Victorian terms "responsibility" was custodial, classist, ageist, and hierarchical.[14] Feminism and female reform ideology virtually dictated the existence of dependent clients on whom to confer aid, comfort, and (hopefully) the status of having been saved. In the imperial context, guardianship held out the promise of moral redemption; this, as the feminists framed it, was contingent upon the female sex in its capacity as redeemer. Most female reformers of the period believed that the guarantor of social progress, *the* agent of civilization, was woman herself, and they adhered to a rather clinical view of their sex as the vessel of a better — which was to say more "civilized" — society. British feminists' sense of mission cannot, of course, be divorced from the evangelical Christian enthusiasm which informed the mainstream of the movement. But again, middle-class feminists deliberately cultivated the civilizing responsibility as their own modern, womanly, and largely secular burden because it affirmed an emancipated role for them in the imperial nation-state. From their point of view empire was an integral and enabling part of "the woman question."

As the title of this essay indicates, British feminists felt they had a special responsibility toward Indian women. The reasons for this are not far to seek; India had always been important to British imperial confidence. After 1857 this was even more true. Rebellion on the part of native troops deepened British distrust of Indians while at the same time heightening the conviction that the British presence alone could bring progress to India.[15] As the second half of the century drew to a close and Britain felt its imperial status threatened by outside competitors, India became the linchpin of empire,[16] as well as a symbolic responsibility upon which Britain's success or failure as an imperial power would be judged. Florence Nightingale's evaluation of India in 1879 as "a home issue . . . a vital and moral question"[17] justly reflects the attitude of nineteenth-century feminists toward Indian women.

Josephine Butler and India

India was the object of concerted female reform effort beginning in the 1860s with Mary Carpenter's Indian visit and subsequent promotion of Hindu female education.[18] Educational improvements for Indian women were an ongoing concern among feminists until World War I and beyond, as was the need for female medical aid.[19] Although her domestic campaign has received much attention,[20] Josephine Butler's crusade against the Contagious Diseases Acts in India (1886–1915), which was the best organized and most prominent of feminist reform movements for Indian women, has never been examined in depth. Waged as it was at the height of British imperial expansion *and* British imperial self-doubt, the campaign for India offers one example of British imperial feminism in action.

The C.D. Acts were a series of measures originally legislated in the 1860s and applicable within England as well as the colonies, which authorized the detainment and medical examination of women designated by local authorities to be "common prostitutes." They were an exercise in social and sexual control that operated in port and garrison towns (like Plymouth and Southampton) where the incidence of venereal disease was feared to be high because of the influx of soldiers, sailors, and other transients. Butler and her co-workers, in both the predominantly male National Association and the Ladies' National Association (LNA), objected to the Acts because they considered them to be a violation of personal liberty, a humiliation for the women obliged to submit to them, and, not least, an ineffective solution for reducing venereal disease or eliminating prostitution. For, of course, the repealers hoped to eradicate prostitution: their method was moral suasion rather than state regulation, which they argued only promoted sexual vice by implying it was a necessity that had to be provided for.[21] By insisting on an equal standard of sexual morality for men and women, Butler and the associations she led not only achieved repeal by act of Parliament, but in the process shaped considerably the sexual premises of feminist arguments for female emancipation.[22]

With the eighteen-year-old domestic campaign finally concluded in April 1886, Butler and hundreds of repeal workers in London and all over the British Isles found themselves in danger of becoming suddenly redundant. They turned almost immediately to empire as a focal point for their continued repeal efforts. Although Butler herself had never been to India (nor was she ever to go), she had been aware of the effects of the C.D. Acts there as early as 1870, when a Hindu magistrate wrote to her detailing the horrors Indian women suffered as a result of the compulsory medical examinations.[23] Butler mentioned the possibility of turning the LNA into an organization for the colonies in a letter to her friends the Misses Priestman in May 1886, and her imperial concerns were fueled by revelations in the ensuing months that in spite of repeal at home, the Acts were still in effect in military cantonments throughout India.[24] Writing from Switzerland in October 1886 she called for an LNA circular to be issued on the subject, declaring, "we must never give up til we have avenged the wrongs of Indian and Chinese women as well as others. . . . For twenty years Indian women have been oppressed and outraged . . . and by a *Christian* nation!"[25] The situation in India necessitated the continued existence of the LNA, which Butler urged be maintained as "a separate *woman's* organisation" for at least a year. As it turned out, unlike the men's National Association, which disbanded almost at once, the LNA lived on with its local and regional networks virtually intact, justifying itself at least partly in imperial terms for the next thirty years.[26]

Butler's Indian crusade followed the model of the original "home" campaign, using the same tactics that had eventually brought success in Britain. This meant that the initiatives on behalf of Indian prostitutes were chiefly parliamentary, and at first involved working for a House of Commons resolution that would compel the government of India to abide by the repeal statute passed at home. Repeal in India was officially declared in 1888, but several species of "Cantonment Rules" continued to operate there under the direction of army officials—rules that permitted brothels to operate within regimental lines and subjected Indian women to the, by now infamous, compulsory examination.[27] Hence throughout the period 1888–1915 the LNA and the affiliated British Indian Committee lobbied Parliament to enforce repeal in India and tried to keep the "Indian scandal" prominently before the public. Together they dispatched agents to India, submitted memorials to the Indian and home governments, published several journals and a steady stream of pamphlets, and organized meetings all over the British Isles. As Butler observed in 1893, "All Abolitionists . . . by this time are aware that the question of highest interest presented . . . [to them] is that of India."[28]

At this point the imperial rationale behind the Butlerites' Indian commitment requires further elaboration. It may appear that the ladies of the LNA were concerned with the condition of Indian women, and to some degree they were. They railed against the exploitation of their Indian "sisters" at the hands of regulationists and made the liberation of Indian women from organized prostitution their main objective over the years, resisting attempts by Anglo-Indian officials and the British medical community to divert their attention to the British soldier in India. "For us women of the LNA," wrote Butler in 1897, "the question can never be so narrowed down. . . . We feel deeply for the ill-guided and corrupted young soldiers but we feel as deeply for the Indian women. Their cause is our cause, their griefs are our griefs."[29] With the same singularity of conviction she had displayed in the English campaign, Butler insisted that the mistreatment of Indian women must remain the vitally important issue.

Still, most repealers, Butler included, did not view the cause of Indian women as an end in itself, but rather as a means of ensuring the well-being of their own England. Immediately after the Acts were repealed at home fears arose about a counter-movement to reinstate them. From its beginning the repeal crusade for India was advocated on the grounds that regulation anywhere in the empire meant its sure return to England.[30] Anxiety about neoregulation ebbed and flowed until World War I, and the panic that ensued frequently inspired renewed enthusiasm for the Indian cause.[31] Reformers for India argued that even though England was an island, it could not afford to be complacent: "The water flows in from all sides," cautioned one observer, "and . . . we in England must either be militant in this matter to keep the tide off, or else the tide will come in upon us."[32] This essentially defensive posture can also be seen in the argument most commonly advanced for Indian repeal—i.e., that soldiers who had consorted with Indian women would return home physically diseased and morally corrupted.[33] Petitioners in one "mothers' memorial" for Indian repeal worried that the impact of the Acts "cannot be confined to the Army, but must permeate the whole of our social life . . . [and] cannot leave unimpaired the sanctity or happiness of the English home."[34] From the perspective of these reformers the health of the home county was as important, if not more so, than the health of Indian women.

It could be argued up to a point that Butler and company extended their campaign naturally to empire because they perceived little distinction between "home" society and, in this instance, India. Butler often referred to Indian women as "our Indian fellow subjects," echoing longstanding ideals of imperial citizenship and indicating her belief that Indians and Britons were all members of equal status in the larger comity of nations. And yet the imperial power relationship was inescapable. Nor was it strenuously denied. On the contrary, the preservation of imperial rule seemed to be at the heart of the Indian cause. In the first memorial presented by the LNA to the government of India in 1888 Butler and her supporters declared:

> We, as women, desire to protest in the strongest and most solemn manner possible against the wrong done to our sisters and fellow subjects in India. At the same time we venture to warn you of the danger to our Indian rule in thus trifling with the best instincts of the people. We have reason to believe that the seeds of rebellion are being rapidly propagated, especially in the Punjab, the inhabitants of which have hitherto been among the most loyal of our Indian subjects. Nothing so surely produces a spirit of rebellion as trampling on the womanhood of a subject race by its conquerors.[35]

The LNA here and elsewhere articulated late nineteenth-century fears about imperial instability and reinforced post-Mutiny imperial ideology that claimed to rely on moral influence rather than military force to guarantee Britain's civilizing presence in India.[36] Butler and her followers offered support for the imperial/moral enterprise by pledging English women's philanthropic activity on behalf of colonized peoples. To do so was to ally the female reform cause to the imperial one by making the two mutually dependent. For Butler tended to view empire as a field of opportunity for English women, a place for them to exercise their philanthropic skills among deserving natives. "Have you leisure? Have you strength?" she inquired of her audience in 1887. "If so . . . . there is a career open, a wide field extending to many parts of the world, a far-off cry of distress waiting for response."[37] The British empire and its dominions provided the occasion for "a just and purifying victory for Imperial England" even as it presented a vast and uncharted workplace for female reform efforts.[38]

For most LNA workers, however, India remained an imaginative landscape. Repeal work was mainly litigative; Butler and her co-workers had little or no direct contact with Indian women. They relied on the accounts of agents they sent to India to observe conditions and gather evidence of ongoing state regulation in the cantonments. But lack of personal contact did not prevent them from claiming to know and to understand their Indian "sisters," whose half-glimpsed lives fascinated them. One of the most telling consequences of the repealers' long Indian crusade was the image they constructed of "the Indian woman" and the hierarchical relationship they presumed to exist between themselves as Western feminists and their "backward" Indian counterparts.

Significantly, this feminist-imperial hierarchy was rooted in contemporary feminist notions of "woman's" role in the advancement of civilization. According to the feminist reform ideology shaped by Butler and her national repeal movement, society progressed by women ministering to each other and thus uplifting social conditions as a whole. Underlying this vision was the belief that only women could know the true needs of women (and interestingly enough, by implication, the true needs of society as well). As Butler remarked toward the end of her life, "it is perfectly true that women will see things in connection with our betrayed sisters which men do not so easily see, and that they will have influence in . . . drawing information from them which one would not expect men to have in the same way."[39] In the case of Indian women, Butler equated commonality of gender with knowledge about Indian women's lives, even though the LNA only received such "knowledge" secondhand. Given the fact that such secondhand knowledge was based mainly on Indian women designated as or assumed to be prostitutes, the repealers' claims to have learned "The Truth about Indian Women" is somewhat problematic.[40]

To their credit, some women working for Indian reform tried to dispel the myth that Indian women were inherently licentious and immoral. Katharine Bushnell and Elizabeth Andrew, two American women who traveled to India in the early 1890s on behalf of the LNA, recounted their conversations with Indian prostitutes (via interpreter) in the cantonments and assured their British public that, contrary to what military officials reported, Indian women were *not* without shame. Of all the Indian prostitutes they interviewed, Andrew boasted, "*not one* ever defended her way of living."[41] The extent to which these interpretations were broadcast may be evidenced in the speaking tours Bushnell and Andrew made throughout Britain after their return from India. One of their favorite lectures was entitled "The Inextinguishable Sentiment of Dignity in Eastern Womanhood." During the course of these talks Bushnell and Andrew typically described the terrible conditions in the cantonments and detailed the miserable lives of Indian women connected to them. They also testified to native women's hostility to the system of regulated prostitution, concluding that "This resistance is, in itself, proof of the imperishable dignity of woman's nature, to be found alike in the untutored slave of the Orient and in the freer representative of the Western world."[42]

These characterizations could not be persuasive, however, without the implicit understanding of some marked imperial assumptions. As much as we might appreciate Bushnell and Andrew's challenge to negative Western male stereotypes of "Oriental" female sexuality, they set themselves up in judgment over it, blaming what they saw as Indian women's degradation on Indian cultural and religious backwardness. The repealers did not deny that the imported European system of regulation was responsible for the suffering of Indian women, but neither did they spare what they perceived as the oppression of native custom. "On *every* Oriental woman's head is set a price, she is regarded merely as a *chattel*," lamented Bushnell and Andrew, "she has no rights in herself, and no liberty of choice as to whether she will be pure or not." Criticism of native custom had the familiar ring of British superiority and moreover implied that Indian culture was in need of "cleaning up" by feminist reformers. In a culture where child-marriage and widow-burning still persisted, they asked themselves, how could women be expected to progress unless reform occurred? In the meantime, the publicity Butler and her reform organizations gave to the "authentic Indian woman" contained devaluations of Indian culture which perpetuated assumptions about Indian "barbarism" and prescribed a distinctly subordinate position for Indian women in relation to their liberated English "sisters."

At times their critical judgments were not very subtle. In an editorial comment in *The Storm-bell* (an LNA publication) of June 1898, Butler lamented that Indian women were

> indeed between the upper and nether millstone, helpless, voiceless, hopeless. Their helplessness appeals to the heart, in somewhat the same way in which the helplessness and suffering of a dumb animal does, under the knife of a vivisector. Somewhere, halfway between the Martyr Saints and the tortured 'friend of man,' the noble dog, stand, it seems to me, these pitiful Indian women, girls, children, as many of them are. They have not even the small power of resistance which the western woman may have . . . who may have some clearer knowledge of a just and pitiful God to whom she may make her mute appeal.[43]

While this comment tells us something about Butler's sympathy for the anti-vivisectionist movement, it is also an un–self-conscious disclosure of how she perceived the ordering of a world which she believed to contain imperial and colonial peoples, as well as imperial and colonial women. Expressing sentiments that neatly parallel the logic of Britain's imperial presence in India, Butler hoped that under the tutelage of British female social reformers, Indian women would be led "into a position of greater freedom and light, which will enable them to fight their own battles."[44] In the interim, she viewed India's women as helpless victims, and repealers like Bushnell and Andrew as "the mothers of the orphaned girls in India."[45]

In both her activities on behalf of Indian women and in the high profile she gave the Indian cause for two decades, Butler helped to shape a brand of maternal imperialism whose premises were shared by many feminists and female reformers of the period.[46] At the time of Butler's death in 1906 the British Committee and the LNA both undertook a re-evaluation of their goals and principles, and decided that as long as regulation still operated, whether officially or unofficially, in the empire, they would continue to make imperial concerns the focus of their activities. What had begun as an escalation of imperial rhetoric in 1887 was by the twentieth century fully established in the LNA's platform. As the lifelong repealer Helen Wilson phrased it in 1908: "England is still the mother country, and has the mother influence. She has that influence for both good and evil; mistakes she made years ago, though she may have repented them, are apt to be perpetuated in her children beyond the seas."[47]

Feminist Writings and "The Indian Woman"

The LNA's campaign against the Indian C.D. Acts was unique in many respects, but its attention to matters of empire was not unusual among middle-class feminists of the period. Feminist periodical literature from 1865 to 1915 featured scores of items about Indian women, many of which depicted them as the special imperial burden of Englishwomen and, more particularly, of British feminists. Relying on the subjection of "the Indian woman" as evidence, many feminists of the period imagined, as Butler did, that the larger world of women was an imperialized one. The repeated invocation of Indian women as enslaved, degraded, and in need of salvation by their British feminist "sisters" indicates how pervasive imperial assumptions were among middle-class feminists. It also suggests that in addition to being liberatory for English women, the new feminist world order which late Victorian British feminists championed was distinctively imperial as well.

Feminist periodicals were an important site for the production and reproduction of feminist ideology, of which images of Indian, Eastern, and "Oriental" womanhood were an essential part. What Lisa Tickner has written about the spectacle of the early twentieth-century suffrage movement applies equally to the self-consciously constructed space of the weekly and monthly magazines: in a climate where notions of "femininity" and "womanliness" were appropriated and distorted by detractors, both spectacle *and* text were media that feminists authorized themselves.[48] By creating visual images of women which embodied industry and competence, for example, feminist artists rejected the caricature of the hysteric and argued for the right to establish their own definitions of themselves as women. In a similar way feminist periodicals, whose purpose could be programmatic or purely informational, were arenas where feminist argument could be worked, reworked, and ultimately controlled. As with spectacle, control over the textual space was a means of empowerment and authority. The genre itself was among the most powerful weapons in the feminist arsenal and must be seen as it was used—not as a passive showcase but as an instrument of power and legitimation.

The Englishwoman's Review (1866–1905), one of the first feminist periodicals,[49] presented articles on India and Indian women within the first two years of publication. "The Position of Women in India" was part of a series on national types by a Mrs. Bayle Bernard and was based on two books about Indian women that had recently been published in England.[50] Mary Carpenter's two-volume *Six Months in India* is the basis of her article. Bernard quotes extensively from Carpenter's work, sharing the author's relief at the discovery that polygamy is "almost obsolete among the upper classes" in India but hastening to note that, uneducated and imprisoned in the harem all their lives, "the women of an Indian household [are] a constant source of bad influence."[51] On the whole, the picture Bernard paints is a dismal and disparaging one, emphasizing the "sunless, airless" existence of the *zenana* (women's quarters), hinting at child-marriage and remarking that the most enlightened Indian women are those married to Christian converts. She does, however, share Carpenter's confidence that Indian women are educable (hence, redeemable) and that their education is a task to which English women in and outside of India must address themselves: "let them throw their hearts and souls into the work, and determine never to rest until they have raised their Eastern sisters to their own level; and then may the women of India at last attain a position honourable to themselves and to England, instead of, as is now so generally the case, filling one . . . [sic] with feelings of sorrow and shame."[52] Her concluding exhortation to the women of England underlines her self-interested attitude toward Indian women, who appear to be most valuable for the possibilities of charitable rescue and imperial pride they promise.

Bernard's article was the first of many in the *Englishwoman's Review* to examine the lives of Indian women; following it were such features as "The Burmese Woman," "Women under Mahommedan Law," "Women Doctors in India," "Zenana Societies," and the like. Books on India were often reviewed and news about India continuously appeared in the columns "Events of the Period" and "Foreign and Colonial Notes." These latter began as brief features but developed over time into full-fledged sections of the quarterly magazine. The Indian column usually contained synopses from Indian newspapers or from the journal of the Indian National Association, noting important events in India, advertising lectures in England pertinent to Indian questions, or announcing Indian visitors to London. Here the focus was on Indian women, their activities in England, and, increasingly after the 1880s, their academic successes at Indian universities and British institutions. The career of Pandita Ramabai, an Indian social reformer who studied at Cheltenham Ladies' College and later opened a school for Hindu widows at Poona, was followed quite closely in this column, as were the activities and achievements of Rukhmabai, the Sorabji sisters, and others.[53] For the readers of the *Englishwoman's Review*, many if not most of whom we can presume never went to India, this magazine provided a steady diet of information, analysis, and speculation about Indian women for nearly half a century.

The *Women's Suffrage Journal*, edited 1870–90 by Lydia Becker, was a more political, more specifically suffragist periodical.[54] Though its life was shorter and its individual issues briefer than the *Englishwoman's Review*, it too gave frequent notice to Indian women. In October 1871, for example, the *Women's Suffrage Journal* reported that "a Hindu caste lady" by the name of Sree Rungamba Garu delivered a public lecture on the need for female education and improvement to an audience of men in India.[55] No editorial comment was made and in general the journal reprinted excerpts from newspapers like the *Indian Daily News* or the *Madras Mail*, rather than writing its own pieces on Indian women. A recurrent and clearly popular figure was the Begum of Bhopal, whose leadership and administrative good sense should, it was argued, recommend her to skeptics of women's political capabilities. "Illustrious Indian Ladies" like the Begum were cited as "proof of what even Indian women, with all their disadvantages, can become."[56]

The *Women's Penny Paper* (later the *Woman's Herald*), which has been called "the most vigorous feminist paper of its time," ran from 1888 to 1893 and appealed to probably the most diverse group of Victorian women who called or thought of themselves as feminists. Suffrage, temperance, prostitution, women in the professions, vegetarianism, Rational Dress—the *Women's Penny Paper* embraced all of these in, as David Doughan and Denise Sanchez have written, a spirit of "lively and uncompromising feminism" unequaled by any other journal of the period.[57] Its founding editor, Henrietta Muller, had a well-developed interest in India, and so the columns of the paper sponsored a wide variety of pieces on Indian women. An overview of the magazine's five-year run turns up articles on Pandita Ramabai, Hindu child wives, medical women in India, "How to Help Indian Women," lectures on Indian women, debates on theosophy, travel descriptions of Ceylon and Burma and, very occasionally, interviews with Indian women, such as the excerpt on Sonderabai Powar in 1893.

What all this attention to Indian women represents is an objectification of "the Oriental woman" by English feminist interpreters. Largely as a result of the journalistic exposure given to the topic, by the 1890s discussion of "the position of Indian women" had become so formulaic that one writer feared, "There is perhaps some danger of . . . [the public] becoming wearied by a too frequent repetition of the story."[58] The recital of woes usually began with a description of the inside of the *zenana*, followed by observations of the relationship between an Indian husband and his wives, then commentary on the practice of child-marriage, culminating in what was perceived as the final condemnation of Indian life: the treatment of widows as outcasts. In these narratives the voices of Indian women appear only erratically, and when one is quoted it is rarely mentioned whether the

woman in question spoke to the interviewers in English or through an interpreter. The number of English women who spoke Indian vernaculars
was notoriously—and by their own admission, deplorably—small.[59]

As with Josephine Butler, there was an assumption on the part of many
British feminists that their "femaleness" gave them an understanding of
Indian women that transcended national and racial boundaries. The common bond of motherhood was also considered a transcendent link. This
may appear to be a spontaneous reaction between women of different cultures; indeed, it became a tenet of "international sisterhood."[60] But in this
instance it must be located in its specifically British feminist-imperial context. British feminists of the period *posited* "woman" the world over as one
class, one race, one nation—a static type that, in "less civilized" societies
than Britain, was corrupted by heathen cultures and religions. In light of
this construct, the attention lavished on India and its women in periodicals
like the *Women's Penny Paper* had the effect of stripping Indian women of
their foreignness, their exoticism, thereby domesticating them for a British
audience. Much like Bushnell and Andrew, feminists writing for periodicals were concerned with defusing the eroticism often attributed to women
of the East by Western male commentators. But since Indian women rarely
spoke for themselves in these controlled textual spaces, British feminists
robbed them of their power to name themselves, effectively silencing them
in the name of feminist "sisterly" protectiveness. In the process, they underscored their own moral purity and legitimized themselves as the imperial authorities on "Indian womanhood."

The quest for feminist imperial authority was not limited to feminist social reformers or constitutional suffragists. *Votes for Women*, which was the
organ of the National Women's Social and Political Union between 1907
and 1918 (and, until 1912, the official mouthpiece of the Pankhursts), represented militant feminists' concern for Indian women and imperial matters. From the outset it was dedicated to "all women all over the world, of
whatever race, or creed, or calling, whether they be with us or against us in
this fight."[61] A column entitled "Women of Other Lands" was a regular
feature of this monthly journal. And, considering the level of domestic suffrage activity—including marches, window-smashing, petitioning, and the
arrest and forcible feeding of many suffragettes—pieces like "The Changing East," "The Awakening of Indian Womanhood," "Woman's Place in
Hinduism," and a variety of articles on Turkish women appeared with remarkable regularity.

The militants proclaimed that the cause of woman was one throughout
the world, and by the twentieth century they were noting with pride the
progress made by their Eastern "sisters," many of whom were quitting the
harem, becoming educated, and leaving the life of *purdah* (seclusion) for
good.[62] The editors of *Votes for Women* were greatly intrigued by the up-
heavals in Turkey and observed with approbation that Turkish women
were being included in the new reform councils. Their enthusiasm, how-

ever, was tempered. In an editorial in September 1908 Christabel Pankhurst warned that Eastern women should not expect to be given political equality when their Western sisters were still denied this fundamental right. British women, she wrote,

> have nothing to say against the enfranchisement of their fellow creatures in any part of the world, but they feel it hard, that being the rightful heirs to the constitutional liberty built up by their foremothers and forefathers, they should have that inheritance withheld, while men of other races are suddenly and almost without preparation leaping into possession of constitutional power.[63]

Both moderates and militants advocated the vote for white women over black men but rarely were their priorities (or their resentments) so baldly spelled out.[64] Pankhurst went on to claim that the British had created the very idea of sex equality, and therefore to British women emancipation would and should come first.

Pankhurst voiced a sentiment that was expressed by many suffrage workers, both militant and nonmilitant, during the first decade of the twentieth century—namely, that England was the "storm-centre" of the international women's movement and that British feminists should fight their own sex equality battles first, so that they could then aid women of other nations in doing the same.[65] It seemed fitting to this generation of feminists that, since England was the Mother of Parliaments *and* the mother country of the empire, it should be acknowledged as the "Mother of the new world-wide movement" as well.[66] They saw it not only as the role of women of other nations, both West and East, to fall in behind, but also as part of the natural order of things in a world where Britain was the imperial leader. Feminists' preoccupation with the condition of women in India and the East not only expresses their imperial assumptions but also underscores a militant national and racial pride which characterized the diverse campaigns for female emancipation in Britain.

This pride is immediately apparent in suffrage literature, where feminists, in claiming their right to citizenship, also claimed their right to be part of the political nation and empire. At times suffragists conflated the idea of nation with the idea of empire. In other words, they believed that the nation into which they sought admission did not just extend to empire, but that citizenship in the nation meant citizenship in the empire as well.[67] Winning the vote "for the women of the empire," bringing female emancipation to "England and her Dependencies"—these were standard feminist cries. It went without saying that the "women" who were to receive the grant of citizenship hoped for by suffragists were the white women of England and the colonies.[68] For late nineteenth- and early twentieth-century middle-class feminists, as for many of their contemporaries, whether they sympathized with votes for women or not, pride in empire was as "natural" and as "right" as pride in nation, since empire and nation could be taken as one and the same. As a speaker at a woman's suffrage rally in Manchester in 1880 reminded her audience, "At Westminster . . . the clock of empire strikes; every time it sounds it marks an epoch in the history of nations, and far and wide, to the very ends of the earth, men hold their breath and listen for the voice of England pealing out in power from Westminster."[69] What feminists wanted above all was to share in this national and imperial power, to participate in what one suffragist called "the moral government of the world."[70]

It bears emphasizing here that feminists believed in the idea of racial progress, and that for them as for many Victorians empire itself was an outward and visible sign of Britain's racial supremacy. Even if the idea of conquering native peoples offended some sensibilities,[71] the promotion of enlightened government through moral example appealed enormously to feminists who believed that the redemptive power of their sex lay in its superior moral qualities. Progress, as the language of Butler's campaign indicates, did not, could not exist in a vacuum. It had necessarily to function in comparison to something else, something less well developed and, ultimately, something less "civilized." For British feminists of the period that point of comparison was the woman of the East. She was a pivotal reference in arguments for female emancipation and she became the embodiment of personal, social, and political subjection in a decaying civilization—the very symbol, in short, of what British feminists were struggling to progress away *from* in their own struggle for liberation.

At first glance these references seem incongruous because they crop up in apparently unlikely places. Sometime in the 1870s Sidney Smith read a paper entitled "The Enfranchisement of Women the Law of the Land." By the third page of his speech he had referred to the status of Turkish women twice, and had this to say about women of the East:

> I well remember the plenipotentiary of an Indian prince declaring to me that he had discovered the reason for the subjection of the Hindoos to the Saxons. "In the zenana," he said, "we have secluded our women, and made them wholly unfit to make intelligent men and women of their children." . . . What [asked Smith] has ruined Turkey and every Eastern country but leaving the culture of each rising generation to the sultans and female slaves of the seraglio and the harem?[72]

Harriet Taylor, the early suffrage theorist, refers several times in her essay "Enfranchisement of Women" to Asian women, who

> were and are the slaves of men for the purposes of sensuality . . . [and who] instead of murmuring at their seclusion, and at the restraint imposed upon them, pride themselves on it, and are astonished at the affrontery of women who receive visits from male acquaintances, and are seen in the streets unveiled. Habits of submission make men as well as women servile-minded.[73]

Not all feminist observers believed that Indian women were powerless simply by virtue of their confinement in the *zenana*. Emily Pfeiffer claimed they had just as much power within the walls as any Englishwomen did inside her home.[74] While this was not an uncommon interpretation of what was perceived as an unhealthy situation, even sympathetic feminists tended to fall back on familiar stereotypes. Millicent Fawcett agreed with Pfeiffer but, she reminded, "Among savage races [which she apparently felt Indians to be] women have little better lives than beasts of burden" and "in the semi-civilisations of the East we know that women are valued principally as inmates of the Seraglio."[75] The embeddedness of references to "the Indian woman" throughout British feminist writings should not blind us to the centrality of this female Other in British feminist thinking. Although Indian women of the period were active in social reform and feminist causes of their own making, many British feminists insisted on creating them as passive colonial subjects partly in order to imagine and to realize their own feminist objectives within the context of the imperial nation into which they sought admission.

Toward a British Imperial Feminism

The implications of the British imperial context for the development of middle-class British feminism are difficult for many of us in the late twentieth century to countenance—despite the ongoing insistence of non-Western feminists that we look critically at the historical roots and Orientalist presumptions of our own feminist ideologies.[76] Josephine Butler was clearly not alone in her generation when she conceptualized Indian women as lower on a scale of human development than her European "sisters"—somewhere "between the Martyr saints . . . and the noble dog." Middle-class British feminists of the period added another dimension to this imperial "great chain of being" by reinforcing already accepted racial/cultural hierarchies with a feminist-justified hierarchy of "civilizedness" rooted in the (perceived) status of women in a culture. It is not too much to say that in so doing, they appropriated to themselves as imperial Britons the highest and most legitimate form of "feminism," in the same way that they appropriated, as imperial Britons, the highest forms of "civilization" and "culture."

Any study of women's interest in empire shadowboxes with both an imperial and a feminist historiography, neither of which has sufficiently noted the degree to which British women, and in this case, Victorian feminists, were conscious of and affected by living in an imperial culture. Bourgeois feminists of the period certainly did not believe that empire was "no place for a white woman."[77] To the contrary, her influence there was thought to be essential if empire was to flourish. Identification with Britain's empire was implicit in a variety of middle-class feminist programs as

they grew and developed from the 1860s onward, with imperial ideals unit-
ing feminists of different stripes who appeared at times to have little else in
common. While it may be remarkable to us, conditioned as we have been
to conceive of empire as a masculine space, feminist interest in India did
not, I think, seem particularly exceptional to this class and generation of
British feminists (which may in part explain feminist historians' neglect of
it). Their concern for Indian women was part of a complex of cultural assumptions which, shaped also by an emerging middle-class feminist perspective itself, dictated a "white woman's burden" that was as natural to
them as empire itself appeared to be.

Historians must not lose sight of the fact that feminism(s) are and always
will be as much quests for power as they are battles for rights. Nineteenth-
century feminists sought empowerment by a variety of means—education,
the vote, welfare legislation—not the least of which was by allying their
cause with British imperial rule. The international feminist vision which reformers like Butler cherished held out the promise of global sisterhood
based on equality and "womanly values." That promise went largely un-
fulfilled because their particular, historically specific brand of feminism depended on the relative, if temporary, powerlessness of non-white women.
In the context of the long, bitter, and fundamentally revolutionary struggle
for female emancipation, British feminists' strategic use of "the Indian
woman" will no doubt be considered by some to have borne little relation
to their real attitudes toward "real" Indian women. The very important distinctions between rhetoric and practice, between tactical expedience and
personal philosophies, are certainly matters for future consideration. In a
crucial sense, British feminists of the period were trapped within an imperial discourse they did not create and perhaps which they could not escape.
That they collaborated in the ideological work of empire implicates them
and the legacy of Western feminism we have inherited from them.

NOTES

1. This essay has profited from the insights and continuing interest of Peter
Marshall, Emmet Larkin, Barney Cohn, Barbara Ramusack, Nupur Chaudhuri, Peg
Strobel, Deb Rossum, David Doughan, Emie Aronson, George Robb, Steve John-
stone, and Gerri and David Burton. Leora Auslander's critical comments on several
versions of this piece for both the Annual Meeting of the AAS, April 1990, and the
Berkshire Conference of Women Historians, June 1990, have made all the difference. A version of this article appeared in *Women's Studies International Forum* 13,
no. 4 (1990), 295–308; reprinted with the permission of Pergamon Press.

2. Valerie Amos and Pratibha Parmar, "Challenging Imperial Feminism." *Feminist Review* 17 (Autumn 1984): 3–17 and Mariana Valverde, "A Passion for Purity"
(review of Sheila Jeffreys, ed., *The Sexuality Debates*), *The Women's Review of Books* 5,
no. 6 (Jan. 1988): 6–7 are two recent exceptions to this rule.

3. The term is Helen Callaway's. See her *Gender, Culture, and Empire: European Women in Colonial Nigeria* (London: Macmillan Press, 1987), 5.

4. Richard Evans, *The Feminists: Women's Emancipation Movements in Europe, America and Australasia, 1840–1920* (London: Croom Helm, 1977), 18–33.

5. See for example John Mackenzie's *Propaganda and Empire: The Manipulation of British Public Opinion 1880–1960* (Manchester: Manchester University Press, 1984), in which he argues that imperialism was "a core ideology" in British culture and society in the period under consideration (1–10). See also Mackenzie, ed., *Imperialism and Popular Culture* (Manchester: Manchester University Press, 1986), together with C.J.D. Duder's review of it in *Victorian Studies* 30, no. 4: 528–29.

6. Olive Banks, *Faces of Feminism* (New York: St. Martin's Press, 1981), especially chap. 6; Jane Rendall, *The Origins of Modern Feminism: Women in Britain, France and the United States 1760–1860* (London: Macmillan Press, 1985); Martha Vicinus, *Independent Women: Work and Community for Single Women 1850–1920* (London: Virago Press, 1985) and Evans, *The Feminists*, 36.

7. Valverde, "Passion," 6–7.

8. Frederic Harrison, "The Emancipation of Women," *Fortnightly Review* (Oct. 1891): 437–52.

9. G. R. Searle, *The Quest for National Efficiency* (Berkeley: University of California Press, 1971), 1–13; R. A. Soloway, *Birth Control and the Population Question in England 1877–1930* (Chapel Hill: University of North Carolina Press, 1982), chap. 2; and Frank Mort, "Health and Hygiene: The Edwardian State and Medico-Moral Politics," in Jane Beckett and Deborah Cherry, eds., *The Edwardian Era* (London: Phaedon Press and the Barbican Art Gallery, 1987), 26 and passim.

10. Mona Caird, *Why Do Women Want the Franchise?* (London: Women's Emancipation Union Pamphlets, 1892).

11. Anna Davin, "Imperialism and Motherhood," *History Workshop Journal* 5 (Spring 1978): 9–65.

12. Helen Blackburn, *Women's Suffrage: A Record of the Women's Suffrage Movement in the British Isles* (London: Williams and Norgate, 1902) and Charlotte Carmichael Stopes, *British Freewomen: Their Historical Privilege* (London: n.p., 1894).

13. Brian Harrison, *Separate Spheres: The Opposition to Women's Suffrage in Britain* (New York: Holmes and Meier, 1978).

14. Judith Walkowitz, "Male Vice and Feminist Virtue: Feminism and the Politics of Prostitution in Nineteenth-Century Britain," *History Workshop Journal* 13 (Spring 1982), 79–93.

15. By the twentieth century Lord Minto considered India to be governed less by force than by the "mere prestige of British authority." Quoted in Ronald Hyam, *Britain's Imperial Century 1815–1914: A Study of Empire and Expansion* (New York: Barnes and Noble, 1976), 160.

16. Frances Hutchins, *The Illusion of Permanence: British Imperialism in India* (Princeton: Princeton University Press, 1967), 137, 139.

17. I first found this quote in Arnold P. Kaminsky, *The India Office 1880–1910* (New York: Greenwood Press, 1986), 160, but he acknowledges his source as P. Sen, *Florence Nightingale's Letters* (Calcutta, 1937), 16–17.

18. Mary Carpenter, *Six Months in India,* 2 vols. (London: Longman's Green, 1868); Jo Manton, *Mary Carpenter and the Children of the Streets* (London: Heinemann Educational Books, 1976); and Barbara Ramusack, "Cultural Missionaries, Maternal Imperialists, Feminist Allies: British Women Activists in India, 1865–1945," this volume.

19. Margaret Balfour and Ruth Young, *The Work of Medical Women in India* (Oxford: Oxford University Press, 1929).

20. Judith Walkowitz's *Prostitution and Victorian Society: Women, Class and the State* (Cambridge: Cambridge University Press, 1980) is the pioneer work on the C.D. Acts in England. She makes brief mention of the repeal movement in the empire but her study ends with the repeal victory at home in 1886. Margaret Forster's chapter on Butler in her *Significant Sisters: The Grassroots of Active Feminism 1839–1939* (New York: Alfred Knopf, 1985), 197, alludes to Butler's interest in India, and Butler's grandson refers to the Indian campaign briefly. See A.S.G. Butler, *Portrait of Josephine Butler* (London: Faber and Faber, 1954), 142–48.

21. Walkowitz, *Prostitution and Victorian Society*, chap. 5 and especially p. 110.

22. Ibid., epilog and especially p. 255. See also Susan Kingsley Kent, *Sex and Suffrage in Britain 1860–1914* (Princeton: Princeton University Press, 1987) chaps. 2 and 6.

23. Josephine Butler, *The New Abolitionists* (London: Dyer Brothers, 1876), 192–94. The letter was written by Keshub Chunder Sen, an Indian reformer whom Butler met personally in her home in Liverpool, according to her recollection of the event thirty years later.

24. Butler to the Priestman sisters, May 2, 1886. Butler Autograph Letter Collection, Fawcett Library, London. All Butler letters referred to are in the BALC unless otherwise specified.

25. Butler to the Priestman sisters, Oct. 19, 1886.

26. The Ladies' National Association became the LNA for the Abolition of the State Regulation of Vice and the Promotion of Social Purity in June 1910 and amalgamated formally with the British Branch of the British, Continental and General Federation in October 1915, adopting the name The Association for the Promotion of Moral and Social Hygiene. *The Shield*, which had been the organ of the original repeal movement, ceased publication in 1886 but was revived in 1897 as the British Committee's publication, though it routinely covered LNA news. After 1915 it became the official organ of the APMSH. See *A Rough Record of Events and Incidents Connected with the Repeal of the 'Contagious Diseases Acts 1864–69' in the United Kingdom, and the Movement against the State Regulation of Vice in India and the Colonies 1858–1906* (Sheffield: "printed for private circulation," n.d.), Fawcett Library (hereafter, FL), London.

27. Maurice Gregory, "The Exact Position of the Regulation of Prostitution at the Present Moment, as Set Forth by the Cantonment Code of October 1st 1899," *The Shield* (Feb. and Mar. 1900).

28. Josephine Butler, "Current Events—India," *The Dawn* (July 1893): 1.

29. Josephine Butler as quoted in the LNA *Annual Meeting* (1897), 27. See also the *Sentinel* for May and September 1887.

30. Josephine Butler, LNA *Annual Meeting* (1887), 40. In the first issue of *The Storm-bell* in January 1898, Butler reminded repealers that India was the "first step" toward bringing repeal home again. In the LNA *Annual Meeting* of the same year it was argued that "You cannot do wrong in India without the effects of it being felt in the Strand."

31. In a letter to the Quaker repealer Joseph Edmonson, Henry J. Wilson wrote that he feared a " 'Regulationists' Flank Movement' of a most dangerous kind. If it remains in India, we shall have attempts on similar lines nearer home. Indeed, in my opinion, the battle ground for England now lies in India; . . . [we must] [*sic*] at once . . . commence an attack on the Cantonment Act." H. J. Wilson to Edmonson, July 30, 1891 (box 80, FL). Wilson was an M.P. and a staunch supporter of both phases of the repeal movement.

32. James Stuart, LNA *Annual Meeting* (1896), 87.

33. James Stuart to H. J. Wilson, August 16, 1893 (box 80, FL).

34. *The Shield*, Dec. 1897.

35. LNA Memorial to Lord Salisbury, April 3, 1888 (box 80, FL).

36. Hutchins, *Illusion of Permanence* and Hyam, *Britain's Imperial Century*.

37. Josephine Butler, *The Revival and Extension of the Abolitionist Cause* (London: Dyer Brothers, 1887): 51–52.

38. Josephine Butler, "Mrs. Butler's Plea" (1893), 8.

39. Reprinted in *The Shield*, May 1903. This was a pre-feminist idea. Sarah Stickney Ellis, author of etiquette books, praised the bond of sisterhood which, she claimed, "arises chiefly out of . . . [women's] mutual knowledge of each other's capacity of receiving pain." Quoted in Vicinus, *Independent Women*, 34.

40. See *The Storm-bell* of January 1898 for an article of that title.

41. Elizabeth Andrew, "Report of the Delegates," *The Dawn* (July 1985): 10–11.

42. Ibid., 8–12.

43. Josephine Butler, *The Storm-Bell* (June 1898): 59.

44. Josephine Butler, *The Sentinel* (Sept. 1887): 113.

45. Josephine Butler, *The Storm-Bell* (June 1898): 60.

46. "Maternal imperialism" is originally Barbara Ramusack's term. See her "Cultural Missionaries."

47. *The Shield*, May 1908.

48. Lisa Tickner, *The Spectacle of Women: Imagery of the Suffrage Campaign 1907–1914* (Chicago: University of Chicago Press, 1988), 81 and passim.

49. David Doughan and Denise Sanchez, eds., *Feminist Periodicals 1855–1984: An Annotated Bibliography of British, Irish, Commonwealth and International Titles* (Sussex: Harvester Press, 1987). See introduction and p. 3.

50. Mrs. Bayle Bernard, "The Position of Women in India," *Englishwoman's Review* [henceforth, *EWR*] (July 1868). "The Position of Women in America," *EWR* (July 1867) and "The Women of Brazil," *EWR* (July 1869) were the other two in the series.

51. Bernard, "Position," 474, 475.

52. Ibid., 477, 482.

53. For references to Ramabai, see *EWR* (Oct. 1878), (Feb. 1880), (Oct. 1887); for notice of Cornelia Sorabji and other "lady lawyers," see *EWR* (Oct. 1902); and for Rukmabai, see *EWR* (Apr. 1887).

54. Doughan and Sanchez, *Feminist Periodicals*, 4–5.

55. *Women's Suffrage Journal* (Oct. 1871): 109.

56. *Women's Suffrage Journal* (Oct. 1878): 174.

57. Doughan and Sanchez, *Feminist Periodicals*, 13.

58. Mrs. E. F. Chapman, *Sketches of Some Distinguished Indian Women* (London: n.p., 1891), 1.

59. While some English women living in India may have taken the time to learn native languages and dialects, the vast majority did not. One Indian women writing in English bemoaned this failure, though she did appreciate the Queen's attempts to learn Hindustani. "Social Intercourse between European and Indian Ladies: Where There Is a Will There Is a Way" (no author given), *The Indian Ladies' Magazine* (Aug. 1901): 29.

60. Many of the major British women's organizations—the NUWSS, the WSPU, the WFL—belonged to the International Women's Suffrage Alliance, whose very raison d'être was its commitment to international sisterhood. Carrie Chapman Catt, an American suffragist and president of the IWSA, warned England to beware of excessive national pride: "So long as there is one woman in the world who is taught that she was born an inferior being . . . there is work for you." Quoted in *Common Cause* (July 13, 1911). The rhetoric of "one great sisterhood" was everywhere in suffrage writings—see *The Vote* (Nov. 30, 1912) or *Common Cause* (July 10, 1914)—but in practice the world of women was an imperialized one for many British feminists,

and imperial assumptions often operated in "international" feminist contexts. An Indian woman named Marie Bhor attended the International Council of Women meetings in 1899, but at the introductory session said nothing while the famous Anglo-Indian novelist Flora Annie Steele spoke on her behalf. Judging from the reprint of her paper in the minutes of the meeting, Bhor could speak English and probably delivered her paper on education in English as well. See *International Council of Women: Report of the Second Quinquennial Meeting* (1899): 71–72. See also Winifred Harper Cooley, "The Internationalism of the International," *Jus Suffragi* (July 1, 1913). This was the journal of the IWSA, one of whose anthems contained the lyrics "Whatever race our country be/ . . . one nation, Womanhood." Leaflet with songs from the IWSA, Fawcett Library.

61. *Votes for Women* [henceforth, *VFW*], "Dedication," (Oct. 1907): 1.

62. Lady Muir Mackenzie, "The Women of India in Modern Thought," *VFW* (Sept. 22, 1911): 26.

63. Christabel Pankhurst, "Shall This Country Lead the Way?" *VFW* (Sept. 3, 1908): 425–26.

64. See for example Emmeline Pethick-Lawrence, "We Are Not Hottentots," *VFW* (Dec. 2, 1910): 1, where she argues "We have the right to vote. We are not aboriginal subjects. We are not Hottentots. We are not children in schools. . . . Never let it be said that women of British name and descent were so tamed by brutal handling that they chose submission and humiliation rather than revolt. Let us thank God they have chosen revolt, and have thus vindicated their blood and race." Pethick-Lawrence borrowed the phrase "We are not Hottentots" from a contemporary speech by Winston Churchill and adapted it here for use in the emancipation context.

65. Teresa Billington-Greig, "The Storm-Centre of the Women's Suffrage Movement," *The International* (Sept. 1908). Henrietta Muller, one-time editor of the *Women's Penny Paper*, told the Marleybone Radical Club that "When English women are free, all other women will follow. England is the centre, the 'Hub' of the world; all other nations take their cue from her." *Women's Penny Paper* (Nov. 22, 1890): 75.

66. Elizabeth Robins, "The Signs of the Times," part 1, *VFW* (Mar. 19, 1909): 445.

67. This is my elaboration of the idea, suggested by Dorothy Thompson, that the demand for women's suffrage was a demand "for entry into the political nation." "Women, Work and Politics in Nineteenth-Century England: The Problem of Authority," in Jane Rendall, ed., *Equal or Different: Women's Politics 1800–1914* (Oxford: Basil Blackwell, 1987), 75.

68. Suffrage advocates in the twentieth century often raised the question of how men of "coloured" or "so-called subject and inferior" races in places like South Africa could be permitted some limited franchise while white women there enjoyed no such privilege. The rights of native women to the vote was rarely discussed. See Emmeline Pethick-Lawrence, "Women or Kaffirs," *VFW* (July 9, 1909): 912.

69. Jessie Craigen, excerpted from a speech on women's suffrage given at a demonstration in the Free Trade Hall in Manchester, Feb. 14, 1880. In Jane Lewis, ed., *Before the Vote Was Won* (London: Routledge Kegan Paul, 1987), 372.

70. Mrs. Duncan McLaren, "Are Women Not a Part of the People?," Women's Suffrage Pamphlets (1875–76), vol. 5 (Fawcett Library, bound green volumes).

71. Josephine Butler, "Our Christianity Tested by the Irish Question" (London, 1887), 28 and passim.

72. Sidney Smith, "The Enfranchisement of Women the Law of the Land," *Women's Suffrage Pamphlets* (1871–80), 6–7.

73. Harriet Taylor, "Enfranchisement of Women," *Westminster Review* (Oct. 1850): 309. Reprinted in *Women's Suffrage Pamphlets* (1867–82), 14 f.

74. Emily Pfeiffer, "Woman's Claim" (originally published in the *Contemporary Review* of Feb. 1881), in Lewis, ed., *Before the Vote*, 381.

75. Millicent Garrett Fawcett, "Mrs. Fawcett on Women's Suffrage," speech delivered in the Town Hall at Birmingham, Dec. 6, 1872, *Women's Suffrage Publications* (1871–72), vol. 2, 5 f.

76. Amos and Parmar, "Challenging Imperial Feminism," 3–17; Chandra Mohanty, " 'Under Western Eyes': Feminist Scholarship and Colonial Discourses," *Feminist Review* (Autumn 1988): 61–88.

77. Callaway, *Gender, Culture, and Empire*, 5.

COMPLICITY AND RESISTANCE IN THE WRITINGS OF FLORA ANNIE STEEL AND ANNIE BESANT

Nancy L. Paxton

In her 1978 essay "Disloyal to Civilization: Feminism, Racism, Gynephobia," Adrienne Rich describes the tangled guilt and complicity that has inhibited American feminists in our analysis of the relationships between race and gender.[1] She writes, "In the history of American slavery and racism, white women have been impressed into its service, not only as the marriage-property and creature-objects of white men, but as their active and passive instruments" (p. 282). Nonetheless, she argues, American feminists "have a strong anti-racist tradition" which has caused some black and white women in the past to defy their culture by assuming a position that was defined as "disloyal to civilization."

Rich defines this tradition of resistance by recovering marginal voices, by asserting that the "white women in revolt against the ideologies of slavery and segregation have most often worked from positions of powerlessness, or from a false sense of our own power and its uses" (p. 283). Middle-class feminists, she argues, have frequently been charged with overemphasizing their powerlessness and victimization by critics who argue that their "oppression is meaningless beside the oppression of Black, Third World, or working-class men and women" (p. 289). Rich demonstrates that marginality has been useful in countering this charge and in authorizing feminists' "anti-racist" critiques, and she has chosen to define herself repeatedly as marginal: as woman, as lesbian, and, more recently, as Jew.

The abolitionist campaign that Rich describes led many nineteenth-century women, on both sides of the Atlantic, into the feminist movement in the years before the American Civil War.[2] Nineteenth-century feminism provided a vocabulary that allowed these women to define black women as their sisters and to recognize their shared oppression while at the same time it provided a means to power by offering a rhetoric that justified resistance to the gender, race, and class systems and to the social, economic, and political institutions that oppressed them. After the abolition of slavery in America, this rhetoric of powerlessness was harder to appropriate. For the white women in the American South that Rich mentions, for the upper- and middle-class women in the more class-stratified world of Victorian England, and, perhaps most of all, for white women living in colonies abroad, the position of powerlessness or marginality could not easily be assumed or sustained. Nowhere were these conflicts more difficult to ignore, I would argue, than in British India under the raj. By focusing, then, on the writing of two English women who lived in India between 1868 and 1933, and by comparing the positions assumed by Flora Annie Steel (1847–1929), on the one hand, and Annie Besant (1847–1933), on the other, we can see how the analysis of race, class, and power was challenged when white feminists were faced with the evidence of their power to dominate others, especially the men and women of the Third World.

Flora Annie Steel and Annie Besant were contemporaries; they were both born in 1847, married when they were twenty years old, and bore two children each, though Steel's first daughter died. They both lived in India for at least twenty years, learned several Indian languages, wrote numerous books about India, and sustained long, productive careers that brought them fame and some fortune. Both achieved some of their fame by writing about women's issues, both worked to improve women's education and advocated greater civil rights for Indian as well as English women, and both identified themselves as feminists in their autobiographies.

Annie Besant came to feminism much earlier in her life than Flora Annie Steel; she lectured frequently about women's issues and worked to advance them in England in the 1870s and 1880s. In her *Autobiographical Sketches* (1885), she summarizes her career working to provide better employment opportunities and union protection for working-class women and to promote greater civil rights, including suffrage, for women. Flora Annie Steel, in her autobiography, *The Garden of Fidelity* (1930), written in the last few years of her life, calls herself a "suffragette," but she, unlike Besant, did not play a significant leadership role in British feminism. While Steel presents her efforts to improve women's education in India and her support for women's suffrage as well as her success as a novelist as evidence of her feminism, her life story shows how the ideology of the women's movement had broadened and diversified between 1868 and 1920 so as to allow Steel to see herself as a feminist while at the same time maintaining her otherwise racist, elitist, and politically conservative analysis of British and Anglo-Indian society. Besant, by contrast, demonstrates in her

life as well as in her writing a remarkable transcendence of many of the
racist and classist assumptions that Steel, and many other British feminists
of the period, held.

Steel and Besant came of age during what Olive Banks defines as the crucial decades of the women's movement in England.[3] They were young
women on the verge of marriage in 1866 when J. S. Mill presented the petition for women's suffrage, and their experiences are perhaps characteristic of a generation of English women that followed the heroic pioneers of
the first campaign for women's emancipation, inspired, for example, by
Harriet Taylor (1808–58) and other intellectuals, and led by women like Barbara Smith Bodichon (1827–91), Jessie Boucherett (1825–1905), Lydia Becker
(1827–90), and Frances Power Cobb (1822–1904), to name only a few. While
most of these older women continued their work to improve women's education, employment opportunities, and working conditions, and advocated women's suffrage and property rights as well as reforms in marriage
and divorce laws, this second generation of feminists also initiated work on
issues more directly related to women's sexuality, as seen, for example, in
the campaign for the repeal of the Contagious Diseases Acts led by Josephine Butler (1828–1906). Annie Besant's sensational role in publicly de-
fending women's right to birth control information in 1877, nonetheless,
set her beyond the pale of respectability, even among the feminists who
allied themselves with Butler.

The feminism of this second generation of Englishwomen was characterized, as Olive Banks has argued, by tensions between "authoritarianism
and voluntarism," between conservativism and radicalism, and between
egalitarian sisterhood and maternalistic protectionism.[4] Banks summarizes
the changes that occurred during this period as follows:

> During the years between 1870 and 1914 most of the radicalism that the pi-
> oneering feminists had inherited from the Enlightenment disappeared. As
> feminism grew in influence and became, in the great suffrage campaign of
> the early twentieth century, something of a mass movement, it shed not
> only its more radical goals but its more radical conception of womanhood.
> (Banks, *Becoming*, p. 84)

These tensions are played out in the lives and writing of Flora Annie Steel
and Annie Besant, especially in their contradictory and compromising
analyses of women's sexuality and its impact on the positions they take on
women's suffrage.

Both Steel's and Besant's experiences in India under the raj were decisive
in shaping their feminism, and their examples thus suggest the largely undocumented role that imperialism played in shaping British feminism in
the second half of the nineteenth century.[5] Steel and Besant came to India
when the political, cultural, and economic imperialism of the British Empire was most uninhibited, and they observed its effects on Indian society

and the place of women in it. Flora Annie Steel came to India in 1868, and her response to the problems posed by Indian women's conditions was, in many ways, constrained by her role as the wife of a British civil servant under the raj.[6] Besant, in contrast, chose a much more independent position as a woman permanently separated from her husband at twenty-five and already a committed feminist activist. She settled in India in 1895 in order to serve as the president of the Esoteric Section of the international Theosophical Society, living in Benares until 1906 and later serving as the president of the Theosophical Society as a whole in Adyar from 1907 until her death in 1933. Unlike most of her compatriots, Besant was free of much of the complicity that apparently inhibited Steel. As early as 1879 she began to voice her criticism of England's role as an imperialist power, was imprisoned by the British in 1917 for publishing seditious articles in her newspaper, *New India,* and was a powerful advocate and leader in the Indian nationalist movement.

From the following more detailed comparison of the conflicts in their feminism, moreover, we can see the power of the nation-state to force not only Flora Annie Steel but also, to some degree, a woman as strong and independent as Annie Besant, into a position of complicity by demanding that both women define themselves, to borrow the words of Adrienne Rich, as either "loyal or disloyal to [British] civilization" (p. 275). The strategy each woman chose in responding to this choice of loyalties reveals how each adopted and acted on what Rich calls "internalized gynephobia," that impulse to despise the feminine in the self and to see the feminine Other as the "rejected part," as the "anti-self" (p. 300).

As young women, both Steel and Besant experienced the economic insecurity and cultural marginality of women under patriarchy when they became what Rich describes as the "marriage-property and creature objects of men" (p. 282). Both were kept utterly ignorant about their sexuality, married apparently unwisely at twenty, and found themselves in loveless marriages. Steel was born in Harrow, and spent her teens in Burnside, Scotland; she was one of eleven children. Noting in her autobiography that her mother quarreled with her father over the control of the money she brought to her marriage, and that nearly three years separated her from her elder brother, Steel concludes by suggesting that her own distrust of female sexuality was inherited: "I have often wondered if this voluntary cessation of marital relations on my father's part had anything to do with my inborn dislike of the sensual side of life" (p. 1). Steel entered marriage, she reports, "ignorant of natural happenings" and commented, "Why I married I cannot say: I never have been able to say, I do not think either of us was in love. I know I was not; I never have been" (p. 1).

Steel's marriage, however, allowed her to go out to India immediately after her marriage in 1867, and during her husband's twenty-two year tour of duty there as a civil engineer, she was able to find many compensations for her choice of a loveless marriage. While motherhood provided many

Victorian women, including Annie Besant, with some compensations for a less than satisfactory marriage, Steel's experience of motherhood was more equivocal. When she had been in India less than two years, she bore her first daughter, who died in delivery. Almost sixty years later, in her autobiography, Steel describes her grief, guilt, and pain over the loss of her first child, saying that the sacrifice of her daughter's life to save her own was one of only two things she regretted about her life in India.

Her experience with her second daughter indicates the pressure that colonial society exerted in defining the lives of what Hilary Callan and Shirley Ardener describe as the "incorporated wives" of the servants of empire. In December 1870, Steel bore her second and only surviving child, Mabel. When her daughter was sixteen months old, she took her to England to be raised by her maternal grandmother, and in her autobiography, Steel characterizes her separation from her young daughter as a "wound" that would not heal. Steel explains that women of her generation commonly faced the choice of living either with their husband or with their children since it was argued, at the time, that the hot weather posed too many hazards for young children and that they could not be educated properly in India. In her bestselling guide to Anglo-Indian life, *The Complete Indian Housekeeper and Cook* (1898), Steel acknowledged that most Anglo-Indian women chose to leave their husbands for part of the year in order to take their children to enjoy the cooler weather of the hill stations of India, but she, rather unaccountably, argues that the "wiser course" is to set "the claims of the husband above those of the children" (p. 199). There is perhaps a kind of feminism underlying her insistence that English women can bear the heat as well as, "or perhaps better than" (p. 199) their husbands, but Steel was not blind to the damage that this separation caused not only to the children but also to their mothers when she notes, matter-of-factly, that many Anglo-Indian mothers felt that "though their children have been good, considerate, friendly, it seemed as though something were lacking" in their bonds with their children (p. 105). Thus, Steel's analysis of women's duty under the raj and the choices she made personally in managing the conflicting roles of wife and mother indicate her predisposition to see masochism as heroic self-sacrifice.

Steel's domestic choices suggest that the most attractive compensation for her loveless marriage was the prestige she enjoyed as the mistress of a large household, staffed by many Indian servants, and the power she could claim by virtue of her race, class, and position as the wife of an English sahib. In her housekeeping guide, Steel argues that the "Indian household can no more be governed peacefully without dignity and prestige than an Indian Empire" (p. 9). She asserts that the "first duty" of the English mistress of the house is "to give intelligible orders" and the second is "to insist on her orders being carried out" (p. 2). Throughout the guide she reproduces the conservative defense of the British right to rule India in her description of the Anglo-Indian household, insisting repeatedly that the Indian servant "is a child in everything but age" (p. 2).

Steel's autobiography too provides telling evidence of what Rich describes as "the capacity of privileged women to delude themselves as to where their privilege originates and what they are having to pay for it . . . as the buffer between the powerful and their most abject victims" (p. 287). We can see the racism that coexisted with Steel's feminism, for example, when she unabashedly describes horsewhipping an Indian servant who mistreated her mule and admits: "I confess that I never do get angry without an intense desire to hit, but I know it is unladylike, and condemn myself, as a rule, to inaction" (p. 155).

Steel's feminism also justified her desires to work outside the home in India, but her racism, elitism, and authoritarianism constantly compromised her efforts to improve the lives of Indian women. She asserts her conservative politics in her autobiography, when she writes, "I saw clearly that everything—order, method, punctuality, efficiency—depended upon one's individuality only. So I gripped the fact, to which I have held ever since, that the best form of Government is beneficent Autocracy. Democracy went by the board as a thing of mediocrity, the Apotheosis of Bureaucracy" (p. 46). The stance she takes in relation to the Indian subjects of the raj thus reproduces the role she prescribed for the mistress of a household of Indian servants; she insists that in relationships outside the home, too, there is an "absolute necessity for high-handed dignity in dealing with those who for thousands of years have been accustomed to it. They love it. It appeals to them" (p. 133). Without apparently investigating the sources of her own authority, Steel accepts the prevailing justification for British domination of India by concluding that because colonial subjects submit to her authority, it is "legitimate" (p. 133).

Steel's autobiography consequently reveals how her efforts to act on her feminism were compromised not only by her racism and elitism but also by her evident pleasure in exercising what she regarded as her legitimate authority as memsahib. While her descriptions in her novel, *On the Face of the Waters*, show, for example, more than usual insight into and sympathy with the lives of her Indian characters, her autobiographical accounts of her work as nurse and inspector of girls' schools in the Punjab betray a self-importance inflated by the authority she claimed as a memsahib. She identifies herself as the "only woman outside the ranks of the mission ladies who could read and write the vernaculars" in the Punjab (p. 161) and claims the credit for organizing government sponsored girls' schools throughout the region (p. 167). Because she fails to investigate the source and limits of her own personal power, Steel underestimates the work of other British women in less privileged positions in the hierarchy of the raj and criticizes missionary women, in particular, for their "lack of dignity in dealing with their clientele" (p. 165).

In describing her career as school inspector, Steel narrates several episodes that expose the limits of her freedom and authority under the raj, but in telling her story she does not recognize the evidence that her power was derived from her husband's position and limited by the conventions that defined the memsahib's proper role. Steel explains that because her husband's posting was changed shortly after she accepted her position as inspector of girls' schools, she felt duty-bound to live apart from him for nearly a year in order to complete the term of her appointment. Her husband's superiors protested their separation and urged him to "keep his wife in order" (pp. 177–78), to which he responded with a little disloyalty of his own, writing back, "Take her for a month and try" (p. 173). Steel's work as school inspector ended, she reports melodramatically, when the Anglo-Indian police discovered that a group of disaffected Indian men were plotting her "assassination." After an inconclusive official investigation, Steel resigned and returned to her husband (pp. 72–73). Her recounting of these events indicates no awareness that the opposition to her work may have been exacerbated by her racism and authoritarianism.

Like the complicit white Southern woman that Rich describes, Steel thus often appears in her autobiography to be "turning and turning in her cage of bitter knowledge, contempt, defensiveness, and consciousness of collusion, . . . part and parcel of a sexual, racial, and economic tangle she had not created" (p. 294). Certainly, the most disturbing feature of Steel's analysis of Indian women is her analysis of *purdah,* which apparently held up a mirror reflecting her own gynephobia and fear of female sexuality. Summarizing her experiences living among the Muslims near Kasur who secluded their women, Steel writes that "the Mohomedan women in towns and therefore in the purdah were inevitably over-obsessed with sex. It was not their fault; they were strangely unaffected by the fact; but they had nothing else about which to think" (p. 121). In speculating about how Indian women were "to be released from this stagnation," however, Steel proposed that *purdah* should be made "less endurable" to them. Arguing that "pain is Nature's strongest fulcrum," Steel explains that she always opposed "zenana missions or zenana doctors" because she "firmly" believed that "but for our efforts to make seclusion more bearable, India would not be half free of the curse of purdah" (p. 245). While more radical political activists may make similar arguments, Steel's reliance on the brutal—and imaginary—mechanics of social Darwinism in this passage reveals her only partially repressed violence and aversion to "the sensual side of life" which allowed her to recommend increasing the suffering of her secluded sisters.

Steel indicates her fear of uncontrolled female sexuality not only in her assessment of Indian society but describes it as a destructive force in Anglo-Indian society as well. In her autobiography, she defends the uprightness of the British officers in India during the 1870s and 1880s by noting that though a young man may be "quite ready to make love to the woman if she asks him to do so; otherwise he is—or was—a gentleman. Not that there are no matrimonial troubles in India. On the contrary, there are many though admittedly, I think, it is invariably the woman who begins them" (p. 130). Later, Steel reveals the consequences of the self-hatred that was fostered and intensified by her position as memsahib in the patriarchal structure of the British raj when she generalizes, in her old age, about women's sexuality. Her daughter reports her final conclusions, saying that in the end Steel regarded all women as "the victims of sex" and saw "women's jealousy" as the "primal cause" of conflict between the races, since female sexuality, in her view, lay at "the root of so many of our social evils" (p. 292). Unable to see British imperialism from the international perspective that Besant assumed, Steel ultimately identified female sexuality as one of the most powerful forces undermining civilization.

The effects of Steel's complicity with the patriarchal raj may also be seen in her analysis of her own authority as a writer. Steel returned to live permanently in England in 1889, and began her career as a novelist when she was forty-two, writing more than a dozen bestselling novels, short story collections, and *The Complete Indian Housekeeper and Cook*. Though she was, to use her word, "lionized" in the years following the publication of *On the Face of the Waters*, Steel continued to feel, despite her success, that she was a fraud. Regarding herself as ill-educated, she concluded that her novels "therefore must in some ways be poor" (p. 197). Moreover, in contrast to Besant, Steel, after so many years of enjoying borrowed authority, could not take full responsibility for her creative power with words. In fact, like many women writing spiritual autobiographies, Steel claimed that some of her work was not written by her but rather was dictated to her, but since she did not see herself as the recorder of God's words, Steel did not feel elevated by being chosen as the transcriber of another's words. The voice that spoke to her, she explains, was a male "figure in the white uniform of an Indian railway guard" who told her "word-for-word the story called *The Permanent Way*" (p. 197), and in this fantasy, we see the literal internalization of male authority.

Finally, Steel's position as a suffragette expresses similar inconsistencies. By 1907, Steel was able to find a position in the women's suffrage campaign that accommodated her elitism and political conservatism while at the same time allowing her to twice justify acts of civil disobedience to protest her lack of legal rights by refusing twice to pay "rates and taxes" (p. 265). To her credit, Steel's affection for individual Indian women may have helped her overcome some of her racism when she supported the limited franchise for Indian as well as English women, which Provincial Assemblies were allowed to grant to a few Indian women in 1919,[7] but Steel's analysis of the fitness of Indian women for the vote demonstrates her internalization of the ideology that justified British rule in India and her inability to recognize the overly restrictive terms of suffrage that she endorsed. She notes that though "many" Indian women "doubtless are as intelligent and as well educated as the males," their "dependent position precludes them at present from outside interests" so that "few women in India" can properly qualify for suffrage because they do not meet the "property qualifications" (pp. 252–53).

In contrast to Steel, Besant settled in India when she was forty-six years old, after more than twenty years of work as a Radical, feminist, and socialist organizer. Her career as a public speaker and social activist in England gave her a far more comprehensive perspective on the condition of Indian women and practical insight into politically expedient ways to improve their lives. Besant was the second child of Emily and William Wood and, as she explains in her *Autobiography*, three-quarters of her blood and "all of her heart" were Irish (p. 193). Her father died when she was five, leaving the family in precarious financial straits, though Besant was brilliantly educated by Ellen Marryat.

When she was twenty, Annie entered marriage "as ignorant as a baby" about "all questions of sex" (p. 54), but she analyzed the causes of the failure of her marriage to Frank Besant with far more clarity and self-awareness. While she had a warm and supportive relation with her mother, Besant identified her mother's role in maintaining her innocence about her sexuality: "My darling mother meant all that was happiest for me when she shielded me from all knowledge of sorrow and of sin, when she guarded me from the smallest idea of the marriage relation" (p. 39). Besant found that her marriage brought a "rude awakening" (p. 54), but she also acknowledged her own defensiveness by noting that she learned to "live and work in armour that turned the edge of the weapons that struck it" (p. 67).

Moreover, in contrast to Steel, Besant chose rebellion rather than complicity and gradually resigned her place in the patriarchal institutions that she saw as compromising or corrupt. After the birth of her son and daughter, Besant began publishing pamphlets on religious subjects and suffered a religious crisis. In 1867, she left the Anglican church and became estranged from her husband, who was a clergyman, as a result. By 1873, she was separated permanently from Frank Besant and attempted to become financially self-sufficient by working first as a seamstress and later as a journalist. By 1874, Besant also recognized many of the class privileges she enjoyed as a middle-class woman and began to work for political reform by writing for the Radical newspaper, *The National Reformer*. Through this paper, she established a close Platonic friendship with Charles Bradlaugh, and she worked for free speech and other Radical causes under his mentorship.

Besant's recognition and renunciation of her privileges as an Anglican, wife, and middle-class woman were deeply empowering for her. In her *Autobiography*, she describes how, in 1873, she delivered her first lecture to a row of empty pews in her husband's church, and shows how she, in contrast to Steel, was able to claim the "power that was to mould much of [her] future life" when she recognized her own authority as speaker and writer:

> I shall never forget the feeling of power and delight—but especially of power—that came upon me as I sent my voice ringing down the aisles. . . . And as though in a dream the solitude was peopled, and I saw the listening faces and the eager eyes, and as the sentences flowed unbidden from my lips and my own tones echoed back to me from the pillars of the ancient church, I knew of a verity that the gift of speech was mine . . . and that if ever the chance came to me of public work, this power of melodious utterance should at least win hearing for any message I had to bring. (P. 97)

Shortly after this experience, Besant began her career as a public speaker and it provided her, as she explains, "one of the deepest delights of life" (pp. 98–99).

In 1874, Besant further demonstrated her "disloyalty to civilization" by espousing her feminism in her first public lecture, "The Political Status of Women." Besant traveled widely in England in the next three years, speaking about any political question that "touched on the life of the people" (p. 153), but she was most notorious for her advocacy of birth control. In 1877, she and Charles Bradlaugh were brought to trial for printing and distributing the birth control information contained in Charles Knowlton's *The Fruits of Philosophy*. At the trial, she spoke in her own defense, arguing that withholding birth control information from men and women who wished to limit the size of their families was truly immoral: "We think it more moral to prevent the conception of children, than, after they are born, to murder them by want of food, air, and clothing. We advocate scientific checks to population, because, so long as poor men have large families, pauperism is a necessity, and from pauperism grow crime and disease." (p. 122). In contrast to Steel, Besant also felt empowered by her feelings of solidarity with working-class women, and in her *Autobiographical Sketches*, she describes the "touching letters from poor women" that came to her "from all parts of the kingdom" in order to express their thanks and appreciation for showing them "how to avoid over-large families" (p. 134).

Though Bradlaugh and Besant were unsuccessful in their defense at the Knowlton trial, the charges were later dismissed.[8] Besant faced a second trial, however, when Frank Besant sued to remove their two children from her custody and won on the grounds of his wife's immorality as a proponent of birth control. Thus, Besant was forced to see that she could not escape from the patriarchy entirely or from the laws and political processes of the nation-state. Nonetheless, in contrast to Steel, who resisted any recognition of her victimization as a wife and mother under the British raj and recommended submission and repression, Besant persisted in choosing marginality and endorsing rebellion. Her *Autobiographical Sketches*, written in 1885, ends with Demeter's cry for her lost daughter, but it also expresses her faith in women's power to create a better world: "I live in the hope that in her womanhood she may return to the home she was torn from in her childhood, and that, in faithful work and noble endeavor, she may wear in future years in the Freethought ranks a name not wholly unloved or unhonored therein, for the sake of the woman who has borne it in the van through eleven years of strife" (p. 169).

By 1885, Besant's "disloyalty to civilization" was also expressed in her critique of capitalism, as she moved from Bradlaugh's Radicalism to the socialism of the Fabian Society, where she befriended George Bernard Shaw. Though her adoption of socialism ruptured her mentorship with Bradlaugh, Besant decided to "profess socialism openly and work for it" with all her heart because "the cry of starving children was ever in my ears; the sobs of women poisoned in lead works, . . . driven to prostitution by starvation, made old and haggard by ceaseless work. I saw their misery was the result of an evil system, was inseparable from private ownership of the instruments of wealth production" (p. 277).

In summarizing her political work from 1885 to 1893 in her *Autobiography*, Besant describes her role in establishing the Matchmakers' Union and her narrative shows how the abolitionist rhetoric of sisterhood continued to persist in the radical feminism of the 1880s. For an article entitled "White Slavery in London," published in the *Pall Mall Gazette*, Besant interviewed some of the matchmakers at Bryant and May's matchworks and documented their appalling working conditions. When the manufacturers pressured the workers to deny Besant's reports, the matchgirls went on strike. Besant describes the touching loyalty and sense of sisterhood that inspired and sustained workers during the strike, by citing one worker who told her, "You had spoke up for us . . . and we weren't going back on you" (p. 305). As a result of this strike, the Matchmakers' Union was eventually established, with Besant as its secretary.

Because of this work, Besant achieved a far more sophisticated international perspective on English politics than most of her contemporaries, both inside and outside the women's movement. As early as 1879, she criticized England's role as an imperialist power in the following terms:

> Against our aggressive and oppressive policy in Ireland, in the Transvaal, in India, in Afghanistan, in Burmah, in Egypt, I lifted up my voice in all our great towns, trying to touch the consciences of the people, and to make them feel the immorality of a landstealing, piratical policy. Against war, against capital punishment, against flogging, demanding national education instead of big guns, public libraries instead of warships—no wonder I was denounced as an agitator, a firebrand, and that all orthodox society turned up at me its most respectable nose. (p. 154)

Throughout her career in England, Besant showed much of the "disloyalty to civilization" that Rich describes and anticipated many of the causes taken up by second-wave feminists, for, like them, she was committed to promoting a "profound transformation of world society" (p. 179).

By 1889, however, Besant was in despair about the limitations both of her socialism and agnostic materialism. In her *Autobiography* she tried to identify the source of her despair: "The Socialist position sufficed on the economic side, but where to gain the inspiration, the motive, which should lead to the realisation of the Brotherhood of Man? Our efforts to really organize bands of unselfish workers had failed. Much indeed had been done, but there was not a real movement of self-sacrificing devotion, in which men worked for Love's sake only, and asked but to give, not to take" (p. 308). It is in this year that Besant fell under the influence of H. P. Blavatsky and found a source of inspiration in the Theosophical Society that transformed her feminism and sustained her for the rest of her long and incredibly active life.

Like many spiritual autobiographies, the version of her life story that Besant wrote in 1893 is framed in retrospect by the revolution in her political and spiritual views that followed as a consequence of her meeting with Madame Blavatsky in 1889, when she experienced a spiritual conversion that allowed her to come "home" to Theosophy. Besant describes her first encounter with the charismatic founder of the Theosophical Society as a fascinating seduction: "I was conscious of a sudden leaping forth of my heart—was it recognition?—and then, I am ashamed to say, a fierce rebellion, a fierce withdrawal, as of some wild animal when it feels a mastering hand" (p. 310). While Besant reports that she felt "nothing special to record, no word of Occultism, nothing mysterious" during the interview, when she rose to go, she felt "for a moment the veil lifted, and two brilliant, piercing eyes met mine," prompting Besant to feel a "well-nigh uncontrollable desire to bend down and kiss her, under the compulsion of that yearning voice, those compelling eyes" (p. 311). Though her "old unbending pride" (p. 311) caused Besant to resist this initial appeal, she returned on May 10, 1889, and asked Blavatsky to accept her as her "pupil." Thus Besant began a long career that led her out of England, prompting her to settle in India in 1895 and, by 1907, to assume the presidency of the Theosophical Society based in Adyar.

The explicit goals of the Theosophical Society make Besant's conversion seem innocuous enough since the group was devoted to promoting "Universal Brotherhood; the study of comparative religion, philosophy, and science; the investigation of unexplained natural laws."[9] However, Besant was quickly drawn into the inner circle of Blavatsky's group, the Esoteric Section, as it was called, which required her profession of belief in occult "Masters" and her submission to "absolute obedience" to an "Inner Head of this group." Thus, Theosophy legitimized Besant's search for a spirituality that was more female-centered; it opened the priestly role to women like Blavatsky and later to Besant herself and it authorized the study of female goddesses (the Society's International Headquarters in Adyar, for instance, honors Minerva, Saraswati, Isis, and Ishtar). In her intimate and loving association with Blavatsky, Besant was apparently able to heal some of the pain she experienced because of the place she elected to take in the patriarchal society of Victorian England, and in this association, she apparently experienced the "real transcendence" that Rich describes so eloquently as "love experienced as identification, as tenderness, as sympathetic memory and vision, as . . . nonexploitative, non-possessive eroticism which can cross barriers of age and condition, the sensing of our way into another's skin, . . . against the censure, the denial, the lies and laws of civilization" (p. 307). However, Esoteric Theosophy also required that Besant, like other devotees, submit entirely to the authority of the spiritual teacher, and Besant's relationship with Blavatsky also proved to be profoundly inhibiting because of the authoritarianism of her teacher and the prominent male members of this inner circle.

The most painful immediate consequence of this discipleship was that Besant renounced her support for birth control in 1891, and in her struggle to accept Blavatsky's uncompromising rejection of neo-Malthusianism, we can see how Theosophy, which taught Besant to honor the power-within, was subverted by some of the same tensions that, according to Olive Banks, characterized late nineteenth-century feminism. Besant's voluntarism and sense of sisterly solidarity apparently made her vulnerable to her teacher's maternalistic authoritarianism. Blavatsky argued that although birth control might be justified if man is seen only "as the most perfect outcome of physical evolution, it was wholly incompatible with the view of man as a spiritual being, whose material form and environment were the result of his own mental activity" (p. 211). Hoping to find a way out of her earlier religious skepticism, Besant submitted to Blavatsky's direction. Feeling that the theory of reincarnation that Blavatsky taught invalidated her previous materialistic understanding of the source and nature of human life, Besant sadly conceded: "My heart somewhat failed me at withdrawing from the knowledge of the poor, so far as I could, a temporary palliative of evils which often wreck their lives and bring many to an early grave, worn old before even middle age has touched them—yet the decision was made. I refused to reprint the 'Law of Population' or to sell the copyright, giving pain to the brave and loyal friends who had so generously stood by me in that long and bitter struggle" (pp. 217–18). While Besant's life in India must have increased her sense of the evils of overpopulation, she maintained this position even after Blavatsky's death in 1891. By 1927, however, Besant had achieved sufficient confidence in her own spiritual authority and publicly renewed her support for birth control when she was honored by the Malthusian League fifty years after the Knowlton trial.

Though Besant provided a new preface for her *Autobiography* in 1908, she never wrote the promised second volume about her astonishing life in India, so the only primary evidence we have about how her move to India affected her feminism must be inferred by comparing the versions of her autobiography written in 1885, 1893, and 1908, and by analyzing her voluminous writings about India. Just before her death, Blavatsky named Besant as the Secretary of the Esoteric Group, and this appointment gave Besant considerable power in the organization as a whole. Yet for the next twenty years Besant devoted herself to the study of Sanskrit and Pali in order to better understand Eastern religious traditions. She first became a student of the Brahmin thinker, G. N. Chakravarti, and later of her countryman, Charles Webster Leadbeater; both teachers claimed they could interpret the will of the Esoteric "Masters" with absolute authority in their studies with Besant.

Thus, through her serious study of the religious traditions of India, Besant was able to achieve a cultural relativism that allowed her to transcend much of the racism and "white solipsism" that limited Steel. But in submitting herself to Chakravarti and later to Leadbeater, whom Gertrude Williams calls Besant's "astral Svengali," Besant also agreed to renounce all political work.[10] By depriving Besant of an audience, both men acted to protect their own authority in the organization, and Besant's submission to them clearly silenced her criticism of the most patriarchal aspects of Indian culture, especially in her analysis of caste restrictions and woman's place in contemporary Indian society.

It was only after Besant was elected president of the Theosophical Society as a whole in 1907, after Leadbeater engineered her break with Chakravarti, and after he was himself exiled to Australia because of persistent scandals about his overly ardent relationships with several young male students, that Besant began to translate her earlier feminism more freely to the Indian context. Gradually, Besant began to reenter the political arena and to develop a sexual and nationalist politics of her own. In 1904, she established the Central Hindu Girls' School and published the cautious *Education of Indian Girls*, but by 1913, she gave feminist issues prominence in the reforms promoted by the "Brothers of Service." The predominantly Hindu members of this organization were required, for example, to pledge themselves not to marry their sons or daughters before their seventeenth year, to educate their wives and daughters and "discountenance the seclusion of women," and to "oppose any social ostracism of widows who remarry," as well as to "disregard all restrictions based on caste" and color, promote the education of "the masses," and support the Indian National Congress.[11]

In 1913, Besant also initiated a series of lectures, later published under the title *Wake up, India*, which included "Child-Marriage and Its Results" and "The Education of Indian Girls." In this work Besant is much more outspoken in her criticism of the "degraded" Hindu customs, which promoted the marriage of girls of eight or ten who are so young that they are "utterly unfit to enter into the married condition" (p. 49). She detailed the physical and social consequences of such sexist practices by reporting that in the Presidency of Madras alone, there were over twenty-four thousand widows under the age of fifteen (p. 65). In both published speeches, Besant justified her call for feminist reforms by citing ancient Vedic texts, which represented women as "the equals of men, trained, cultivated, and educated to the highest point" (p. 52). She concluded by exhorting the fathers and husbands in her audience "for India's sake to save the girls and boys and let them marry in full age" (p. 76). "The shame of modern India," she declared, is to have to have "such women as you have, and to handicap them as you do, to have brains so bright and give them no chance of education, to have bodies so fair and ruin them by imposing motherhood on them while still they ought to be at school" (p. 52). In 1917, Besant joined with her friends Margaret Cousins and Dorothy Jinarajadasa to establish the Women's Indian Association, devoted to women's suffrage and other feminist reforms, and served as its first president.[12]

In 1917, however, Besant was also faced with the ultimate test that, according to Adrienne Rich, reflects the partriarchy's hegemony by forcing feminist critics to define themselves as either loyal or "disloyal to civilization." Faced with this choice, Besant, like Steel, was torn by divided loyalties as she tried to act on her feminism and on her support for Indian nationalism. Since 1879, Besant had written volumes exposing the brutal exploitation that was disguised by British paternalism in India and criticized the cult of male heroism that helped to justify the East India Company and later the British raj at its most aggressive and militaristic, calling Robert Clive, for example, "a very wicked man, careless of suffering, careless of justice, careless of principle, careful only to gratify his own lust of blood, of power and wealth."[13]

By 1917, Besant joined with moderate Indian nationalist leaders like Gopala Krishna Gokhala in openly criticizing British policy in India. In these years, Besant editorialized persuasively and persistently in support of Indian Home Rule in her public speeches, her writing, and her newspaper, *New India*. As the First World War wore on, taxing British resources and leadership, the Indian Nationalist movement seemed to pose more of a threat to the raj, and when British officials attempted to quell the movement by, among other measures, imposing stricter censorship of the press, Besant's newspaper became a conspicuous target. On June 14, 1917, Lord Pentland, the governor of Madras, demanded that Besant silence her criticism of British policy in her newspaper and return to England or be interned. Asserting her belief in the right to a free press, as she had many years before in the Knowlton trial, Besant indignantly refused to leave India. As a result, she was sent to Ootacamund, where she was kept under house arrest for ninety-four days.

Before her internment, Besant delivered a "stirring farewell address," which concluded:

> I go into enforced silence and imprisonment because I love India and have
> striven to arouse her before it is too late. It is better to suffer than to consent

to wrong. It is better to lose liberty than to lose honour. I am old, but I believe that I shall see India win Home Rule before I die. If I have helped ever
so little to the realization of that glorious hope I am more than satisfied.
VANDE MATARAM. GOD SAVE INDIA.[14]

Raj Kumar estimates the effects of Besant's internment on the nationalist
movement as decisive: "What Mrs. Besant could not have achieved in
twenty years, her internment achieved in just one day. . . . Prominent Indian politicians who had kept away from the Home Rule League joined it
and took up its leadership" (p. 113). When Besant was released, her return
was a celebrated triumph and huge crowds of her Indian supporters
greeted her at Madras. In December 1917, she was elected to the presidency of the Indian National Congress and addressed 4,690 delegates and
thousands of guests in Calcutta.

The strategies that Besant adopted in the three years that culminated in
her election as president of the Indian National Congress, nonetheless,
demonstrates the power of the patriarchy to compel the complicity even of
a woman as formidable as Annie Besant. A few months before her imprisonment, Besant, as president of the Home Rule League, refused to accept
suffrage for Indian women as a plank in the group's political platform even
though her friends Margaret Cousins and Sarojini Naidu urged her to take
this step. Besant's position, thus, mirrored the political dilemma faced by
socialist feminists in England during the war years who had to decide
whether to accept women's limited enfranchisement as an intermediate
goal or to press for universal suffrage for men and women. Ironically,
while Besant apparently felt that Home Rule was the more expedient cause
and preferred to work for women's suffrage and better education through
the Women's Indian Association that she had helped to found, many male
as well as female nationalists supported women's suffrage. As one member
of the Provincial Assembly explained a few years later, "It is gratifying to
find that in a county where men are accused of treating women as chattels
the political progress of women has been more rapid than in England."[15]

By 1918, Besant was also more conservative than other nationalists in her
analysis of Indian suffrage in general, and this position ultimately lost her
the support of moderates in the Indian National Congress who gradually
shifted their allegiance to Mohandas Gandhi. Besant consistently opposed
democratic voting plans that "permitted a vote of equal weight to every individual" and recommended a system that granted individuals "a share of
the power of guidance, over the things he understood, in which knowledge, experience, and high character would be the credentials for
power."[16] In her four-tier system of enfranchisement, based on Indian traditions of village governance, Besant recommended granting universal suffrage to twenty-one-year-old males only at the lowest level of the village
panchayat. Electors for the highest office of national parliament members
would be restricted to men who were at least thirty-five years old with mas-

ter's degrees. Besant's years in the authoritarian hierarchy of the Theosophical Society clearly affected her analysis of suffrage and prompted her,
like Steel, to endorse an overly restrictive plan for suffrage in India. By
1919, Besant lost further credibility with moderate nationalists because of
the temporizing position she took over the Montagu-Chelmsford Report
and thus, by 1923, her political career in India was virtually over. In setting
the precedent of female leadership in the Indian National Congress, however, Besant clearly prepared the way for her friend Sarojini Naidu, who
was elected in 1925 as the first Indian woman to serve as president of this
organization.

Besant's feminist position, in contrast to Steel's, demonstrates her cou-
rageous commitment to self-examination and her willingness to assume all
the responsibilities of her power. But it shows as well her compelling need
to find a source of inspiration that would allow her to reconcile the demands of her reason with the urgent needs of her spirit. While Besant's
surrender to the occult mysticism of Madame Blavatsky and the Theosophical Society may appear to us, with the advantage of hindsight, to be a fat-
uous or credulous mistake, the flattering appeal of a self-defined vision of
"past lives" and the seductiveness of a vision of an entirely "self-created"
reality offered by Theosophy is very much alive today.

Besant's life makes us question, finally, why the gratification of her spiritual needs prompted her, as other needs prompted Flora Annie Steel, to
counter or oppose women's right to "determine how, when, and for whom
she will exercise her sexuality and her reproductive powers" (Rich, p. 179).
The riddle Besant's life poses is, why does an enlightened feminist who has
freed herself of so much continue to evidence, in Adrienne Rich's termi-
nology, an "internalized gynephobia," which finds expression in the view,
shared by Steel, that women's sexuality is a dangerous force?

Besant's and Steel's autobiographical writing about India demonstrates
ultimately, then, how the politics of empire worked to circumscribe not
only the rhetoric of feminism but also their discourse about love and sexuality. Both Besant and Steel came to regard their resistance to sexual desire
as a sign of spiritual enlightenment or racial superiority, and their examples suggest the central role British imperialism played in defining and imposing an ideology of sexual as well as racial identity that persisted well
beyond Besant's death.

NOTES

1. An earlier draft of this chapter was first presented at the National Women's
Studies Conference in Minneapolis on June 24, 1988. A version of this article appeared in *Women's Studies International Forum* 13, no. 4 (1990): 333–46; reprinted with
the permission of Pergamon Press. I would like to thank Jane Rudd, Indira Jung-

hare, Joy Huntley, Laura Quinn, Helen Callaway, Nupur Chaudhuri, Peg Strobel, and Kumari Jayawardena for their helpful suggestions. I would also like to thank Nancy Fix Anderson for sharing her essays-in-progress on Annie Besant with me.

Research for this essay was supported by the Fulbright-Hayes Summer Seminars Abroad Program. Special thanks go to Sharada Nayak for making my first visit to India both wonderful and productive. Finally, I would like to thank Harvard University for granting me a Mellon Fellowship in 1988–89, which provided both the resources and the time to develop this article in its present form.

2. Olive Banks, *Becoming a Feminist: The Social Origins of First Wave Feminism* (Athens: University of Georgia Press, 1986), p. 109.

3. Olive Banks, *Faces of Feminism: A Study of Feminism as a Social Movement* (New York: St. Martin's Press, 1981), p. 59.

4. See Olive Banks, *Faces of Feminism*, p. 84. See also Judith R. Walkowitz, *Prostitution and Victorian Society: Women, Class, and the State* (Cambridge: Cambridge University Press, 1980) and Susan Kent, *Sex and Suffrage in Britain, 1860–1914* (Princeton: Princeton University Press, 1987).

5. Antoinette Burton's essay, included in this volume, explores one of the most promising avenues in the analysis of the relationship between English feminism and imperialism. On feminism and Indian nationalism more generally, see Kumari Jayawardena, *Feminism and Nationalism in the Third World* (London: Zed, 1986) and Partha Chatterjee, "The Nationalist Resolution of the Women's Question," in Kumkum Sangari and Sudesh Vaid, eds., *Recasting Women: Essays in Indian Colonial History* (New Brunswick, N.J.: Rutgers University Press, 1990), 233–53.

6. Hilary Callan and Shirley Ardener's analysis in *The Incorporated Wife* (London: Croom Helm, 1984) has been especially helpful to my understanding of the shape and ideology underlying Flora Annie Steel's fiction and life story.

7. For an excellent analysis of women's suffrage in India see Joanna Liddle and Rama Joshi, *Daughters of Independence: Gender, Caste, and Class in India* (London: Zed, 1986), p. 35.

8. For details on the trial, see Gertrude Williams, *The Passionate Pilgrim: A Life of Annie Besant* (London: John Hamilton, 1932), p. 91.

9. Geoffrey West's analysis of theosophy was especially helpful; see *Mrs. Annie Besant* (London: Gerald Howe, 1927), p. 55.

10. Gertrude Williams, *The Passionate Pilgrim*, p. 283. See also Geoffrey West, *Mrs. Annie Besant*, p. 64.

11. Raj Kumar, *Annie Besant's Rise to Power in Indian Politics* (New Delhi: Concept Publishing, 1981), pp. 73–74.

12. Barbara N. Ramusack, "Women's Organizations and Social Change: The Age-of-Marriage Issue in India," in Naomi Black and Ann Baker Cottrell, eds., *Women and World Changes: Equity Issues in Development* (Beverly Hills, Calif.: Sage Publications, 1981), p. 203.

13. Annie Besant, *India: A Nation, a Plea for Self Government* (London: T. C. Jack, 1915), p. 17.

14. Gertrude Williams, *The Passionate Pilgrim*, p. 297.

15. Joanna Liddle and Rama Joshi, *Daughters of Independence*, p. 35.

16. Raj Kumar, *Annie Besant's Rise to Power*, p. 89.

WORKS CITED

Banks, Olive. *Becoming a Feminist: The Social Origins of First Wave Feminism*. Athens: University of Georgia Press, 1986.

_____ . *Faces of Feminism: A Study of Feminism as a Social Movement.* New York: St. Martin's Press, 1981.

Bauer, Carol, and Lawrence Ritt, eds. *Free and Ennobled: Source Readings in the Development of Victorian Feminism.* New York: Pergamon Press, 1979.

Besant, Annie. *Autobiographical Sketches.* London: Freethought Publishing Company, 1885.

_____ . *An Autobiography.* 1879. Rpt. Adyar: Theosophical Society, 1939.

_____ . *England, India, and Afghanistan.* 1879. Rpt. Adyar: Theosophical Society, 1931.

_____ . *India: A Nation. A Plea for Self-Government.* London: T. C. Jack, 1915.

_____ . *Wake up, India: A Plea for Social Reform.* Adyar: Theosophical Society, 1913.

Callan, Hilary, and Shirley Ardener. *The Incorporated Wife.* London: Croom Helm, 1984.

Jayawardena, Kumari. *Feminism and Nationalism in the Third World.* London: Zed, 1986.

Kent, Susan. *Sex and Suffrage in Britain, 1860–1914.* Princeton: Princeton University Press, 1987.

Kumar, Raj. *Annie Besant's Rise to Power in Indian Politics.* New Delhi: Concept Publishing, 1981.

Liddle, Joanna, and Rama Joshi. *Daughters of Independence: Gender, Caste, and Class in India.* London: Zed, 1986.

Nethercot, Arthur. *The First Five Lives of Annie Besant.* Chicago: University of Chicago Press, 1961.

_____ . *The Last Four Lives of Annie Besant.* Chicago: University of Chicago Press, 1963.

Ramusack, Barbara N. "Catalysts or Helpers: British Feminists, Indian Women's Rights, and Indian Independence." In Gail Minault, ed., *The Extended Family: Women and Political Participation in India and Pakistan.* Columbia, Mo.: South Asia Books, 1981, pp. 109–50.

_____ . "Women's Organizations and Social Change: The Age-of-Marriage Issue in India." In Naomi Black and Ann Baker Cottrell, eds., *Women and World Change: Equity Issues in Development.* Beverly Hills, Calif.: Sage Publications, 1981, pp. 198–216.

Rich, Adrienne. "Disloyal to Civilization: Feminism, Racism, Gynephobia," in Adrienne Rich, *On Lies, Secrets, and Silence: Selected Prose, 1966–78.* New York: W. W. Norton, 1979.

Steel, Flora Annie. *The Complete Indian Housekeeper and Cook.* London: Heinemann, 1898.

_____ . *The Garden of Fidelity: Being the Autobiography of Flora Annie Steel, 1847–1929.* London: Macmillan, 1930.

Walkowitz, Judith R. *Prostitution and Victorian Society: Women, Class, and the State.* Cambridge: Cambridge University Press, 1980.

West, Geoffrey. *Mrs. Annie Besant.* London: Gerald Howe, 1927.

Williams, Gertrude. *The Passionate Pilgrim: A Life of Annie Besant.* London: John Hamilton, 1932.

THE "WHITE WOMAN'S BURDEN" IN THE "WHITE MAN'S GRAVE"

THE INTRODUCTION OF BRITISH NURSES IN COLONIAL WEST AFRICA

Dea Birkett

In the late nineteenth century, the consolidation of the British Empire and the growth of European communities abroad brought an immediate cry for appropriate medical care. In 1896, through the efforts of leading colonial officials' wives, the Colonial Nursing Association (CNA) was established to meet this need. The voluntary board of the CNA was to raise funds for and administer the provision of qualified nurses to British colonial communities worldwide, working in close alliance with the Colonial Office. Committees were also formed in the colonial communities themselves to facilitate administration and encourage local sponsorship of the scheme. Alarmingly high death rates among European residents in West Africa, which had led the Coast to be nicknamed "the white man's grave," and the British objection to being nursed by Africans, soon made this arena of imperial expansion by far the largest area of employment for CNA nurses. But the conflict between the CNA and colonial authorities', and the nurses', own desires and ambitions in West Africa quickly became apparent. Within a few years, the energies of the lady founders of the CNA were consumed in trying to quell "the scandal of the nurses on the Coast."

In the 1890s, the qualifications required of a nurse were still a matter for debate.[1] In 1888, the British Nursing Association, which campaigned for the recognition and standardization of nursing as a profession, began to agitate for the formation of a national registration of nurses. To register, nurses would need a certificate of three years' training in a general hospital and would have to demonstrate their medical competency through examination. In opposition to this move, a lobby, with the figurehead of aging nursing pioneer Florence Nightingale, maintained that nursing should be carried out by "ladies" who qualified on the grounds of their character and feminine sensibilities. With conflicting arguments over the essential qualities of a nurse and her function within the medical hierarchy, the class and educational background of nursing recruits varied considerably. Both upper-class single women and former domestic servants were employed at different ranks. The battle between nursing as a career, requiring medical skills, and as a vocation, relying upon innate womanly attributes, continued through to the first decade of the twentieth century.

The CNA committee fluctuated between supporting the Nightingale and British Nursing Association's definition of a good nurse. Experience at midwifery was compulsory for all CNA candidates, although in the West African postings rarely called upon. Some training from the Schools for Tropical Disease at Greenwich or Liverpool was looked upon favorably, and many candidates went on a short course of a few weeks to one of these institutions. By July 1899 it was unanimously agreed that an applicant without a three-year certificate of training in an approved hospital should not be interviewed, a standard as high as those expected of any nurse in Britain. But less than three months later this decision was reconsidered, and within a year rescinded.[2]

In general, the CNA nurses who went to West Africa were well qualified and would have not found it difficult to find similar positions in Britain, where nurses were in high demand. Most candidates, in addition to short specialist courses in tropical medicine, had several years' training in a major hospital, such as St. Thomas's or Guy's in London. But in the interview notes taken before the CNA board, appearance, manner, and accent receive more of an emphasis in the assessment of these candidates than their nursing experience. Typical notes read, "A short woman with high cheek bones and small nose" or "dark, very young looking, not a lady. Not very suitable."[3] Although lack of training was rarely considered sufficient reason for declining an applicant by the CNA, "not a lady" was.

The major contribution being asked from the nurses was not medical skills but feminine talents. The Chief Medical Officer of the Gold Coast outlined how

> Good looks and a cheerful disposition conjoined go a long way in the successful management of cases of illness in this Colony; indeed in my experience of practice here, I have found that a tender touch, a sympathetic look . . . have done more good to their patients than the drugs, or other therapeutic measures prescribed by them.[4]

An appointment in the empire, however, endowed this feminine undertaking with a mightier mission. From the outset, the employment of European nurses in West Africa was seen as integral to and supportive of the imperial endeavor. Colonial Secretary Joseph Chamberlain elucidated how the nurses were crucial in helping the men at the forefront of British expansion overseas:

> The conclusion I wish to press upon you is that, lives such as these so precious to the Empire, the lives of those who are the successors of those who gained the Empire for us, such lives ought not to be wasted. We owe it to them and to ourselves to do all in our power to preserve them, and to see, so far at all events may be possible, when they are struck down as unfortunately they often are in the course of their duty, by sickness, that at least they shall not want the tending of skilful and kindly hands and that sympathy, and womanly attention, which will be found to be the best anodyne for their pain and perhaps the most effective cure for their disease.[5]

The nurses' attachment to the West African Frontier Force (WAFF) and Ashanti Expedition, enabling the military to better carry out their expansionist maneuvers, was a more obvious example of their involvement in imperial development. But there were also more subtle, yet just as important and central ways, in which the nurses could contribute. "Any movement which has for its object the prevention or cure of disease is therefore a matter of Imperial as well as of private concern," wrote Mary Chamberlain, wife of the colonial secretary and founding member of the CNA.[6] Addressing the CNA 1899 Annual Meeting, Sir George Goldie of the Royal Niger Company summed up the work of the European nurses in West Africa, with apologies to Kipling, as "the white woman's burden."[7] The imperial bard was himself approached for a "pathetic little story to be inserted in one of the papers" to raise money for the association.[8]

While working in the colonial setting, the nurses would hold a greater responsibility than to their profession; they would be visual representatives of the British imperial enterprise. "More, far more than in England," they were told, "will her actions, her behaviour, and her general tone, be criticised." The presence of European nurses at the front edge of imperialist expansion would help to ensure that rigid racial divisions were not threatened. Writing in a nursing magazine, Mary Chamberlain explained:

> For educated Englishmen or their wives to find themselves in a hospital among natives or other uncongenial companions, is an ordeal from which they may well shrink. . . . Strong men, who have never had to think of themselves, are struck down by that hateful and deadly foe, tropical fever, far away from all the comforts to which they have been accustomed, with no friend at hand, with no white woman within reach—only natives near them who are totally incapable. . . . The terror of helpless loneliness is added to the misery of a wasting disease.[9]

The racial hierarchy would in turn protect the nurses from any threat of defeminization. "They will not," the acting colonial secretary was reminded, "be required to do work entailing much physical exertion: native assistants will be provided for such duties under their immediate supervision."[10]

The large number of applicants to the CNA were drawn by the ideal of serving empire and securing British interests abroad. But the particular appeal of West Africa can be attributed to an allure beyond the call of queen and country. In late nineteenth-century Britain, images of Africa as a land of adventure were purveyed through popular literature, exhibitions, and lectures catering to working as well as middle-class audiences.[11] Within this portrait of the "Dark Continent," women missionaries were presented as heroines in the field, to be admired and even emulated. Although essentially a continent for male endeavor, Africa could accommodate the more daring and devoted women who were prepared to sacrifice the security of Britain for the dangers of and service to a far continent.

Letters from nurses published in the CNA's magazine conjured up and confirmed this image of an exotic land free from many of the restrictions of British society. One nurse wrote from Jebba:

> We have a tent to eat and sit in, and it looks quite nice with paper pictures fastened round and a few tables and deck chairs and photos and some native works of art. There are mats about the floor. Of course there are creepy-crawly things everywhere, in the food, on the floor, and in our beds—but for all that, and in spite of the fact that we have no rain for months and the heat is great and every day becomes greater—we are very happy together. . . . We have each a black boy to do things for us, and they are very quaint. We get a Reuter's telegram now and then, and our newspapers from home take months to come and sometimes never turn up at all.[12]

A nurse in Nigeria sent back a particularly spicy account of her pet monkey being eaten by a hyena. "What with fevers, hyenas and an occasional leopard," she wrote, "life can hardly be dull in Nigeria."[13] As the first nurses were sent to communities where there were often no other white women, it is not surprising that they saw themselves in some sense as pioneers; the word itself was often used to describe them in CNA literature. All these attractive images, usually reserved for white male travelers, must have been part of the lure to those seeking nursing positions in "the white man's grave."

For many women, the sense of importance instilled by imperial duty, combined with the promise of adventure, was strong enough to draw them away from more comfortable positions in Britain. It was even the less cushioned postings in West Africa that proved to be the most successful, while in the colonial comfort of the Nursing Home in Freetown and in Lagos Hospital problems soon arose with the nurses employed. When three "Lady Nurses" from Guy's Hospital were appointed to the WAFF up-country, where living was basic, the principal medical officer reported, "The employment of nursing sisters under such rough conditions and so far from civilisation, was an experiment which was fully justified by the results . . . I am of the opinion that several lives were saved by their care."[14]

The WAFF nurses worked a twelve-hour day from 6:30 A.M. to 6:30 P.M., comparable with the hours they would have been expected to work at Guy's. In contrast to the luxury of Lagos Hospital's European Nurses Quarters where the furniture "had pretensions to elegance,"[15] in Jebba "each [WAFF] nurse has a bed, table and chair or stool, no other furniture whatever."[16] In these remote stations, the nurses' images of Africa were matched by reality. When one nurse was moved from a posting with the Ashanti Expedition, which had won her an Order of the Red Cross, to an established hospital, soon her actions and reputation were being brought into question and she was forced to resign.[17]

Although living conditions in West Africa would for many be primitive, and the pay for a matron—£100–120 per annum—was at the lower end of the scale for a similar position in Britain, there was no shortage of applicants. It was reported in *Nursing Notes:*

> One of the most encouraging features in the work of the Colonial Nursing Association has been the ease with which posts on the West Coast of Africa have been filled. These districts are acknowledged to be unhealthy, but there has never been a time when the Association has not received special petitions from nurses to be sent out there. "West Coast of Africa preferred," is a phrase often to be found in the application forms.[18]

When one post at Lagos became vacant, six candidates were selected for interview.[19]

Nurse Lucy Clarke, who had trained at Guy's, and Nurse O'Flynn were the first private nurses sent to West Africa, arriving in Lagos in 1896. They were quickly followed by appointees to Accra in early 1897; to the West African Frontier Force in Northern Nigeria; and to Freetown, Sierra Leone. Within five years of the commencement of West African service, forty-eight nurses were employed, over half of the CNA's total worldwide register for that period.

The ladies of the CNA's voluntary board were concerned to emphasize to the applicants that they must not harbor ambitions in West Africa that could not be realized in Britain. Mary Chamberlain warned:

> A woman of firm, steady, capable character, sound religious and moral principles, an equitable pleasant disposition combined with adaptability and tact, is the stamp of candidate in her private capacity that the Association would like to employ.
>
> On the other hand, the girl who merely wishes to escape from the restrictions of home or life in England, who desires to place first "seeing the

world" and "enjoying life," should not be encouraged to imperil the fair fame of nurses by seeking service abroad.[20]

Their newsletter underlined, "Let them never be tempted to claim abroad liberties that, as nurses or as women, they would never think of taking at home. Let them realize that climate and circumstance breed temptations that are only to be resisted by devotion to work and loyalty to the best traditions of their profession."[21]

The nurses themselves, however, soon demonstrated that they intended to exploit any opportunities of greater autonomy and liberty than had been offered them in Britain, and refused to conform to the role expected of them. When the new chief medical officer arrived in Lagos eighteen months after Nurses Clarke and O'Flynn, he found "that there was a tendency on the part of the nurses to regard social pleasures as being of primary importance and to resent any restriction, however salutary, being placed on their movements; or the imposition of any disciplinary measures."[22] The governor complained, "many of the nurses have been giddy and restive beyond all expectation."[23]

The nurses expressed their rebellion in small gestures of defiance.[24] But the importance of such minor actions as dressing inappropriately or staying out late is demonstrated in the extreme disapproval they met as a result. One manner in which the nurses refused to conform was in the clothes they wore. In Freetown, it was said that Sister Austin "attends dances and dinners in startling and vivid costumes." The governor lamented the "jaunty and unprofessional costumes" of the CNA, which consisted of a modest white skirt and shirt, a navy belt and white sailor's hat, much preferring the sober gray worn by a nursing sisterhood to ensure "no breath of scandal touches them."[25]

While nurses were asked to display all the feminine values of nurturing in their hospital work, they were not supposed to display their female sexuality. The image of Africa proferred in popular books and travelogues was of a land of rampant sexuality, and one in which Europeans were particularly susceptible to temptations of the flesh. It was imperative, therefore, that European nurses desexualize and thereby distance themselves from the surrounding lascivious landscape. Requests were made for lady nurses of "mature years and less attractive appearance."[26] The chair of the CNA Nursing Committee wrote of the importance of wearing uniforms "which tend to the protection and safe guarding of the Nurses."[27] Nuns' veiling was suggested as suitable material for the tropics.[28]

Despite these strictures, the nurses persisted in exploiting opportunities of sensual and sexual freedom, and, soon, to the accusations of improper appearance were added more substantial charges of sexual impropriety. The experiences of the Colonial Hospital at Accra, Gold Coast, were typical. Matron Fladgate, who had trained at Leamington Hospital, was appointed to the Colonial Hospital in January 1898. Within a year, the chief medical officer was writing to the colonial secretary in London complaining of her "indiscreet" behavior.[29] Chamberlain, whose wife had been central in founding the CNA, wrote anxiously to the governor that "statements have been made to the effect that Miss Fladgate's conduct on the Gold Coast has given rise to scandal; and that owing to these statements the system of employing European nurses on the West Coast of Africa is being brought into disrepute."[30] It had been claimed that Miss Fladgate had an "unguarded way of talking" and "the habit of frequenting the officers' quarters." She was forced to resign.

Within weeks of Fladgate's dismissal, Nurse Deeks, who had been promoted to acting matron in her place, was also being interrogated. Deeks had received exemplary reports from Fladgate when working under her, again suggesting the very different perceptions and ambitions of the colonial communities and the nurses themselves. Two CNA nurses serving in Northern Nigeria were called before the CNA committee on their return to London to give statements against Deeks, neither of whom had worked with her. (They had received their information, they said, from "a wife of an official" whose name they refused to disclose.) The charges brought against Deeks were of sexual liaison with a married man, Dr. Henderson, who worked in the Colonial Hospital and had given evidence against Fladgate. At Deeks's "trial" in absentia, it was alleged that "Miss Deeks has, on several occasions, spent the night or portions of it at Dr. Henderson's house, and has been seen by reliable witnesses leaving it in the early hours of the morning." The result, it was claimed, was "that great scandal has been caused."[31] The Colonial Office recommended that Deeks be employed in another region—anywhere *but* West Africa. Dr. Henderson remained at his post. A year later, one of the nurses who had given evidence against Deeks was herself forced to resign on the grounds that she had "no idea of discipline."[32]

Measures were taken by the local European communities and the home body of the CNA to try to prevent any further challenges to acceptable behavior on the part of the nurses. The CNA believed that it was by reinforcing class status, rather than the nurses' professional abilities, that the nurses' and the association's reputation could be saved. The association's Council was a Who's Who of London society, packed out with the titled and wealthy. Princess Henry of Battenberg was made Patroness. The wives of the colonial secretary and his under secretary Reginald Antrobus, the prominent campaigner Emily Hobhouse, and Ladies Ampthill, Musgrove, and Norman were among the distinguished members of the Executive Committee. While rumors may have been rife, the home body was determined to prop up its flagging public image.

It was also felt by the CNA and colonial authorities that by employing a certain class of nurse, many of the difficulties so far experienced might be overcome. Having initially agreed to draw only "lady" recruits, the CNA was soon receiving frequent complaints from the local committees about the problem of reconciling the status of middle-class ladyhood with paid employment. The ambivalence of the nurses' class led to a request from the governor of Lagos that "trained nurses of the servant girl class or members of a nursing religious sisterhood would be more likely to give satisfaction." The chief medical officer suggested "that possibly a more satisfactory state of things would result if the European nurses were not 'lady nurses' but trained nurses of a class that would not look for or demand social recognition and entertainment in Lagos anymore than England."[33] The Colonial Office ultimately rejected such suggestions, however, on the grounds that nurses from "the class to which domestic servants in England belong . . . would be less able than nurses of somewhat higher social standing to resist the temptations of which they would be exposed in a Colony."[34]

While debates in Britain continued between "lady" vocationists and career nurses, in West Africa a nurse may have hoped to improve and consolidate her social standing. To many recruits, imperialism promised, much as patriotism had to British Military nurses, a common cause that could overcome social distinctions.[35] But if the CNA nurses believed that the colonial context would provide them with enhanced social status denied them in Britain, they were to be disappointed once again. One of the first reactions of the CNA to the scandal was to issue a "Letter of Conduct" to local committees giving guidelines for the reception of a nurse in their community. The CNA suggested that, rather than being incorporated into the colonial community and enjoying the status and benefits that implied, the nurses should be kept strictly apart from it. The CNA felt,

> that regulations should be made locally that the Nurses wear their uniform at all times even when off duty. . . . There are certain forms of amusement such as card parties at the Club, Bachelor's entertainments and frequent dances to which Nurses should not be asked and the Local Committees or other Authorities are earnestly requested to discountenance such invitations being given or accepted.[36]

In giving evidence against Deeks, one of the nurses had blamed this case on "one English nurse being frequently left alone in the hospitals." Recommendations were soon made that, contrary to previous practice, nurses should be posted in pairs. "When left entirely alone, as the nurses have been on the Gold Coast," Nurse Ward pointed out, "it has led very naturally to their continually frequenting the Officers' quarters in order to find companionship and amusement."[37] Solutions were sought in replicating the conditions in which a nurse would work in Britain, where nurses would be encouraged to live together in the nurses' home and conduct their own separate social life.[38]

To Mary Kingsley, a traveler who had herself nursed in West Africa and was a supporting member of the CNA, it was not their class but the lack of professionalism which was to blame for the nurses' poor reputation. In support of the British Nursing Association's campaign, she wrote to the acting governor of Sierra Leone:

> I am miserable beyond words about the latest developments of nurses in West Africa. . . . The organisation of the nursing profession is in an awful mess all round. That general mess is at the back of this W[est] A[frica] one. Nurses ought in this measure to be like doctors—examined accredited registered—a Profession. This is not the case, largely owing to . . . a pack of amateur society ladies putting their oars in. . . . What is wanted is a professional board, in whose hands the selection of the individuals should be.[39]

But as the nurses' role in West Africa was perceived to be one of feminine comfort, supplementing the medical attention of the male European doctors as well as undertaking tasks formerly done by African staff, those who did have experience and training were often frustrated in the exercise of their skills. The tension that arose from differing expectations is expressed in complaints lodged against nurses, usually against those who held senior positions as matrons. The medical superintendent at the nursing home in Freetown made a complaint against Sister Emily Jessop:

> It has been a rule since the Home was started that the serving of the food of patients should be supervised, if not actually taken in by the Nurse on duty, and not left to the boys, and that it should be as nicely and daintily served as possible, for it has been my object to make this Institution a place where the patients can count on receiving those little Home attentions which go so far to alleviate the discomfort of illness in a tropical climate. I may state that I had occasion to speak to Sister Jessop on this very point before I went on leave, but I am very sorry to say that I have heard from patients that during my absence in many cases matters were left almost entirely to the boys.[40]

At the same nursing home, Matron Jardine had her contract terminated because "she appears to have taken the appointment under a misapprehension of the duties of Nurse Matron."[41] Given very little authority within the hospital, Jardine, who had specifically stated on application to the CNA that she "wants Matron post only," had demanded a written list of her duties.[42] This in itself was judged by the local European community to constitute demands for professional status they did not believe her position deserved. After Jardine's dismissal, the title of Matron, which implied a certain freedom from more mundane nursing duties, was replaced by Senior Sister. Women were not to be granted the prestige and autonomy they had in part come to West Africa to find.

The nurses themselves were often confused in their ambitions. They looked for a certain freedom from forms of behavior considered appropriate at home, stirred by the image of abandon that Africa offered. At the same time, they sought to enhance their status through inclusion in a colonial culture that emphasized their difference, and superiority, over the surrounding population. Although drawn by tales of living in tents, most were pleased to find the European nurses' quarters in Lagos equipped with sugar tongs, crumb brush, napkin rings, and a tea service.[43] Their own conflicting expectations must also explain in part the hostile reaction to their behavior and demands.

In the first five years of CNA appointments, one-third of the nurses stationed in West Africa were recalled or "retired," in many cases because of pressure from members of the white communities in which they served.[44] One nurse, giving evidence in London in a case that led to dismissal, pinpointed the cause of this embarrassing statistic: "ignorance on the part of most of the nurses who go out, and who think they may do things there which they would not dream of doing here."[45]

In their expectations of West Africa, the nurses were to be disappointed. Denied autonomy, authority, and professionalism in their home hospitals, they hoped their role in the imperial endeavor would give them greater status. At the same time, the image of a land free from the restrictions of their home society led many to believe that they could enjoy a social and personal freedom they did not enjoy as single women in Britain. But instead they found a closely controlled and ordered European society which sought a nonprofessional, separate place for them within it. Yet even within the rigid regulations facing them on arrival in West Africa, they found ways of rebelling. Their exploitation of chances for sexual freedom was an indication of women taking control of an area of their lives usually denied them. The cost of such action, however, would be scandal, reprimand, and dismissal. The personal, feminine arm of the imperial endeavor it was hoped the nurses would be had failed. "The white woman's burden" had proved to be a load the British nurses to West Africa were not prepared to bear.

NOTES

1. There is a large literature covering the politics of nursing in the late nineteenth century, most importantly Martha Vicinus, *Independent Women: Work and Community for Single Women 1850–1920* (Chicago: University of Chicago Press, 1985); Celia Davies, ed., *Rewriting Nursing History* (London: Croom Helm, 1980); Monica Baly, *Nursing and Social Change* (2nd ed., London: Heinemann, 1980); and Brian Abel-Smith, *A History of the Nursing Profession* (London: Heinemann, 1960).

2. Nursing Committee Minutes, Mar. 1899–July 1901, Overseas Nursing Association (formerly CNA) Records. Rhodes House, Oxford. All further references are to box numbers in these records, unless otherwise indicated.

3. Ibid.

4. Chief Medical Officer (Gold Coast) to Acting Colonial Secretary, 23 Sept. 1896, box 123.

5. Minutes of CNA Annual Meeting 1899, box 120.

6. Mary E. Chamberlain to "Sir," 19 Oct. 1903, box 120.

7. *Times*, 26 July 1899, p. 12.

8. CNA Executive Minute Books, 6 Mar. 1900.

9. Mary E. Chamberlain, "In Obligation of Empire," *Nursing Notes*, Aug. 1900.

10. Chamberlain, "In Obligation of Empire."

11. See John M. Mackenzie, *Imperialism and Popular Culture* (Manchester: Manchester University Press, 1986).

12. *Nursing Notes*, Apr. 1901.

13. *Nursing Notes*, Mar. 1902.

14. Quoted by F. Lugard to Chamberlain, 14 June 1900, box 122.

15. George C. Denton (for Governor, Lagos) to Chamberlain, 12 May 1901, box 122.

16. Lugard to Chamberlain, 14 June 1900.

17. "Half Yearly Report on Nursing Sisters, Northern Nigeria," 16 Aug. 1902, Lugard to Chamberlain, box 122.

18. "Colonial Nursing Association," *Nursing Notes*, Aug. 1899.

19. Draft letter from CNA to Mr. Read, n.d., box 123.

20. Mary Chamberlain to "Sir," 19 Oct. 1903.

21. "Colonial Nursing Association," *Nursing Notes*, Feb. 1900.

22. Quoted in "Half Yearly Report of Chief Medical Officer," Lagos Hospital, 12 May 1901.

23. William MacGregor to Chamberlain, 17 Oct. 1899, box 123.

24. For the importance of small gestures such as decoration of a room or mode of dress as indicators of rejection of colonial culture, see Helen Callaway, *Gender, Culture, and Empire: European Women in Colonial Nigeria* (Oxford: Macmillan Press, 1987).

25. C. A. King-Harman (Governor) to Chamberlain, 10 Jan. 1903, box 121.

26. Mabel Piggott to Colonial Office, Dec. 1902, box 121.

27. "Letter on Conduct," 5 May 1903, box 120.

28. *Nursing Notes*, May 1900.

29. W. B. Henderson to Chamberlain, 20 Jan. 1900, box 122.

30. Chamberlain to Governor, 13 Mar. 1900, box 122.

31. Gold Coast Nursing Service, statement by Miss E. K. Nevill to CNA Committee, London, 25 May 1901, box 122.

32. "Half Yearly Report on Nursing Sisters, Northern Nigeria," Lugard to Chamberlain.

33. Quoted by R. L. Antrobus to Honorary Secretary CNA, 5 Feb. 1900, box 123.

34. Antrobus to Honorary Secretary CNA, 19 Feb. 1900, box 123.

35. For military nursing, see Anne Summers, *Angels and Citizens: British Women as Military Nurses 1854–1914* (London: Routledge, 1988).

36. "Letter on Conduct."

37. Gold Coast Enquiry, Miss A. M. Ward to CNA Committee, 7 June 1901, box 122.

38. See Vicinus, *Independent Women*.

39. Mary Kingsley to Matthew Nathan, 8 Mar. 1900, Nathan Papers, Bodleian Library, Oxford.

40. W. T. Prout, "Report on the Nursing Home," Sierra Leone, Jan. 1903, box 121.

41. Resolution passed at Local Committee of Sierra Leone Nursing Home, 28 Dec. 1899, box 125.

42. Jardine's statement, 20 Dec. 1899, box 125.

43. "Inventory of Furniture etc. European Nurses Quarters, Lagos Hospital," 1900, box 122.

44. "Statistics relating to Nursing Service: West Africa: December 1902," box 121. From 1897 to 1902, of the forty-eight European nurses employed in West Africa through the CNA, fifteen retired or resigned, eleven were invalided home, and four died.

45. Gold Coast Enquiry, Miss A. M. Ward to CNA Committee.

Missionaries

A NEW HUMANITY

AMERICAN MISSIONARIES' IDEALS FOR WOMEN IN NORTH INDIA, 1870–1930

Leslie A. Flemming

William Hutchison, in his analysis of the development of American Protestant mission theology, *Errand to the World,* identifies two key motifs in American mission thinking: an emphasis on direct evangelism and an emphasis on the civilizing activities thought necessary for making evangelism more effective. While early European missionary efforts reflect both motifs and American mission thinking has variously emphasized one or the other,[1] both motifs received almost equal emphasis in late nineteenth- and early twentieth-century mission thinking. Suggesting that Americans felt themselves a chosen people, Hutchison argues that mission theorists expressed a strong sense of both the superiority of American culture and Americans' responsibility to save the world by imposing their own culture on it. Equally impelled by a strong sense of millennialism, mission theorists also felt compelled to share Christianity, and especially the American version of Christian culture, with the rest of the world's peoples. Clearly marked in the work of missionaries in Asia, the Middle East, and Africa, this twin concern for evangelism and social change is reflected both in the number of mission personnel engaged in direct preaching and teaching of the Bible and in the considerable portion of mission resources committed to institutions dedicated to concrete social change.

An additional distinctive feature, perhaps *the* distinctive feature, of the American mission enterprise was the heavy involvement of women. Contributing substantial amounts of time, effort, and money to the activities at every level of American mission boards, after the American Civil War women also made up an increasing proportion of the overseas mission personnel. By 1910 about two-thirds of the American mission force was composed of women, a majority of whom were single.[2]

In general, women accepted the goals of mission activity articulated by the leading spokesmen of the movement. Heavily influenced by the Student Volunteer Movement, which began recruiting college-age women and men into overseas mission service in 1887,[3] women were strongly committed to evangelization. Many of them graduates of the Moody Bible Institute or other similar mission-oriented training institutions, women missionaries engaged in a variety of evangelical activities, frequently finding in mission work a wider range of permissible activities than was then available in most American churches. At the same time, most women missionaries were convinced of the need for missions to accomplish social change. Strongly influenced by the cult of domesticity, most women involved in mission work, either as supporters in the United States or as overseas missionaries, believed that, as women, they occupied an exalted position in American culture. Attributing their exalted position to Christianity, especially American Protestant Christianity, they constructed women in the cultures of Asia and the Middle East as downtrodden and oppressed by their traditional religions.[4] In addition to evangelizing Asian and Middle Eastern women, therefore, American missionaries were also motivated by a desire to extend to them the superior social position they saw as promised by both American-style domesticity and Christian identity.

While the development of American mission thinking in general and the history of American missionary activity in China in particular have both received substantial scholarly attention, little attention has as yet been paid to how these interlocking concerns of evangelism and social change in women's lives played themselves out in the cultures of the rest of Asia and the Middle East.[5] Focusing particularly on American Presbyterian women missionaries in north India between 1870 and 1930, I provide here a more context-specific example of the attempt to transplant American social and religious norms to another culture. Examining the values American women missionaries brought to the mission encounter, the human material with which they saw themselves working, the new human beings they hoped to create from that encounter, and the aspects of Indian culture they criticized most strongly, I will detail how missionaries' values shaped their encounters with Indian women and encouraged them to pursue particular institutional directions in their work. I will argue that because the vision of womanhood missionaries offered Indian women was strongly oriented toward domestic roles, they did not, despite their self-construction as agents of change, offer Indian women radically new roles. However, because of their emphasis on education, physical well-being, and voluntary activities that took women outside their homes, the missionaries encouraged Indian women to begin breaking down the strong public-private distinctions characterizing much of north Indian life and to assume roles not previously available to them in Indian culture.

The Setting

Somewhat smaller than its sister mission in the Panjab, the North India Mission of the American Presbyterian Church included eleven stations, all in central Uttar Pradesh (U.P.),[6] founded between 1836 and 1913. Between 1870 and 1930 nearly one hundred women worked in these stations. Initially, most of these women were the wives of male missionaries, the majority of whom were ordained Presbyterian ministers. However, by 1910 most of the women in the field were single. Unlike their married sisters, who usually subordinated their own sense of missionary call to their husbands' activities, the single women were often professionally trained and felt a distinct sense of vocation.

Generally from small town, middle-class families, most American Presbyterian women missionaries were well educated. Almost all had had post-secondary education, and many had trained as teachers, nurses, or physicians. Some had completed B.A.s, while others had obtained specialized evangelical training, through either the deaconess movement or by attending the Moody Bible Institute or other mission training school.

Women in the North India Mission were generally engaged in four spheres of activity. Reflecting both Board of Foreign Missions policy and their own orientation, the first was a cluster of activities involving education. Most important of these activities was running a variety of schools for girls. Varying considerably in size and quality, many of these schools were small local day schools for high-caste Hindu and Muslim girls in provincial cities that deliberately combined education with evangelism. The North India Mission also ran three boarding schools for Indian Christian girls, the Elizabeth Prentiss School at Etah, the Rakha Orphanage and School near Farrukhabad, and Mary Wanamaker School at Allahabad.

A second sphere of activity was the provision of Western medical care to women and girls. Missionary physicians ran, often with only a skeleton staff, the Sara Seward Hospital at Allahabad and a full dispensary at Fatehgarh. Others provided outreach medical services at smaller dispensaries in provincial towns. Using the home nursing skills typically possessed by nineteenth-century American women, most missionaries also ran "veranda dispensaries" and dispensed simple medicines on their evangelical tours through the rural areas. Usually the only medical facilities available to women, these institutions, along with their conscious evangelism, provided a distinct, and often life-saving, service to Indian women and their families.[7]

A third activity, usually carried out by married women, was *zenana* visiting, i.e., regularly visiting secluded upper-class women confined to the women's quarters of houses. The object of these visits was unabashedly evangelistic: missionaries taught Bible stories, prayed, and sang religious songs, refusing to visit any houses where these activities were forbidden or restricted. However, they also encouraged literacy, and made the teaching of reading, albeit through religiously oriented texts, an essential part of their visits.

Finally, despite the Presbyterian ban on women's public preaching, women missionaries also engaged in itinerant evangelism. For some, this involved selling tracts and singing hymns during occasional visits to religious fairs and pilgrimage places. For others, the primary evangelistic activity was instructing low-caste converts during distinct itinerations, i.e., periodic tours of rural areas during the winter months.

Changing Women's Status in Society

Reflecting their sense of chosenness both as Americans and as Christians, most missionaries came to India committed to effecting substantial change in the social norms affecting Indian women. That commitment was often couched in a rhetoric that stressed women's low status in Indian society and urged conversion to Christianity as a means of raising women's status. Without distinguishing between high- and low-caste lifestyles, and without recognizing the specific legal rights at least theoretically enjoyed by Muslim women, missionary women identified several key areas of Indian social life that to them particularly reflected women's low status and in which they wished to effect change. Having come to India at a time when the marriage age for women in the United States had already begun to rise, many missionary women saw the custom of early betrothal, then common among all religious communities in India, as the area of social life most in need of change. Throughout this period, while rarely criticizing the institution of arranged marriage itself, missionary writers criticized Indians for bowing to social pressure in the age at which betrothal arrangements were made, decrying the loss of carefree childhood and the interruption of education that early marriage frequently represented.

Like most of their Anglo-American secular contemporaries, as well as many prominent Hindu social reformers, missionaries also criticized the position of Hindu widows. While custom with respect to remarriage varied widely among Hindus and Muslims in north India, these missionaries focused on the customs of high-caste Hindus, most of which strongly encouraged celibacy for all widows. Particularly moved by the fate of young widows who had been betrothed as children and often faced a lifetime of poverty and neglect, missionaries frequently described their own attempts to make these women economically independent. Missionaries were equally critical of the lifestyles of high-caste Hindu and Muslim married women, who were almost completely secluded in their husband's family's houses, and in their writings they contrasted these women's lives with what they considered to be their own enviable freedom of movement. Missionary writings also referred to the sorrow and suffering, especially the hidden suffering, of secluded *zenana* women. Seemingly unaware of the parallels with their own lives, missionaries also frequently criticized Indian women's subordination to male family members, especially citing their lack of physical freedom, their economic dependence on their husbands, and male family members' prevention of their access to medical care. Reflecting their own class bias, however, missionaries seemed scarcely concerned with the needs of working-class women, who were not only *not* confined to the domestic sphere, but often provided the sole support of their families. The labor contribution of rural women was also similarly overlooked.

While clearly asserting Indian women's low status, missionary women articulated less clearly the means Indian women ought to pursue to change their status. Themselves relatively well educated, they argued that the school experience was beneficial in increasing women's sense of self-respect. They also argued for greater physical freedom for women and more opportunities for them to experience intellectual growth. However, these missionaries were imbued with a commitment to women's responsibility for the management of domestic life and reproduction, and they did not hope to see education and physical freedom lead Indian women into roles that excluded them from those responsibilities. Even highly educated single women missionaries, whose work helped to provide new options for some Indian women, accepted the domestic role as the primary one for women. Thus the physician Adelaide Woodard told the Board, in her allusion to a *purdah* club (a club for secluded women at which no men would be present) that met at her house, "We hope it is the beginning of a larger movement for better homes, better babies and more freedom for the women."[8]

The missionaries thus did not, perhaps could not in the context in which they were working, advocate radical change in Indian women's roles. Nevertheless, they represented many of their activities as producing a higher valuation of women by Indian society. Those who were parents saw their own families as models of a care and concern for daughters that they felt Indians lacked.[9] While strenuously arguing against early marriage for girls of all communities, they expressed a particular responsibility to attempt to change the practices of Indian Christians. They arranged the marriages of Christian orphans only for girls in their late teens or older, they refused to take part in early betrothals arranged by families, and they did not allow couples in which the wife was very young to attend training schools for village workers.[10] They also attempted, against prevailing Indian social norms, which permitted only a weak bond between husband and wife, to foster an egalitarian, conjugal marriage style among Christians. Offering their own marital relationship as ideal, they encouraged wives and husbands to eat, speak, socialize, worship, and attend public meetings together. Finally, without mentioning the similar work of other Indian reformers, they engaged in much rescue work, adopting orphans and young girls abandoned by their husbands' families and attempting to equip the many widows whom they sheltered with usable economic skills.

Changing Caste Relations

The rigid structure of relations between the various Hindu *jatis* (kin-based subcastes) and between Hindus and members of other religious communities was another area of Indian social life in which missionaries saw themselves as agents of change possessing a superior ethos. In their earliest observations of caste, missionaries were generally concerned with the ways in which caste barriers inhibited their interactions with Indians. Christine Belz, for example, an itinerant evangelist in Etah district, called the caste system "a strong bulwark of the devil to keep the people away from Christ."[11] While some missionaries optimistically expected caste identities to weaken gradually, others saw the divisions created by caste as justification for continued British presence in India. As the rise of the Social Gospel movement after the turn of the century increased their awareness of some of the social and economic dynamics of Indian caste and community relations, and especially after the mass movements brought large numbers of members of untouchable *jatis* into the church,[12] many missionaries became aware of the economic relations built into the caste system. Mary Bandy, for example, although denying any similarities between American slum dwellers and rural untouchables (which was actually an apt comparison), treated *Women's Work* readers in 1906 to a relatively sophisticated analysis of the ways in which higher land-owning castes prevented members of lower castes from rising economically. Other missionaries, especially those engaged in district work, i.e., ministering to rural Christians, stressed the need of formerly lower-caste Christians for social and economic uplift. By the 1920s, many had also begun to suggest that the persistence of former caste identities would prove divisive in the Indian church, and they advised mixing classes and castes in schools, hospitals, and voluntary associations.

Although these women, perhaps because of their tacit assumption of the superiority of American culture, were seemingly unconcerned with the rigid racial segregation then common in the United States, they held up a strongly egalitarian ideal for India, looking forward to the day when caste lines would no longer divide either the Indian Christian community or Indian society as a whole. In institutions serving Indian Christians in particular, missionaries consciously strove to create groups mixed by caste and class. In addition to encouraging desegregated reception of communion, in the villages they often hosted *prem bhajan* (love feast) dinners, in which Christians of all castes, contrary to prevailing Hindu norms, publicly ate together. District and provincial meetings and revivals often brought together Christians of many different backgrounds and of both genders.

In their attack on the economic and social consequences of caste relationships, the differing activities of male and female missionaries reflect the division of labor in their own lives. Many male missionaries worked to narrow economic gaps and were active in agricultural institutes, industrial cooperatives, and other programs offering economic benefits primarily to lower-caste men.[13] Women, on the other hand, emphasized the mixing of castes and classes in educational institutions and charitable voluntary organizations. Almost all the educational institutions for Christian girls that the missionaries ran contained student bodies mixed by class and caste origin, and in their reports and articles the missionaries pointed out their contribution to the breakdown of caste, community, class, and denominational barriers among the students. Those working with voluntary organizations frequently described the mix of castes and classes of the people attending the meetings, praising the spirit of unity prevailing in the meetings.

Missionaries also stressed their contribution to the blurring of caste lines in the wider community. In annual reports, they took particular pride in the caste and community mix brought together in the audiences for programs in schools for Hindu and Muslim girls in Farrukhabad, Gwalior, and Jhansi. They also believed that their concern for low-caste people, especially reflected in the education offered low-caste girls at the Prentiss School in Etah and in the dispensaries serving low-caste people, would loosen caste barriers by encouraging high-caste Hindus and Muslims to evince similar concerns and establish parallel institutions. These missionaries also believed that their participation in such voluntary associations as temperance societies and *purdah* clubs, whose focus cut across caste and community lines, significantly contributed to caste and community integration.

Changing Attitudes toward Health and Physical Well-Being

Although even the earliest missionaries, as good middle-class American women, expressed disgust at what they considered the almost unbearable dirt and poverty of India, missionaries felt compelled to attempt to change Indian attitudes toward health, hygiene, and general physical well-being only after 1900. This greater concern for health-related issues reflects both their heightened social awareness, as a result of the influx of low-caste groups into Christian institutions, and the involvement of middle-class women in the health reform movement in the United States. As Regina Morantz-Sanchez reminds us, "By the end of the nineteenth century, reform ideas about personal cleanliness, public health, and family hygiene had become familiar axioms of middle-class American culture."[14] Although missionaries were concerned with health and hygiene for all women, they had different expectations for the larger community of women, on whose lifestyles they usually had little influence, than for the Christian schoolgirls, over whose lives they exercised significant control.

Throughout this period, missionary women remarked on the dirtiness and poverty of Indian women, and especially of the rural Christians whom they visited on district tours. Seemingly unaware of the ways in which traditional economic relations and Hindu beliefs created a kind of culture of poverty for low-caste people, they complained of women's smelliness, lack of attention to dress, and lack of care of their own and their children's hair.[15] They also expressed great dismay at the several famines India experienced, although they seemed unaware of the contribution of colonial government policies to the development of famines.

Unfamiliar with the vast body of Hindu belief, these women failed to perceive the competing Hindu attitude toward health and disease, which assumed the intimate involvement in personal health of various deities and the operation of the laws of karma in individuals' lives. They also had little regard for traditional Hindu or Muslim medicine. They were convinced of the superiority of Western medicine and were fully imbued with American health reform attitudes that encouraged individual responsibility for health maintenance. The missionary physicians, as well as those who kept veranda dispensaries or dispensed medicines on district itinerations, were most vocal in their call for changes in Indians' health and medical practices. Appalled by the number of Indians with physical deformities, especially blindness, and by the frequent epidemics of cholera, smallpox, and plague, these women were especially critical of what they saw as Indians' lack of concern with proper hygiene. Mary Forman, for example, lamented Indians' fatalistic abandonment to smallpox, while Nellie Binford told *Women's Work* readers that Indians' opposition to segregation of the sick and disinfection of houses made it impossible to stop the spread of disease. Strongly critical of both traditional midwifery and prevailing methods of childcare, missionaries also deplored the reinforcement of deleterious health care practices by religion and superstition and the resistance to Western medicine they often encountered, especially among mass-movement Christians. Although few of these missionaries expressed political opinions, many blended their American valuation of physical well-being with an imperialist sense of cultural superiority. They saw Indians' lack of proper concern with health and hygiene as further justification not only of their own presence, but also that of the British government, with its structure of municipal and provincial health-care institutions.

Inspired by their Christian concern for both body and soul,[16] and committed to a sense of individual responsibility for health maintenance, missionaries in north India persuaded home boards to commit substantial resources to changing Indians' attitudes toward health and Western medicine. In their homes, missionaries not only ran veranda dispensaries but also promoted higher standards of cleanliness and good grooming among their servants. Actively involved in famine relief work and in the treatment of victims of infectious diseases, they made instruction in hygiene and Western methods of childcare part of hospital treatment sessions, *zenana* visits, and district itinerations. In addition, they trained local

midwives in Western childbirth methods and, in the 1920s, held public exhibitions, called "baby shows," demonstrating Western techniques of
childcare and hygiene. They also included articles on preventive medicine
in Christian publications, especially in the Hindi newspaper *Dehati*, published from Fatehgarh by Louisa Lee. Most productive of potential change,
in the mass-movement areas they trained both men and women as nurses,
dressers (of wounds), compounders (lay pharmacists), and hygiene in-
structors, encouraging them to live among village Christians to help them
combat disease.

Extending these same values to the pupils in their schools, the missionaries criticized Indian culture for confining girls to a retiring, inactive role.
Echoing Helen Holcomb's Christian concern for both body and soul, many
educators emphasized teaching girls to sit and stand upright, breathe
deeply, and get regular exercise. Against the objections of some parents,
they added calisthenics and drills to the curricula of mission schools, dis-
tributed primers on proper sanitary practices, and included instruction in
temperance and Western hygiene methods in their visits to girls' homes.
Mission physicians annually examined all boarding school pupils, regularly inoculating them against the common infectious diseases. In order to
combat tuberculosis and isolate sick pupils, educators urged the renovation
of mission structures, especially at Rakha. Not only did death rates from
tuberculosis drop dramatically among boarding school pupils after 1910,
but their general level of health, as described in mission reports, was consistently higher than that of girls in surrounding communities.[17] Following
similar developments in American schools, basketball and other team
sports were introduced at Wanamaker and Rakha after the turn of the
century.

A Vision of Christian Womanhood

The values that women missionaries articulated in the areas of women's
status, caste relations, and physical well-being were values they wished to
make operative in Indian society for all women, irrespective of community
identity. However, in addition to these, missionaries also articulated a set
of values that applied chiefly to Christian women. Drawing on both their
own vision of Christian womanhood and their perception of the needs of
the Indian church, they promoted these values particularly in the institutions that served primarily Christian women and girls, and most especially
in the boarding schools for Christian girls. While the new Indian Christian
woman whom the missionaries wished to create in these institutions
closely resembled her Hindu and Muslim sisters in some respects, she differed markedly from them in others. While neither radically innovative nor
revolutionary, this new vision of Christian womanhood encouraged a partial liberation from some indigenous constraints on women. More impor-

tantly, this new vision of womanhood, combined with membership in a minority religious community, strengthened Christian women's sense of themselves as agents of change and encouraged them to provide other women with the means to assume new social roles.[18]

The social context of west-central U.P. appeared decidedly hostile to the missionaries as they attempted to create new Indian Christian women among boarding school pupils. Part of both the traditional heartland of Sanskritic culture and the central area of Mughal political control, this region experienced relatively little of the British presence before 1857. Moreover, the usual family structure for both Hindus and Muslims was the patriarchal, joint family, i.e., one in which sons held family property in common, with the oldest male presiding over a multigenerational household. Strict patrilocal marriage was the norm, and all family members were expected to subordinate their individual desires to the needs of the entire family, especially as those needs were articulated by senior males. Education for Hindus was restricted to the males of certain castes. Intimate familiarity with religious texts was prescribed for Brahmins and compositional and mathematical skills for members of the scribal *jatis*. Members of untouchable *jatis* were strictly forbidden to pursue education of any kind. For Muslims, education was directed toward learning to read the Qur'an and was available almost exclusively to males. Most of these social norms, and especially the views of education, carried over into the early Christian community of this area.

For most of these missionaries, education was the primary avenue for social change among Indian Christians, the primary arena in which the new Christian woman would be created. Working in a cultural context that not only discouraged education for women but also hindered formal education for members of untouchable *jatis*, the missionaries often felt frustrated in their attempts to spread the gospel of education and complained bitterly about the parental opposition (particularly among mass-movement Christians), family and ritual obligations, early marriages, and frequent illnesses that regularly interrupted girls' education. However, the spread of Western education among middle-class Indian males of all communities led after 1900 to increased interest in girls' education among middle-class Indian Christians. This increased interest is reflected in the steadily rising enrollments at both the Rakha and Wanamaker Schools after 1900. While enrollments at the Prentiss School also rose after 1900, chiefly as a result of intense lobbying by itinerating missionaries, mass-movement Christians accepted the value of education for their daughters more slowly.[19]

Early missionaries were often equally frustrated by the unpromising human material Indian Christian girls themselves provided. Because girls were subject to the tight control of their mothers-in-law after marriage, their families tended to indulge them as young children. Consequently, to American women strongly imbued with the Protestant ethic, these girls seemed particularly unprepared for the school experience. Earlier missionaries, who often were working with the first generation of school-going girls, were especially likely to describe their pupils as wild and undisciplined. Later missionaries, working with second- or even third-generation Indian Christians, found them better prepared for the school experience but were critical of their pupils' relations with the Indian church. They regularly criticized the girls' lack of interest in evangelization and charitable service and their maintenance of caste and class distinctions despite missionaries' attempts to foster Christian unity.

While expressing their frustrations to their American readers, the missionaries nevertheless also articulated their vision of the new Indian Christian woman. Most wanted to create "useful" women. By "useful" they typically meant having an enhanced domestic role similar to that ideally prescribed for middle-class American women, i.e., one that combined at least minimal literacy[20] with the ability to cook, keep a clean house, sew, teach one's children, and, above all, find satisfaction in the role of village pastor's wife. Initially espoused by those running almost all the Christian boarding schools, this ideal particularly continued to be operative at Prentiss, whose mass-movement pupils were expected to return to their villages and later marry. Until it became a middle school in 1914, endowing Christian girls with a modest degree of literacy, domestic skills, and contentment with the helpmeet role was also the primary goal of Rakha School, which, having begun as an orphanage, continued as a source of brides for Christian men.

These missionaries were also acutely aware that the north Indian cultural context devalued women's education. Taking their own culture as the standard, they also wished the school experience to provide Indian Christian girls with an orientation toward education that matched their own. Thus, two other key elements in their definition of "usefulness" were the acquisition of teaching skills and the desire to use those skills to benefit the Indian Christian community. The need to turn girls and women into teachers for the Christian community was particularly addressed not only at Wanamaker, but also at Rakha after 1914, at the Mainpuri and Fatehgarh training schools (for the wives of village pastors and teachers), and even partially at Prentiss. Stressing the importance of education in both effecting changes in women's status and building up the Indian church, these missionaries forcefully articulated, for both American readers and their Indian pupils, their expectation that all school graduates would be prepared to teach others. Those attending the training schools and Prentiss were expected to return to their home villages able to teach minimal literacy to their neighbors. Those passing the middle school examinations from Rakha were strongly encouraged to take normal school training and return to teach at Rakha or other mission schools. Those passing the matriculation and entrance examinations from Wanamaker were expected either similarly to return as teachers or to continue on with college-level and professional education. A measure of the missionaries' success in inculcating this value, as well as Indian women's enthusiastic response to professional involvement in education, is the missionaries' frequent report of a significant number of former pupils occupying teaching positions. Holding up some as particularly exemplary in their accomplishments, they also expressed profound disappointment when early marriages or other similar circumstances prevented promising pupils from becoming teachers.

Secluded within patriarchal families and encouraged to play a largely domestic and reproductive role within those families, most Indian women had little experience of voluntary organizations. Indeed, few such organizations existed in India before the British presence. While some of the late nineteenth-century Hindu and Muslim reformers had founded women's organizations, the activities of most of these were concentrated among high-caste Hindu and well-to-do Muslim women in the large British cities, i.e., Bombay, Calcutta, Madras, and, to a lesser extent, Delhi. Such organizations were rarely available in the west-central U.P. provincial towns that made up the North India Presbyterian Mission, nor were low-caste women likely to be involved with them.[21] Again taking their own heavy involvement in voluntary charitable organizations as the standard, these missionaries strongly encouraged, indeed expected, Indian Christian girls and women to participate in activities benefiting the Indian Christian community. Thus "usefulness" also meant the ability to lead voluntary organizations, especially those in the church. Boarding school teachers continually encouraged girls' leadership of Christian Endeavor Societies, branches of the Indian National Mission Society, the Girl Guides, the Y.W.C.A., and many local charitable efforts. More importantly, like their counterparts in the United States, the Indian girls appear to have found in these organizations valuable opportunities to gain leadership and organizational skills, work collectively on projects not directly benefiting their own families or *jatis*, and gain public visibility unavailable elsewhere in Indian society. In addition, membership in organizations like the Girl Guides and the Y.W.C.A., which had national and international ties, gave these girls a rare opportunity to broaden their social and intellectual horizons through participation in all-India, and even all-Asia, conferences.

North Indian culture valued a submissive role for women, and girls were generally socialized to be docile and passive. Pushing women and girls into more visibly activist roles, these missionaries strongly encouraged them to follow in their own footsteps by involving themselves in the expansion of the Indian church. Thus a final element in their definition of usefulness was engaging in missionary work and taking individual responsibility for evangelism. Older pupils at Rakha and Wanamaker were encouraged to conduct Sunday schools for servants' children and visit nearby villages and *zenanas*. Those returning to their home villages from Prentiss or the Mainpuri and Fatehgarh training schools were expected to help their husbands in rural evangelization. While all pupils and teachers were expected to be "earnest" in their desire for the salvation of others, and while most students and teachers did engage in local evangelization and teaching, students and teachers were apparently not always as earnest as the missionaries desired. Recounting their own attentiveness to the evangelistic task, missionaries frequently lamented the lack of earnestness, zeal, and spirituality among the Indians.

Again, missionaries articulated similar values for adult Christian women with whom they interacted, although they had fewer opportunities to influence these women than they did their pupils. Often reacting strongly to the class differences between themselves and these women, they characterized them, and especially those who had converted in the mass movements, as disappointingly ignorant, superstitious, and dirty. Consequently, the missionaries defined their first task as encouraging a higher standard of cleanliness than these women generally observed. After that, however, these women were expected to be useful in much the same ways as the schoolgirls were. Christian women were urged both to broaden their range of domestic skills and, regardless of their community, to become literate. Once literate, they were expected to teach their relatives and neighbors to read. Christian women were also expected to understand basic Christian beliefs and practices and to divorce themselves from their indigenous community identities by giving up old customs and beliefs. They were also encouraged to be active in church causes, especially in charitable work and evangelistic activities, or in serving as Bible women; and they were to exercise leadership in the Indian church through women's organizations and through offering advice and counsel. In addition to these expectations of usefulness, missionaries also encouraged other more traditional values for these women: they should be truthful, gentle, loving, patient, trusting, quiet, orderly, and unselfishly devoted to their husbands and children. Indian women who fulfilled all these expectations were held up as examples to other women in mission reports and magazines and in Christian newspapers in the regional languages.

American women missionaries brought a cluster of values to north India that informed their desire and ability to function as agents of change for women in late nineteenth- and early twentieth-century India.[22] Viewing themselves as bearers of a superior culture in which women occupied an exalted place, they felt a responsibility to change not only the religious identities of Indian women, but their social roles as well. However, because the missionaries strongly identified themselves with the domestic role, they did not advocate radical changes in Indian social structures but rather encouraged values that largely reinforced and upheld the already domestic identity accorded to women in Indian culture. On the other hand, through their insistence on education, and especially on literacy, for as wide a cross-section of women as possible, through their encouragement of professional training for women, and through their encouragement of women's participation in voluntary organizations that gave them access to communications media and opportunities to develop organizational skills, the missionaries enabled Indian women to assume leadership roles that afforded them much greater personal liberty and public visibility than their culture traditionally allowed them and that ultimately let Indian women see *themselves* as potential agents of change.

The account presented here rests on the writings of the missionaries, their reports to mission boards in the United States, and their writings in various mission magazines. Clearly, what is missing is an assessment of Indian women's *response* to the values articulated by the missionaries. Mission papers do report some Indian responses, and I have alluded here to missionaries' sense of success in encouraging women to enter the teaching and other professions, to engage in evangelism, and to join voluntary organizations. I have also alluded to a progressive world view articulated by some Indian Christian women. Obviously, however, such sources as Christian newspapers in Indian languages, alumnae reports in newsletters of boarding schools and colleges, biographies and autobiographies, diaries, and oral histories must now be tapped to gauge the Indian response. If we are to understand fully the dynamics of the encounter between American missionaries and Indian women, much research still needs to be done.

NOTES

1. William Hutchison, *Errand to the World* (Chicago: University of Chicago Press, 1987); R. Pierce Beaver, "Missionary Motivation through Three Centuries," in *Reinterpretation in American Church History,* ed. J. C. Brauer (Chicago: University of Chicago Press, 1968); C. W. Forman, "A History of Foreign Mission Theory in America," in *American Missions in Bicentennial Perspective,* ed. R. Pierce Beaver (Pasadena, Calif: Carey, 1977).

2. H. P. Beach and B. St. John, eds., *World Statistics of Christian Missionaries* (New York: Foreign Missionary Conference of North America, 1916); R. Pierce Beaver, *American Protestant Women in World Mission* (Grand Rapids, Mich.: Eerdmans, 1980); Patricia R. Hill, *The World Their Household* (Ann Arbor: University of Michigan Press, 1982).

3. R. W. Braisted, *In This Generation* (New York: Friendship Press, 1941).

4. Barbara Welter, "The Cult of True Womanhood, 1820–1860," in *Dimity Convictions* (Athens, Ohio: Ohio University Press, 1976); Joan Jacobs Brumberg, "Zenanas and Girlless Villages," *Journal of American History* 69 (1982): 347–71; Joan Jacobs Brumberg, "The Ethnological Mirror: American Evangelical Women and Their Heathen Sisters, 1870–1910," in *Women and the Structure of Society,* ed. B. J. Harris and J. K. McNamara (Durham, N.C: Duke University Press, 1984) pp. 108–28.

5. To date Jane Hunter, in *The Gospel of Gentility* (New Haven: Yale University Press, 1984), is the only one to have provided a detailed analysis of the intersection of these themes, here for American women missionaries in turn-of-the-century China.

6. Before 1947 this area was called the United Provinces (of Agra and Oudh). Both before and after 1947 this area is usually referred to as U.P.

7. Access to adequate medical care for women and girls is still an issue for South Asian women. Among many references, see, e.g., Doranne Jacobson, "The Women of North and Central India: Goddesses and Wives," in *Women in India: Two Perspectives*, ed. Doranne Jacobson and Susan Wadley (New Delhi: Manohar, 1977), pp. 17–111; Madhu Kishwar and R. Vanita, *In Search of Answers* (London: Zed Books, 1984); Barbara D. Miller, *The Endangered Sex: Neglect of Female Children in Rural India* (Ithaca, N.Y.: Cornell University Press, 1981).

8. Quotations from missionary sources before 1910 came from Board of Foreign Missions microfilm records (BFM-MR). Sources after 1910 are contained in record group 83, boxes 1 and 4. Both sources include station reports (SR), personal labor reports (PLR) and calendared correspondence (CC). Missionary quotations are also taken from *Woman's Work for Woman* (called *Woman's Work* after 1920 and abbreviated here as *WW*), all housed at the Presbyterian Historical Society. Adelaide Woodard, PLR 1925.

9. Many missionary anecdotes describe the abuse of young girls, in both their parents and their in-laws' homes. Miller's work on neglect of female children in north India, as well as contemporary accounts in Kishwar and Vanita, suggest that the missionaries' accounts may well have been accurate.

10. Indian Christians seem to have responded positively to these concerns of the missionaries. Christian girls were gradually allowed to remain longer in school, with many completing their middle or matriculation examinations before marrying (see below). Some worked as teachers or physicians before marrying, and a small minority never married at all.

11. PLR 1891.

12. In the mass movements, which began in the 1880s, whole families or even clans of usually untouchable *jatis* were converted to Christianity at the same time. These mass conversions often caused great consternation among Protestant missionaries, who were accustomed to individual conversions, and who hoped to convert high-caste Hindus and Muslims. In north India, the Methodists were the first to experience and accept these mass conversions. For Presbyterian experiences with the mass movements, see John C. B. Webster, *The Christian Community and Change in Nineteenth-Century North India* (Delhi: Macmillan, 1976).

13. Sam Higginbottom, for example, spent most of his more than thirty years in India running the Agricultural Institute in Allahabad. William Wiser, who later became well known for his descriptions, with his wife Charlotte, of rural life in north India, began his mission career working in industrial cooperatives in Kanpur. Charlotte, predictably, began hers with running baby shows, i.e., fairs demonstrating Western hygiene and childcare techniques.

14. Regina Morantz-Sanchez, *Sympathy and Science* (New York: Oxford University Press, 1985).

15. I use the term "culture of poverty" fully aware of its meaning in the United States. While this term is not generally used in descriptions of low-caste life-styles in India, one can argue that traditional economic relationships between high and low castes (*jajmani* relationships) and the doctrine of *karma* strongly discouraged members of low-caste *jatis,* and especially untouchables, from attempting to change their economic status.

16. Helen Howe Holcomb, *WW*, Sept. 1897, 249.

17. Although scarcely statistically rigorous, annual station reports unfailingly comment on the health of boarding school pupils and the deaths from the various epidemics of the Hindu and Muslim girls in the day schools for non-Christian girls. Explicit comparisons between these two groups are also common. The assertion by

the physician Mabel Sammons Hayes that, in comparison to the cases coming to her dispensary, the girls at Wanamaker, Rakha, and Etah Schools "are monotonously healthy," (PLR 1928) is typical.

18. Preliminary study of the autobiographies of Indian Christian women reveals a strongly progressivist identity among them, with a conscious articulation of the need for change in women's roles. While these women do not attribute their progressive viewpoint *directly* to their Christian identity, they do exhibit a strong sense of detachment from Indian tradition and a desire to look forward rather than backward. For more discussion of this point see my paper, "Visions of Grace and Power: Autobiographies of Indian Christian Women," given at the 1989 meeting of the Association for Asian Studies, Washington, D.C. Preliminary study of the *Lal Bagh Chronicle*, the alumnae newsletter of Isabella Thoburn High School and College in Lucknow, suggests similar attitudes.

19. The oldest of the three institutions, Rakha reported enrollments of 77 in 1879, 125 in 1915, and 238 in 1927. Mary Wanamaker reported 75 in 1900, 119 in 1913, and 151 in 1927. Prentiss School opened in 1903 with 8 and reported enrollments of 50 in 1917 and 96 in 1927. However, much of the enrollment at Prentiss represented a rapid turnover of girls, with few staying the full four possible years and some even dropping out after the first vacation. By contrast, during this period a steadily increasing proportion of pupils at Rakha and Wanamaker stayed through the entire course and sat for the government examinations. BFM-MR, Allahabad, Etah, and Farrukhabad Station Reports.

20. These writers did not define the skills involved in literacy, beyond that of being able to read the Bible. Clearly those who sat for the government middle and (university) entrance examinations possessed substantial abilities in both reading and writing, as well as knowledge of such other standard school subjects as mathematics, history, and geography (although relatively little of science). Although readers and standard levels are mentioned in station reports for the Prentiss School and the training schools, there is little concrete information on the level of literacy these girls and women actually possessed as a result of the school experience. On the problems of the definition of literacy in historical perspective see H. J. Graff, *Literacy in History* (New York: Garland, 1981) and K. A. Lockridge, *Literacy in Colonial New England* (New York: Norton, 1974). For a summary of the issues from a contemporary educational perspective see J. A. Langer, "The State of Research on Literacy," *Educational Research* 17 (1988): 42–46.

21. Patricia Caplan, "Women's Organizations in Madras City," in *Women United, Women Divided: Cross-Cultural Perspectives on Female Solidarity*, ed. Patricia Caplan and Janet M. Bujra (Bloomington: Indiana University Press, 1979), pp. 99–128; Gail Pearson, "The Female Intelligentsia in Segregated Society: Early Twentieth-Century Bombay," in *Women in India and Nepal*, ed. Michael Allen and S. N. Mukherjee (Canberra: Australian National University Monographs on South Asia, 1982), pp. 136–54.

22. The argument here is based on only the case of American *Presbyterian* women missionaries. However, accounts of the activities of women in other denominations, or even in nondenominational groups, reveal similar attitudes and emphases. In addition to *The World Their Household*, see, e.g., Barbara Fassler, "The Role of Women in the India Mission, 1819–1880, in *Piety and Patriotism*, ed. J. W. Van Halen (Grand Rapids, MI: Eerdmans, 1976), pp. 149–62; A. R. Gracey, *Eminent Missionary Women* (New York: Eaton and Mains, 1898); J. N. Hollister, *The Centenary of the Methodist Church in Southern Asia* (Lucknow: Lucknow Publishing House, 1956); and Charlotte Dennett Staelin, "The Influence of Missions on Women's Education in India: The American Marathi Mission in Ahmednagar, 1830–1930," Ph.D. dissertation, University of Michigan, 1977.

GIVE A THOUGHT TO AFRICA
BLACK WOMEN MISSIONARIES IN SOUTHERN AFRICA

Sylvia M. Jacobs

The late nineteenth and early twentieth centuries witnessed the European partitioning and subsequent colonization of the continent of Africa. A small segment of the African-American community, including journalists, religious and secular leaders, diplomats and politicians, missionaries, and travelers and visitors, addressed themselves to the issue of the impact of the establishment of European imperialism in Africa. Although they may have viewed the different elements of imperialism (cultural, social, economic, political) in various ways, most middle-class blacks, believing that Africa needed to be "civilized and Christianized," generally concluded that if the interests and welfare of the indigenous African populations were being considered, European activity on the continent would be beneficial. They therefore supported the European imperialists in Africa as long as exploitation was not their only goal. Black American views on the European partitioning of Africa varied only slightly from tacit approval to partial rejection. This chapter will discuss the response of one African-American group—black American women missionaries—to the European colonization of Africa, and how imperialism, gender, and race limited their roles as missionaries in Africa.

In the nineteenth century, white American and European Protestant church boards began to establish missions in Africa. These churches gave serious consideration to using African-Americans as missionaries on the continent. Thus began many successive attempts to appoint blacks to missionary work in their ancestral homeland. The largest number of African-American missionaries sent to Africa went during the late nineteenth and early twentieth centuries. Black American missionaries were affected by the prevailing Western image of Africa as a "Dark Continent" in need of "civilizing." Their relationship with Africa and Africans was both ambivalent and contradictory. On the one hand, these black American missionaries, women and men, believed that Africa needed to be "civilized and Christianized" and that it was their "duty," as descendants of the continent, to assist in that redemption. Race, then, was a factor in their commitment to Africans. But they had to wrestle with their Western orientation and their biases about African culture and society, and thus they initially held Africa and Africans at arm's length.

Although more than half of the American Protestant missionaries who went to Africa during this period were males, they were assisted by their wives, who were designated "assistant missionaries." But even single women sent as missionaries had secondary roles. The mores of the late nineteenth and early twentieth centuries prescribed that women be engaged in "women's work": that meant teaching in day, Sunday, and industrial schools; maintaining orphanages and boarding schools; making house-to-house visitations; and dispensing medical care to women and children.[1]

Between 1880 and 1920 almost eighty African-American women were assigned to or accompanied their husbands as missionaries to Africa. Of that number, fourteen went to five southern African countries: Angola and Mozambique, which were under Portuguese colonial rule; and the British colonies of Nyasaland, Southern Rhodesia, and South Africa. They represented six mission-sending societies. But only nine African-American women missionaries are discussed in this essay because there is little information on three of these women, who accompanied their husbands to South Africa—Celia Ann Nelson Gregg (1904–6, 1924–28), Mattie E. Murff (1906–10), and Lucinda Ernestine Thomas East (1909–20)—and the two others served the major portion of their terms of service after 1920—Julia Cele Smith (1918?–48) and Bessie Cherry Fonveille McDowell (1919–37). Were the views of these black female missionaries about European imperialism in Africa any different from their black male or white counterparts? Were there major differences in the experiences of African-American women missionaries in African mission work? Did these women have to adjust in any way to the European presence on the continent? Because of the nature of available sources, it is not always easy to distinguish the views of black female missionaries from those of black male missionaries. Of the nine women discussed here, only five sent home letters or reports, or wrote about their experiences in Africa. What this means is that often we are left with only the writings of black male missionaries. Thus to understand the views of some of these women, we need to look at other things, such as applications, letters to newspapers and magazines, college and university catalogues and histories, and unpublished manuscripts.

The American Board of Commissioners for Foreign Missions (ABCFM) was the first American board to send missionaries to Africa. The ABCFM, one of several Congregational missionary societies, was organized in 1810 and two years later sent out its first foreign missionaries to India. At its

1825 annual meeting, the board voted to open a mission in Africa. In 1834 missionaries set up the first ABCFM mission at Cape Palmas, Liberia. ABCFM missionaries reached Natal in 1835 and subsequently set up the Zulu Mission, the first American-sponsored mission in South Africa.[2]

In 1882, the Reverend William C. Wilcox asked for and received permission from the board to explore the region around Inhambane, located between the cities of Sofala and Lorenço Marques in the southeastern corner of Mozambique, five hundred miles east of the Umzila kingdom and about six hundred miles north of Natal on the seacoast. Inhambane was at first a part of the Zulu Mission, but eventually the name East Central African Mission was adopted to designate this area, with the idea that it was only a stopover point from which an advance later would be made into the interior. Though not having received formal permission from the Portuguese government to open the mission, representatives of the ABCFM secured a location a few miles outside the city of Inhambane and employed Africans to begin building mission houses. Several locations around the bay were ultimately occupied, and three African-Americans—Benjamin Forsyth Ousley, Henrietta Bailey Ousley, and Nancy Jones—pioneered one such station of the East Central African Mission at Inhambane, that of Kambini.[3]

Benjamin Ousley, born a slave of the brother of the Confederate States president, in Davis Bend, Warren County, Mississippi, was the first ordained black missionary of the ABCFM. Ousley earned a B.A. degree and an M.A. degree from Fisk University and a B.D. degree from Oberlin Theological Seminary.[4]

Henrietta Bailey was born to slave parents, Henry and Harriet Bailey, on October 4, 1852, in Washington County, Mississippi, although during the Civil War her family escaped to Knoxville, Illinois. She united with the African Methodist Episcopal (AME) Church in 1875 but was not fully accepted until 1878. Bailey studied at Knoxville High School and Fisk University, and before going to Africa she was employed as a teacher in Corinth, Mississippi. On August 14, 1884, she married Reverend Benjamin Ousley, who was under appointment by the ABCFM to the East Central African Mission. On her application of September 24, 1884, for mission service, in reply to the question—"When did you decide to go to the heathen, and what led you to think of the subject?"—Henrietta Ousley answered: "It had been brought to notice first by the departure of some missionaries for the West Coast of Africa, then an appeal was made to me personally by a friend to fit myself for a teacher for the Mendi Mission [mission of the American Missionary Association in Sierra Leone], then finally this request of Mr. Ousley's that I would share with him the life of a foreign missionary."[5] Benjamin Ousley apparently had sought a wife when he was commissioned to go to Mozambique. Henrietta Ousley, the first black woman sent out by the ABCFM, served in Mozambique with her husband from 1884 to 1893.

The last of the African-American pioneer missionaries in Mozambique appointed by the ABCFM was Nancy Jones. Jones, the first unmarried black woman commissioned by the American Board, was born in Christian County, near Hopkinsville, Kentucky, in 1860 and during her childhood moved with her family to Memphis, Tennessee. She was baptized at the age of fourteen while a student at Lemoyne Institute (now Lemoyne-Owen College), and united with the First Colored Baptist Church of Memphis soon afterwards. Jones also attended Fisk University, graduating from the Normal Department course in 1886. At the same time, she taught in Alpika, Mississippi, commuting to Fisk. Although a Baptist, she applied to the Congregational American Board for a missionary appointment. In her letter of application she stated: "I have wanted to be a Missionary ever since I was twelve years old. . . . I have earnestly prayed to the Lord to teach me my duty, show me just what he would have me do and I received in answer to these petitions an urgent longing for work in a Mission field in Africa." Jones served the board in Mozambique, and later in eastern Rhodesia, from 1888 to 1897. The Ousleys and Jones worked together at Kambini for over five years. Henrietta Ousley and Jones had known one another at Fisk and apparently both had given some thought to their "duty" to assist in the "religious uplift" of Africa before their appointment.[6]

On September 25, 1884, the Ousleys departed from New York to join the East Central African Mission. They arrived at Durban, Natal Colony, South Africa, three weeks later, on November 14, and sailed for Inhambane on November 28, reaching the bay on December 2. Benjamin Ousley and William Wilcox traveled into the interior and Ousley selected the station at Kambini that he and his wife, and later Nancy Jones, eventually occupied. In the 1885 annual report of the East Central African Mission from the Kambini station, Ousley noted that because the Portuguese government in Mozambique was so restrictive of foreigners, missionary activities were limited to religious instruction, and only in those areas surrounding the mission; ABCFM missionaries were forbidden to preach outside these boundaries.[7]

In the Reports of Committees on the Annual Report in 1885, the Committee on Missions in Africa, chaired by James Powell, made the following observation:

> The East Central Mission . . . has been marked the past year by the exploration, selections of new stations, and the reinforcement of the mission by Mr. and Mrs. Ousley, colored graduates of Fisk University, Nashville; Mr. Ousley being also a graduate of Oberlin. We note the possible significance that the lives of these missionaries, trained in the schools of our denomination at the South, are to play in the future in the evangelization of the Dark Continent.[8]

Obviously, the Committee was reflecting the positive feelings, at that time, of the Congregational Church toward assigning African-Americans as missionaries to Africa.

In 1886, the Ousleys completed their mission compound at Kambini, and having learned to speak the Sheetswa language, opened a school, which numbered about fifty students by the end of the year. Henrietta Ousley's duties, because of her training, included teaching in the mission school. She taught alone in the mornings, but because of a larger number of students, Benjamin Ousley joined her in the afternoon. He spent his mornings studying and translating an English Bible study and a book of catechisms into Sheetswa, the language of the people around the bay of Inhambane. In view of the nature of nineteenth-century mission responsibilities for women, Henrietta Ousley also worked with the children and women of the area. But she found great disappointment in the work, partly because of her own Western biases. In a report to the board, Benjamin Ousley pointed out: "It is sad, but nevertheless true, that woman seems more degraded here, and harder to reach, than man. . . . We often commiserate the degraded condition of these poor women; yet they do not appreciate our pity, or even desire to live different lives. They are satisfied with their present lot."[9]

A few explanations may help to clarify black missionaries' negative views about African women. First was the issue of labor roles. African-American missionaries were distressed over the fact that African women did agricultural work, which these missionaries viewed as "man's work." During slavery, African-American women had been forced to work side-by-side with male slaves in farming on plantations, and consequently, among African-Americans, female farm labor became an indication of low status. However, in African agricultural societies women who farmed had a high economic and social status. Second, black American missionaries viewed African women as inferior in African society because of polygamy. Often in African societies polygamy was beneficial to women because they assumed a higher social status as wives and because it resulted in the sharing of "women's work" among more persons. Because of their own cultural limitations, these missionaries failed to see the social and economic benefits to African women of agricultural work and polygamy. Third, African-American missionaries were disturbed by nudity and sexuality among African women.

On January 28, 1888, Francis W. Bates and his wife, Laura H. Bates, along with Nancy Jones, departed from Boston, the location of the headquarters of the ABCFM, to join the East Central African Mission.[10] In several letters written before her departure, Jones pondered her life's work. In one to President E. M. Cravath of Fisk University, she discussed missionary work and asked for his advice about her decision to go to Africa.

> I have prayed to the Lord and asked Him what He would have me to do ever since I became a Christian and I believe He has given me the work of a missionary and He directs my mind and heart to Africa, the land of my Forefathers. To those who are calling to their sons and daughters to come

and help them. . . . I am willing to go to Africa as a Missionary and I offer myself to any Missionary Society who wants some one to go to any Foreign Mission Station.[11]

Cravath directed Jones to the Congregational American Board, and she began communicating with Dr. Judson Smith, corresponding secretary of the ABCFM. She explained that she hoped to be useful to the Ousleys and would like to be associated with them in their mission work.[12]

After a short stay in Natal, Jones arrived at the Kambini station on May 18, 1888, immediately began studying the Sheetswa language, and soon began teaching with the Ousleys. After two weeks, she took charge of the school's primary department. Besides her regular school work, she also visited nearby areas and read to the village women. Like the Ousleys, Jones expressed regret that she had been unsuccessful in reaching the African girls and women. Unbeknownst to some missionaries, African women often viewed education as a male's prerogative, which may explain some of the resistance the missionaries encountered. Jones proposed setting up, on a small scale, a boarding school for the girls and boys, the "Kambini Home," and affirmed: "I do not know whether I shall be successful, but as it has not been tried here I feel that the good Lord will bless the effort." Unfortunately, Jones never realized her dream. Although she and the Ousleys took many abandoned and orphaned children into their homes, they were never successful in persuading the American board of the necessity and benefit of a boarding school. The Ousleys, however, did adopt one of the children and took him back to the United States with them when they returned.[13]

In July and August of 1888, Jones and Henrietta Ousley were left alone at the Kambini mission when Benjamin Ousley visited Natal for health reasons. Because there were not enough children in the Kambini school to keep both Henrietta Ousley and Jones busy, Jones, in October 1888, opened another school across a nearby stream, two miles from the Kambini station. Since a schoolhouse had not been built, the class met outside under a large tree, with over sixty children sitting on the ground. Jones taught them the commandments, the Lord's Prayer, verses of Scripture, reading, and sewing.[14]

Benjamin Ousley continued to suffer from an illness that he had contracted in the United States. Finally, in 1890, the Ousleys withdrew from Kambini, seeking medical relief in America and arriving in Boston on May 27.[15] During their absence, Jones continued the work among the younger children and visited the women in nearby villages. She criticized the Portuguese government for not providing food for the people that it had brought south to work. She declared, "I think it would be better for the people if this country was in the hands of a more judicious government." John D. and Hattie F. Bennett (who were white) joined Jones during the Ousleys' absence so that she would not be left alone on the Kambini station. The Bennetts and Jones took a furlough in Natal during the spring of 1891.[16]

In the 1890 Reports of Committees on the Annual Report, the Committee on Missions in Africa complimented the Ousleys and Jones for the work they were doing in Africa. It insisted that, "From the colored students of our country are coming forward some of the most useful workers for this field [Africa], three out of five missionaries in the East Central African Mission being graduates of Fisk University. These facts emphasize the importance of larger work in this land, and suggest that we may properly expect that the gospel will be carried thence by the descendants of the African race."[17] After six years experience with African-American missionaries in Mozambique, the American board evidently was pleased with the results.

Upon their return to Kambini, the Ousleys resumed their work at the mission, but found the situation somewhat worsened since they had left the station two years earlier. Because of the failing health of Benjamin Ousley, the Ousleys were again compelled to return to the United States. On July 8, 1893, they arrived in New York and later withdrew from their connection with the ABCFM. They returned to Mississippi.[18]

The Inhambane region proved too unhealthy for continued missionary activity. Since missionaries of the East Central African Mission had not lost sight of their original plan for settling on higher ground away from the coast, the year 1893 was spent in selecting a new mission site in the elevated region of Gazaland. The area selected was located in eastern Rhodesia, on the northern slope of Mt. Silinda, at an elevation of four thousand feet above sea level, and nearly two hundred miles inland, at the mouth of the Pungwe River. Gazaland occupied the region adjoining the eastern coast from Delagoa Bay northward to the mouth of the Zambezi River. The new mission was within the jurisdiction of the British South Africa Company and its president, Cecil Rhodes, rented more than thirty thousand acres to the ABCFM for their mission station. Missionaries of this station were under British administration, while the remaining part of the mission field was subject to Portuguese control.

Jones joined the other members of the new Gazaland mission, and the Inhambane stations were permanently closed. The missionaries set forth from Durban on June 21, 1893; a portion of the party, including Jones, arrived at Mt. Silinda on September 25, 1893, the remainder twenty-four days later. Houses were built, land cleared, crops planted, roads marked, and all of the main activities of mission work were begun.[19]

At Mt. Silinda, a day school was opened with Jones as teacher, and she continued to be in charge of the school throughout 1895 and 1896, despite poor attendance. She also organized a literary club among the people of the region. Although Jones's house was called "Silinda Hall" because of her continuing interest in caring for abandoned children, she again was unable to interest this mission station in the idea of a children's home and commented: "It seems that my hopes for seeing a Boarding school started for

. . . girls and others will never be realized. Yet I am not discouraged entirely. It may not be in my time. But I feel that it will be established."[20]

On September 10, 1896, the Bateses and H. Juliette Gibson arrived at Mt.
Silinda. Eight months later, on May 27, 1897, Nancy Jones submitted her
resignation from the East Central African Mission to the Prudential Committee, giving as her reason: "on account of my aged mother needing my
help and realizing that I am unable to work in harmony with the mission."
On October 25, 1897, she arrived in Boston.[21]

Back in the United States, Jones admitted to Judson Smith, corresponding secretary of the board, that her reason for resigning was prejudice
against her by several of the white missionaries who did not want to live
with her at Mt. Silinda. After the Bateses and Gibson arrived on the station,
Jones was no longer allowed to teach in the school or work with the children. Gibson took over these duties. At the same time, Jones was given the
tasks of cooking, buying food, planting a garden, and supplying the mission with vegetables. The Bateses insisted that she pay for the room and
board of the children and African friends who visited her at the mission
station. Jones complained that although she knew the language, and the
people liked her, these missionaries were claiming that she was an unfit
missionary. She admitted that their racism had made it so uncomfortable
for her that she had resigned. But she asked the Prudential Committee to
allow her to withdraw her resignation and assign her to an area where
white missionaries could not live well. There, she claimed, she could work
alone or with other African-American missionaries.[22]

Apparently, the Prudential Committee did not reconsider her resignation, because Jones was never reassigned to Africa; she returned to her
home in Memphis. In a series of addresses given in Alabama in 1898, Jones
discussed pioneer missionary work on the coast of southeastern Africa.
She testified that wherever white men were in control, Africans, as a rule,
were discriminated against and treated with prejudice. Jones claimed that
Africans regarded missionaries of their own race with confidence and asserted that Africa was a wide field that called loudly for intelligent, Christian African-American women and men, not only as teachers, but as leaders in every line of industrial, educational, religious, and social life. This
view was not shared by all Africans, since some saw African-American
missionaries simply as "white men and women in black skin."[23]

During this period, 1880 to 1920, two African-American women missionaries served in Angola, a Portuguese colony. Susan Collins, of the Methodist Episcopal Church's Pacific Coast Conference, was a graduate of the
Chicago Missionary Training School (Illinois). Collins first was mentioned
in the Methodist missionary report of 1890 as a missionary worker who was
not a member of the Methodist Episcopal African Conference. She initially
stopped at Dondo in the Angola District but immediately was transferred
to Malanje. The missionaries in Angola were to plant industrial missions
and establish nurseries for children in order to accomplish the dual mission

goals—self-support and evangelism—of the third Methodist missionary bishop of Africa, William Taylor.[24]

Malanje, the last settled of the five original Methodist stations opened in Angola, was organized in September 1885. When Collins arrived in 1890 the church at Malanje had over twenty members. In 1893 Collins began working at Canandua. Mission property consisted of a house, two trading buildings, and farm land valued at over $2,700. At Canandua, Collins was a teacher at the girls' home. She was able to raise a few vegetables in the gardens of the home toward their support.

On April 19, 1898, Collins was formally recognized by the Methodist Board of Managers as a missionary in Angola. The girls' school at Canandua was transferred and formed a part of the school at Quessua. After her certification by the church, Collins was transferred to the Quessua station. This station was opened in 1890 as part of Bishop Taylor's scheme of African industrial nursery missions. Originally connected with the Malanje Mission, it was first called Munhall and eventually came to be known as Quessua. It was located at the foot of a mountain, about six miles from Malanje. To the Quessua mission house and farm there was ultimately added a common school and a nursery mission for Angolan girls. In the fields, sugar cane, Indian corn, and fruit trees were grown. At Quessua, as matron and teacher, Collins was in charge of the boarding school and orphanage for girls where there were about twenty students. She also did industrial work.[25]

In 1901, after a furlough in the United States, Collins returned to Angola under the auspices of the California branch of the Woman's Foreign Missionary Society (WFMS) of the Methodist Episcopal Church. Management of the girls' home and school at Quessua had been assumed by the WFMS in 1901. By 1904 Collins taught over twenty girls in the WFMS school at Quessua. The WFMS home at Quessua, with Collins as matron, constantly housed about sixty girls by 1917, almost all of whom attended the WFMS school. Collins eventually was joined at Quessua by another African-American woman missionary sent out by the WFMS, Martha Drummer.

At Quessua there was a farm of over six hundred acres with an industrial school for boys and young men, taught by an Angolan helper, in addition to the WFMS home and school for girls. In 1918 an eight thousand acre parcel adjoining the original property was secured by Quessua. The following year, Collins left Angola.[26] It is not clear why Collins was retired home, but it is possible that it was her advanced age, since she had been in the field twenty-eight years.

Martha Drummer, of Barnesville, Georgia, was graduated from Clark University (now Clark Atlanta University, Atlanta, Georgia) in 1901. She continued her training at the Northeastern Deaconess Training School (Boston, Massachusetts), where she specialized in nurse training.

In 1906 Drummer sailed for Angola as a missionary of the Women's Foreign Missionary Society. She spent sixteen years at the Quessua station working at the girls' boarding home and school. She retired in 1922 from missionary service. On December 11, 1937, Drummer died in Atlanta, Georgia, with the last words: "Say Africa when you pray."[27] Apparently neither Collins nor Drummer, as unmarried, black female missionaries without church-related administrative responsibilities, had any dealings with the Portuguese government in Angola; they rarely discussed European imperialism in their letters home.

Two other American churches initiated mission work in southern Africa during this period. The National Baptist Convention and the Seventh-Day Adventist Church opened mission stations in Nyasaland. The former, a black board, and the latter, white, both sent African-American missionaries into this area. The agents of the National Baptist Convention were Landon Cheek and Emma Delaney, and the Seventh-Day Adventists were represented by Thomas Branch and his wife, Henrietta Paterson Branch.[28]

Black American Baptists first became interested in African mission work in the nineteenth century. After the organization of the Baptist Foreign Mission Convention in 1880, its first missionaries were sent to Liberia in 1883. In the late nineteenth century, the National Baptist Convention made plans to open an African Baptist industrial mission in the Shire highlands of Nyasaland.[29]

Reverend Landon N. Cheek was the first African-American missionary to arrive in Nyasaland. Cheek applied to the National Baptist Convention for a missionary assignment, was accepted in 1899, and after a year of soliciting funds from African-American churches, left New York on January 23, 1901, arriving in Nyasaland in April. In the Chiradzulu district in the southern province of Nyasaland, Cheek found an able and willing assistant in the American-educated African, John Chilembwe.[30]

When Landon Cheek arrived in Nyasaland, his advanced formal education, in conjunction with general European misgivings about African-American missionaries, assured colonial mistrust. In a letter to John Mitchell, Jr., editor of the *Richmond Planet* (Virginia), Cheek wrote: "The Negroes are looked upon [by the European colonialists] with suspicion as they hoist even the banner of Jesus in heathen Africa."[31]

The other National Baptist Convention missionary and the second African-American missionary in Nyasaland, arrived in 1902, a year after Cheek. Emma Bertha Delaney was born in Fernandina Beach, Florida, in 1871, the same year as Cheek. She was graduated from Spelman Seminary (now Spelman College) in 1894 and its missionary training course in 1896. She spent six years completing the Spelman nurse training course, from which she received preliminary instructions for the mission field. After graduation, she worked for several years as a matron at Florida Institute (Live Oak). Delaney was sent out and supported by the Baptist women of Florida, serving in both Nyasaland (1902–6) and Liberia (1912–20).[32]

In an address delivered before she left for Africa, entitled "Why I Go as a Foreign Missionary," Delaney discussed mission work. She commented

that, "my interest in missions was awakened in early childhood by a returned missionary who spoke on behalf of his work in Africa." She continued:

> At the age of thirteen, . . . I united with the [Baptist] church, and the spirit
> of missions increased. After entering Spelman Seminary and spending
> twelve years there, where our duty to God and humanity, both at home and
> abroad, is daily set forth, the mere desire for this work was changed to duty
> and a longing for the work that nothing else would satisfy. After more than
> three successful years of work at home, I stand to-night as a full-fledged
> candidate for Africa in obedience to the great command.[33]

At the Chiradzulu mission station, Delaney taught school. Eventually,
extra teachers were added. Delaney was influential in establishing a women's society and weekly sewing classes for girls. Certainly she was responsible for arousing interest among African-American women for African redemption, through her letters from Africa and her lectures in the
United States. Four years after her arrival in Nyasaland, Delaney could see
considerable improvement in the area surrounding the mission, and there
were students in regular attendance at the schools.[34]

After Cheek and Delaney had been at Chiradzulu for two years, the mission station was renamed the Providence Industrial Mission (PIM). The arrival of these missionaries had shown Africans and European colonialists
that the National Baptist Convention was prepared to support the mission
financially and by 1904 regular remittances arrived from the church. Thus,
by the time the missionaries left in 1906, a promising mission station existed. Cheek had married Chilembwe's niece, Rachael, and fathered three
children, one of whom died before they left Africa. When Cheek returned
to the United States, he took two PIM boys with him and educated them.
Delaney was followed to the United States by one of her students, Daniel
Malekebu, who earned a medical degree in the United States and returned
to Nyasaland in 1926 as head of the reopened Providence Industrial Mission. With the foundations of the mission secure, Cheek, his family, and
Delaney left Nyasaland in June of 1906 for a well-deserved furlough.[35]

Considering her visit to the United States in 1906 only temporary, Emma
Delaney asked the Baptist board to reappoint her to mission work in Nyasaland, but permission was denied by the British government. By this date
the European imperialists were beginning to question the African-American and African-Caribbean presence in Africa. These colonialists feared
that Africans would identify with their better educated, politically conscious brothers and sisters. Delaney then applied for a mission position in
Liberia, was accepted, and worked there for eight years. Cheek, after his
return to the United States, apparently did not reapply for African mission
work.[36]

The Seventh-Day Adventist Church first sent six missionaries to Africa in

July of 1887. Arriving in Cape Town, South Africa, this corps later was re-inforced. In 1892 the South African Union Conference was organized with headquarters at Cape Town. Buildings were erected, a training school opened, an orphanage founded, and two periodicals, the *South African Sentinel* and the *South African Missionary*, were established. The first Seventh-Day Adventist to enter Nyasaland was George James, a student of Battle Creek College (Michigan) who went to that country in 1892. Unluckily, he died in 1894 of malaria on the return journey to the coast.[37]

At the beginning of 1902 the Seventh Day Baptists sold their mission near Cholo (about thirty miles south of the Blantyre region in southern Nyasaland) to the Seventh-Day Adventists. The third African-American missionary appointed to Nyasaland, Thomas H. Branch, and his wife, Henrietta, and family sailed from New York on June 28, 1902, on the *RMS Saxon*, arriving at Cholo, Nyasaland, on August 29, 1902. Branch had been chosen by the American missionary organization of the Seventh-Day Adventists to open their initial mission in Nyasaland. The Colorado Conference had recommended Branch and his family and had offered to support them in the field. Branch was sent as superintendent of the newly acquired Plainfield Mission Station in Nyasaland, a name given to it by the Seventh Day Baptists in honor of Plainfield, New Jersey, headquarters of that denomination. Branch was probably the first African-American Seventh-Day Adventist to be sent overseas as a missionary.[38]

Branch initially noticed that many Africans were indifferent to alien religions but were eager to secure an education. It was for this reason that older missionary societies had established schools, which attracted many young men. In these missionary schools, African students were exposed to Christianity and some accepted the new religion. Many Africans recognized a direct relationship between obtaining an education for the purpose of advancement within the colonial system and conversion to Christianity, and some were willing to convert as a means of securing that education. Branch hired teachers who had been trained by the older societies, and a Plainfield Mission school, with twenty-five students, was opened. Initially, the classes were held under the trees but eventually a school building was constructed. Henrietta Branch, and the Branches' daughter, Mabel, worked in the school. By the time the Branches left Nyasaland in 1907 the mission school numbered seventy-five pupils, and there were two out-schools located several miles from the mission.[39]

For five years the Branches faithfully carried on the work of the Plainfield Mission, but because Thomas Branch protested mistreatment and abuse of Africans, local journalists accused him of also being militant in his religious teachings. Because the Seventh-Day Adventist Church wanted the mission to be viewed in a positive light by the colonial government and remove all doubts of loyalty, in 1907 the General Conference decided to send a white man, Joel C. Rogers, to Nyasaland to take charge of the mission. Within four months of Rogers's arrival in May 1907, Branch and his family left

Nyasaland. They worked a short time at the Seventh-Day Adventist South African Mission in Cape Town before eventually returning to the United States.[40]

On January 23, 1915, racism, taxes, forced labor, famine, drought, and conscription for World War I resulted in the highly significant but abortive Nyasaland Uprising led by John Chilembwe, who instructed his patriots: "This very night you are to go and strike the blow and then die." Chilembwe and a few of his followers were killed and the uprising was crushed eleven days later on February 3, 1915.[41]

After the Chilembwe uprising many white colonialists in Nyasaland believed that the teachings of black American men and women missionaries in that country had induced a spirit of independence and insubordination among Africans. They argued that the protectorate had been free of such subversive elements until African-American missionaries entered the country, and they accused them of teaching revolution rather than religion. The six member Nyasaland Native Rising Commission, appointed by the governor of the colony to inquire into the causes of the Chilembwe uprising, recommended that "only properly accredited missions should be allowed in the Protectorate" and stated that black American missionaries were "politically objectionable." The commission believed that black male missionaries encouraged African men to protest their political status and that black female missionaries made African women unhappy with their educational status.[42]

Another area in southern Africa where African-American women missionaries were stationed from 1880 to 1920 was South Africa. Mamie Branton of North Carolina married John Tule, a South African missionary educated in America, and the couple traveled to South Africa in 1897 as missionaries of the National Baptist Convention. They were first located at Cape Town. In 1899 Reverend Tule transferred his affiliation and initiated the work of the Lott Carey Baptist Home and Foreign Mission Convention in South Africa. Little information exists on Mamie Tule's activities in the country but she obviously assisted in her husband's work.[43]

Lillie B. Johns, born in Wilmington, North Carolina, in 1877, traveled to Africa on January 26, 1897, with her husband, G.F.A. Johns, a South African missionary also educated in America, as a missionary of the National Baptist Convention. It is possible that Lillie B. Johns was the sister of Mamie Branton Tule. Both women were from North Carolina and bear a striking resemblance. After seven months in South Africa, three months spent in a sick bed, Lillie B. Johns died on September 21, 1897, only twenty years old. She had stated before she left the United States: "Should I not return home, do not grieve for me; it is just as near heaven from Africa as from America."[44]

Fanny Ann Jackson was born a slave in Washington, D.C., in 1837. Her freedom was purchased by an aunt and she was sent to New England to live with relatives. Jackson attended school in Massachusetts and Rhode

Island. She earned an A.B. degree and an A.M. degree from Oberlin College. From 1865 to 1902 she taught at and eventually became principal of the Institute for Colored Youth in Philadelphia, Pennsylvania.[45]

In 1881 Jackson married Levi Jenkins Coppin, who was licensed to preach in the AME Church in 1876 and edited the *A.M.E. Church Review* from 1888 to 1896. Levi Coppin was elected the first bishop of South Africa in 1900 and assigned to the recently created Fourteenth Episcopal District (Cape Colony and Transvaal). His main responsibility was to oversee the merger of the South African Ethiopian Church with the American AME Church. Since it was common practice in the AME Church to assign a certain portion of missionary duties to wives, Fanny Coppin accompanied her husband to South Africa. The couple arrived at Cape Town on November 30, 1902.[46]

Before journeying to the continent, Fanny Coppin admitted that she thought of Africa, like most missionaries, black and white, as a place devoid of any religious development. Later, she was surprised to find that Africans had engaged in theology before the arrival of missionaries. She dedicated herself to preserving African indigenous cultures and felt that missionaries should structure religious training for Africans around the patterns that already existed. Many African-American missionaries came to respect African culture and society after their stays on the continent.

Fanny Coppin was involved in issues and activities relating to all aspects of African life, including: living conditions for Africans in Cape Town, the establishment of a school and mission in the city, the development of women's organizations, and the impact of white colonial rule upon the lives of black South Africans. But most of her attention was directed toward the organization of Women's Christian Temperance Union Societies and Women's Mite Missionary Societies. She also formed small missionary groups among the wives of AME South African ministers.[47]

Like many black American missionaries working in Africa during this period, the Coppins questioned the benefits of European rule. Fanny Coppin asserted that after the imposition of British colonial rule in South Africa, no portion of the country remained the same. The Coppins were under constant surveillance by British officials. Fanny Coppin claimed that the British feared that religious and educational training would result in resistance by black South Africans to white rule. And she believed that repercussions could indeed be expected when colonial subjects became educated and began to question their inferior status in society. She cautioned:

> I think, however, the authorities finally came to understand that we were missionaries pure and simple, and not politicians, and if there was any cause for alarm it must grow out of the fact that enlightenment does indeed enable people to see their true condition, and that they do sometimes become dissatisfied when convinced that injustice and a general lack of Christian spirit of brotherhood, is responsible for much of their misery.[48]

Fanny Coppin felt that education was a vehicle for the expression of discontent among oppressed people. After the Coppins left South Africa, a 1915 law, passed by the Union of South African government, provided that "colored people, including missionaries, shall not immigrate" into the country.

It is clear from the applications, speeches, and letters written by these African-American women missionaries before they traveled to southern Africa that they believed that they were assisting in the redemption of the continent. They hoped to transfer Western gender-linked roles and functions to African women and many times they could not understand why African women rejected them and wanted to maintain their traditional way of life. Black American women missionaries often viewed African women's responsibilities and duties in their own societies as foreign, alien, and even unacceptable.

A significant influence in their decision to pursue a missionary career was the colleges that they attended. Of the six women who are known to have received a post-secondary education, four graduated from southern black institutions. These schools promoted the idea that it was the "special mission" of African-Americans to help in the redemption of Africa. Fisk University, a privately controlled liberal arts institution, was founded in 1865 by the American Missionary Association (AMA) and historically has been associated with the Congregational Church. E. M. Cravath, Fisk's first president, was also field secretary of the AMA. Nancy Jones recalled the words on a banner in the dining room at Fisk, "Her Sons and Daughters are ever on the altar," and confessed that she felt that she was included in that number.[49] At Spelman College, a private women's school, students sang a song:

> Give a thought to Africa,
> 'Neath the burning sun—

which typified a spirit prevalent throughout the institution, that of the duty of African-American women to help "Christianize and civilize" their ancestral homeland. The motives of individual women missionaries may have been various, but it is clear that the overriding theme of duty helped to explain why so many African-Americans volunteered for mission work in Africa. These African-American women who served in southern Africa, like most women missionaries, were trained as teachers, nurses, and deaconesses.

Additionally, African-American women missionaries most times did not fully understand the nature of European imperialism in Africa. Missionaries had the goals of economic, social, educational, and religious development for Africans, but these did not coincide with the main objective of European imperialists in Africa before 1920, which was simply to maintain control in the African colonies, with as little cost as possible to the home governments. European administrators were not concerned about African societal growth. The Ousleys and Jones were critical of the Portuguese government in Mozambique for being restrictive, for not providing for African workers, and for being unfair in its dealings with Africans. Delaney, Cheek, and the Branches in Nyasaland and Fanny Coppin in South Africa reprimanded the British government for its lack of educational opportunities for Africans.

By the end of World War I, the general consensus of European colonialists in Africa, who by that date had occupied all of the continent except for the Republic of Liberia and Ethiopia, was that African-Americans caused too many disruptions to warrant their effective use as missionaries in Africa. Generally, there were no legislative restrictions directed against black American missionaries after 1920, but most European governments began to exclude them based on the belief that the African-American presence caused unrest among Africans and was dangerous to the maintenance of law and order on the continent.

European imperialists accused black missionaries of encouraging political revolts, and colonial governments, believing that they preached revolt rather than religion, discouraged their entry. But in southern Africa, where revolts occurred before 1920—such as the Herero Rebellion in Southwest Africa from 1904 to 1907, the Bambata (Zulu) Rebellion in South Africa in 1906, and the John Chilembwe Uprising in Nyasaland in 1915—African-American missionaries either were not present or did not exert enough influence to stage such uprisings. It is probably true, though, that the presence of educated black American missionaries was a constant reminder to Africans of the opportunities denied to them in their own land. Furthermore, by 1910 over 150 southern Africans had been educated in American black colleges and universities and exposed to African-American protest.

But other changes occurring in southern Africa and in the United States made the post–World War I world quite different from the prewar one. In southern Africa, Africans began to form political organizations at the end of the nineteenth and beginning of the twentieth centuries. The principal one was the African National Congress (ANC), founded in 1912. In the United States, Booker T. Washington, the conciliatory black leader, died in 1915. A year later, the Jamaican, Marcus Garvey, arrived in the United States with his more militant stance. In 1919 W.E.B. Du Bois called the first Pan-African Congress in Paris, emphasizing the poor conditions under which worldwide blacks lived and calling for unity among this group. The post–World War I period also witnessed an increase in black American self-consciousness with the New Negro movement and the Harlem Renaissance. Additionally, Africans and African-Americans had fought in World War I and returned to their countries after the war with a much more militant outlook. European imperialists, hoping to maintain law and order and develop Africa's resources with little resistance, feared the consequences if these two groups, Africans and African-Americans, both with increasing political awareness, were to get together. Europeans feared the rise of Ethiopianism, or the independent African church movement, in southern Africa. In the late nineteenth century, the Ethiopian Church united with the American based African Methodist Episcopal Church. Colonialists were also frightened by the popularity and spread of the Garvey movement throughout Africa with its "Africa for the Africans" philosophy. Attempting to keep "troublemakers" out of Africa, European governments in Africa concluded that African-American missionaries upset the status quo and were dangerous to the maintenance of law and order in Africa. Therefore, these colonialists discouraged the entry of not only black missionaries, but all black visitors to Africa.[50]

Black American women missionaries faced triple jeopardy. In addition to having to deal with European colonial policy in Africa, African-American women missionaries in southern Africa from 1880 to 1920 also faced sexism and racism from other American and European missionaries. Women were discriminated against as missionary workers. They were viewed by their mission boards and by their male colleagues as second-class missionaries. In this age of imperialism, racism also became a dominant issue in European and American thought. Whether they worked with white missionaries or at segregated mission stations, African-American missionaries were constantly being scrutinized by whites.

Some conclusions can be made about these African-American women missionaries who were stationed in southern Africa from 1880 to 1920. All served in countries—Angola, Mozambique, Nyasaland, Southern Rhodesia, and South Africa—with little or no previous experience with African-American missionaries. In almost all instances these women were among the first black women missionaries in the country (Ousley and Jones were the first in Mozambique, Jones was the first in Southern Rhodesia, Delaney and Branch were the first in Nyasaland, Collins and Drummer were the first in Angola, and Tule and Johns were among the first in South Africa). Five of the nine women were married (three of them wed immediately before they sailed with their husbands to Africa) and four were unmarried. The age when they went to Africa is known for five of the nine women. The average age for four of those was twenty-eight years old. Because Drummer was graduated from college in 1901, she probably also fit into this average. Coppin was sixty-five years old when she went to South Africa. Only the Branches took children to Africa with them. All of the women appeared to have been ignorant of the situation in Africa before their arrival and not only had to adapt their attitudes to a partial acceptance of the African way of life in order to be effective among them, but also had to take care not to offend the European imperialists. In this age of imperialism and racism, the perceptions and experiences of African-American female and male missionaries in Africa were not dissimilar. With the assumption of Europeans of the "white man's burden" and the rise of Jim Crow in the United States, Africans and African-Americans were treated with the same prejudice. There was really no difference between the exploitation of and discrimination against Africans on the continent and the degradation and oppression of diasporic Africans throughout the world. African-American women missionaries in Africa faced this discrimination, as well as the sexism inherent in this imperialistic age.

NOTES

A version of this article appeared in *Women's Studies International Forum* 13, no. 4 (1990): 381–94; reprinted with the permission of Pergamon Press.

1. For a discussion of African-American views on the establishment of European imperialism in Africa during the late nineteenth and early twentieth centuries, see Sylvia M. Jacobs, *The African Nexus: Black American Perspectives on the European Partitioning of Africa, 1880–1920* (Westport, Conn: Greenwood Press, 1981). See also Sylvia M. Jacobs, "Afro-American Women Missionaries Confront the African Way of Life," in *Women in Africa and the African Diaspora,* ed. Rosalyn Terborg-Penn, Sharon Harley, and Andrea Benton Rushing (Washington, D.C.: Howard University Press, 1987), p. 122.

2. In *Black Americans and the Missionary Movement in Africa,* ed. Sylvia M. Jacobs (Westport, Conn.: Greenwood Press, 1982) there is a discussion of the role of African-Americans in the American Protestant mission movement in Africa before 1960. See also Wade Crawford Barclay, *History of Methodist Missions,* vol. 1: *Missionary Motivation and Expansion, 1769–1844* (New York: Board of Missions and Church Extension of the Methodist Church, 1949), pp. 165–66; and William E. Strong, *The Story of the American Board: An Account of the First Hundred Years of the American Board of Commissioners for Foreign Missions* (Boston: Pilgrim Press, 1910), pp. 124–25, 132.

3. Strong, *American Board,* p. 342; *The Missionary Herald, Containing the Proceedings of the American Board of Commissioners for Foreign Missions* 80, Editorial Paragraphs (March 1884): 85, and (October 1884): 383; "Zulu Mission," *Annual Report of the American Board of Commissioners for Foreign Missions,* no. 73 (1883), p. 27; and "East Central African Mission," *Annual Report,* no. 74 (1884), pp. 20–21.

4. American Board of Commissioners for Foreign Missions Papers, Biography File, Benjamin Forsyth Ousley, Houghton Library of Harvard University, Cambridge, Mass. Samuel Miller, who taught in Angola from 1880 to 1884, was the first ABCFM black missionary.

5. ABCFM Papers, Memoranda Concerning Missionaries, volume 9, Henrietta Bailey Ousley, Houghton Library of Harvard University, Cambridge, Mass. "Notes for the Month," *Missionary Herald* 80 (Oct. 1884): 406 mentions the marriage of the Ousleys.

6. Strong, *American Board,* pp. 343–44 and Nannie Jones to Mr. E. K. Alden, July 19, 1887 (no. 612), ABCFM Papers, 6, vol. 35, Candidate File, Nancy Jones, Houghton Library of Harvard University, Cambridge, Mass. Nancy Jones's nickname was Nannie.

7. See "Notes for the Month" *Missionary Herald* 80 (Nov. 1884): 465; "Notes for the Month," ibid., vol. 81 (Feb. 1885): 79; and Editorial Paragraphs, ibid., vol. 81 (Apr. 1885): 135. See also "East Central African Mission, Kambini," *Annual Report,* no. 75 (1885), pp. 20–21.

8. "Reports of Committees on the Annual Report: The Committee on Missions in Africa" *Missionary Herald* 81 (Dec. 1885): 508.

9. See *Missionary Herald* 83, "East Central African Mission: A Day At Kambini" (Apr. 1887): 142 and "East Central African Mission: Degradation of Women" (Aug. 1887): 309. See also, "East Central African Mission,'" *Annual Report*, no. 77 (1887), p. 60.

10. "Notes for the Month," *Missionary Herald* 84 (Mar. 1888): 127.

11. Nannie Jones to Pres. E. M. Cravath, March 20, 1887 (no. 610), ABCFM Papers, 6, vol. 35, Candidate File, Nancy Jones.

12. Nancy Jones to Dr. Judson Smith, November 1, 1887 (no. 63), ABCFM Papers, 15.4, vol. 12, East Central Africa File.

13. "Notes for the Month," *Missionary Herald* 84 (July 1888): 318; and "East Central African Mission: A Hopeful Outlook," ibid. (Sept. 1888): 387–88. See also "East Central African Mission," *Annual Report*, no. 78 (1888), pp. 19–21. Jones gives an account of her first four months at Kambini in Nancy Jones to Dr. Judson Smith, May 2, 1888 (no. 70); Nancy Jones to Dr. Judson Smith, May 29, 1888 (no. 71); and Nancy Jones to Dr. Judson Smith, September 20, 1888 (no. 72), ABCFM Papers, 15.4, vol. 12, East Central Africa File.

14. "East Central African Mission: Kambini," *Missionary Herald* 85 (Mar. 1889): 110 and Nancy Jones to Charles E. Swett, October 19, 1888 (no. 73), ABCFM Papers, 15.4, vol. 12, East Central Africa File.

15. "East Central African Mission: From Kambini," *Missionary Herald* 86 (June 1890): 237–38; "Notes for the Month," *Missionary Herald* 8 (July 1890): 296; "East Central African Mission," *Annual Report*, no. 79 (1889), p. 31; and Nancy Jones to Rev. Judson Smith, January 9, 1890 (no. 63), ABCFM Papers, 15.4, vol. 20, East Central Africa File.

16. "East Central African Mission," *Missionary Herald* 86 (Dec. 1890): 515; ibid., vol. 87 (Feb. 1891): 62–63 and (Oct. 1891): 421; "East Central African Mission," *Annual Report*, no. 80 (1890), p. 28, and no. 81 (1891), p. 22; and Nancy Jones to Rev. Judson Smith, Feb. 6, 1890 (no. 64), ABCFM Papers, 15.4, vol. 20, East Central Africa File.

17. "Reports of Committees on the Annual Report: The Committee on Missions in Africa," *Annual Report*, no. 80 (1890), p. xv.

18. "Notes for the Month," *Missionary Herald* 89 (Aug. 1893): 336; and Nancy Jones to Judson Smith, Jan. 4, 1893 (no. 80), ABCFM Papers, 15.4, vol. 20, East Central Africa File. See also, "East Central African Mission, *Annual Report*, no. 82 (1892), pp. 25–26; no. 83 (1893), pp. 26–27; and no. 84 (1894), p. 23.

19. Strong, *American Board*, pp. 342–44; Editorial Paragraphs, *Missionary Herald* 89 (Aug. 1893): 304; and ibid., vol. 90 (March 1894): 96; and "East Central African Mission," *Annual Report*, no. 82 (1892), pp. 225–27; "Mt. Silinda (Gazaland)," ibid., no. 83 (1893), p. 26; and ibid., no. 84 (1894), pp. 23, 27.

20. "Letters From Mission: East Central African Mission, Gazaland," *Missionary Herald* 90 (July 1894): 286, ibid. (Oct. 1894): 426, and ibid., vol. 91 (May 1895): 189–91; "East Central African Mission," *Annual Report*, no. 85 (1895), p. 31; and no. 86 (1896), p. 28; and Nancy Jones to Rev. Judson Smith, March 8, 1894 (no. 81) and March 26, 1895 (no. 82), ABCFM Papers, 15.4, vol. 20, East Central Africa File.

21. "East Central African Mission," *Missionary Herald* 93 (Feb. 1897): 68 and "Notes for the Month," ibid. (Dec. 1897): 523; "East Central African Mission," *Annual Report*, no. 87 (1897), p. 28; and no. 88 (1898), p. 28; and Resignation—Nancy Jones, May 27, 1897 (no. 87) and Nancy Jones to Rev. Judson Smith, Dec. 2, 1897 (no. 92), ABCFM Papers, 15.4, vol. 20, East Central Africa File.

22. Nancy Jones to Rev. Judson Smith, Nov. 1, 1897 (no. 90), ABCFM Papers, 15.4, vol. 20, East Central Africa File.

23. "On the Dark Continent," *Indianapolis Freeman*, Feb. 5, 1898.

24. Collins is listed almost every year from 1890 to 1906 in the *Annual Report of the Missionary Society of the Methodist Episcopal Church.*

25. *Annual Report on the Board of Foreign Missions of the Methodist Episcopal Church* (1907–19), passim.

26. Walter L. Williams, *Black Americans and the Evangelization of Africa, 1877–1900* (Madison: University of Wisconsin Press, 1982), p. 14.

27. James P. Brawley, *The Clark College Legacy: An Interpretive History of Relevant Education, 1869–1975* (Atlanta: Clark College, 1977), p. 61.

28. I would like to extend sincere thanks to George Shepperson of the University of Edinburgh for his invaluable assistance in helping me to research this topic and for the priceless photographs of the Branch family in Nyasaland that he so generously shared with me.

29. W.E.B. Du Bois, ed., *The Negro Church* (Atlanta: Atlanta University Press, 1903), p. 111; Miles Mark Fisher, *A Short History of the Baptist Denomination* (Nashville: Sunday School Publishing Board, 1933), p. 117; Joseph R. Washington, Jr., *Black Religion: The Negro and Christianity in the United States* (Boston: Beacon Press, 1964), pp. 52–53; Edmund F. Merriam, *A History of American Baptist Missions* (Philadelphia: American Baptist Publication Society, 1913), p. 189; Henry C. Vedder, *A Short History of Baptist Missions* (Philadelphia: Judson Press, 1927), p. 270; Lewellyn L. Berry, *A Century of Missions of the African Methodist Episcopal Church, 1840–1940* (New York: Gutenberg Printing Co., 1942), pp. 225–28; and George Shepperson and Thomas Price, *Independent African: John Chilembwe and the Origins, Setting and Significance of the Nyasaland Native Rising in 1915* (Edinburgh: University Press, 1958), pp. 134–36.

30. Shepperson and Price in *Independent African* erroneously state that Thomas Branch was the first black American in Nyasaland, "arriving at the beginning of April 1901" (p. 135). My research has indicated, however, that Cheek arrived in April 1901 and Branch reached Nyasaland in August 1902. Kings M. Phiri in "Afro-American Influence in Colonial Malawi, 1891–1945: A Case Study of the Interaction between Africa and Africans of the Diaspora," in *Global Dimensions of the African Diaspora,* ed. Joseph E. Harris (Washington, D.C.: Howard University Press, 1982), p. 255 repeats Shepperson and Price's mistake. See also, Lewis Garnett Jordan, *Up the Ladder in Foreign Missions* (Nashville: National Baptist Publications Board, 1901), p. 132.

31. "Rev. Cheek Writes," *Richmond Planet* (Virginia), June 3, 1905; and Shepperson and Price, *Independent African,* pp. 137–38.

32. Florence Matilda Read, *The Story of Spelman College* (Atlanta, Ga.: n.p., 1961), pp. 352–53, 357–58; and C. C. Adams and Marshall A. Talley, *Negro Baptists and Foreign Missions* (Philadelphia: Foreign Mission Board of the National Baptist Convention, U.S.A., Inc., 1944), p. 23.

33. See "Sketches of Spelman Graduates—Emma B. Delany," *Spelman Messenger,* Oct. 1901, p. 2; "Why I Go as a Foreign Missionary," ibid., Feb. 1902, p. 5; and "Spelman Women in Africa," ibid., Feb. 1945, pp. 2, 7, 8.

34. Read, *Spelman College,* pp. 354–55; Shepperson and Price, *Independent African,* pp. 139–41; Du Bois, *The Negro Church,* p. 120; and Adams and Talley, *Negro Baptists and Foreign Missions,* p. 23.

35. Shepperson and Price, *Independent African,* pp. 139–42. Roderick J. Macdonald in "Rev. Dr. Daniel Sharpe Malekebu and the Re-Opening of the Providence Industrial Mission: 1926–29: An Appreciation," in *From Nyasaland to Malawi: Studies in Colonial History,* ed. Roderick J. Macdonald (Nairobi, Kenya: East African Publishing House, 1975), pp. 215–33 discusses the reopening of the Providence Industrial Mission (PIM) in 1926. There has been some recent controversy concerning the PIM. The question centered on the issue of whether Daniel Malekebu reopened the PIM in

1926 on his own or as a representative of the National Baptist Convention, U.S.A., Inc. (NBC). After his death, Malekebu's followers took over the mission property, despite the protests of the NBC. In the court decision, Judge L. A. Chatsika sustained the claim of the NBC. See William J. Harvey III, *Sacrifice and Dedication in a Century of Mission: A History of One Hundred Years of the Foreign Mission Board, National Baptist Convention, U.S.A., Inc., 1880–1980* (Philadelphia: Foreign Mission B ˑˑd, National Baptist Convention, U.S.A., Inc., 1979), pp. 92–93; and Civil Case 〔 ⁱ977, High Court of Malawi at Blantyre. The final court decision was ˑt. 6, 1978, pertinent pages, 18–20.

Spelman College, pp. 357–58. Emma Delaney's name is spelled DeLany)lications.

lsworth Olsen, *A History of the Origin and Progress of Seventh-Day Advent-* on, D.C.: Review and Herald Publishing Association, 1925), pp. . E. Robinson, "Historical Sketch of the Work of the Seventh-Day Ad-asaland, 1902–1915," typescript, General Conference of Seventh-Day /ashington, D.C., pp. 3–4. I would like to thank Alta Robinson for a usband's manuscript.

urray, *Handbook of Nyasaland* (London: Waterlow and Sons, 1932), p. ·venth-Day Adventists, p. 493; and N. Olney Moore, "Seventh Day Bap-ion Work in Nyasaland, Africa," (Plainfield, N.J.: Seventh Day Baptist :iety, n.d.), pp. 2–3. I am grateful to Thomas H. Merchant of the Sev-ⁱtist Historical Society for a copy of the latter report. See also Shepper-ˑ, *Independent African*, pp. 86–87, 137.

·anches wrote many letters and reports from Nyasaland which were the *Advent Review and Sabbath Herald* (Seventh-Day Adventist Church, D.C.) from 1902 to 1907.

. Neufeld, *Seventh-Day Adventist Encyclopedia* (Washington, D.C.: Re-erald Publishing Association, 1966), p. 151; William J. W. Roome, *A pation: A Missionary Survey of Nyasaland, Central Africa* (London: World ress, 1926), p. 46; Olsen, *Seventh-Day Adventists*, p. 494; Murray, *Hand-* and Robinson, "Historical Sketch," pp. 10, 12. I am indebted to Mau-ⁱ, Associate Secretary, General Conference of Seventh-Day Adventists, , D.C. for his assistance in my research on Thomas H. Branch.

ⁱrt I. Rotberg, ed., in *Strike a Blow and Die: A Narrative of Race Relations in Colonial Africa by George Simeon Mwase* (Cambridge: Harvard University Press, 1967), pp. 23–24 mentions Cheek and Delaney's relationship with Chilembwe. Chilembwe's uprising is discussed on pp. 29-52. See also, Shepperson and Price, *Independent African*, pp. 267–319, 399.

42. Johannes Du Plessis, *Thrice through the Dark Continent: A Record of Journeyings across Africa during the Years 1913–1916* (London: Longmans, Green and Co., 1917), p. 346; Shepperson and Price, *Independent African*, p. 135; and George Shepperson, "Notes on Negro American Influences on the Emergence of African Nationalism," *Journal of African History* 1 (1960): 305. See also Native Rising Commission, *Report of the Commission [on] . . . the Native Rising within the Nyasaland Protectorate* (Zomba: Government Printer, Nyasaland Protectorate, c. Jan. 7, 1916), pp. 4, 6, 8. William J. Harvey III, executive secretary of the Foreign Mission Board of the National Baptist Convention, U.S.A., Inc., contends that his reading of Emma Delaney's letters and descriptions of her by other people led him to believe that she was very militant for her time and could have encouraged Africans at Chiradzulu to protest their position in Nyasaland. Interview, William J. Harvey III, March 9, 1983, Philadelphia, Pa.

43. Williams, *Black Americans and the Evangelization of Africa*, pp. 71, 190.

44. L. G. Jordon, comp., *In Our Stead* (Philadelphia: n.p., 1913), p. 21, 36.

45. Fanny Jackson Coppin, *Reminiscences of School Life and Hints on Teaching* (Philadelphia: A.M.E. Book Concern, 1913), pp. 122–23; Martin Kilson and Adelaide Hill, *Apropos of Africa: Afro-American Leaders and the Romance of Africa* (Garden City, N.Y.: Doubleday and Co., 1971), pp. 281–82.

46. Margaret E. Burton, *Comrades in Service* (New York: Missionary Education Movement of the United States and Canada, 1915), p. 160; and Josephus R. Coan, "The Expansion of Missions of the African Methodist Episcopal Church in South Africa, 1896–1908" (Ph.D. diss., Hartford Seminary Foundation, 1961), pp. 293–94, 327–28.

47. Fanny Coppin, *Reminiscences*, pp. 125, 129–30; Burton, *Comrades*, p. 160.

48. Fanny Coppin, *Reminiscences*, pp. 124–28.

49. Nannie Jones to Mr. E. K. Alden, July 19, 1887 (no. 612), ABCFM Papers, vol. 35, Candidate File, Nancy Jones.

50. Jacobs, ed., *Black Americans and the Missionary Movement in Africa*, pp. 20–22.

Wives and "Incorporated Women"

SHAWLS, JEWELRY, CURRY, AND RICE IN VICTORIAN BRITAIN[1]

Nupur Chaudhuri

In British colonial discourse scholars usually discuss colonizers' impact on the colonized people. Thus the centrifugal effects of imperialism have come in for much more attention than the centripetal. This has created nearly a vacuum in understanding the role of imperialism in British social history,[2] although some scholars have shown that the lasting images of the latter half of the nineteenth century are those associated with the achievements of empire and British people's apparent delight in these accomplishments.[3] British performances in the empire shaped the public's world view. In *Imperialism and Popular Culture,* several authors have analyzed the influence of imperialism on a variety of media and leisure activities between the late nineteenth century and the Second World War. They have demonstrated the ways popular cultural vehicles conveyed an imperial world view to the British public. But none of these authors has examined the role British women played in creating an imperial world view. By focusing on the parts taken by English women, especially housewives or memsahibs, in transferring Indian artifacts and gastronomic cultures to various segments of Victorian society in mid- and late Victorian England, this paper demonstrates that memsahibs were also a significant force in shaping the imperial world view of the Victorians.[4]

To protect their status as rulers and defend British culture in India, the Anglo-Indians during the nineteenth century chose racial exclusiveness and altogether rejected Indian goods and dishes.[5] Scholars of Indian colonial history have blamed the memsahibs for this ethnocentricism. Reflecting on these women's perception of their own cultural superiority, one late nineteenth-century observer noted: ''No Collector's wife will wear an article of Indian manufacture . . . and all her furniture, even to her carpets, must be of English make.'"[6] Extending this snobbish attitude, Flora Annie Steel and Grace Gardiner wrote in the standard household manual of 1888, *The Complete Indian Housekeeper and Cook*: "Of course, if Indian [Anglo-Indian] bairns are fed upon curry and caviare, their taste for simple dishes will become impaired, but there really is no reason *why* they should be fed."[7] They also recommended that housekeeping in India should be organized on a British model with only minimum modifications. Thus even when the Victorians at home decorated their homes with Indian decorative objects and started to eat curry, nineteenth-century memsahibs, to create a British lifestyle in the Indian subcontinent, seem to have collectively rejected Indian objects in their colonial homes and refused Indian dishes in their diets.[8] These expressions of intransigent ethnocentrism among memsahibs have led scholars of Indian colonial history to conclude that British women were largely responsible for maintaining social distance between the rulers and the ruled.[9]

Yet the memsahibs' negative attitude regarding the use of Indian goods and dishes was almost totally confined to the colonial environment. Newspaper and magazine articles, letters to the editor, cookery columns, "exchange columns," and advertisements in women's periodical literature in Victorian Britain reveal memsahibs' antipodal view toward Indian material and gastronomic cultures outside the colonial environment. These sources show that memsahibs served as a conduit for the flow of culture from India to Britain beginning around the mid-nineteenth century. When accounts from women's literary periodicals, newspaper advertisements, cookbooks, household manuals, and memsahibs' private letters are read as a corpus, what becomes evident is that memsahibs served as a major channel through which a range of Indian artifacts, such as shawls and jewelry, flowed to a segment of middle-class Victorian women in Britain who previously could not afford such items. This material transport fostered a mutually beneficial economic system, outside the mainstream economic structure of the country, for memsahibs and their sisters at home. From the mid-nineteenth century the imperial ethos became so strong that many English families from different socioeconomic backgrounds began to include Indian foods in their diets. Memsahibs were a major force in nurturing this newly acquired culinary taste.

This essay explores the complex reality of memsahibs' lives, which has been largely ignored by historians of colonial India, and oversimplified even by historians of memsahibs.[10] Diffusion of a subordinate, not to imply inferior, culture into a dominant one is a major effect of colonial rule. The exportation of aspects of Indian cultures by memsahibs was one significant dimension of such diffusion. Tracing the impact of one group of female colonialists on their own "native" culture suggests the larger importance of women as agents of cultural exchange between colonizers and the colonized.

Around the mid-eighteenth century, British men returning from India introduced shawls from Kashmir into Britain.[11] The Kashmir shawl, as it provided extra warmth, became a desirable accompaniment to dresses for wealthy British women, who often wore shortsleeve, low-cut dresses made of light-weight cotton or muslin.[12] Genuine Kashmir shawls were expensive, costing between seventy and one hundred pounds each in the 1810s.[13] Since the cost of an Indian shawl was so high, its market was limited to wealthy women. In October 1819, 611 Kashmir shawls were shipped from Calcutta to London.[14] Yet the fancy for Indian shawls also generated home-based production of shawls, patterned after Indian motifs but manufactured in mills in Lyons, Norwich, Edinburgh, and Paisley.[15] Paisley shawls, which overshadowed both Norwich and Edinburgh products during the 1810s, were priced at twelve pounds each, considerably less than Kashmir shawls in the same period. The price of a Paisley shawl declined further over time, and by the late 1850s, the cost of a Paisley shawl ranged from 17s. 6d. to 27s., making it possible for upper-middle-class women of lesser means to be elegantly dressed with a shawl that appeared to have been made in India.[16]

Several shawl emporiums opened in response to the popularity of the new item. These shops sold both English-made and Indian shawls. J. & J. Holmes in Regent Street, established in the 1820s, advertised shawls of one guinea to one hundred guineas, including "an immense variety of Indian shawls." Soon after the Holmes opened their store, three other stores with stocks of Indian shawls appeared, one in Regent Street, the second in New Bond Street and the third in Fleet Street. Farmer and Rogers took over the J. & J. Holmes sometime between 1849 and 1854 and renamed the store The Great Shawl and Cloak Emporium, focusing customer attention on its collection of Indian shawls and scarves.[17]

In the mid-nineteenth century, the shawl remained a popular outdoor covering for women in Britain, and an authentic Kashmir was preferred by the most fashionable. Women's desire for Kashmir shawls was evidenced in both private letters and popular magazines. Residents in England wrote relatives and friends on the subcontinent, requesting not only assistance in obtaining shawls but also attention to the latest fashion trends. "Do you know, my shawl is getting very shabby," wrote one lady. "When you can afford it, think of me for a Cashmere . . . if you send me a Cashmere, do not let it be *black;* I should so greatly prefer a red or white. Let it be square, and of the Harlequin pattern, which is most admired in England."[18] Admiring the high quality of the Indian shawls, *The Ladies Companion* of September 21, 1850, remarked: "There is a minority who do know, and duly esteem a beautiful shawl . . . and perhaps they are Anglo-Indians, or the relatives and near friends of Anglo-Indians, who know well a 'Cashmere,'—measuring every other shawl in the world by and from it." *The Ladies' Treasury* of December 2, 1867, claimed "Nobody [in Britain] but provincials buy French Kashmeres in the present day. The shawl must be undeniably and manifestly, Indian, or the world of fashion will have nothing to do with it."[19] The same feeling of admiration was expressed in the "Conversazione" column of *The Englishwoman's Domestic Magazine (EDM)*, a monthly periodical with a very large number of middle-class subscribers, in October 1870, when it wrote: "Indian shawls are now selling at very moderate prices, and should be 'secured' as we [are] so often told, while they are really cheap." *EDM* further claimed: "Shawls are daily resuming their forever importance in the wardrobes of *elegantes,* and we must all have an Indian shawl if we would [want to] avoid the unlucky fate of the unfortunate lady who is confined to the house when it is windier than usual, because her shawl is not Indian."[20] Its aesthetic value aside, the Kashmir shawl was also considered to be an item of tangible wealth. The shawl from India was listed in *trousseaux,* and the item was regarded as a valued inheritance.[21]

Although the Indian shawl was a popular fashion article, it was too costly for most Britons. Lacking the resources to buy a new one, yet desiring the genuine article over an English imitation, some women began exploring "Sale and Exchange" columns in popular monthly and weekly periodicals like *EDM* and *Queen.*[22] Requests for Indian shawls could be repeatedly found in publications of *Queen* during the 1870s. The "wanted" columns often contained such advertisements as: "Wanted, a long-full sized Indian shawl—good offer," or "Want an Indian shawl—can offer jewelry, double smelling bottle with silver gilt tops, ornamental jars for toilet and many other things."[23] Such demands for Indian shawls naturally offered an opportunity for memsahibs to obtain goods they wanted in exchange. One memsahib wrote to *EDM* in July 1870:

> I have just returned from India and have a handsome Punjaub shawl to dispose of i.e. to exchange for a couple of good dresses. . . . This shawl is made of the fine camel-hair, and beautifully worked all over in pine leaves patterns with a fringe. . . . It has never been worn. A gift from my husband, but he told me if I cared to exchange it for a couple of good dresses I could do so. The shawl was 15 pounds in India.

In exchange columns of the *EDM* and the *Queen,* many memsahibs repeatedly expressed their willingness to either sell Indian shawls for a fixed price or exchange them for items meeting their own needs. "Indian shawl for sale or exchange. Cost 25 pounds," read one advertisement. Another read, "Indian shawl cost 75 rupees [approximately seven pounds, ten shillings] offer requested for a value of 6 pounds." One woman wanted to exchange an "Indian white cashmere shawl for a seal skin jacket and muff."[24] Another memsahib sought a Persian or Turkish carpet, drawing room furniture, a carriage clock, or a sewing machine in exchange for her shawl.[25] The last item had become almost an essential household implement in the 1860s for a middle-class woman who wished to make her own fashionable clothes. One memsahib expressly requested a Weir's hard-lock stitch sewing machine as payment for a shawl. Such requests may have come most often from widows of soldiers and other low-ranking personnel, who occasionally earned their livelihood by sewing after returning to Britain. Mrs. William, for example, a widow whose husband had been a sergeant in the First Battalion Eighth the King's Regiment of Foot in India, supported herself and her daughter by dressmaking following her return to England.[26] To such a woman, an Indian shawl became an important source of capital to buy a sewing machine. Others, with less concern for earning a living, wanted to exchange their shawls for precious stones and jewelry.[27]

Some memsahibs brought home Rampore chuddars, which were shawls uniform in color, without pattern, and made in Rampore in northwestern India. One memsahib advertised, "[I have] 3 red Rampore shawls value each 3 pounds. What offers in exchange?" Indian shawls became so popular that even used shawls were of much value to memsahibs. One advertisement noted, "I have very handsome cashmere shawl, cost 40 pounds and not been worn more than half a dozen times. Offer requested."[28] Rampore chuddars were sold in commercial stores, such as Lewis Allenby and the Farmer & Rogers stores as well, though at higher prices, only new, and only for cash, as the advertisements indicated.[29] According to notices in exchange columns, authentic Indian shawls sold or exchanged by memsahibs varied in price from five pounds to fifty pounds, as opposed to seventy pounds or more for the same articles bought in a store. Due to the high prices, the commodities were clearly beyond the reach of the lower middle- and working-class women.

Victorian fashion also enhanced the value of Indian fabrics. Fashionable women of the era wore dresses that draped softly, for which they often admired very light-weight Delhi or Madras muslin and tussore silk, the last imported from India to make summer skirts.[30] The demand for Indian fabrics with fine needlework created an opportunity for memsahibs to sell or exchange their Indian-made dresses as well as shawls. A memsahib wrote to the editor of *EDM*, "Rawal Pindi wishes to exchange a white muslin ball dress (Indian), embroidered with beetle's wings and gold thread; corseted body of green satin and tulle, worn twice, a perfectly new upper skirt of Tussore silk, handsomely embroidered for a sewing machine." Another memsahib tried to sell a dress made of Lahore silk for two pounds and another silk dress for one pound, five shillings, or was willing to exchange these for "a real black lace mantilla or shawl and an evening dress suitable for a person over thirty and of a very fresh complexion," provided the articles were not soiled.[31]

In the early 1870s, cloaks and scarves for evening wear were popular among Victorian women. Notices of sale or exchange of these items were often found in newspapers and magazine columns. One woman wanted to exchange her Indian cloak worth ten pounds for a gold ring.[32] Between 1869 and 1872 especially, the "exchange columns" of both *EDM* and *Queen* frequently carried advertisements for sale or exchange of these items, such as "Indian scarf in exchange for child's silver cup or a little silver candle stick" and "Indian Scarf—rather dirty—but can be cleaned—good offers requested."[33]

Knowing that hats trimmed with ribbons, flowers, and feathers were also cherished by Victorian women, some memsahibs brought back already mounted peacock feathers for a hat hoping to be able to exchange these hat accessories for things they wanted.[34] Thus, as in the case of Indian shawls, dress fabrics and accessory items were introduced by memsahibs to women in Victorian society who could not afford to buy these imported items from regular stores. In the process, memsahibs served as catalysts in popularizing Indian artifacts.

Throughout the nineteenth century, jewelry was as essential to the fashionable Victorian woman as shawls, fabrics, cloaks, and scarves. The ornaments worn were generally made of precious or semi-precious stones and precious metals, many of which could be found in the Near East. No record can be found that the East India Company organized any regular trade in jewelry, but the company's display of Indian jewelry at the Great Exhibition of 1851 (which later became a part of the crown jewels) fascinated the British public.[35] Impressed by the splendor of the ornaments and demands for them in the market, Arthur Lasenby Liberty, the owner of the most fashionable shop for the diffusion of Aestheticism, began importing Indian jewelry through his East India House store on Regent Street in 1875.[36] The disciples of the Aesthetic movement, detesting machine-made products, were attracted to the rich appearance of Indian jewelry, which was achieved by putting irregularly shaped precious stones in hand-made settings.[37] Mrs. H. R. Haweis, a follower of the Aesthetic movement and author of *The Art of Beauty* wrote, "No two pendants are alike . . . but this does not strike obnoxiously on the eye; it requires a second glance to observe it."[38] When Queen Victoria became the empress of India in 1876, Indian jewelry became fashionable in circles beyond the artistic world of the Aesthetes.[39]

The most popular Indian jewelry in the 1870s were jeweled and enameled works from Jaipur, Delhi pavé-set pieces in which the whole front of the ornament is covered with or paved with stones, turquoise and pearl bracelets and earrings, and Mughal jade inlaid with gold and precious stones.[40] The popularity of such accessories in some circles of Victorian society is reflected in a notice published in the *Queen*: "Wanted Indian Jewellery must be of real Indian make. Offer lady's gold watch and other things."[41] Between 1870 and 1880, Indian earrings designed as peapods, of tortoise shell with pearls, were another fashion favorite.

Indian jewelry, like Indian shawls and dresses, were also sold by memsahibs for cash or in exchange for needed items. In the exchange column of *EDM* in July 1870, one memsahib from Rawalpindi wanted to exchange various jewelry items for a sewing machine that was in perfect order and complete with full instructions. Among the items of exchange she offered were "a pair of dark tortoise-shell bracelets, with earrings to match." In the "Conversazione" of *EDM*'s July 1874 issue, a woman, calling herself Bee, offered to sell her matched Indian-made gold crescent brooch, pendant, and earrings for three pounds. Others wanted buyers to make an offer: "Two beautiful bracelets, turquoise set in gold, each value 9 pounds. All quite new. What offers in exchange?" Or, "Very handsome Indian bracelets, set with turquoise and rubies. What offers?"[42] Through offers of sale and exchange, then, memsahibs brought Indian jewelry along with shawls, scarves, dresses and other accessory items of fashion within the reach of many women who could not possibly have afforded to buy these items in regular shops.

Memsahibs not only injected Oriental elements into the Victorian fashion scene, but also introduced new tastes in interior decoration to many Victorian families. Although memsahibs seldom used Indian artifacts in their own homes in the subcontinent, they often sent Indian handicrafts as gifts to their families in Britain. Emily Short Wonnacott, for instance, wife of a school master with the First Battalion Eighth the King's Regiment, sent her parents "a few trifling articles of Indian workmanship. The 'palanquin' and figures will stand very well in the large glass case," she assured them.[43] Minnie Wood, wife of Captain Archibald Wood of the Fourteenth Bengal Native Infantry, sent her mother a chenille cushion, a pen case, and an envelope case.[44] Such gifts were one means by which Indian artifacts became implanted in British domestic decorations. The increased use of Indian goods scattered in Victorian homes then helped to widen the market for similar decorative items throughout Britain. Moreover, during the latter half of the nineteenth century both middle and working class English families started to collect bric-a-brac to decorate their homes, partly because an increasing number of people had more spare cash to buy these objects and partly because collecting decorative objects became a widespread craze, not just confined to a few wealthy.[45] Some memsahibs saw this as an opportunity to sell or trade Indian goods, which they brought with them when they returned home. Ivory carved objects were especially popular.[46] Memsahibs brought home Indian ivory card cases, ivory fans, and ivory glove stretchers, which they tried either to sell or exchange for jewelry.[47] Wooden carved jewelry cabinets and Indian statuettes were other common goods that some memsahibs sought to sell or exchange: "Poona figures exquisitely modelled and dressed in exact native costume elegant and interesting for drawing room cabinets."[48] Thus, through gifts sent to their friends and family members and by sale or exchange, memsahibs introduced and popularized Indian artifacts as well as clothes.

The impact of colonial culture on fashion and interior design was readily apparent to nineteenth-century Britons. Memsahibs were a major force in accelerating the infusion of Indian culture into the society. Their influence was even more critical to the popular adaptation of Indian cuisines to British tastes.

By publishing recipes for curry and rice and other Indian dishes in an array of popular periodicals, memsahibs helped to modify the food habits of many middle-class Britons. Since the fifteenth century, spices such as cinnamon, ginger, pepper, cloves, mace, and saffron had been used in Britain.[49] Although in 1694 a recipe for Indian pickle described the use of powdered turmeric, only in the late eighteenth century did Britons who wanted to make "curry the Indian way" begin to use imported turmeric.[50] The Norris Street Coffee House at Haymarket had served curry as early as 1733, but the population that had a taste for it was apparently quite limited.[51] Like Indian shawls, curry—as we use the word today to indicate an admixture of spices—was not in vogue in England until officials of the East India Company began to return home on leave in the early part of the nineteenth century.[52]

Then the general population began to get a taste for curry. During this period, Miss Hill's *How to Cook or Serve Eggs in [One] Hundred Different Ways* (1825) provided Britons with a recipe for egg curry, and at the same time, the amount of turmeric, the main ingredient in curry, imported from India began to increase. In 1841, for instance, 26,468 pounds of turmeric were imported from India (compared to 8,678 pounds in 1820).[53] As the mid-nineteenth-century taste for curry became widespread more cookbooks and household manuals included recipes for this and other Indian foods. Eliza Acton's *Modern Cookery* (thirteenth edition in 1853) provided its readers with several choices of curry recipes including Bengal curry, dry curry, common India curry, Selim's curry, and curried egg. The book also contained a recipe for boiled rice to accompany these different dishes. Similarly, *The Practical Housewife* (1855) and Mrs. Beeton's *Household Management* (1861) contained several curry and rice recipes. Some household manuals like *The Young Housekeeper's Essential Aid to the Thorough Understanding of the Duties of Her Maidservants* (1852), gave curry powder recipes which the authors claimed "will be found quite equal to that Indian curry provides."[54] Publications of curry recipes in cookbooks and household manuals by a few women, who most likely had never been to the Indian subcontinent, and readers' queries in women's periodicals about preparation of Indian dishes prompted memsahibs to publish recipes for Indian food in popular journals. The Anglo-Indian wives usually rejected Indian cuisine in the subcontinent. And now in this period of heightened interest in curry at home they presented themselves as experts in Indian dishes. Most likely memsahibs acquired this knowledge from their cooks.

Memsahibs' involvement in the diffusion of curry and rice into the British diet is revealed in a variety of weekly journals which contained sections on cookery, household hints, letters to the editor, and notes and queries. The *Ladies' Own Paper* (1866–72), the *Queen* (1861–99), and such monthly periodicals as *EDM* (1852–78), *The Young Ladies' Journal* (1864–86), *The Ladies' Treasury* (1857–84), and *The Ladies' Companion* (1864–86) often contained recipes for meat, poultry, fish, egg, or vegetable curry and for rice accompaniments. Between February and November, 1866, *The Young Ladies Journal* published ten booklet-sized supplements providing recipes for daily menus. Six of these booklets contained at least one method of cooking curry. Many of the recipes used were obtained from memsahibs who often sent their favorites for publication in *Queen* and other magazines.[55]

Requests for curry and curry powder recipes were also frequent.[56] W.M.B. from Bath wrote in *Queen*, "Madame, you supply me at times with such excellent recipes, I should be glad if you favour me with a good one for dressing meats with Indian curry powder."[57] Writers who provided curry powder recipes commonly characterized these as "original Indian recipes."[58] To emphasize the distinctive Indian character of the curry powder, writers often named their curry powders after notable Indian reformers, such as "The Late Baboo Sir Dwarkanath Tagore's Highly Esteemed Curry Powder," or after places, such as "Genuine Madras Curry Powder—a recipe supposedly received from Warris Khan, the Khansama of late Prince Jummodin, a son of Tipoo Sahib."[59] Dishes were variously called "Bombay Curry," "Curried Beef—Madras Way," "Lord Clive's Curry," "Bengal Curry," or "Burdwan Curry."[60] Many authors claimed that they learned their culinary secrets from "natives."[61] Besides the recipes for curried dishes, periodicals also published recipes for other Indian foods such as kedgiree or kitchery, mulligatawny soup, dal, chappatis, Indian pickle or chutney, and omelet.[62] Sometimes the same dish appeared with different names, such as Bengal omelet and Madras omelet.[63]

The authors of curry recipes often recommended boiled rice as the perfect accompaniment to curry. *The Ladies' Companion* of March 16, 1850, for instance, printed an "excellent Indian recipe for boiling rice to serve with curry." Similarly, in May 1863 and February 1865, the *Ladies' Treasury* urged their readers to serve mutton curry with "boiled rice, separate, not on it." *Queen* of January 3, 1868, informed its readers that curry should not only be served with rice but should be eaten with a spoon. By September 12, 1868, the *Ladies' Own Paper* could report that "boiled rice is mostly served with curry." In recommending the use of rice with curry, many authors suggested substituting Indian Patna for Carolina rice, as the former was less expensive. In the 1860s, Patna rice was sold for four pence per pound, while Carolina rice cost seven pence per pound.[64]

As can be expected, Indian cuisine was adapted both to British palates and to the availability of ingredients. An author of a curry recipe wrote that any kind of meat including sweetbread could be used for curry, pointing out that sweetbread was never used for curry in India.[65] Curried dishes in Britain were often made with chicken, rabbit, pork, or beef, and less frequently with egg or fish. Thus the memsahibs transformed as well as transmitted Indian culinary culture. In response to a reader's query on how to make a Bengal chutney, *Queen* published two recipes from two separate authors, one of whom recommended apples and the other gooseberries in place of mangoes.[66] By informing readers how to improvise Indian dishes, memsahibs were helping their sisters at home to adapt a culinary culture from the colony.

An advertisement in the *Morning Post* shows that curry powder was commercially sold at least as early as 1784, but not until the 1860s was it, or curry paste, mulligatawny paste, or Indian chutney, sold on a mass scale. By the mid-nineteenth century, Fortnum and Mason's was selling Bruce's Vapory Paste, "which was most savoury to an Indian palate"; Reece's Medical Hall sold Trompe's Curry Powder; Halls of London sold their own brand of curry powder; and Crosse and Blackwell sold Captain White's Curry or Mulligatawny Paste.[67] Prices of these items varied considerably. For instance, Reece's Medical Hall sold curry powder for 4s. 6d. per pound, while Halls of London sold it for 7s. 6d. per pound.[68] Stembridge's Oriental Depot at Leicester Square was a specialty store for Indian foods. It sold "all kinds of Indian condiments and pickles, including a great variety of chutnees—Lucknow, Pindaree, tamarind, green mangoe, Col. Skinner and Major Grey's, and also dried fish from Bombay, known also as called Dundary or Bombay Duck."[69]

But even these large commercial stores could not satisfy the needs of some women who craved "authentic" Indian curry powder. In *EDM*'s "Conversazione," someone called Leona wanted to know where she could procure in London real Indian curry powder and pickles sent directly from India. Leona had tried Crosse and Blackwell's, but they were made differently from Manoekjee Poojajee's of Bombay, which she thought nothing could equal.[70] Having found a high demand for genuine Indian curry powder, one Miss Kilfeather of Harbour View, Sligo, wanted to exchange four bottles of Bombay-made curry powder for goods she needed.[71] The existence of such a substantial market for different varieties of Indian spices and curry powder during the latter part of the nineteenth century clearly resulted from the dissemination of Indian curry and rice recipes by memsahibs to their sisters at home, who were eager to adopt this colonial culinary culture. It also revealed a growing cosmopolitanism.

Until the early nineteenth century, the entreé of Indian cuisine to British society was generally among elites. In 1815, mulligatawny soup was served to exclusive groups such as members of the Prince Regent's set.[72] Later, as more British women began to travel to India and then return home, tastes for Indian dishes became widespread among all classes. By the mid-nineteenth century memsahibs were able to popularize curry and rice among middle-class and lower middle-class families. This acceptance of Indian food by middle-class Victorians can be partly attributed to a concern for economy.[73] The incomes of these families ranged between one hundred and one thousand pounds.[74] Women's periodical literature informed their readers how leftover meats could be used for curry. In February 1865, the

Ladies' Treasury wrote that "curry is one of the most useful and inexpensive modes of using up remnants of meat which will form no other dish." In 1890, *The Housewife* also noted that "curry is an invaluable aid in re-cooking cold meats."[75] The *Domestic Economy and Cookery for Rich and Poor* (1827) included a number of recipes for mulligatawny and Indian curries, and these were "inserted with the view of introducing a less expensive, a more wholesome, and a more delicate mode of cookery."[76] Both Mrs. Eliza Warren and Mrs. Isabella Beeton made similar suggestions about using leftover meat or fish in curries.[77] But these women could easily cook stew with leftover meat. Why, then, did they cook curry? Since the latter half of the nineteenth century, the imperial ethos was so strongly grafted on to most people irrespective of their class and gender that the English families embraced curry and rice in their diets.

Attention to nutrition was yet another reason for adaptation of foreign foods into the British diet. Fish was considered a nutritious food, and by the late 1860s fish curries became a new type of health food.[78] Turmeric, the main ingredient in curry powder, was generally perceived as having anti-bilious properties.[79] Thus, both curry powders and curried foods were regarded as nutritious as well as economical. The Duke of Norfolk made rather exaggerated claims on both accounts when, apprised of dire food shortages in 1845, he recommended that the poor take a bit of curry powder: "a pinch of this powder mixed with warm water . . . warms the stomach incredibly . . . and a man without food can go to bed comfortably on it."[80]

Both contemporary and subsequent observers perceived British cookery in the Victorian era as mediocre and plain.[81] Victorian women apparently tried to change that perception by adding curry and other items from Indian cuisine to their daily menu. The publication by memsahibs of recipes and articles on cookery in women's periodicals helped infuse the cookery of the colonized into the dietary world of the dominant culture. The memsahibs' ability to make the unfamiliar accessible to their sisters at home added novelty to many English dinner tables and eventually promoted the incorporation of curry and rice into the list of national dishes. If in 1815 mulligatawny soup was served only to the Prince Regent's set, by 1885, the same soup mix could be bought from Thomas Nelson Company for four pence by middle-, lower middle-, and working-class patrons. Memsahibs made a marked contribution, then, to a major development in Victorian culinary culture.

As with cuisine, the initial diffusion of Indian material cultures into British society was generally limited to the elite and wealthy sectors. From the 1860s on, however, diffusion of both Indian material and culinary cultures into the worlds of fashion and furnishings became more widespread. By selling Indian goods or exchanging articles from India for other goods, memsahibs created opportunities for many to procure fashionable dress items or decorative pieces at prices considerably lower than those charged in commercial emporiums. While the economic system created by memsa-hibs served their own interests, it also had the effect of popularizing colo-nial material culture in their society at home.

Since the 1850s, India had become synonymous with the "empire" to many Britons. Before this time the imperial experience was felt mostly by the elite or the wealthy. From the beginning of the second half of the nine-teenth century, memsahibs served as important agents for many upper middle- and middle-class families to acquire the tastes of Indian material culture. They played even a larger role in the transfer of culinary culture. By providing recipes of Indian dishes they enabled even the lower middle-class and working-class women to have a share in the imperial experience and the benefits of empire. In 1876, when Victoria became the empress of India, British newspapers and periodicals published a plethora of articles on Indian manners and customs and Indian flora and fauna. India became a household word in Britain. But the foundation for the growth of this na-tional euphoria had been partly laid out in previous years by memsahibs who served as catalysts in popularizing Indian artifacts and culinary cul-ture in Victorian society.

Memsahibs' role in this diffusion of a colonized culture into a dominant culture sheds some light on the relationship that these women had with imperialism. Anglo-Indian men believed that it was their duty to maintain Britain's imperial interest in India. Fully conscious of their husbands' re-sponsibilities to uphold these interests in the subcontinent, memsahibs faithfully created an ethnocentric "home" environment that facilitated their husbands' obligations.[82] Yet many of these wives knew that once they returned home, the special context for which they had to be overtly ethno-centric by displaying a certain indifference to the surrounding culture would no longer bind them. At home, no longer directly involved in the imperialistic enterprise, they were free to transmit a culture that thereto-fore they seemingly had rejected.

NOTES

1. This is a revised version of a paper I presented at the American Historical Association Conference in Washington, D.C., on Dec. 28, 1987. I am grateful to Nancy Hewitt and Peg Strobel for their advice and suggestions.

2. John M. Mackenzie, ed., *Imperialism and Popular Culture* (Manchester: Man-chester University Press, 1986), p. 2.

3. James Walvin, *Victorian Values* (Athens: University of Georgia Press, 1987), p. 113; John Saville, "Imperialism and the Victorians," in *In Search of Victorian Values: Aspects of Nineteenth-Century Thought and Society*, ed. Erick M. Sigsworth (Man-chester: Manchester University Press, 1988), p. 168.

4. The term *memsahibs* was used originally to show respect for a European mar-

ried woman in the Bengal Presidency, the first portion denoting "ma'am"; over the years the usage spread throughout the British colonies in Southeast Asia and Africa.

5. Here I am using the term *Anglo-Indian* in the nineteenth-century sense—a Briton in India and not a Eurasian.

6. Wilfred S. Blunt, *India under Ripon, A Private Diary* (London: T. Fisher Unwin, 1909), p. 248.

7. Allen G. Greenberger, "Englishwomen in India," *British History Illustrated* 4 (1978): 42.

8. Ibid., 42–51; Francis G. Hutchins, *The Illusion of Permanence: British Imperialism in India* (Princeton University Press, 1967), p. 108.

9. P. Spear, *The Nabobs* (London: Oxford University Press, 1963), p. 140; M. Nadis, "Evolution of the Sahibs," *The Historian* 19 (1975): 430; J. K. Stanford, *Ladies in the Sun: The Memsahibs in India, 1790–1860* (London: The Galley Press, 1962), p. 131.

10. V. Bamfield, *On the Strength: The Story of the British Army Wife* (London: Charles Knight, 1974), P. Barr, *The Memsahibs: The Women of Victorian India* (1976; reprint, Bombay: Allied Publishers, 1978), and Margaret MacMillan, *Women of the Raj* (London: Thames and Hudson, 1988) are merely descriptive accounts of British women's lives in India without much analysis.

11. Caroline Karpinski, "Kashmir to Paisley," *The Metropolitan Museum of Art Bulletin* (1963): 121; C. H. Rock, *Paisley Shawls: A Chapter of the Industrial Revolution* (Paisley Museum and Art Gallery, 1966), p. 9.

12. Elizabeth Ewing, *Everyday Dress, 1650–1900* (London: B. T. Batsford, 1984), p. 9.

13. John Irwin, *Shawls: A Study in Indo-European Influences* (London: Her Majesty's Stationery Office, 1955), p. 24; Karpinski, p. 121.

14. "Principal Exports from Calcutta," *Calcutta Exchange Price Current*, no. 114, Nov. 16, 1820 entry,.

15. Rock, p. 9; Karpinski, p. 121. These centers were opened between 1790 and 1804.

16. Rock, p. 11.

17. Alison Adburgham, *Shops and Shopping, 1800–1914*, (London: Allen and Unwin, 1981), pp. 98–99; see *Queen*, Nov. 2, 1861: "Farmer and Rogers invites attention to several large lots of India shawls and scarfs, recently imported which they are selling at greatly reduced prices."

18. *The East India Sketch-Book*, by a Lady, vol. 2, (London: Richard Bentley, 1833), p. 12. Emphasis is in original.

19. Between 1850 and 1860 many visitors to Kashmir noted that the French were influencing Kashmir shawls with their oriental style patterns and colors. But many of them did not believe the influence was an improvement. See John Irwin, pp. 15–17.

20. In 1852 the *The Englishwoman's Domestic Magazine* first appeared on the London scene. By 1860 the number of subscribers reached to sixty thousand and the majority of the readers were from the middle class.

21. Dale Carolyn Gluckman and Sandra L. Rosenbaum, "As Good as Landed Property—Socio-Economic Aspects of the Kashmir Shawl" (Paper delivered at Symposium on Kashmir and Related Shawls at the Textile Museum, Washington, D.C., November 14–15, 1986), p. 3.

22. Samuel Orchard Beeton, editor of the *EDM*, founded *Queen*, the weekly journal, which aimed at a "wide and wealthy" readership. In "Edward William Cox and the Ride of Class Journalism," Charlotte C. Watkins claims that Queen Victoria and the royal princesses were supposed to have contributed to the early issues of

Queen and Buckingham Palace was said to approve the court information published in its pages. *Victorian Periodicals Review* 15 (1982): 91.

23. *Queen*, May 21, 1870, Jan. 10, 1874; similar notices were published on July 9, 1870, Sept. 3, 1870, June 24, 1871, Oct. 14, 1871.

24. *Queen*, May 27, 1871, June 10, 1871.

25. *EDM*, Jan. 1869; *Queen*, Mar. 26, 1870, Sept. 16, 1871.

26. Emily Louisa Short Wonnacott to her parents, Apr. 29, 1870, Wonnacott Collection, MSS. Eur.C 376/2, India Office Library.

27. *Queen*, Feb. 12, 1870, Apr. 9, 1870, June 18, 1870, Oct. 29, 1870, June 10, 1871, and June 24, 1871.

28. *EDM*, Feb. 1869; similar notices appeared in *Queen*, Feb. 12, 1870, Mar. 5, 1870, Apr. 9, 1870, Mar. 11, 1871, Apr. 29, 1871, July 29, 1871.

29. *The Morning Post*, Jan. 11, 1865; *Illustrated London News*, July 1, 1865.

30. Ann Buck, *Victorian Costume and Costume Accessories* (New York: Thomas Nelson, 1961), p. 72.

31. *EDM*, July 1870 and Sept. 1870.

32. *Queen*, Jan. 14, 1871.

33. *EDM*, Aug. 1869; *Queen*, Feb. 25, 1871; similar notices were published in *Queen*, Mar. 26, 1870, Oct. 8, 1870, Oct. 29, 1870, Nov. 12, 1870, July 22, 1871, Aug. 19, 1871, Aug. 24, 1872.

34. *Queen*, Jan. 14, 1871.

35. Charlotte Gere, *Victorian Jewellery Design* (London: William Kimber, 1972), p. 187.

36. Ibid., p. 242.

37. Bernard Denver, *The Late Victorians: Art, Design and Society, 1852–1910* (London: Longman, 1986), pp. 206–7.

38. H. R. Haweis, *The Art of Beauty* (London: Chatto and Windus, 1878), p. 107.

39. Gere, p. 186; Margaret Flower, *Victorian Jewellery* (London: Cassell and Co., rev. ed. 1967), p. 30.

40. Gere, p. 241.

41. *Queen*, May 4, 1872.

42. *Queen*, Jan. 10, 1874, and July 1, 1877.

43. Emily Louisa Short Wonnacott to her parents, Oct. 4, 1869, MSS. Eur.C 376/2, India Office Library.

44. Minnie Wood to her mother, Nov. 2, 1857, MSS. Eur.B 210/B, India Office Library.

45. Susan Lasdun, *Victorians at Home* (London: Weidenfield and Nicholson, 1981), p. 19; Walvin, p. 143; J. M. Golby and A. W. Purdue, *The Civilization of the Crowd: Popular Culture in England, 1750–1900* (London: B. T. Batsford, 1984), p. 149.

46. Bea Howe, *Antiques from the Victorian Home* (New York: Charles Scribner, 1973), p. 89.

47. Following notices appeared in *Queen*—on Feb. 26, 1870: "Indian Ivory card case elaborately carved in 2 medallions on each side. Price two pounds and two shillings. Offer requested to the value of twenty-five shillings"; on July 23, 1870: "has carved Ivory Indian fan, wanted gold earrings with or without stones"; and Oct. 29, 1870: "Indian Cabinet for jewellery, 5 and 1/2 inches high, 7 inches wide, and 4 inches deep, and ivory glove stretcher for jewellery."

48. *Queen*, Oct. 8, 1870, Mar. 26, 1870, and Oct. 29, 1870.

49. C. Anne Wilson, *Food and Drink in Britain: From the Stone Age to Recent Times* (1973; reprint, Middlesex, England: Penguin, 1984), pp. 254–55.

50. Ibid., p. 265.

51. Sorlie's Perfumery Warehouse, 23 Piccadilly, near Air Street, advertised of selling curry [powder] in *Morning Herald*, May 4, 1784. In her *History of Shopping*

(London: Routledge, Kegan and Paul, 1966), Dorothy Davis writes: "The cargoes of the East India Company's ships auctioned off at East India House, contained not only coffee, tea, and spices but many ornamental goods from both India and China, and many traders, but especially tea and coffee dealers, bought some of these to sell in their shops. There were even one or two Indian or Chinese specialty stores. Peter Motteaux, translator of *Don Quixote*, operated one such shop in Leadenhall Street in early eighteenth century." (p. 199). See also James M. Holzman, *The Nabobs in England: A Study of the Returned Anglo-Indian, 1760–1875* (New York: Privately published, 1926), pp. 90–91.

52. Dorothy Harley, *Food in England* (1974; reprint, London: Macdonald and Janes, 1975), p. 219.

53. "Statements of Principal Articles of Exports to Great Britain from First May to Thirty-First December, 1841," *The Calcutta Monthly Journal* 7 (1841): 397; *Calcutta Exchange Price Current*, Nov. 16, 1820 entry.

54. *The Young Housekeeper's Essential Aid to the Thorough Understanding of the Duties of Her Maidservants* (London: Thomas Dean and Son, 1852), p. 51.

55. *Queen*, June 25, 1864, Nov. 4, 1871, May 12, 1877.

56. *Queen*, January 8, 1870, Dec. 18, 1875, Jan. 8, 1876.

57. *Queen*, Jan. 3, 1863. Throughout the latter part of the nineteenth century readers wanted to know the process of making curry powder. Following are some of the issues in which this weekly periodical published curry recipes in response to readers' requests: Jan. 6. 1866, Jan. 8, 1870, Jan. 28, 1871, Nov. 4, 1871, Feb. 19, 1876. Even in the early 1880s (Jan. 10, 1880) one reader requested: "Can anyone recommend me a curry powder possessing the Indian flavour, without the excessive heat, by which all powders, I have ever tested in England are spoilt."

58. *Queen*, Jan. 6, 1866.

59. *Queen*, Apr. 26, 1862, June 25, 1864.

60. *The Ladies' Companion*, June 1850, Feb. 1851; *The Ladies' Own Paper*, Aug. 27, 1870; *The Queen*, Nov. 14 and 21, 1868; *The Young Ladies' Journal*, June 1, 1868.

61. *Queen*, Nov. 4, 1871.

62. *Queen*, July 30, 1864, Sept. 17, 1864, Nov. 5, 1864, Sept. 26, 1868, Oct. 3, 1868 (three different recipes for kitchree), Oct. 10, 1868, Nov. 28, 1868, Dec. 19, 1868, May 25, 1870, Nov. 11, 1871, Nov. 18, 1871, Mar. 2, 1878, Apr. 20, 1876; *The Young Ladies' Journal*, Oct. 18, 1865.

63. *Queen*, July 9 and Sept. 10, 1864.

64. Eliza Acton, *Modern Cookery* (London: Longman, 1853), p. 36; Isabella Beeton, *Book of Household Management* (London: n.p., 1861), pp. 78, 677–78.

65. *EDM*, July 1869.

66. *Queen*, Nov. 28, 1868.

67. The advertisements published in the *Morning Post*, Jan. 4, 1862; *Queen*, Sept. 3 and 17, 1864, and Jan. 6, 1866.

68. Ibid.

69. *Queen*, Apr. 20, 1876: "Soojee [cream of wheat] used for Bombay pudding can be procured from a grocer at Talbot Road at Bayswater." On July 9, 1870, and on Jan. 3, 1874, this weekly journal published advertisements for Indian tea, condiments, and chutnees available at 3 Hanover Street, Edinburgh.

70. "Conversazione," *EDM*, Feb. 1872; *Queen*, Jan. 10, 1880.

71. *Queen*, May 4, 1872.

72. John Burnett, *Plenty and Want: A Social History of Diet in England from 1815 to the Present* (1966; reprint, London: Scolar Press, 1979), p. 82.

73. How economics influences people's food habits is explored by the Annales School. See Maurice Aymard's "Toward the History of Nutrition: Some Methodological Remarks," and Jean-Paul Aron's "The Art of Using Leftovers: Paris,

1850–1900," in *Food and Drink in History: Selections from the Annales,* ed. Robert Forster and Orest Ranum (Baltimore: Johns Hopkins University Press, 1979), pp. 1–16 and 98–108.

74. John Burnett, p. 124.

75. *The Housewife* 5 (1890): 125.

76. *Domestic Economy and Cookery for Rich and Poor,* by a Lady (London: Longman, Rees, Orme, Brown, and Green, 1827), p. iv.

77. Eliza Warren, *Comfort for Small Incomes* (London: 1866), p. 67; Beeton, pp. 459, 469–70, 925, 936.

78. *The Ladies' Own Paper,* Mar. 16, 1867.

79. *Domestic Economy and Cookery,* p. iv.; see also, "My Great-Aunt Receipt Book" *Queen,* July 11, 1863: "My Great-Aunt always had a great idea of the advantage of adding a curry to her bill of fare in hot weather. It is good for the digestion, she would say, and that is why hot things are so relished in India. Excessive heat interferes with the vital functions, and the digestive powers require a stimulent when enervated by the heat. She was very proud of her home-made curry powder, the receipt for which had been given to her by some of her East Indian friends in her younger days."

80. David Roberts, *Paternalism in Early Victorian England* (New Brunswick, N.J.: Rutgers University Press, 1979), p. 107. Roberts cites *Sussex Agricultural Express,* June 15 and Dec. 14, 1844, June 13, 1846. I am grateful to Ellen Huppert for bringing this citation to my attention.

81. Stephen Mennel, *All Manners of Food: Eating and Taste in England and France from the Middle Ages to the Present* (London: Basil Blackwell, 1985), pp. 206, 213.

82. Nupur Chaudhuri, "Memsahibs and Motherhood in Nineteenth-Century Colonial India," *Victorian Studies* 31, (1988): 519–20; cf. Beverley Gartrell, "Colonial Wives: Villains or Victims?" in Hillary Callan and Shirley Ardener, eds., *The Incorporated Wife* (London: Croom Helm, 1984), pp. 170–71.

WHITE WOMEN IN A CHANGING WORLD

EMPLOYMENT, VOLUNTARY WORK, AND SEX IN POST-WORLD WAR II NORTHERN RHODESIA

Karen Tranberg Hansen

> "Doing?" he asked, astonished, "What
> should she be doing? after all, she is old
> So-and-So's wife!"[1]

Colonial white women have made ambivalent copy in the works of social scientists and popular writers: admiration for the eccentrics like Karen Blixen and Beryl Markham who stood out from the crowd, daring, within obvious limits, to flout accepted standards of "white civilization" and received patterns of respectability;[2] and trivialization, contempt, if not vilification of those far larger numbers of white women whose hidden work in constructing class[3] and whose insistence on decorum helped keep colonialism going.[4] The ironic point about my crude characterization has been made by Ann Stoler: "sources in which colonial women receive little or no mention accord to these otherwise marginal actors the primary responsibility for racial segregation."[5]

As discussed in the introduction to this book, recent scholarship has begun to qualify the stereotype of white women, shifting the blame for the loss of empire from their alleged racism to other developments in colonial society or to problems antedating their arrival. These works view the deepening black-white rift as the product, and not the cause, of political and economic developments in society at large. In the case to which I turn shortly, I argue that it was class relations, and in particular the insistence on British class-bound practices, that contributed to growing racial tensions in Northern Rhodesia during the late colonial period.[6] Acknowledging that racism was already deeply sedimented in the structure of colonial society, my argument neither accords primacy to class nor subsumes the effects of

racism under it, but recognizes that there were numerous intersections between the two. And gender played a complicated role in these processes,
for colonialism was a fundamentally gendered enterprise. As we grapple
with the implications of this for our interpretation of colonialism, gender
relations and the ambiguous place of colonial white women became critical
loci for a more detailed analysis of colonialism as class practice.

This chapter explores such an analysis during the post–World War II era
in Northern Rhodesia and, in particular, the decade leading up to the exchange in 1964 of the colonial flag for that of independent Zambia. I weave
together a variety of archival sources I collected in Zambia and Great Britain between 1982 and 1989, oral interviews, and correspondence with ex-
colonial wives and their husbands now retired to Britain, mostly from the
colony's civil service ranks. Although my sources are disparate, they reveal
many shared assumptions about gender, race, and class. After discussing
the ambiguous problem white women pose for analyses of colonialism, I
sketch the political and economic situation of post–World War II Northern
Rhodesia. Then I examine white women in three types of activity: wage
employment, voluntary work, and sex. Touching on problems of retrieving
colonial ethnography, of availability and omission, the conclusions comment on my study of gender and colonialism, raising the question of
whether and, if so, how such scholarship may matter.

The Problem: Mr. So-and-So's Wife

The concern of Elizabeth Knowles, author of the epigraph, was the lack of
encouragement that wives of colonial officers received to take on employment or pursue a career. Annoyed about "a certain attitude which dies
hard in a man's country [Kenya]," the epigraph reports the answer of one
of her husband's male colleagues in response to her question about what a
well-educated woman, who had spent many years in India and was an accomplished writer, was now doing.[7] Before her marriage to a district officer
in Kenya, she had been a welfare officer in that colony. Writing in 1954 in
Corona, the journal of the British Overseas Service, she took to task the notion of the "silent partner" that informed the advice of Emily Bradley in an
epistolary novel of 1950 addressed to an imaginary god-daughter just
about to join her junior civil servant husband in some tropical colony. In
Dearest Priscilla, Mrs. Bradley drew on her own experience as wife of a civil
servant in Northern Rhodesia between 1929 and 1942.[8] In the colonial
scheme of things, the husband came first, for, as Mrs. Bradley told young
Priscilla, "it was the rule rather than the exception out there . . . that the
men can get along without us." A married woman in a colony "must be
interested in the [husband's] work, and yet a refuge from it, knowing nothing and yet everything about it. . . . Your husband is 'the master,' the work
is his life. You really are going to a man's world in which you will be very

much the lesser half of this imperial partnership . . . although you command half a dozen pairs of willing hands . . . merely running a house is presumed to be a full-time job, the be-all and end-all of your feminine existence."[9]

Although it was unpaid, the importance of the silent partner's "full-time job" has not been overlooked. In the words of Sir Charles Jeffries, the deputy undersecretary of state for the colonies, such women made their contribution by supporting husbands: "looking after their health and comfort, keeping house, dispensing hospitality, enduring when need be separation in order that children may be brought up the way their fathers would wish."[10] Clearly, such work had importance beyond wifehood. Mrs. Bradley was well known in Northern Rhodesia for her skills in colonial housekeeping and provided quite specific household management advice in her 1939 *Household Book for Africa*. The book was written especially for the bachelor "faced with the bewildering problem of housekeeping" before the days when wives commonly accompanied their civil servant husbands out to Africa.[11] Sir Ralph Furse, long-time recruiting officer for the Colonial Service, had encouraged Mrs. Bradley to write this book when, on a 1935–36 tour of Africa, he made a stop at the Bradleys at Mumbwa, a tiny *boma* (administrative headquarters) some fifty miles west of Lusaka. So impressed was Furse "by the heart of a lettuce in the midst of a desert" that he there and then talked her into the project.[12]

Colonial officials such as Charles Jeffries and Ralph Furse thus understood intuitively the complex gender connections between domestic labor and capitalism which social scientists have struggled to conceptualize over the last decade.[13] Searching for a language with which to engender economistic notions of class based on workplace interaction between workers and management, feminist scholars have brought the family/household, its work, and ideologies about male/female relations into class analysis, casting new light on the relationship between gender inequality and class reproduction.[14] Much of this scholarship suggests similar conclusions, even if the language differs. Mrs. Bradley's notion of the silent partner captures the contradiction: colonial white women worked hard at keeping house, but behind their men, and without questioning their superior standing. The notion of "incorporation" throws light on the way such wives' experience is given shape "within the institutional and moral frameworks associated with their husbands' occupations" (e.g., the police, academia, diplomatic service, and colonial settings).[15] In Hilary Callan's formulation, incorporation refers to "the condition of *wifehood* in a range of settings where the social character ascribed to a woman is an intimate function of her husband's occupational identity and culture."[16] In a settler colonial situation structured hierarchically by race and class, this formulation captures the dilemma of the wife's incorporation as a member of a sex considered to be inferior within a race that held itself to be superior. The ambiguous role white women had beyond wifehood in shaping standards of "civilization"

contributed to reproduce racially divided and class-structured colonial societies. At the same time as they were acting as wives and housekeepers,
such women were engaging in what Hannah Papanek has called "family
status production work" that is, they were constructing the culture and
life-style appropriate to their class level.[17]

The notion of incorporation helps us to highlight the centrality of gender
in the colonial enterprise. But while it may be helpful, the concept itself is
also problematic. Its generality prevents us from recognizing that there are
significant differences between the various situations it lumps together. It
assumes too much class homogeneity and ignores the effects that changes
in political and economic structures may have on gender and race relations.
Last, but not least, the notion of incorporated wife hides a tension between
personal agency and the cultural norms and expectations of subordination.
Here, I explore in more detail the usefulness or lack thereof of the notion of
incorporated wife to an analysis if white women's activities in the late colonial period in Northern Rhodesia. Apart from their rigidly delineated
roles as women and wives, what scope was there for colonial white women
to act as individuals and acquire an identity of their own, not overdeter-
mined by being "old So-and-So's wife"? And if there was scope, to what
extent did women's activities support the status quo or contribute to
change the oppressive race and gender relations that marked colonial
society?

Background

By all accounts, the years during and after World War II and particularly
the decade leading to independence in 1964 were a period of upheaval on
many fronts in Northern Rhodesia. The colony experienced unprecedented
economic growth, prompted by increased world market demand, in the
late 1940s through the mid-1950s, for copper, the colony's chief resource.
Labor was scarce in spite of increased immigration of white workers from
Britain and South Africa as well as of African laborers from the rural areas.
The urbanization process was so rapid that in the boom years of 1951–56,
the population of Lusaka increased by over 100 percent, and that of the
chief Copperbelt towns of Kitwe and Ndola by about 90 and 140 percent
respectively.[18]

During these same years, the relationship of black to white was gradually redefined in economic and political terms. The policy of the Colonial
Office in London since the 1930s of giving priority to African rather than
settler affairs had had noticeably few effects.[19] The policy was now reinvig-
orated, in part prompted by new thinking in the metropole about the future of empire and fueled by the Colonial Development and Welfare Acts of
1940 and 1945, which made funds available to colonial governments for
economic development. The newly established welfare department (1952)

helped extend Western-derived notions about gender-appropriate work to African women in the townships. The very limited educational system, both for Africans and whites, was expanded and, for the first time, some emphasis was placed on African women's education. For the African population, new opportunities opened up: more occupational differentiation, limited advancement, and union rights; representation in politics, first in African Representative Councils and Urban Advisory Committees, and later membership in the Legislative Council; and party politics, developing from African Welfare Societies to full-fledged political parties: the African National Congress in 1949, and its rival, the Zambia African Congress; when it was banned in 1959, its successor, the United National Independence Party, grew quickly. In general, the 1950s were highly charged in racial and political terms, prompted first by widespread African opposition to plans for a federation of the Rhodesias and Nyasaland, which the Colonial Office nevertheless imposed from 1953 to 1963. This opposition contained the seeds of rapid political mobilization and a nationalist struggle, resulting in political independence in 1964.[20]

The immigrants who arrived on this scene contributed to a remarkable growth in the white population: from 21,907 to 37,079 between 1946 and 1951, and 65,277 to 72,000 between 1956 and mid-1957. It peaked at 77,000 in 1962, dropping to 70,000 in 1965, one year after independence. In 1956, people born in South Africa constituted approximately 41 percent; British-born, 26 percent; and persons born in the colony, 17.5 percent of the total white population. The skewed female/male sex ratios characteristic of the previous decades (48:100 in the 1920s and 1930s) had become more balanced with 91 women per 100 men in 1946, and 83 women per 100 men in 1956.[21]

In spite of different national and class backgrounds, most of these new immigrants adjusted quickly to the local white scene. The dominant attitude of racial exclusivity had been propped up by a legal framework, instituted at the turn of the 1920s, structuring the division of labor, space, and responsibility in terms of race. In this setting, white residents had fashioned a "civilization" of their own design in the attempt at "keeping house like in London."[22] White society in the late 1920s was "very long on ritual and precedence, calling, entertainment, etc., in strict order of rank."[23] Such practices reinforced relative rank in the colonial hierarchy and helped to establish, and maintain, a "them and us" difference between whites and blacks. This sense of racial exclusivity had not become less marked by the postwar years. In the words of Kathleen M. Crawford-Benson, one of the very few white women to hold a senior administrative post in Northern Rhodesia during the early 1950s: "The great populace of indigenous Africans of whom I was almost unaware, lived in a different world; or, rather I should say, that we, in our tiny European enclave, perpetuated our own culture, without imposing on theirs."[24]

Although colonial white society did have its divisions (most notably between persons associated with the colonial service, the mines, commerce, farming, and missions) and most branches had a hierarchical organization, commentators on life in the 1950s have noted the blurring of class distinctions in leisure-time activity. The unprecedented economic prosperity of the postwar boom, especially in the mining industry, enabled white workers "not only to maintain the cherished values of the 'European way of life,' but to raise their material standards to a general level probably unequaled elsewhere in Africa." The egalitarian character of leisure life was "vigorously expressed in a multiplicity of organizations and in a spirit of lavish and competitive conviviality."[25] Here, racial distinctions functioned almost akin to class distinctions when judged in terms of wealth and comfort. Household interaction with African male servants provided many white women with the chief, if not only, model of gender and race relations in the colony: a one-sided affair in which women issued orders that servants were supposed to execute, obligingly, and with no questions asked.

How did white women live through these years of rapid change when at least the metropolitan vision of empire had altered and a new external discourse on African needs and capabilities had been initiated? The pursuit of the "European way of life" took place in a political climate that was growing increasingly hostile to it.[26] Local and external observers have commented on the atmosphere of heightened racism, worse even than in Southern Rhodesia and South Africa, that characterized white/black relations in Northern Rhodesia during the decade leading up to independence.[27] Robin Short, a former district commissioner, writing of his experiences during the breakdown of the federation, described the Copperbelt as an inhuman place that paid lip service to culture, good causes, racial harmony, and welfare, but only worshiped money, and where "Dog-bites, guns, odious treatment in shops and even post offices, poor education, insurance, housing, lack of social equality, federation even, all hung around the African's neck."[28] John Stonehouse, the British Member of Parliament for the Labour Party who was declared a prohibited immigrant and deported from Northern Rhodesia when on a study tour of conditions in the Federation in 1959, was glad to get away "from that atmosphere of mistrust and racialism, where the techniques of the police state are all too much in evidence." The white politicians, he wrote, were prejudiced, and the settlers "have failed to tackle the psychological and social problems of adjusting themselves to the millions of Africans in Africa."[29]

Employment

To what extent did white women in this rapidly changing colonial situation fit the bill of the incorporated wife? Mrs. Bradley's picture of the colonial wife who was "married to the job"[30] was drawn primarily from outstations where such wives might have been the only white women or members of communities containing few white women. But already in 1931, 90 percent of the white population lived along the line of rail and on the Copperbelt; most of them were town dwellers, and over two-thirds of the white population lived in the seven largest towns.[31]

Many of the British wives who came to the colony during those years had given years of active war service, and several had been self-supporting before marriage. In fact, a large proportion of them had been gainfully employed. Unmarried women arrived as well, specifically to pursue jobs, chiefly as nurses, teachers, and from the early 1950s on, welfare workers. A small number of women combined missionary activity with philanthropy since the early days of settlement and continued doing so in the postwar era when the major growth in female employment occurred in lower government ranks. Much beyond the scope of this paper, questions about their place in the colonial class and gender hierarchy require a study in their own right. According to the 1956 census, "the proportion of the female European population which is economically active is amongst the highest in the world. The figure of 25.2 per cent. in the Federation [of the Rhodesias and Nyasaland], in 1956 may be compared with 27.6 per cent. in England and Wales in 1951. . . . Approximately 53.8 per cent. of the European women in the Federation in 1956 were married and of all married European women 28.2 per cent. were in employment."[32] In Northern Rhodesia, the economically active male and female population as of 1956 was enumerated as 22,169 and 7,116, respectively.[33] Even Mrs. Bradley reckoned with these changes. She directed the 1948 edition of her household management book, *A Household Book for Tropical Colonies*, "Also to the wives, especially beginners who are equally worried by housekeeping and the bachelor girls who have both homes and jobs to look after."[34]

The number of white women in paid employment grew from 382 to 987 between 1921 and 1931 and, again, to 1,734 between 1931 and 1946.[35] Even in the 1946 census, personal services composed a large sector of women's wage employment since many of them worked as governesses, housekeepers, ladies' companions, and children's nurses.[36] But the bulk were employed between 1946 and 1956, when the number of women workers more than quadrupled and that of men tripled.[37] These women's employment clustered in such gender-typed fields as nursing, teaching, shop assistance, and clerking.

My sampling of the Northern Rhodesia *Staff Lists* indicate that very few women were employed as "temporary woman assistant secretary" (WAS), the post the Colonial Office in 1944 granted women with the "manpower" shortage of the war.[38] These assistant secretaries worked in junior positions in the secretariats and had to resign at marriage. When Kathleen Crawford-Benson came to Northern Rhodesia in 1947, the only other WAS was Ina "Topsy" Wilkie. Wilkie was born in Natal and had come to Lusaka before the war as stenographer in the secretariat. When the decision was made to appoint WASs, she got the first appointment.[39] She served at least through 1958 (not on 1960 list), along the way receiving an M.B.E., the lowest decoration for Commonwealth civil servants, as Member of the Order of the British Empire.

Career civil servants like "Topsy" Wilkie were a minority. Most women workers were "local appointments" with contracts for fixed periods, which were renewable, or on less well rewarded agreements. About the lowest form of employment term was the "temporary local appointment." Within this category, whose label crowds the women's slate in the *Staff Lists*, were wives and daughters of civil servants, private businessmen, and local white farmers. Finally, some women workers were on "secondment" from one section or department to another, but would in time go back to their own section.[40]

The term "seconded from home service" figures prominently for women's employment in one particular branch of the colonial civil service in Northern Rhodesia: the police force. Aside from the growing number of women who did clerical work in this branch, the employment of women assistant police inspectors experienced a sudden spurt: from 12 in 1956, 24 in 1957, 40 in 1958, to 43 in 1959. In addition, 1962 saw the appointment of 5 women senior inspectors who increased to 7 in 1963.[41] Several of these women were seconded from home service from places like the Hampshire Constabulary, West Riding constabulary, and the Bradford City Police. But the majority held temporary local appointments. This expansion of the police force in general, and of women officers, was dictated by events. The Chiefs' and Urban Native Courts that had dealt with customary law cases concerning bridewealth, adultery, and witchcraft accusations were incapable of handling the kind of infringements that were among the results of a rapidly urbanizing colonial society, such as burglaries, fraud, and political riots. By the early 1950s, some women were locally employed as assistant inspectors. Mr. Woolcott, an ex-inspector in the colony, recalled that most of them were either police or administrative wives, who did sterling service. By the late 1950s and early 1960s, the need for trained police women whose primary loyalty would be to the force became apparent: "it was under these circumstances that trained women police officers from the British County Forces were recruited." He explained: "As African women became increasingly involved in political protest so the male European officers found that they were increasingly being compromised by African women offenders who alleged brutality and sexual harassment; complaints which were easy to make and very difficult to disprove. Therefore many officers demanded female 'chaperones' before they would become involved in any cases involving market boycotts, political meetings and rallies."[42]

Women like Kathleen Crawford-Benson had terms of employment that required them to stop working at marriage. Many others did stints of paid work, like Emily Bradley who once filled a staff vacancy at a Lusaka school.[43] Barbara Carr took a temporary job in the secretariat in Lusaka.[44] When Frances Greenall found a reliable nanny, she felt free to work on the newspaper *Mutende*.[45] And Mary Thompson did a stint of work for the census.[46]

These women, together with those who held full-time employment, worked in settings where during the postwar years and particularly by the mid-1950s, African men began to be appointed at entry levels. The rapid growth in white women's office employment thus coincided with the decrease of white men in the top clerical positions, while small numbers of African men entered at the bottom. Between the mid- to late 1950s, names of African men began to appear in the staff lists outside of the clerical ranks. While these men clustered in the African education department, some reached the rank of assistant executive officers in the secretariat. Others worked in the provincial administration, in cooperatives, social welfare, and the native courts. Yet few found advanced employment in the technical fields that expanded in the 1950s. Throughout those same years, the appointments of African women were negligible.

Certainly, being "So-and-So's wife," was not the only basis on which colonial white women might identify themselves. As we have seen, many women, single and married, were working outside the home. Gender identity could in part be drawn from the work relationship. Most employed white women were remunerated at worse terms than white men and had fewer opportunities for advancement. Did they see themselves as sharing the class position of the African men who were entering these formerly all-white settings at even lower wages? Did they see themselves as helping to create a place for African women in the world of work? The available evidence is negative. Although the color bar in Northern Rhodesia eventually was forced to yield in response to a combination of metropolitan and local African reactions, white racial pride constituted a barrier against interaction that work only exceptionally could mitigate.

Most white women were not so much working for personal fulfillment as to earn money to enhance and enjoy the high standard of "European living" many considered their cultural birthright and saw as a symbol of "civilization" in the African colony. Participation in the swirl of society, with its clubs, sports, amateur theatricals, *braaivleis* (Afrikaans for barbeque), home entertainment, and vacations, placed pressures on modest civil service salaries. Many wives worked in order to earn spending money and to contribute toward holiday savings. Emily Bradley took her job as a substitute teacher when she and her husband were "very young, and poor, and stationed in the capital" which was "gay and expensive." It was up to her to "make no new clothes, to cut down amusements, petrol, the club, books, records, and to see if I couldn't spend less and less on the house and garden." Tired of "enforced economy," she taught till the "targets of solvency and early leave were reached."[47] Barbara Carr got her job at a time when the family was "hard up" after a holiday in Britain when husband Norman filled in, at no extra salary, for the director of the game department at Chilanga, fourteen miles south of Lusaka.[48]

The perceived need to keep up with the Joneses was especially marked on the Copperbelt where white mining employees drew fabulous wages. After Chilanga, the Carrs were posted at Ndola, the government seat on the Copperbelt, but not a mining town. There, wrote Barbara Carr, "we of the government huddled in our derelict houses . . . and tried to pretend that we were shabbily genteel and very much more important in the scheme of things than our flashy, rich neighbours in the nearby mining towns. . . . Government wives counted their pennies (and the days to their next leave) and dressed in 'good' clothes bought in England on their last leave. They drove to town in little rattling cars, but the mining wives did their shopping in Cadillacs and Chryslers and came back from frequent holidays on sunny South African beaches or continental week-ends in Lorenzo [sic] Marques or Elizabethville with beautiful, up-to-date outfits."[49] There was lavish entertainment and parties all the time, recalled Ishbel Stokes. She lived with her civil servant husband Roy in Kitwe on the Copperbelt during the mid-1950s, including that phenomenal year of 1956 when the white miners' copper bonus was 100 percent.[50] She enjoyed the conviviality but recalled how difficult it was for civil servants to reciprocate.[51] Kathleen Crawford-Benson also had a good time although the social life of Lusaka presented a scaled-down version of that of the Copperbelt. She remembered white society in Lusaka in the early 1950s, where "my servant was the only non-European with whom I had any contact." In her recall, the "chief leisure activity of the European community was drinking. I think," she continued, "we all developed a considerable capacity for holding liquor, as there was seldom any obvious drunkenness, outside one's home, though at times there were some hilarious parties."[52]

Voluntary Activities

Whether or not they worked for wages, most colonial white women had time for pursuits outside the home. Almost all the wives I interviewed spoke of "helping out" in many capacities: handling problems concerning servants' households; dispensing remedies; typing reports; filing documents; and accompanying husbands on district tours. Their language captures their culturally delineated place *behind* their men in roles appropriate to the circumscriptions of the colony's class and race hierarchy.

Having praised their wifely support of husbands, Sir Charles Jeffries emphasized white women's opportunity to "set an example which can be of great help to their colonial sisters." A wife of the "right sort" should find "common interests and take real pleasure in getting to know the people of the country and entering into their lives." She should go out "feeling that she has a great responsibility and a worthy object in giving to women of the country the best of our civilization, and in learning to understand and encourage all that is valuable in their own ideas and civilization. . . . Women all the world over," he waxed, "have much in common, and in these common interests, outside the administrative, educational, medical, nursing, or social-service duties of a post, the most valuable contacts can be made. The home, housekeeping, dress, music, art, literature, sport—all these give an opening for real friendship and understanding among women of all races."[53]

To men like Jeffries, the role white women might play in bridging cultural relations across the colonial race and class divide was perfectly obvious. It was premised on the idea that women's place was in the home. This construction of gender could allow a reform program at the same time as it kept women's behavior within acceptable limits. While this assumption (itself a historically constructed stereotype) was an ideal that did not always, as I discuss shortly, reflect the rapidly changing social reality, it does help to explain the approach of many white women to voluntary work aimed at effecting change in the colony.

White women in Northern Rhodesia had the opportunity to participate in organized voluntary activity aimed at improving life in the colony, some of which they considered might (in Jeffries's words) be of great help to their colonial sisters. White women were, however, very slow to develop outreach work to African women. Such work was long considered to be the job of missionaries, teachers, and welfare officers.

Even a skimpy account of the Federation of Women's Institutes (FWI) in Northern Rhodesia throws into dramatic relief many of the class issues that contained white women's intercultural work. The Women's Institute (WI) movement originated in Canada in 1897, spreading to England by 1915. WIs were established in Kenya shortly after World War I, and in Southern Rhodesia in 1925.[54] White women in Mazabuka, a small town in a commercial farming district along the railway line between Livingstone and Lusaka, established the first branch in Northern Rhodesia in 1935. By 1936, branches had opened in the major towns.[55] The FWI in Northern Rhodesia was formed in 1936 and became a constituent member of the Associated Countrywomen of the World in 1938.[56] Aimed at making women effective partners in the life and development of the country, the activities of WIs focused on turning women into good mothers and homemakers; teaching them to help themselves; creating good relations among neighbors and friends; and making life more interesting for all.

Local WIs decided on which activities to focus on, say, arts and crafts or welfare work. Through regular meetings, held almost every month, and annual conferences, WI members developed skills in committee work, in working together, and in exchanging and presenting ideas. They organized lectures, demonstrations, outings, and competitions. These activities included, among others, handicrafts and cooking, gardening, horticultural exhibits, arts and crafts displays, and welfare projects. During the war years, for example, members of the Livingstone WI made care packages for the troops.[57] In 1949, members of the Lusaka WI listened to a lecture on

"Women in Africa" by a newly appointed YWCA education secretary who had spent twelve years in East Africa.[58] At its annual conference in 1951, the FWI passed a resolution on the question of African women replacing men in domestic service, an issue that, at a time of acute labor shortage, was hotly debated. The resolution encouraged the colonial government to include hostels for African women domestics in the general plan to expand urban African housing.[59] A related issue came up at the 1955 annual meeting when the question of employing African women rather than men in girls' school hostels was discussed and a resolution was passed to urge the government to do just that.[60]

FWI activities received frequent mention in the almost all-white press that rarely reported on African affairs. But WI garden tours and craft exhibits were featured, along with the bazaars and raffles staged to raise funds. The FWI called attention to such public interest issues as the rising cost of living, cleanliness of towns, and education.[61] The annual FWI meeting usually included the governor of the colony and a few other men of local renown. The FWI received some support from the government and from the mining managements. One result was the building in the early 1950s of Winrow House, a home for sixteen elderly white women in Ndola, maintained by the WIs throughout the colony.

Organized voluntary activity was not every white woman's cup of tea. The lower ranks of the colonial service experienced frequent transfers. Some wives may have been more concerned to establish continuity in their own households, especially if they had children below school age. Yet WIs included women both from the civil service and from business and commerce. Those who reached prominent rank in the FWI were what one of them termed "natural leaders."[62] Their visibility was in part conditioned by their husbands' position and through them they had ready access to the old boys' networks. Elizabeth Morton, an early example, the president of the Lusaka WI in 1937, was a wealthy business woman who on her husband's death in 1930 carried on his firm, in the lime works.[63] Betty Clay headed the Livingstone WI branch in the mid-1950s when her husband Gervas was district commissioner. Married since 1936, the youngest daughter of Lady and Lord Baden-Powell (of fame from the Boer War and founder of the Boy Scouts), she not only knew about standards, but also how to teach the correct way of enacting them. Joan Hanford, national president of the FWI for several years, was also well connected. Her husband, a doctor at the Roan Antelope copper mine in Luanshya from 1945 to 1974, advanced to become director of medical services of the mine. He had been induced to work in Northern Rhodesia by his uncle, Steward Gore-Browne (later, Sir Steward), one of the most prominent, and eccentric, white politicians of the colonial era.[64]

In this cultural enclave, race functioned almost akin to class, at least in the WI discourse. At the Luanshya WI, recalled Joan Hanford, occupational differences did not matter. Many members were highly educated, that is to say, they had highly educated husbands. They called each other by first names, and among them were wives of officials and businessmen, as well as of artisans, i.e., skilled white workers of the mines. The mines, she said, had no white working class as we think of it in the West. They were "one of us," she explained, and aside from gradations between the houses of persons in upper-level positions and artisans, all whites lived segregated from Africans. Such an insistence on minimizing the importance of class in the structure of opportunity for volunteer work stuck Arlene Daniels in her recent study of women in California. Her observations concerning women's reluctance to consider their place in the class structure also apply to this case: they thereby "obscure their own place in the construction of class."[65]

Although I have not seen any WI membership lists, and pending more research, I am inclined to agree with other ex-colonial wives who detected class snobbery in the attitude of the WI leading women. There was indeed, at least in objective terms, a white working-class segment of daily paid mine workers, many of them recruited from South Africa. Their lower "standards" might effectively have excluded their wives from the category of "one of us."

Compared to the FWI in the two settler colonies of Southern Rhodesia and Kenya, local WIs in Northern Rhodesia were tardy in reaching out to African women.[66] Their tenuous efforts were shaped by terms that reflected the motherhood and housewifery roles, delineating the ideal stereotype of woman's place. From the beginning of the fifties and onward, most WI branches intermittently organized activities aimed at promoting African women's welfare. Such involvement often included the identification, through white women missionaries, educators, and welfare assistants, of "advanced" African women living in the townships who might gather a group of African women.[67] The emphasis was placed on the "domestic arts": hygiene; baby care; cooking; and knitting, embroidery, crocheting, and sewing. Both the Livingstone and Luanshya WIs raised funds to purchase sewing machines and materials, and WI members taught groups of African women in regular classes. The results were shown at the annual WI exhibition.[68]

These classes were not particularly popular with African women.[69] Some of the white women understood that something was wrong with the approach. They felt helpless, as Betty Clay explained, "because we did not know about them."[70] The opportunity to establish personal contacts across race (other than with one's servants) was limited, for white women then did not go into the African townships. Given the racial segregation of their time, contacts had to be mediated. There was little cross-communication, and few white women went to the trouble of learning any of the local languages, a fact which some bemoaned in retrospect. The white women I spoke to recalled how hard they had to work to inveigle African women to take an interest in WI activities; they just did not see it, did not understand,

and it was of no use trying to force them. The African women, said one, would not do things on their own, but only have them done for them. Having always been considered the underdog, they might have been afraid to come forward. There was a difference in culture between the two sides and Africans were not particularly keen to mix with whites. And, being on the receiving end, African women lagged far behind their men. The few who had been educated were far too busy, probably got snapped up by the teaching service, and did not see the point of WI activities. The rest were really backward, and the men kept them at home to take care of children.

As *post hoc* rationalizations, these statements reveal some unquestioned assumptions in white women's definitions of African women's needs and capabilities, their backwardness and ignorance.[71] FWI activities glorified a domestic ideal that introduced a gender dichotomy between public and private that was foreign to rural African lives and applied poorly to the changing livelihood of urban African households. Most male African workers earned substandard wages, which many wives supplemented by income-generating activities from home, yards, and markets (single women earned money in similar ways).[72] African women's lack of enthusiasm for WI activities might be due to the fact that they had enough to do already, and that most saw little use in learning skills without being consulted about their needs and desires. The abridged version of the "European way of life" they were imparted in WI classes did not lessen but accentuated their dependence on men.

In short, cultural chauvinism and paternalistic attitudes prevented WI efforts and WI members from entering the hearts and minds of urban African women during the last decade of colonial rule. They did not, in more ways than one, speak the same language. We are almost entirely without records as to African women's experience of these well-intentioned but insufficiently thought out activities. Hortense Powdermaker offers a rare glimpse of one African woman's reaction on the occasion of an exhibit from an African women's homecraft class in Luanshya in 1954. After inspecting the display, the European visitors were served tea and cake; the Africans sat on benches, or stood, outside. Before the distribution of certificates, the Africans were invited inside to see the work and to drink soft drinks. Not all those present saw any value in the certificates: "Look at our friends. . . . The winners are given only pieces of paper which have no use at all. . . . If they were not given money, it would have been nicer if they would have been given needles and cotton. These women are no better than we, who do not go to classes."[73]

It is ironic to notice that at a time when increasing numbers of white women worked away from home, spectacularly few attempts were made either by the FWIs or the education and welfare departments to prepare African women for autonomous roles and wage labor. Not until the late 1950s did white women like Betty Clay and her friends in the small white enclave of about a hundred persons at Mongu in Barotseland realize that their outreach approach had missed something. Knowing how limited contacts there had been, they staged "social classes," showing Lozi women the social etiquette associated with drinking tea and eating cake; preparing and taking sundowners; organizing buffet suppers; and organizing party games.[74] But upgrading the "domestic arts" and shifting them from poor African women to the likely upper crust of African society in preparation for independence does not change the story of colonial white women's voluntary activity in Northern Rhodesia. It merely highlights the group's general failure to engage in reform activity with political ramifications, activity that would aim at changing the lives of their colonial sisters and developing friendship and understanding rather than express class chauvinism in patronizing disguise.

"Proper Homes" and Sex

The white women who reached prominence within the FWI played the role of incorporated wives to the hilt, using their husbands' occupational status and the culture of "civilization" with its norms of male domination and female dependency to their advantage in creating a particular public role for themselves. But the notion of incorporated wife does not exhaust the full range of male/female relations offered by life in an African colony undergoing rapid change. Just as white women began to work away from home in substantial numbers, Africans and whites were increasingly thrown together at work, to be sure still on unequal terms, and white immigrant workers not socialized into British class-based practices arrived in large numbers.

There were other options than playing the role of incorporated wife. Some marriages went on the rocks, and some wives left the colony. Another choice was extramarital affairs with white men. While Northern Rhodesia does not come close to Kenya's Happy Valley in this respect, the practice, judging from my interviews, gave cause to gossip.[75] Liaisons between white women and African men were still another choice, one regarded as so despicable and mentioned so rarely in "civilized society" that I have found limited evidence, other than anecdotal, testifying to its incidence.

As the pace of change quickened, the stereotype whose ideal gender construction placed colonial white women in domestic roles, subordinate to white men, corresponded less and less to reality. A survey of white family life in the early 1950s showed a high incidence of instability: breakups or divorce, and especially problems of rearing children and youth. White women who worked, and servants, were blamed for these problems. "In something like 9 cases out of 10 women go out to work, usually leaving their children in care of servants," commented Mrs. M. G. Rabb of the FWI in 1955:

> We insist not only on the motor cars, refrigerators and telephones of the West, but also on [a] plenitude of domestics and other servants. . . . In order to keep up with even the most average Jones, wives feel they must go out to work to meet the monthly bills, savings toward holidays, the sudden emergencies. Not to mention the inevitable entertaining at home, the parties at clubs. . . . Is it surprising that a child left in the care of a servant whose mental agility is lower than its own, should . . . develop a bullying, tyrannical sense of superiority?[76]

Women like Mrs. Rabb had less time to supervise their servants than the generation of white women who came to the colony between the wars. It is perhaps noteworthy that the second edition of Emily Bradley's book on household management was published in 1948, at a time when more women of working-class background and unfamiliar with employing household servants joined the labor force in larger numbers than ever before. Uncertain about the place and role of servants and unfamiliar with the mores and manners of the segment to whose life-style they aspired, they are likely to have treated servants with a mixture of familiarity and crudeness, rather than distance and firmness as was usual in domestic service.

If white women had problems with servants, so they had in their own lives. Commenting on a report from the welfare department that showed the "perilous state of [white] family life in the territory," Governor Sir Gilbert Rennie in a speech at the Lusaka Business and Professional Women's Club in 1952 warned young wives of the disadvantages of going out to work. "The family," he said, "is the basis of our social structure, and any undermining of that basis will imperil the future welfare and prosperity of the country." To safeguard the interests of the children and the home he suggested that white women should pay attention to social services and voluntary work. This would give "the home—the right type of home—its proper place in our lives."[77] His view of the home as woman's place was held by others. A member of the legislative council complained that child care was too easily pushed on to African servants. "I hope," he said, "that young married people may not feel obliged to deny themselves the greatest joy and privilege of home life for fear of the cost of bringing up a family."[78]

Judging from newspaper reports, the white colonial home was far from what it was supposed to be. In the mid-1950s, drinking and petting parties among teenagers in Lusaka caught the headlines. Teenagers were accused of five-minute love competitions, in which "boy and girl are paired off for that time under the gaze of other teenagers. The pair who do it best are then acclaimed." There were also "petting parties," and the teenagers held drinking sessions in one another's homes "where beer, spirits and cocktails are the order of the day." According to the news report, parents said they could not control their children and that "their daughters won't cook, knit or sew," but attended teenage parties instead, often until the small hours. The lack of parental influence was blamed, as was the absence of youth community centers and the generally unsettled character of town life, with new immigrants coming and going.[79] Yet one member of the legislative council squarely blamed career mothers for neglecting their children.

The change in the white sex ratio between 1946 and 1956 is likely to reflect an influx of single immigrant men who may have contributed to "the perilous nature" of urban family life in the 1950s. For one thing, some of the "problematic" teenagers might have emulated the behavior of adults. Few white women cooked their own food; and African men cooks did not train the employer's daughters. Some women had extramarital affairs and some single women more than one partner. A "callgirl racket" was revealed in 1955 among white women and girls in Lusaka. Operating from one of the suburbs, a dozen women and girls as well as some who worked independently took assignations by phone and met both white and African men for commercial sex.[80] Sex across the color line had always been a touchy issue and became even more so in the fifties' tense political climate and exaggerated concern for maintaining the distinct standards of the multiracial society. The concerns both with "the proper home" and interracial sex must be viewed in that light.

Sex across the color line threatened the persistence of the "European way of life" and the upkeep of "civilized standards." The colonial preoccupation with "degrading practices" was pronounced in the days of heavy white immigration, when some hoped to put an end to it by making miscegenation a criminal offense.[81] Newspaper headlines declaring "Vice Rife in Lusaka"[82] and recurrent questions in the legislative council about prostitution brought evidence of widespread commercial sex also between African women and white men. It was attributed to the coming of "certain people who do not have the same standards as the rest of the community," such as "foreign European labour" and, especially, "Southern European workers."[83] Obviously, such persons were not "one of us." Insisting on class chauvinism right to the end of colonial rule, most white women and their husbands failed to adjust to the ongoing changes that were transforming the colony and the world beyond it. The "loss of Empire" is not to be blamed singularly on white women's racism. Discriminatory economic and political measures both made and unmade colonialism in Northern Rhodesia. Racism nonetheless played an important part in this process, disguised in the garb of class chauvinism and in the insistence, till the very end, by most whites, women *and* men, on the need to view Africa and Africans not in African terms but on their own terms, those of the cherished values of the "European way of life."

Conclusions

The difficulties colonial white women had in entering the hearts and minds of their African sisters are paralleled in my own research efforts to retrieve white women's changing experiences. The language in which they spoke and wrote was layered with received accounts about the nature of African societies and of the capabilities of African women and men that at the level of discourse distanced them from each other. The social science language of race, class, and gender in which I speak was developed in relation to a very different reality than theirs and may not adequately capture the deeper resonances of their lived experiences. My attempt to retrieve content is limited by the kinds of questions I asked and the kinds of records at my disposal as well as by the lack of contextual information. The context includes the numerous white women who also lived in the colony and whom the records of the dominant class leave out, among them, Afrikaner women, the wives of skilled white workers, those who married African men, and women who were single heads of households.

While the challenge to generate additional colonial ethnography thus remains with us, my focus on white women has sought neither to embellish nor to belittle their activities in the late colonial situation in Northern Rhodesia. From my vantage point in the 1990s, British colonialism in Northern Rhodesia seems far away and long ago, and the preoccupation of many white residents with maintaining proper standards appears at best elusive. Yet standards were among the central concerns of colonial class practice and this helps to explain why some women were content to play the role of incorporated wife[84] and why others, although they worked away from home, saw employment as a means to enhance their "European way of life." The great majority of colonial wives gave wifely support to husbands, managed homes, took care of children, dispensed hospitality, and observed manners and mores. The quotidian dimensions of such domestic work hide its public face: the part it played in reproducing class practice and thus the insistence on the superiority of the "European way of life" in Northern Rhodesia till the very end of colonial rule.

This observation does not lessen the tension between cultural norms and expectations of dependency and the desire for autonomy that individual women might have experienced. Although I suggest that their status, qua their husbands' position, as incorporated wives contributed to many white women's view of themselves and of their paid and voluntary work in the colony, the distinction between home and work as loci for identity formation is likely to be too crude and to underestimate the coexistence of plural ideologies that might have allowed some women to hold alternative views of their place in society. Much more contextual information is needed about white women such as those I have described and about the other groups of white women in the colony before we can unpack the notion of incorporated wife and assess its relevance or irrelevance.

In voluntary social activity the status of incorporated wife allowed some women to become publicly visible by bridging the spheres of domestic and public life that colonial gender ideology glorified as distinct for both white and African women. The voluntary work white women did under the auspices of the FWI was aimed primarily at improving the "European way of life" rather than altering exploitative relations in the colony. And in general, the colonial government did not begin addressing African women's educational and welfare needs until the 1950s and then largely in response to metropolitan prompting. Perhaps both the government and the FWI considered African women to lag so much behind their men as to be a lost cause—in the words of a labor officer in 1948: "very much more trouble that [they are] worth."[85]

Although British colonialism in Northern Rhodesia was dismantled more than a quarter of a century ago, the observations of this paper bear directly upon the present. The colonial era's invidious racial distinctions may have gone, yet gender and class remain salient principles of social organization. In post-colonial Zambia the concern for class reproduction and the maintenance of status privilege produce tensions, rather than sharing and cooperation, over access to scarce resources between Zambian women who are separated by class position, and not perceived notions of race. As we seek to create more and better texts in colonial ethnography, the task of tracking the unfolding of today's gender constructions against the uneasy backdrop of economic shifts, political changes, and ideologies disseminated by local and Western mass media remains equally challenging.

NOTES

This research has been made possible by grant no. BNS-8303507 from the National Science Foundation, 1983–85, and supported by grants-in-aid from the McMillan Fund of the Graduate School, University of Minnesota, and by three faculty grants from Northwestern University, 1985, 1986, and 1989. I thank the many individuals in Great Britain who in correspondence and/or personal interviews were willing to share insights with me from their lives and times in Northern Rhodesia, and I am grateful to Bruce Fetter, Elizabeth Schmidt, and Peg Strobel for comments and criticism.

1. Elizabeth Knowles, "Jobs for the Girls," *Corona* 6 (Sept. 1954): 336–38.

2. See Mary S. Lovell, *Straight on to the Morning: The Biography of Beryl Markham* (New York: St. Martin's Press, 1987), and Judith Thurman, *Isak Dinesen: The Life of a Storyteller* (New York: St. Martin's Press, 1982).

3. Arlene Kaplan Daniels used this formulation in *Invisible Careers: Women Civic Leaders from the Volunteer World* (Chicago: University of Chicago Press, 1988), p. xxi.

4. For example, Lewis H. Gann and Peter Duignan, *The Rulers of British Africa, 1870–1914* (Stanford: Stanford University Press, 1978), p. 242.

5. Ann Laura Stoler, "Rethinking Colonial Categories: European Communities and the Boundaries of Rule," *Comparative Studies in Society and History* 31 (1989): 147.

6. Anthony Kirk-Greene, "Colonial Administration and Race Relations: Some Reflections and Directions," *Ethnic and Racial Studies* 9 (July 1986): 284.

7. Knowles, pp. 337–38.

8. Emily Bradley, *Dearest Priscilla: Letters to the Wife of a Colonial Civil Servant* (London: Max Parrish, 1950). After their stay in Northern Rhodesia, the Bradleys held colonial service postings in the Falkland Islands and the Gold Coast.

9. Ibid., pp. 112; 119–20.

10. Sir Charles Jeffries, *Partners in Progress: The Men and Women of the Colonial Service* (London: George G. Harrap, 1949), pp. 155–56.

11. Emily Bradley, *A Household Book for Africa* (London: Oxford University Press, 1939).

12. Sir Ralph Furse, *Aucuparius: Recollections of a Recruiting Officer* (London: Oxford University Press, 1962), p. 252, in which Furse also told that Emily Bradley was an American. Furse misidentifies the book, referring to *Dearest Priscilla* and not *A Household Book*.

13. See, for example, Henrietta L. Moore's excellent discussion of "Production and Reproduction" and "Women and 'Domestic Labour' " in her *Feminism and Anthropology* (Minneapolis: University of Minnesota Press, 1988), pp. 46–54 and 82–89.

14. Belinda Bozzoli, "Marxism, Feminism and South African Studies," *Journal of Southern African Studies* 9 (1983): 139–71, and Karen B. Sacks, "Toward a Unified Theory of Class, Race, and Gender," *American Ethnologist* 16 (Aug. 1989): 534–50.

15. Shirley Ardener, "Preface," in *The Incorporated Wife*, eds. Hilary Callan and Shirley Ardener (London: Croom Helm, 1984), p. i.

16. Hilary Callan, "Introduction," in *The Incorporated Wife*, p. 1. Italics in the original.

17. Hannah Papanek, "Family Status Production Work: The 'Work' and 'Non-Work' of Women," *Signs* 4 (Summer 1979): 775–81.

18. J. F. Holleman with S. Biesheuvel, *White Mine Workers in Northern Rhodesia 1959–60* (Leiden: Afrika-Studiencentrum, 1973), p. 81.

19. *Report of the Commission Appointed to Enquire into the Financial and Economic Position of Northern Rhodesia* (London: His Majesty's Stationery Office, 1938), Colonial no. 145.

20. Colin Leys, "The Growth of Police Powers and the 1959 Emergencies," in *A New Deal in Central Africa*, ed. Colin Leys and Cranford Pratt (London: Heinemann, 1960), pp. 126–37.

21. George Kay, *A Social Geography of Zambia* (London: University of London Press, 1967), pp. 26–29.

22. Karen Tranberg Hansen, *Distant Companions: Servants and Employers in Zambia 1900–1985* (Ithaca, N.Y: Cornell University Press, 1989), p. 57.

23. Dorothea Irwin, *Far Away and Long Ago* (privately published, n.d.), p. 68.

24. Rhodes House, MSS, Afr. S. 1799. Women Administrative Officers: Colonial Development Records Project, box 1, file no. 7, Kathleen M. Crawford-Benson.

25. Holleman, pp. 66–67.

26. Ibid., p. 13.

27. Some of the deep tensions of the late colonial period have been captured from different perspectives by Arnold L. Epstein, "Unconscious Factors in Response to Social Crisis: A Case Study from Central Africa," *The Psychoanalytic Study of Society* 8 (1979): 3–39; Doris Lessing, *Going Home* (London: Michael Joseph, 1957); Hortense Powdermaker, *Copper Town: Changing Africa* (New York: Harper and Row,

1962); Robin Short, *African Sunset* (London: Johnson, 1973); and John Stonehouse, *Prohibited Immigrant* (London: The Bodley Head, 1960).

28. Short, pp. 125–26.

29. Stonehouse, p. 201.

30. This term is borrowed from Janet Finch, *Married to the Job: Wives' Incorporation in Men's Work* (London: George Allen and Unwin, 1983).

31. Kay, pp. 33–34.

32. *Census of the Population: 1956: Federation of Rhodesia and Nyasaland* (Salisbury: Central Statistical Office, 1960), p. 9.

33. Ibid., pp. 98–117.

34. Emily Bradley, *A Household Book for Tropical Colonies* (London: Oxford University Press, 1948), p. vii.

35. *Report on the Census of the Population of Northern Rhodesia Held on 15th October, 1946* (Lusaka: Government Printer, 1949), p. 33.

36. Ibid., p. 39. Hansen, pp. 142–49, discusses white women in domestic service.

37. *Report on the Census . . . 1946*, table 8, p. 36, and *Census of the Population, 1956*, table 49, pp. 98–117.

38. Helen Callaway, *Gender, Culture, and Empire: European Women in Colonial Nigeria* (Urbana: University of Illinois Press, 1987), pp. 14; 139–43.

39. Rhodes House, Crawford-Benson, p. 7.

40. Dick Hobson kindly clarified the meaning of these employment terms to me. Personal communication, Dec. 27, 1989.

41. From my sampling of the Northern Rhodesia civil service *Staff Lists*, 1952–63 (Lusaka: Government Printer).

42. O. "Tigger" Woolcott kindly offered me this information. Personal communication, January 1990.

43. Bradley, *Dearest Priscilla*, pp. 220–21.

44. Barbara Carr, *Not for Me the Wilds* (Cape Town: Howard Timmins, 1963), p. 211.

45. Frances Greenall, personal communication, Oct. 4, 1986.

46. Mary Thompson, personal interview, Sept. 6, 1989.

47. Bradley, pp. 220–21.

48. Carr, p. 211.

49. Ibid., p. 217.

50. In addition to wages, white miners received a bonus the size of which depended on the profitability of copper sales.

51. Ishbel Stokes, personal interview, July 12, 1986.

52. Rhodes House, Crawford-Benson, pp. 7–9.

53. Jeffries, pp. 155–57.

54. Winifred J. Needham, *A History of the Federation of Women's Institutes of Southern Rhodesia* (privately published, circa 1959), p. 9; Audrey Wipper, "The Maendeleo ya Wanawake Movement in the Colonial Period: The Canadian Connection, Mau Mau, Embroidery and Agriculture," *Rural Africana* 29 (Winter 1975–76), p. 196.

55. According to letter from Rosemary Young, wife of the governor of Northern Rhodesia, to the secretary of the National FWI in London (Mar. 21, 1936). Consulted at the London files of the NFWI in 1983.

56. According to description in WI membership card/booklet owned by Joan Hanford.

57. *Livingstone Mail*, June 13, 1941, p. 5.

58. *Central African Post*, Oct. 20, 1949, p. 6.

59. As noted in file containing documents NAZ/NR 3/143 Md/14 Labour Department, Native Labour Conditions of Service: Labour Supplies: Woman Power; and Hansen, p. 126.

60. *Central African Post*, early April, 1955.

61. Ishbel Stokes, personal interview, Sept. 11, 1989.

62. Joan Hanford, personal interview, Dec. 18, 1989.

63. *Year Book and Guide of the Rhodesias and Nyasaland with Bibliographies*, (Salisbury: Rhodesian Publications, 1937), p. 618.

64. Robert I. Rotberg, *Black Heart: Gore-Browne and the Politics of Multiracial Zambia* (Berkeley: University of California Press, 1977).

65. Daniels, p. 279.

66. Needham, pp. 24; 30–34; Wipper, p. 196.

67. Stokes, 1989.

68. Stokes, 1986.

69. Neither the FWI nor the education and welfare departments had much success with their homecrafts classes and clubs for women in the African townships. The white staff of the departments realized this, as indicated, for example, in NAZ/NR 2/512 Native Education, Female, 1949–59, and NAZ/NR 2/27 African Welfare, General Correspondence, 1944–54.

70. Betty Clay, personal interview, Sept. 7, 1989.

71. Patricia Caplan highlights the vocabulary of class Indian women used in volunteer work in *Class and Gender in India: Women and Their Organizations in a South Indian City* (London: Tavistock Publications, 1985), p. 207.

72. On this, see, for example, George Chauncey, Jr., "The Locus of Reproduction: Women's Labour in the Zambian Copperbelt, 1927–1953," *Journal of Southern African Studies* 7 (1981): 135–64, and Jane Parpart, "The Household and the Mine Shaft: Gender and Class Struggles on the Zambian Copperbelt, 1926–64," *Journal of Southern African Studies* 13 (1986): 36–56.

73. Powdermaker, p. 109.

74. B. Clay, 1986 and 1989. The term *sundowner* refers to drinks (happy hour) taken at the time the sun is setting.

75. See James Fox's real-life story, *White Mischief* (Harmondsworth: Penguin Books, 1982).

76. *Central African Post*, Mar. 30, 1955, p. 4. Lead article entitled, "Danger to the Future of Our Children."

77. *Central African Post*, May 29, 1952, p. 14.

78. Northern Rhodesia, *Legislative Council Debates* 67 (1950), Jan. 4–13, cols. 140–42; comments by Reverend E. Nightingale.

79. *Central African Post*, Oct. 28, 1955, p. 1.

80. *Central African Post*, Oct. 14, 1955, p. 1; Oct. 17, 1955, p. 1.

81. The matter of legislating against miscegenation had been discussed several times after World War II in the legislative council and in 1957 a motion was even introduced, but not passed, to make it a criminal act. Northern Rhodesia, *Legislative Council Debates* 91 (1957) Mar. 12-Apr. 3, cols. 681–799. For a more detailed discussion of sexual relations across race in Northern Rhodesia, see Hansen, pp. 87–106, 139–40; and for a general statement, Ann L. Stoler, "Making Empire Respectable: The Politics of Race and Sexual Morality in Twentieth-Century Colonial Cultures," *American Ethnologist* 16 (Nov. 1989): 634–60.

82. *Central African Post*, Nov. 14, 1956, p. 1.

83. Northern Rhodesia, *Legislative Council Debates* 91 (1957), Mar. 12-Apr. 3, cols. 681; 793; comments by John Gaunt. The Southern Europeans (*Central African Post*, Aug. 3, 1956, p. 3), are likely to have been the Italian workers recruited to build the Kariba dam.

84. Margaret Derrick, "Unwanted Priscillas?" *Corona* 5 (Dec. 1953): 460–62.

85. NAZ/NR 3/119 Annual Reports, Senior Labour Officer, Lusaka, 1950-60. Tour Reports of Farms in the Mazabuka, Monze, and Pemba Areas, 1948.

CONTRIBUTORS

DEA BIRKETT is a freelance writer with a special interest in women and travel. She is author of *Spinsters Abroad: Victorian Lady Explorers* and is currently writing about British merchant seamen who work the West African route, incorporating her own experiences as a member of a crew aboard a cargo vessel from the Elder Dempster shipping line.

SUSAN L. BLAKE, Associate Professor of English at Lafayette College, is working on a study of white women's narratives of African travel. She is the author of articles on African-American literature and travel narrative, and has written a travel narrative of her own, *Letters from Togo*.

ANTOINETTE M. BURTON, Assistant Professor at Indiana State University in Terre Haute, is revising her dissertation, "British Feminists and India, 1865–1915: Race, Nation, and Empire in the Age of Female Emancipation."

HELEN CALLAWAY is the author of *Gender, Culture, and Empire: European Women in Colonial Nigeria,* which was awarded the Amaury Talbot prize for African anthropology. She has published chapters in several books and is the co-editor of an anthology, *Women and Political Conflict,* all dealing with women's lives and feminist theory. She now serves as Deputy Director of the Centre for Cross-Cultural Research on Women in Oxford.

NUPUR CHAUDHURI, James C. Carey Associate of History at Kansas State University, is the author of "Memsahibs and Motherhood in Nineteenth-Century Colonial India," in *Victorian Studies.* She is at work on a book about memsahibs.

JULIA CLANCY-SMITH is Assistant Professor of Middle Eastern and North African History at the University of Virginia. She has published articles on women, sufism, and sociopolitical movements in eighteenth- and nineteenth-century North Africa and is currently working on a book entitled "Reluctant Rebels: Muslim Notables, Popular Protest, and the Colonial Encounter in Nineteenth-Century North Africa."

LESLIE A. FLEMMING is Dean of the College of Arts and Humanities and Professor of Foreign Languages at the University of Maine. She is currently completing a monograph on American Presbyterian women missionaries in north India.

KAREN TRANBERG HANSEN is Associate Professor of Anthropology at Northwestern University. She is interested in broad questions of political economy, especially concerning the division of labor and its changes in terms of class, race, and gender. Her several rounds of fieldwork in Zambia have resulted in articles on gender, the informal sector, and urbanization, and in the publication of *Distant Companions: Servants and Employers in Zambia, 1900–1985*. She is editor of *African Encounters with Domesticity*.

MERVAT HATEM, Associate Professor of Political Science at Howard University, was born and raised in Egypt. She has written widely on the topics of feminism, nationalism, patriarchy, and gender; she is currently writing a book about state feminism in Egypt.

DOROTHY O. HELLY, Professor of History and Women's Studies at Hunter College, is author of *Livingstone's Legacy: Horace Waller and Victorian Mythmaking* and a co-author with the Hunter College Women's Studies Collective of *Women's Choices, Women's Realities: An Introduction to Women's Studies*. She is co-editing an anthology of essays from the Seventh Berkshire Conference on the History of Women, *Connected Domains: Beyond the Public/Private Dichotomy in Women's History*. She has written about the impact of feminist scholarship on the field of history today.

SYLVIA M. JACOBS, Professor of History at North Carolina Central University, authored *The African Nexus: Black American Perspectives on the European Partitioning of Africa, 1880–1920* and edited *Black Americans and the Missionary Movement in Africa*. She has written nearly three dozen articles on the relationship of African-Americans with Africa and Africans.

NANCY L. PAXTON is Associate Professor of English at Northern Arizona University, where she teaches courses in Victorian literature, feminist theory, and women's studies. Research for this essay and for a forthcoming book on British novels about the raj has been supported by a Mellon Faculty Fellowship at Harvard. She is author of *George Eliot and Herbert Spencer: Feminism, Evolutionism, and the Reconstruction of Gender*, and has published essays on Olive Schreiner and Susan Ferrier.

BARBARA N. RAMUSACK, Professor of History at the University of Cincinnati, has current research interests in the princes of India and in the interaction among British and South Asian women over women's rights issues. She has published *The Princes of India in the Twilight of Empire* and is working on the volume on the princes for the New Cambridge History of India series.

MRINALINI SINHA holds degrees in History and in International Politics. A former Rockefeller Humanist-in-Residence at the University of

Minnesota's Center for Advanced Feminist Studies, she is Assistant Professor of History at Boston College. She is completing a book entitled " 'Manliness': A Victorian Ideal and Colonial Policy in Late Nineteenth-Century Bengal."

MARGARET STROBEL is Professor of Women's Studies and History at the University of Illinois at Chicago. Her book *Muslim Women in Mombasa, 1890–1975* was co-winner in 1980 of the Herskovits Prize awarded by the African Studies Association. She has published *Three Swahili Women: Life Histories from Mombasa, Kenya* (co-edited with Sarah Mirza, in Swahili and English) and *European Women and the Second British Empire.* Her current project is a study of socialist feminist women's unions in the United States, which focuses on the Chicago Women's Liberation Union.

INDEX